Framing Terrorism

Framing Terrorism
The News Media, the Government and the Public

Edited by **Pippa Norris, Montague Kern**
and **Marion Just**

ROUTLEDGE
NEW YORK AND LONDON

Published in 2003 by
Routledge
29 West 35th Street
New York, NY 10001
www.routledge-ny.com

Published in Great Britain by
Routledge
11 New Fetter Lane
London EC4P 4EE
www.routledge.co.uk

Routledge is an imprint of the Taylor and Francis Group.

Printed in the United States of America on acid-free paper.

10   9   8   7   6   5   4   3

Library of Congress Cataloging-in-Publication Data

Framing terrorism : the news media, the government, and the public / edited by
   Pippa Norris, Montague Kern, and Marion Just.
        p.   cm.
      Includes bibliographical references and index.
      ISBN 0-415-94718-9 (alk. paper)—ISBN 0-415-94719-7(pbk.: alk. paper)
      1. Terrorism and mass media.   2. Terrorism in mass media.   3. Terrorism—Press coverage.   I. Norris, Pippa.   II. Kern, Montague.   III. Just, Marion R.

P96.T47F73   2003
303.6'25—dc21

                                                                2003043126

CONTENTS

Part III: The Public's Response

Conclusion

Preface

The events of 9/11 cast such a shadow over America that, in their immediate aftermath, we shared with people viewing or reading about these events elsewhere the shock of the attack, the sorrow for the victims and their families, dismay for the death and destruction, and anxiety about the implications for world affairs. Time, however, has given us all the opportunity to reflect upon the meaning of these events. As scholars of political communications, putting these events in a broader perspective requires us to address a series of questions surrounding how terrorism is commonly depicted by journalists covering terrorism in the U.S., and elsewhere, such as the Middle East, Northern Ireland, or Africa. In particular, how are interpretative frames about terrorism generated and to what extent are they reinforced by the news media? Do common news frames shape patterns of media coverage of terrorism in different contexts and cultures, including the United States, the Middle East, and Africa? Do conventional news frames about terrorism have the power, as many assume, to affect public opinion, including perceptions of risk and security in America? These are the core issues explored in this book.

The editors of this volume owe debts to many friends and colleagues. The idea for the book developed from a colloquium, "Restless Searchlight: Terrorism, The Media, And Public Life" held at the John F. Kennedy School of Government, Harvard University, in August 2002. The meeting was co-sponsored by the Political Communication section of the American Political Science Association and the Joan Shorenstein Center on the Press, Politics and Public Policy and was offered as a Short Course by the American Political Science Association. We are most grateful to all these organizations, especially the support of Darrell West, Steve Livingstone, Alex Jones, and Nancy Palmer and the invaluable assistance of Eric Lockwood and Edith Holway for attending to the practical arrangements for the conference. We would like to thank Dean Joseph S. Nye, Jr. of the John F. Kennedy School, who shared our enthusiasm and gave the conference keynote address.

We would particularly like to thank the panel discussants, chairs, and colleagues at this meeting for providing many critical suggestions and thoughtful feedback to the authors. Among those who participated, we would like to acknowledge the contributions of Sean Aday, Ted Brader, Paul Brewer, Robin Brown, Erik Bucy, Karen Callaghan, Cynthia Coleman-Sillars, Darren W. Davis, Mansour el-Kikhia, Timothy J. Fackler, David P. Fan, Richard Flickinger, Nathalie J. Frensley, Tracey Gladstone-Sovell, Doris A. Graber, Kim Gross, Amy E. Jasperson, Alex Jones, Christopher Kelley, Michael A. Krasner,

Regina G. Lawrence, Steve Livingston, Maria Teresa Martinez, David W. Moore, Brigitte Nacos, Joseph S. Nye Jr., John Peterson, Andrew Rojecki, Frank Louis Rusciano, Todd M. Schaeffer, Frauke Schnell, Brian D. Silver, Katina Stapleton, Oscar Torres-Reyna, Michael W. Traugott, Gabriel Weimann, Darrell West, William R. Wilkerson, Lars Willnat, Liana B. Winett, and Gadi Wolfsfeld. Most chapters were originally presented in draft form at this colloquium, although a few chapters were specially commissioned to improve the overall balance of the volume.

This book would not have been possible without the encouragement and stimulation provided by colleagues at the Joan Shorenstein Center on Press, Politics and Public Policy and the John F. Kennedy School of Government, Harvard University, the Department of Journalism and Media Studies at the School of Communication, Information and Library Studies, Rutgers University, and the Department of Political Science at Wellesley College. Lastly we greatly appreciate the support of Eric Nelson and colleagues at Routledge.

Introduction

CHAPTER 1

Framing Terrorism

PIPPA NORRIS
MONTAGUE KERN
MARION JUST

The events of September 11 ricocheted around the world from satellite to satellite. News spread instantly from the New York studios to London, Rome, and Moscow and from al Jazeera's airwaves to Islamabad, Riyadh, Baghdad, and Kabul. The al Qaeda catalyst triggered massive coverage in the Western news media with hundreds of stories highlighting the grief, suffering, and shock of the victims and their relatives; condemnation by the Bush administration and public officials; speculation about the underlying causes and possible consequences of the events of 9/11; and expressions of sympathy from world leaders. Months later, the reverberations and aftershocks triggered by these events continue to impact international relations, domestic policy, and public opinion. The specter of al Qaeda operations bringing a new form of terrorism to the world has sparked a major debate over the definition of terror, its social and political roles, the ethics of counter-terrorism operations, state complicity, the dangers of future terrorist activities, the failure of democracy in Middle Eastern states, and the underlying reasons fueling religious fundamentalism.[1]

One important issue arising from these events is the role and effects of mass media coverage of terrorism.[2] Journalism often attracts controversy, not least where news coverage becomes part of the contest to define the social meaning of events. Reporting terrorism—whether the destruction of 9/11, suicide bombers in the second Intifada, or violence in Chechnya—raises significant questions about how far news coverage can meet journalistic standards of 'balance', 'truth' and 'objectivity' in cases of extreme political conflict.[3] Debate has centered around two questions. First, does media coverage err on the side of group terrorists, lending them legitimacy and credibility, as well as unintentionally encouraging further incidents through a 'contagion' effect?[4] Alternatively, do journalistic conventions err instead on the side of governments, due to an over-reliance upon the framework of interpretation offered by public officials, security experts, and military commentators, with news functioning ultimately to reinforce support for political leaders and the security policies they implement?[5]

To understand the news coverage of terrorism, this book theorizes that the events of 9/11 can best be understood as symbolizing a critical culture shift in the predominant *news frame* used by the American mass media for understanding issues of national security, altering perceptions of risk at home and threats abroad. We argue that what changed, and changed decisively with 9/11, were American *perceptions* of the threat of world terrorism more than the actual reality. Systematic evidence provided by the U.S. State Department indicates that the actual dangers from international terrorism have fallen substantially around the world, and indeed fallen during the last decade.[6] Yet post 9/11, American fears of the risks of terrorism have sharply risen.[7] Understanding this situation is important, not just for its own sake, but also because perceptions of the growing threat of terrorism in America has created widespread public concern, as well as fueled radical changes in U.S. security and foreign policy. The events of 9/11 moved counter-terrorism to the top of the public-policy agenda in America, leading the Bush administration to boost spending on police, firefighters, and emergency medical teams; to create the Department of Homeland Security; as well as taking steps designed to improve airport security, intelligence gathering, security at US borders, the prevention of bio-terrorism, and reserves of medicines.[8] In American foreign policy, the events of 9/11 initiated the war in Afghanistan, as well as shaping President George Bush's identification of an 'Axis of Evil' with 'state terrorism' linking Iraq, Iran, and North Korea, while simultaneously thawing relations with leaders in Russia, China, and Pakistan.[9] Discussion of issues that used to be regarded as the province of a few specialized, esoteric, and highly-technical security and intelligence experts—such as the potential risks of biological and chemical warfare, 'loose nukes' and 'dirty' bombs, and 'weapons of mass destruction'—are now widely debated in public on the American airwaves. Explaining these developments requires an understanding of perceptions of terrorist threats and, in particular, the role of the news media in this process. This book explores how frames about terrorism are generated and reinforced, compares how far these frames shape patterns of news coverage in different contexts and cultures, and analyzes how far conventional frames about terrorism have the power to affect public opinion.

The heart of our explanation lies in the idea of news frames, representing persistent patterns of selection, emphasis, and exclusion that furnish a coherent interpretation and evaluation of events.[10] Decisions and common practices in newsgathering—determining what and how stories are covered—contribute toward these frames. Out of the myriad ways of describing events in the world, journalists rely upon familiar news frames and upon the interpretation of events offered by credible sources to convey dominant meanings, make sense of the facts, focus the headlines, and structure the story line. Although the specific details surrounding any terrorist occurrence may be unique—a particular suicide bomber in Tel Aviv, a car bomb in Manila, or a kidnapping in Bogotá—the way that journalists observe and report each of these occurrences is shaped by how similar events have been covered in the past and by the reporter's most trusted sources of information. Conventional frames, which become mainstream in the news media, provide contextual cues, giving meaning and order to complex problems, actions, and events, by slotting the new into familiar categories or storyline 'pegs.' Conventional news frames of terrorism are important because they furnish consistent, predictable, simple, and powerful narratives that are embedded in the social construction of reality.

This book seeks to understand the news frames of terrorism. *Part I* focuses upon the extent to which different actors in any incident of political violence manage to shape the interpretation of events provided by the mass media and the balance in news coverage, both in 'one-sided' conflicts within societies where there is a broad consensus about the interpretation of events shared by most leaders, journalists, and the public within one particular nation state (such as mainstream views of 9/11 *within* the United States) and also in cases of 'two-sided' conflicts within societies where leaders, journalists, and the public are deeply divided by long-standing political violence (such as in Northern Ireland or Israel and the West Bank). In *Part II*, chapters compare and contrast alternative news frames about terrorism, presented within different news media, sub-cultures, and countries around the world, to see how far these provide rival visions of 'reality' even when covering the same events, including in the Middle East and United States. Lastly the conventional news frames presented by the mass media are widely expected to influence the public's understanding of terrorism and its threat. *Part III* therefore seeks to establish what the American public learnt about terrorism from the coverage of 9/11, including the dynamics of 'rally round the flag' effects and also widespread perceptions of security and risk. The conclusion considers the main lessons from the analysis and their broader implications for understanding processes of political communications.

No single methodological approach or discipline could hope to do justice to studying all these diverse and complex issues. As a result chapters in this book adopt different research designs, including analysis of the contents of the news in different countries, specially designed panel and cross-sectional public opinion surveys in different countries, experimental designs, rhetorical analysis, and elite interviews, as well as direct experience of journalism, combining communication studies with social psychology, political behavior, and comparative politics. We compare cases as diverse as the Belfast peace process, the Israeli-Palestinian conflict, the battle over Desert Storm, the war in Afghanistan, the U.S. embassy bombings in Nairobi and Dar-es-Salaam, as well as how U.S. news media and the international press framed the story of 9/11. The final chapter summarizes the major findings that flow from this analysis. We begin by outlining the core concepts and theoretical perspective used throughout the study, to set the particular events of 9/11 in a broader context, and then summarize the structure, contents, and plan of this volume.

The Concept of Terrorism

Before we can understand the meaning and implications of how terrorist events are framed in the mass media and before we can distinguish between 'objective' indicators monitoring incidents of terrorism and its 'subjective' perception, we need to deconstruct and clarify the basic concept of "terrorism." This concept is essentially contested, value-laden, and open to multiple meanings located within broader cultural frames, so that, to some extent, terrorism is in the eye of the beholder.[11] The decision to label protagonists forms part of the political tussle over meaning. Groups can be regarded as "terrorists" or alternatively as "liberation movements," "radical activists," "armed rebels," "urban guerrillas," or "extremist dissidents," just as nation states can be labeled 'terrorists' or seen as "repressive regimes," "authoritarian systems," or "dictatorships." Rather than being identified by their tactics, groups present labels focused upon their grievance or cause, such as Hamas, Shining Path (Sendero Luminoso), the Animal Liberation Front, or the Liberation Tigers of Tamil Eelam (Tamil Tigers). Since labeling certain actions or actors as "terrorist" carries strong normative overtones, the social construction of reality cannot avoid being an intensely political contest. Since conceptualization is intimately linked with theory, there can be no single "correct" definition; instead, concepts should be assessed in terms of the fruitfulness of the theoretical insights that flow from the understanding. Ideal conceptualizations of terrorism avoid maximalist definitions (the inclusion of theoretically irrelevant attributes) or minimalist definitions (the exclusion of theoretically relevant attributes), and they should have a clear conceptual logic, avoiding problems of redundancy and conflation. Any empirical measures derived from the concept should ideally be valid, reliable, and replicable.[12] Unfortunately the literature is plagued with partial and incomplete understandings of terrorism that often fit only a few particular cases, as well as the opposite danger, with long and verbose "kitchen-sink" catalogues.[13]

Terrorism is understood here as *the systematic use of coercive intimidation against civilians for political goals.* This concept identifies this phenomenon by the techniques, targets, and goals; and all these attributes are regarded as necessary and sufficient for an act to qualify as terrorism. 'Terrorists' are those who employ the methods of terrorism.

Techniques

Terrorism is a method or tactic involving systematic *coercive intimidation*, including the threat or use of violence in the destruction of property or physical harm to persons used as a mechanism of control. This process is exemplified by the use of sabotage, destructive riots, hijackings, assassinations, kidnappings, arson, mass poisonings, torture, rape, bombings, and unlawful imprisonment designed to instill fear, insecurity, and anxiety among its target population. It is *systematic,* meaning that there is a pattern of such action rather than a single incident. Terrorist acts that coerce others are qualitatively different from peaceful forms of direct protest, even passive techniques such as disruptive demonstrations, sit-in occupations, road-blockages, unlawful wildcat strikes, and indeed extreme acts of self-immolation.[14] In democratic societies, the deployment or threat of terrorist violence represents the ultimate failure of conventional channels of political expression and legitimate forms of authority. In non-democratic societies, areas under military occupation or in the international arena, where opportunities for political expression are constrained, groups opposing the status quo may undertake terrorist activities as a primary means of expression and not as a last resort.

Targets

The main targets of terrorist coercion are the *civilian population,* distinguishing these techniques from conventional acts of war directed primarily against military targets. Members of the public are selected at random, if arbitrarily attacked or harmed, or violence can be directed against specific targets involved in the conflict, such as Israeli settlers living on the West Bank, Catholics who worked for the British government in Ulster, or elected government officials in the Basque region. Terrorism often targets business corporations in the private sector. The often random, unpredictable, and indiscriminate impact of terrorist coercion upon its immediate victims heightens its ability to inspire anxiety, even among members of the public far removed from its immediate vicinity, as well as generating widespread moral repugnance about the use of these techniques. Of course, in conventional acts of war aimed primarily at military targets, 'collateral damage' can often occur, where many civilians are accidentally hurt, but this differs from violent acts that are intentionally directed against the general public. States can also use terrorism as a tactic in wartime, employing torture, assassinations, bombing, and other means to terrorize civilian populations in violation of international norms and law relating to human rights.

Terrorism can be classified as domestic if victims and perpetrators are confined within the borders of a single nation-state or as multinational if involving victims or perpetrators from more than one nation-state. Some official definitions, such as that used by the U.S. State Department, slightly broadens the target population to include all "non-combatants," meaning civilians but also any military personnel who at the time of the incident are unarmed or not on duty. Some chapters in this book adopt this slightly broader understanding, and this classification affects how we regard violence used against military personnel, such as the October 2000 bombing of the battleship USS *Cole* in Aden, Yemen, the 9/11 planes hitting the Pentagon, or snipers shooting soldiers in Belfast or Jerusalem, even in the absence of a legal declaration of war.

Goals

Lastly, terrorism is an instrument adopted to achieve multiple *political* goals.[15] The motivation is often unclear; nevertheless, typically the immediate political goals include, spreading anxiety and alarm among the immediate victims and their families, as well as the wider public; eliminating opponents and destroying symbolic targets such as the Pentagon or Arafat's Palestinian headquarters; and generating direct damage on society, such as depressing business confidence in Wall Street or discouraging international corporate investors in Lima. The most important long-term or primary goals commonly include publicizing issues, communicating demands, and airing grievances to pressure authorities, influence the public policy agenda, and gain concessions; undermining the authority of opponents; reinforcing and mobilizing support among potential sympathizers and coalition partners; all designed with the ultimate objective of gaining political power, status, and legitimacy.[16] Terrorism is sometimes employed, however, simply to shock, demoralize, or otherwise damage a political enemy. The pursuit of politically symbolic rather than instrumental goals may have characterized those who carried out the 9/11 attacks and the Oklahoma City bombing.

The definition of terrorism employed here excludes violent crimes motivated purely by private gain, such as blackmail, murder, or physical assault directed against individuals, groups, or companies, without any political objectives. Clearly some cases fall into a gray area, for example the kidnapping of businessmen in Bogotá is a crime whether designed to raise funds for political dissidents or for drug-cartels, but nevertheless the emphasis on a *political* objective as the long-term goal of terrorist acts remains an important conceptual distinction.[17] This understanding thereby excludes borderline acts that sustain public fear through random violence yet which make no explicit political demands, such as the 'suburban snipers' operating in the Maryland, Washington, DC, area and, arguably, the Anthrax cases where no explicit objective was ever declared.[18] In contrast, the sporadic bombings of abortion clinics by Pro-Life groups, designed to damage medical facilities, deter staff, and discourage clients, can legitimately be regarded as terrorist acts under this understanding, as can the use of violent direct action against scientific facilities and personnel by animal liberation activists, the destruction of property and shop-windows by anticapitalism demonstrators, and violent racist and anti-Semitic vandalism by far-right groups.[19]

Some accounts assume that the function of terrorism is designed to achieve publicity, for its own sake, and argue that an effective counter-terrorism policy is recognition.[20] Yet this perspective seems unduly limited; although certain spectacular terrorist acts can generate massive attention in the public eye, the instigators cannot control the type and direction of news coverage, which often relies upon condemning interviews with relatives and with official sources.[21] Moreover routine types of terrorism, such as the kidnapping of businessmen or a sniper assassination of security forces, are not necessarily intent on receiving publicity *per se*. Terrorist groups can directly achieve some specific goals by using political violence; for example, the destruction of the World Trade Centers damaged a symbol of American wealth and power, as well as generating substantial aftershocks on Wall Street and the broader U.S. economy. Assassinations—like that used by the Red Brigade against former Prime Minister Aldo Moro of Italy, by Irish Republicans against Lord Louis Mountbatten, or by rebels against

Rwandan Prime Minister Agathe Uwilingiyimana—can succeed in destroying powerful antagonists and even in destabilizing states, irrespective of media coverage. Many forms of state terrorism are designed to operate in the utmost secrecy, aiming to repress and control citizens, as in the death squads employed during Pinochet's Chile.

Therefore in this account it is not claimed that the mass media is essential to terrorism: Yet many of the more diffuse objectives of terrorism do depend upon the way that events are communicated, framed, and transmitted to the broader general public, largely through the mass media, which becomes the battleground for political conflict and dissent. Terrorists initiate routine or spectacular cases of political violence, but once this catalyst is launched, the communication and framing of the meaning of the events is largely out of their hands. The role of the media is central for the impact of these events upon the general public. As many have long emphasized, journalists function as facilitators in the sense that without the oxygen of publicity, without the airwaves of al Jazeera or the front-page headlines in the *New York Times,* group and state terrorists would fail to achieve many of their objectives.

Group and State Terrorism

This understanding of terrorism emphasizes that techniques, targets, and ultimate goals define this phenomenon, leaving unspecified the type of actors who adopt these methods. Instigators of terrorism fall into two main categories. In cases of *group terrorism,* radical insurgents and minority dissidents initiate political violence directed against the state, generating 'terrorism from below.' This is the common meaning of the contemporary use of the term in established democracies, including the research community, in part because Western governments seeking ways to counter terrorism have sponsored much policy analysis on this topic.[22] In domestic terrorism, the type of groups initiating political violence typically reflect the major societal cleavages in politics, as in national independence movements, disaffected ethnic minorities seeking local autonomy, conflicts between the interest of capitalist markets and a social class, and by religious cleavages between faiths.[23] Group terrorism is exemplified in the political violence employed by the Islamic Resistance Movement (Hamas) and the PLO during the Israeli-Palestinian conflict, by the Basque Fatherland and Liberty party (ETA) in Spain, by Kashmiri extremists on the Pakistan-Indian border, and by radical splinter groups in the Provisional Irish Republican Army and the Ulster Unionists in Belfast. Group terrorism can be understood as the breakdown of the conventional channels of mobilization, participation, and expression, with violence used as a mechanism of last resort to polarize conflict. At the most extreme, widespread domestic group terrorism turns into open civil war seeking to undermine and overturn the political authorities. Where violence is successfully contained, group dissent can be expressed through more conventional channels, such as the Irish peace process leading the provisional IRA and

Ulster Unionists to contest democratic elections in the province. For dissidents, the threat or use of "bottom-up" violence functions to highlight specific issues, grievances, or demands, thereby gaining concessions from the authorities on certain political issues, such as minority rights and regional autonomy. As is all too apparent since 9/11, there are groups operating internationally whose near-term goals are to demoralize civilian populations and destabilize regimes they oppose on broad grounds. The source of the opposition may be economic, environmental, or religious, such as the al Qaeda attack on the World Trade Center.

By contrast, *state terrorism* involves coercive intimidation initiated by government authorities against civilian populations, representing "terrorism from above." This form of control, most common among repressive authoritarian regimes, is exemplified by Stalin's massive purge directed against Soviet citizens, the death squads used during the 1980s to suppress dissent in El Salvador, Nicaragua, Guatemala, and Chile, Saddam Hussein's gassing of the Iraqi Kurds, or more recently the use of the Fifth Brigade by Robert Mugabe against the Ndebele in Zimbabwe. Although less often labeled as "terrorist" acts per se, violence used by the state (whether the militia, intelligence services, police, or partisan thugs) against the civilian population to suppress dissent and intimidate opponents, shares many similar characteristics to those tactics used by terrorist groups against governments. In extreme cases, state terrorism can also degenerate into outright civil war between competing factions and into ultimate state failure. State terrorism can also be directed against civilian targets located in other countries, for example where governments provide safe havens, weapons, paramilitary training, or funds to encourage acts of political violence outside their own borders. The South African government in the 1980s employed such military action in an effort to destabilize neighboring African states. State terrorism is most commonly deployed by highly repressive regimes, but democratic governments have also adopted these tactics in wartime. For example the Allied carpet-bombing of Hamburg during the Second Word War functioned as an instrument designed to damage enemy morale rather than any conventional military targets.[24] State 'top-down' terrorism typically serves to maintain the control of the political authorities, by suppressing internal dissident groups, silencing opposition movements, and reducing external threats. Given this understanding, how do the mass media report terrorist events and what consequences does this have?

Theories of Framing

The theoretical perspective developed within this book suggests that terrorist events are commonly understood through news "frames" that simplify, prioritize, and structure the narrative flow of events.[25] Understanding mass communications through the concept of framing has become increasingly common, whether in the fields of social psychology, public opinion, or media studies. The idea of 'news frames' refers to interpretive structures that journalists use to set particular events within their broader context. News frames bundle key concepts, stock phrases, and iconic images to reinforce certain common ways of interpreting developments. The essence of framing is selection to prioritize some facts, images, or developments over others, thereby unconsciously promoting one particular interpretation of events. Where conventional news frames reflect broader norms and values common within a particular society, dissident movements challenging the mainstream news culture are likely to prove most critical of their use, providing rival ways to frame and interpret events.[26] Frames serve multiple functions for different actors. Political leaders can respond to events and communicate policy priorities simply and effectively by adopting predominant cultural frames to streamline and simplify their message ("I condemn all such acts of terrorism"). Reporters can also 'tell it like it is' within 60 seconds, or within brief newspaper headlines, rapidly sorting key events from surrounding trivia, by drawing on reservoirs of familiar stories to cue readers. And the public can use frames to sort out and make sense of complex and unfamiliar events, peoples, and leaders.[27] Through frames, apparently scattered and diverse events are understood within regular patterns; to pick just a few examples at random that occurred within the last few months (in January 2002), the terrorism frame can be used to explain the nightclub attack in Bali, the Chechen rebels holding hostages in the Moscow theatre, the bombing of Israeli tourists in a Mombassa hotel, the suicide bombers in Tel Aviv, or the capture of communist insurgents in the Philippines. Without knowing much, if anything, about the particular people, groups, issues, or even places involved, the terrorist and anti-terrorist frame allows us to quickly sort out, interpret, categorize, and evaluate these conflicts. Conventional news frames never provide a comprehensive explanation of all aspects of any terrorist act, leaving some important puzzles unresolved, while accounting for those factors which best fit the particular interpretation of events. In international affairs, framing serves several functions by highlighting certain events as international problems that affect American interests (*agenda-setting*), identifying and explaining the source of any security threats (*cognitive priming*), and offering recommendations for particular policy solutions designed to overcome these problems (*evaluation*).

Although news framing represents an important aspect of political communications, many puzzles remain about the reasons why one frame rather than another becomes adopted and reinforced as the conventional interpretation of a particular event, especially where rival or dissonant interpretations are initially offered by different actors in any political contest. We know still less about what impact news frames have upon public opinion, especially in 'two-sided' conflicts where there can be dissonance between the predominant frames offered by leaders and the news media on different sides of any political conflict, for example whether U.S. news frames about 9/11 are accepted or rejected in the Middle East. Figure 1.1 identifies schematically the key factors expected to contribute towards the creation and reinforcement of conventional news frames of terrorist events, as well as how, in turn, these frames influence public opinion and the policy process.

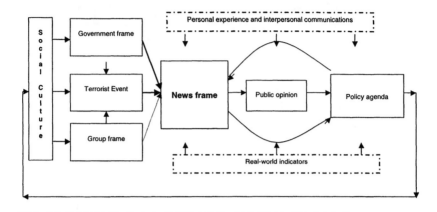

Fig. 1.1 Model of the framing process for terrorist events

In this model, the societal culture is understood to operate at the broadest level, meaning the predominant norms, values, and beliefs in any community. In 'one-sided' cases, there is a broad consensus about how terrorist events should be interpreted *within* any particular community (although not necessarily outside that community), including among most mainstream leaders, including government officials and political interest groups, journalists, and the public, with few voices offering alternative perspectives. Arguably this process was exemplified by coverage of 9/11 presented within the United States by the American major mass media, with broadly similar patterns in framing responsibility and interpreting these events offered in the main outlets for the mass media as well as a broad consensus among political leaders.[28] In one-sided cases, the conventional news frame is likely to be so strong and all pervasive that politicians, journalists, and the public within the community will probably be unaware of this process and media coverage will be relatively uncontroversial.[29] 'One-sided' coverage is also likely where state terrorists control the major mass media, either through direct ownership or through the power of censorship, excluding minority views. By contrast, there is likely to be greater awareness, contest, and dispute about the framing process in 'two-sided' cases, where perceptions and evaluations of acts of political violence differ sharply among sub-cultures deeply affected by the conflict and where divided communities share access to the mass media, for example among Catholics and Protestants in Belfast, among Muslim and Jewish residents in Jerusalem, or among Russians and Chechens living in Grozny.

Within this broader context, the news frame in each society is expected to be shaped by three factors: the basic facts surrounding the terrorist event itself; and the way that these events are interpreted by official sources in the government (including press releases, speeches, and briefings by political leaders and spokespersons for relevant government agencies, including the military, security, law enforcement, and intelligence services, as well as related expert commentators, including representatives of a variety of interest groups, think tanks, and others who offer past experience in these fields); and by communiqués, manifestoes, press statements, or interviews with spokespersons articulating the grievances or demands of dissident groups. Credible sources are expected to shape interpretations of the meaning of the event by providing alternative ways of understanding the "who," "what," and "why" that makes sense of the incident. Some 'facts' about any terrorist event may be relatively neutral (such as the specific timing); but many others may remain highly contested (such as the deeper motivation of the actors or the political grievances underlying their actions), including every aspect of coverage in the news media such as the language used to describe events (was it a lynching, a murder, an assassination, or a killing?), the selection, depiction, and meaning of iconic images, and the choice of "experts" and "authorities" for commentary.

In evenly divided two-sided conflicts, strong emotional reactions to extreme acts of political violence mean each society may offer different interpretations of events and images, sharing almost nothing in common. (Was 9/11 the work of a small group of al Qaeda operatives? Or, as some Arab commentators suggested, was it a Zionist conspiracy to blame Muslims?) The news media serving each community may reflect and thereby reinforce these cultural divisions, especially in societies with strong linguistic cleavages, or journalists and broadcasters may attempt to bridge and overcome community differences by carefully 'balancing' contrasting viewpoints. The role of the international mass media and international agencies adds another layer of complexity to this process, as this can provide another perspective, challenging any 'one-sided' consensus operating within a society. The model suggests that, in turn, the news frame will influence public opinion, especially if there are mainly 'one-sided' messages, including what people learn about any terrorist event, how they evaluate the main actors and issues under contention, and how far this coverage affects public concerns and perceptions of the risks and threats of further terrorist acts. The news frame is also predicted to shape the public policy agenda, including the response to events by government officials and the security services, both directly, and also indirectly via public opinion. The news media frame in any society is only one factor affecting public opinion, which is also influenced by real world indicators and by personal experience and interpersonal communications. Nevertheless the conventional news frame in any society is expected to play a central role in shaping public reactions, especially where there is a broad consensus creating a shared 'one-sided' interpretation among most leaders and those who share a common national culture and identity.[30]

Numerous examples of news framing in other contexts can be easily recognized. To take just a few: Within election campaigns the familiar 'horse race' frame (who is ahead, who is behind) often dominates coverage of U.S.

primaries, allowing the public to identify the strongest contenders, even if they know little about their ideological beliefs, policy platforms, or background and experience.[31] Journalists repeatedly employ certain news frames, such as 'personifying' political conflicts to make them more comprehensible to their audiences.[32] News stories often employ 'conflict' and 'economic' frames to simplify the story lines of complex events.[33]

Western media organizations have been accused of framing news of developing countries only in terms of 'natural disasters' like earthquakes, famines, and tidal floods, while neglecting broader political conditions or economic development issues, such as government corruption or the lack of international investment in public services and economic development, which may have contributed towards events.[34] Counter-culture social movements including feminists, environmentalists, anticapitalists, antiglobalization, peace activists, anti-nuclear groups, and ethnic minorities have also commonly challenged the way that they have been framed in the mainstream mass media.[35] The adoption of 'episodic' frames, focusing upon the specifics of any particular event, has also been applied to understand typical news coverage of political issues, including the Gulf War, crime, poverty, and Iran-Contra, along with the neglect of 'thematic' frames providing a broader and more contextualized understanding of the background factors contributing towards these issues.[36]

In 'one-sided' contexts, conventional frames become so widespread within a society that they are often regarded as natural and inevitable, almost as common sense, with contradictory information or interpretations discounted as failing to fit preexisting views. Functioning in a similar way to scientific paradigms guiding basic research in normal science,[37] conventional news frames can be seen as "journalism as usual," explaining and prioritizing some dominant ways of understanding events while underplaying or neglecting others. Where conventional frames become pervasive within a particular news culture, journalists may well believe themselves to be reporting "just the facts" in the tradition of objective and balanced reporting, as they are unaware of the way that the broader frame shapes their story narratives. Yet just like scientific paradigms, at times long-established journalistic frames can break down, producing confusing rivalry between alternative interpretations of the most appropriate news narrative, or the displacement of one conventional frame by a rival way of understanding events in the world.[38] In 'two-sided' contexts, awareness of rival news frames means that the process of political communications can become extremely controversial, as both communities dispute the meaning and interpretation of similar events.

The War on Terrorism Frame

The book will argue that the events of 9/11 contributed to, but alone were not sufficient to create, a profound and dramatic shift in perceptions of American foreign and security policy. The underlying conditions were already ripe for change. The older Cold War frame, used for understanding international conflict during the post-war era, had been losing its intellectual coherence and narrative power steadily throughout the 1990s, following the dramatic fall of the Berlin Wall and the spread of electoral democracies throughout most of Central and Eastern Europe. But after 9/11, a new 'war on terrorism' frame was rapidly adopted in the White House as the primary standard used to reinterpret and understand "friends" and "enemies" around the globe. This perceptual frame was stretched and used to explain and justify the Bush administration's hostility toward the Taliban regime in Afghanistan, toward Saddam Hussein's Iraq, and Kim Jong-il's North Korea, while simultaneously warming relations and creating new international alliances, notably with Russia, China, and Pakistan. After the fall of the Berlin Wall, the replacement of the older Cold War frame with the newer 'war on terrorism' frame offered a way for American politicians and journalists to construct a narrative to make sense of a range of diverse stories about international security, civil wars, and global conflict. The war on terrorism frame could be applied to events occurring in the Philippines, Chechnya, Indonesia, Israel, Kenya, Iraq, or North Korea, thereby communicating a simplified narrative to the American public as well conveying U.S. foreign policy priorities to the international community.

The use of the terrorism frame serves several functions both cognitive, by linking together disparate facts, events, and leaders, and also evaluative, by naming perpetrators, identifying victims, and, attributing blame. It allows political leaders to communicate a coherent, simple message to the public, while also reshaping perceptions of 'friends' and 'enemies'. In the words of President Bush: *"Every nation in every region now has a decision to make. Either you are with us, or you are with the terrorists."*[39] Clearly numerous and significant problems around the world failed to fall into this frame post 9/11—the AIDS/HIV pandemic decimating many African states; the deep economic crisis and government destabilization evident in many Latin American nations, especially Argentina and Venezuela; or broader issues of poverty, hunger, disease, and illiteracy evident in South Asia. These issues were also affected by the new agenda, since international problems that failed to fit the security frame were often relegated in importance in U.S. foreign policy priorities.

To understand this phenomenon, this book seeks to understand how the process of political communications, particularly the role of the news media, contributed toward the frames used for understanding security issues, political conflict, and international affairs. The first section of the book focuses on the tensions in the relationship between governments and journalists about the framing of terrorism, considering issues of official censorship and curbs on press freedom designed to strengthen national security. The American experience is compared with how journalists have covered long-standing societal conflicts in deeply divided plural societies, including political violence in Israel and the West Bank and in Northern Ireland. *Part II* focuses on how journalists construct and frame news of terrorism, including which events receive attention, how much prominence is given to spokespersons from different sides in any conflict, how news of political violence affects the standard norms and routines for journalists, and how coverage of these events varies systematically in different cultural contexts and media systems, in the United States and elsewhere. The concluding section analyzes how the public responds psychologically to news coverage of terrorism, including the impact of any "rally-round-the-flag" effects in times of crisis, the American public's understanding and comprehension of terrorist events, and their perceptions of risk.

Plan of the Book

The first part of the book focuses on the relationship between governments and journalists in framing terrorist events. In **Chapter 2** Doris A. Graber considers the relationship between terrorism, the First Amendment, and censorship. Press freedom is crucial in times of national crisis such as impending terrorism and war. But press freedom is likely to become a casualty at such times because of legitimate concerns about security for civilians and military personnel and because of fears of compromising the confidentiality of important public policies. Although these dilemmas arise frequently, neither the U.S. government nor the American press has developed an adequate policy to deal with them. The same holds true for other Western democracies. This chapter diagnoses the problem as a typical trade-off dilemma and tracks the record of past U.S. policies. Based on lessons drawn from the analysis of political trade-offs, the study identifies feasible guidelines. Governments and the media can use these guidelines to achieve a workable balance between press freedom and security needs. Citizens can use them to judge the fairness of the process and assess the merits of the outcome.

In **Chapter 3** Robin Brown examines how far Clausewitz can be applied in the age of al Jazeera. The theoretical core of the chapter is drawn from Clausewitz's argument that war is the continuation of politics. His analysis suggested that war must be understood as a process where the political environment within which conflict takes place shapes the dynamics of military action and where the consequences of that action affect the political environment. As a consequence, political change reshapes the nature of conflict. In this chapter Brown finds that the expansion of the number of news outlets over the past twenty years ensures that continuous coverage and commentary accompany military action by Western countries. Most analysis of the relationship between war and the media focuses either on the contentious nature of the relationship between journalists and armed forces or on the disruptive impact of news coverage on military operations. This chapter argues that the relationship between developments in the media and the military should be conceptualized as a dynamic interaction along the lines suggested by Clausewitz. Such an approach suggests that the impact of media developments on the conduct of military operations is more radical than is normally suggested.

In **Chapter 4** Tamar Liebes and Anat First consider conflict and the media in Israel. In the days of terrestrial television, national audiences saw a national framing of conflict. In the new global environment, all sides involved in conflicts enter into a contest of images, in the attempt to influence international public opinion. Television reporters search for such images and sound bites that encapsulate their understanding of the conflict—but they can be easily misled. The paper examines two competing case studies occurring at the start of the second intifada—that of Muhammad Dura, a Palestinian child who died in his father's arms, and the lynching of two Israeli soldiers. It questions the "reality," the "representativeness," and the "effectiveness" of news coverage of these images.

Another well-known case of two-sided internal conflict concerns Northern Ireland. In **Chapter 5** Tim Cooke examines how the press in the province covered paramilitaries during the peace process. The reporting of sustained conflict poses particular challenges for news organizations and journalists in the search for truth, objectivity, accuracy, balance, independence, and responsibility. For news media most closely linked to the arena of conflict, the challenges are unique. While international or foreign media often go largely unaccountable to the society about which they report, indigenous news organizations must wrestle daily with both the short and longer-term consequences of their judgments and actions. The very proximity of news organizations rooted in and broadcasting or publishing to a society affected by conflict, and in particular by political violence, makes them important players in the battle for hearts and minds in a war of weapons and words, of politics and pictures. Reporting on a society attempting the transition to peace offers fresh challenges. What role does the news media play in such a transition and how do the journalists who frame our daily window on the world assess what we should see when we look through it? This examination of the role of news organizations in Northern Ireland in reporting the paramilitary groups—responsible for thirty years of headlines at home and abroad, as they have moved into the political arena—attempts to offer insight into this interactive process in one divided society.

In *Part II* of the book we examine the media's framing of incidents of terrorism in different contexts. **Chapter 6** by Todd M. Schaefer looks at the case study of U.S. Embassy bombings in Africa to compare national influences on the coverage of terrorism, especially how the media in developing countries cover such events. This chapter examines local-versus-foreign coverage by the same media sources in two sets of similar terrorist attacks—the 1998 U.S. Embassy bombings in Kenya and Tanzania and the 9/11 attacks in New York and Washington, DC, respectively. The study compares the major national newspapers headquartered in the cities where the attacks took place: the *New York Times, Washington Post*, Nairobi *Daily Nation*, and the Dar Es Salaam *Daily News*. The chapter establishes that physical proximity and the 'local angle' influenced media framing, especially in terms of the prominence and amount of coverage, although less in the nature of coverage. Cultural influences play a relatively small role in how these events are reported. Most important, national worldviews derived from the international system greatly shape the interpretation of terrorist attacks, especially abroad. Just as terrorism may be in part caused by peoples' perceptions of global political-economic structures of power, the message of terrorist attacks appears to be mediated to diverse publics around the globe through lenses crafted by that very same system.

In **Chapter 7** Amy E. Jasperson and Mansour O. El-Kikhia focus on media coverage of the war in Afghanistan, comparing the framing of the same events by CNN and by al Jazeera. Typically, past research on international crises primarily focused on how American media coverage often reinforces the official admin-istration position and amplifies the natural "rally-round-the-flag" that occurs during an international crisis. This chapter attempts to extend past research by examining how coverage of the "war in Afghanistan" and the military response to the September 11 attacks differs from past coverage of American wars in the Middle East. Had reporters learnt any lessons from the Persian Gulf War of 1991? Was the coverage different in Afghanistan? Moreover, the chapter examines how Western sources of news compare with al Jazeera, which emerged as an impor-tant primary source of news within the Middle East. How did al Jazeera frame the discourse about the war in Afghanistan? Further, how did American media conceptualize news reports presented by al Jazeera and what consequences did this have for the range of information available in the information environment? Did this differ from the way that other domestic sources of non-Western news framed the military actions undertaken by Western nations against the Taliban and al Qaeda in Afghanistan?

Chapter 8 by Brigitte L. Nacos and Oscar Torres-Reyna looks at the framing of Muslim-Americans in the news. Popular fiction and Hollywood motion pictures have perpetuated the stereotype of Muslims and Arabs as villains and terrorists for many years. According to some critics, the news in the United States, too, has long displayed anti-Muslim and anti-Arab bias. The chapter explores how the U.S. news media framed Muslim Americans over an 18-month period and whether this reporting reflected negative biases and stereotypes—especially after the terrorist attacks of September 11, 2001. The study found that the events of 9/11, as horrific as they were, affected the news about American Muslims in terms of volume, themes, stereotypical references, frames, and viewpoints, but in several positive ways.

In **Chapter 9** Frank Louis Rusciano analyzes whether the discourse patterns in discussions of the terrorist acts and their aftermath follow global opinion theory or the 'clash of civilizations' theory by studying the construction, agenda, and content of "world opinion" in newspaper stories. This chapter studied all references to world opinion on the attacks from September 11, 2001, through October 31, 2001, in ten international newspapers. The study concludes that diverse frames were offered to interpret these events in different countries, rather than any clear consensus about the meaning of 9/11.

In *Part III* the book turns to the public's response to news framing of events. In **Chapter 10** Michael W. Traugott and Ted Brader examine American news coverage of 9/11 and its consequences. The attacks on the World Trade Center and the Pentagon on September 11, 2001, were historic events that tested the ability of the American media to cover and explain to their audience what had happened and why. In particular, the study is interested in whether or not elements of the media framing of September 11 help citizens to explain what happened during these events. The study had two interests: to what extent did the coverage provide information about explanations for the attacks and would exposure to media content produce more complex answers about why they occurred? The analysis presented in this chapter is based on a national telephone survey about people's reactions to the events of September 11, 2001, and a content analysis of the American national news coverage of the events. The chapter concludes that individual factors like education can explain the ability of individuals to form complex views of the world, but attention to the news, and perhaps the volume of coverage, also play a role in the ability to explain the events of 9/11.

Pippa Norris and Ronald Inglehart examine in **Chapter 11** some of the first systematic survey evidence for public opinion among Muslim and Western states. In seeking to understand the root causes of the events of 9/11, many accounts have aroused strong debate by turning to Samuel P. Huntington's provocative and controversial 'clash of civilizations' thesis. Evidence from the 1995–2001 waves of the World Values Survey allows us, for the first time, to examine an extensive body of empirical evidence about public opinion in Muslim nations. Comparative analysis of the beliefs and values of Muslim and non-Muslim publics in 75 societies around the globe, confirms the first claim in Huntington's thesis: Culture *does* matter, and indeed matters a lot, so that religious legacies leave a distinct imprint on contemporary values. But Huntington is mistaken in assuming that the core clash between the West and Muslim worlds concerns democracy. The evidence suggests striking similarities in the political values held in these societies. It is true that Islamic publics differ from Western publics concerning the role of religious leadership in society, but this is not a simple dichotomous clash—many non-Islamic societies side with the Islamic ones on this issue. Moreover, the Huntington thesis fails to identify the most basic cultural fault line between the West and Islam, which concerns the issues of gender equality and sexual liberalization. The cultural gulf separating Islam from the West involves Eros far more than Demos.

Chapter 12, by Paul Brewer, Sean Aday, and Kimberly Gross, draws on data from a two-wave telephone survey of Americans to examine the structure of system support in the wake of the September 11 attacks. Past research on trust in government suggests that mutually reinforcing relationships bind various forms of support for the political system. These relationships carried the troubling implication of a vicious circle, wherein a decline in each component of system support fed the downward spiral in political trust we have seen in the United

States over the past three decades. Of course, these mutually reinforcing relationships might also have fed a virtuous circle, helping to raise trust in government after September 11. In particular, this chapter focuses on whether the relationships among various forms of trust differ in the post-September 11 period from other contexts and whether the structure of system support changed as America moved from the rally phase into a period where trust had returned almost to its pre-September 11 levels.

Leonie Huddy, Stanley Feldman, Gallya Lahav, and Charles Taber analyze the politics of threat in **Chapter 13**. Terrorism is a form of psychological warfare. One of its central goals is to frighten people through acts of random brutality and violence that gain broad publicity despite their limited targets. Underlying this objective is a second political goal: to force political elites to negotiate with terrorists and make concessions that will mollify a frightened citizenry. These motives contrast starkly, however, with the objectives of political leaders and governments in countries that have been targeted by terrorists. Political elites in such countries hope to marshal public backing for actions designed to eliminate the threat of terrorism, often through the use of force. Terrorist efforts to incite fear in publics are thus directly at odds with the objectives of political elites who hope to foster pervasive citizen support for retaliation. The focus of this chapter is on American reactions to the attacks of 9/11. The terrorists' actions undertaken to instill fear in the American public and thus undercut support for retaliatory action are contrasted with the success of the government in amassing support for its war on terrorism. The authors examine whether concerns about future attacks simply hardened American resolve against the perpetrators of 9/11. Lastly in **Chapter 14** the conclusion summarizes the major findings throughout the book and considers their implications for understanding the impact of conventional news frames about terrorism on the process of governance, on international affairs and foreign policy, and on public opinion.

Notes

1. These books generated by 9/11 are far too numerous to mention but see, for example, John L. Esposito. 2002. *Unholy war: terror in the name of Islam.* Oxford: Oxford University Press; Rohan Gunaratna. 2002. *Inside al Qaeda: global network of terror.* New York: Columbia University Press; Harvey Kushner. 2002. *Encyclopedia of Terror.* Newbury Park, CA: Sage; Strobe Talbott and Nayan Chanda. Eds. 2002. *The Age of Terror: America and the World after September 11.* New York: Basic Books; Paul R. Pillar, Allison Gilbert, Robyn Walensky, Melinda Murphy, Phil Hirschkorn, and Mitchell Stephens. Editors. 2002. *Covering Catastrophe: Broadcast Journalists Report September 11.* NY: Bonus Books; Fred Halliday. *2002. Two Hours that Shook the World: September 11, 2001: Causes and consequences.* London: Saqi.

2. The major books include, among others, Philip Schlesinger, Graham Murdock, and Philip Elliott. 1983. *Televising Terrorism: Political Violence in Popular Culture.* London: Commedia Publishers; Odasuo A. Alali and Kenoye Kelvin Eke. Eds. 1991. *Media Coverage of Terrorism: Methods of Diffusion.* Thousand Oaks, CA: Sage Publications; Yonah Alexander and Robert Picard. 1991. *In the Camera's Eye: News coverage of Terrorist Events.* Washington, DC: Brasseys; Bethami A. Dobkin. 1992. *Tales of Terror: Television News and the Construction of the Terrorist Threat.* New York: Praeger; Richard W.

Schaffert. 1992. *Media Coverage and Political Terrorists: A Quantitative Analysis.* New York: Praeger; David L. Paletz and Alex P. Schmid, Eds. 1992. *Terrorism and the Media.* Newbury Park, CA: Sage; Robert G. Picard. 1993. *Media Portrayals of Terrorism: Functions and Meaning of News Coverage.* Iowa: Iowa State University Press; Steven Livingstone. 1994. *The Terrorism Spectacle.* Boulder, CO: Westview Press; Gabrielle Weimann and Conrad Winn, 1994. *The Theater of Terror: The Mass Media and International Terrorism.* New York: Longman Publishing/Addison-Wesley; Brigitte L. Nacos. 1996. *Terrorism and the Media: From the Iran Hostage Crisis to the Oklahoma City Bombing.* New York, NY: Columbia University Press; Gadi Wolfsfeld. 1997. *Media and Political Conflict: News from the Middle East,* Cambridge: Cambridge University Press; Brigitte L. Nacos. 2002. *Mass-Mediated Terrorism.* Lanham: Rowman & Littlefield; Bradley S. Greenberg and Marcia Thomson. 2002. *Communication and Terrorism: Public and Media Responses to 9/11.* Hampton Press.

3. For comprehensive overviews of the earlier literature see, for example, Amos Lakos. 1986. *International terrorism: A Bibliography.* Boulder, CO: Westview Press; Odasuo A. Alali and Gary W. Byrd. Eds. 1994. *Terrorism and the News Media: A Selected, Annotated Bibliography.* New York: McFarland & Company.

4. See the discussion in Manus I. Midlarsky, Martha Crenshaw and Fumihiko Yoshida. 1980. 'Why violence spreads: The contagion of international terrorism.' *International Studies Quarterly.* 24(2): 262–298; Martha Crenshaw. 1989. *Terrorism and International Cooperation.* Boulder, CO: Westview Press; Martha Crenshaw. 1995. Ed. *Terrorism in Context.* Pennsylvania: Pennsylvania State University; David L. Paletz and John Boiney. 1992. 'Researchers' Perspectives.' In *Terrorism and the Media.* Edited by David Paletz and Alex P. Schmid. Newbury Park, CA: Sage; Richard W. Schaffert. 1992. *Media Coverage and Political Terrorists: A Quantitative Analysis.* New York: Praeger.

5. The most forceful argument here is presented in Edward S. Herman and Noam Chomsky. 1988. *Manufacturing Consent: The Political Economy of the Mass Media.* New York: Pantheon; see also Edward S. Herman and Gerry O'Sullivan. 1989. *The Terrorism Industry: The Experts and Institutions that Shape Our View of Terror.* New York: Pantheon.

6. The U.S. State Department. *Patterns of Terrorism* 2001. Washington, DC: U.S. Department of State.

7. For example, the News Interest Index survey conducted by the Pew Research Center For the People and the Press periodically asks a representative sample of Americans: *"How worried are you that there will soon be another terrorist attack in the United States?"* In October 2001 three-quarters (73%) of Americans said that they were 'very' or 'somewhat' worried. In December 2002 the proportion expressing concern remained at the same level (73%). The Pew Research Center For the People and the Press. *Public more internationalist than in the 1990s.* 12 December 2002. www.people-press.org. For trends in levels of public concern about terrorism, see also Figure 14.5, in Chapter 14. For a broader discussion and interpretation of this phenomenon, see David L. Altheide. 2002. *Creating Fear: News and the Construction of Crisis.* New York: Aldine de Gruyter.

8. Jane's Intelligence Review. 26 July 2002. www.janes.com.

9. As well as Iran, Iraq, and North Korea, the other four nations that the US has identified officially as 'state terrorists' include Cuba, Libya, Syria, and Sudan. U.S. State Department. *Patterns of Terrorism* 2001. Washington DC: U.S. Department of State. Pp.63–68.

10. In this conception of framing we follow Tod Gitlin 1980. *The Whole World is Watching.* Berkeley: University of California Press; Tod Gitlin, 1994. *Inside Prime Time.* London: Routledge.

11. R. D. Crelinsten. 1998. 'The discourse and practice of counter terrorism in liberal democracies.' *Australian Journal of Politics and History.* 44(3): 389–413.

12. Robert Adcock and David Collier. 2001. 'Measurement validity: A shared standard for qualitative and quantitative research.' *American Political Science Review.* 95(3): 529–546.

13. There are of course multiple alternative conceptualizations of 'terrorism', leading relativists to abandon attempts at any precise definition as meaningless. The concept outlined here shares many similar elements to other common definitions specified by official bodies given elsewhere:
     The U.S. State Department: *"The term terrorism means premeditated, politically motivated violence perpetuated against non-combatant targets by subnational groups or*

clandestine agents, usually intended to influence an audience." U.S. State Department. 2001. *Patterns of Terrorism.* Washington, DC: U.S. State Department.

 The Federal Bureau of Investigation. *"Terrorism is the unlawful use of force or violence against persons or property to intimidate or coerce a government, the civilian population, or any segment thereof, in furtherance of political or social objectives."*

 The U.S. Department of Defense. *"Terrorism is the calculated use of violence or threat of violence to inculcate fear; intended to coerce or to intimidate governments or societies in the pursuit of goals that are generally political, religious or ideological."*

14. In this regard, we follow the conventional understanding of 'protest politics' established by Samuel Barnes and Max Kaase. 1979. *Political Action: Mass Participation in Five Western Democracies.* Beverly Hills, CA: Sage.

15. See, for example, the discussion in Martha Crenshaw. 1990. 'The logic of terrorism: terrorist behavior as a product of strategic choice.' In *Origins of Terrorism.* Ed. W. Reich. Cambridge: Cambridge University Press.

16. See the discussion in Richard W. Schaffert. 1992. 'The transmission of terror and its translation into political power.' Chapter 5 in Richard W. Schaffert *Media coverage and political terrorists: A quantitative analysis.* New York: Praeger.

17. See for example discussions in Martha Crenshaw. 1995. Ed. *Terrorism in Context.* Pennsylvania: Pennsylvania State University; A. George. 1991. *Western State Terrorism.* New York: Routledge; Bruce Hoffman. 1998. *Inside Terrorism.* New York: Columbia University Press.

18. The definition also excludes the use of the term 'eco-terrorism' to describe companies responsible for environmental destruction, although it does cover cases of violent direct action by environmentalists. See D. M. Schwartz. 1998. 'Environmental terrorism: Analyzing the concept.' *Journal of Peace Research.* 35(4): 483–496.

19. For a discussion see U.S. Department of Justice. 1999. *Terrorism in the United States, 1999: 30 Years of Terrorism.* Washington, DC: FBI.

20. See, for example, Brigitte L. Nacos. 2002. *Mass-Mediated Terrorism.* Lanham: Rowman & Littlefield and also B. S. Frey. 1987. 'Fighting political terrorism by refusing recognition.' *Journal of Public Policy.* 7(2): 179–188.

21. Ronald D. Crelinsten. 1992. 'Victims' Perspectives.' In *Terrorism and the Media.* Edited by David Paletz and Alex P. Schmid. Newbury Park, CA: Sage; Louise F. Montgomery. 1991. 'Media victims: Reactions to coverage of incidents of international terrorism involving Americans.' In *In the Camera's Eye: News coverage of Terrorist Events.* Edited by Yonah Alexander and Robert Picard. 1991. Washington, DC: Brasseys.

22. E. O. F. Reid. 1997. 'Evolution of a body of knowledge: An analysis of terrorism research.' *Information Processing and Management.* 33(1): 91–106; Edward S. Herman and Gerry O'Sullivan. 1989. *The Terrorism Industry: The Experts and Institutions that Shape our View of Terror.* New York: Pantheon.

23. In addition, individuals, such as the Unabomber or lone assassins, can also use the techniques of terrorism, although such cases are relatively rare.

24. Edward S. Herman and Noam Chomsky argue that during the 1980s, when supporting regimes in Nicaragua and El Salvador that employed state-organized violence, the United States was associated with these repressive practices. 1988. *Manufacturing Consent: The Political Economy of the Mass Media.* New York: Pantheon.

25. Erving Goffman. 1974. *Frame analysis.* Boston: New England University Press; Robert M. Entman. 1991. 'Framing U.S. Coverage of International News.' *Journal of Communication* 41(4): 6–28; Robert M. Entman. 1993. 'Framing: Towards Clarification of a Fractured Paradigm.' *Journal of Communication* 43(4); Robert M. Entman. 1993. 'Freezing out the Public: Elite and Media Framing of the U.S. Anti-Nuclear Movement.' *Political Communication* 10(2): 155–173; Pippa Norris. 1996. 'The Restless Searchlight: Network News Framing of the Post Cold-War World.' *Political Communication* 12(4): 357–370; William Gamson. 1991. *Talking Politics.* New York: Cambridge University Press.

26. Akiba A. Cohen and Gadi Wolfsfeld. Eds. 1993. *Framing the Intifada: People and Media.* Norwood, NJ: Ablex Publishing.

27. The idea of 'frames' is analogous to information processing theories in social psychology, suggesting that individuals use 'cognitive schema' to organize their thinking, linking substantive beliefs, attitudes, and values.

28. See especially chapters by Michael Schudsen. 2002. 'What's Unusual About Covering Politics as Usual?' In *Journalism After September 11.* Eds. Barbie Zelizer and Stuart Allan. New York: Basic Books. See also James Carey. 2002. 'American Journalism on, before, and after September 11.' In *Journalism After September 11.* Eds. Barbie Zelizer and Stuart Allan. New York: Basic Books.

29. *Indexing* theory suggests predominant government impact on news that American journalists 'index'—the range of voices and viewpoints in both news and editorials according to the range of views expressed in mainstream government debate about a given topic. W. Lance Bennett. 1990. 'Toward a Theory of Press-State Relations.' *Journal of Communication* 40 (2): 103–125. Some research into Cold War crises, which were driven by popular fear or anxiety, like terrorism-related incidents, supports indexing theory, suggesting a strong government role in setting the press agenda. John Zaller. 2000. 'Government's Little Helper: U.S. Press Coverage of Foreign Policy Crises, 1946–1999.' In *Decision-making in a Glass House: Mass Media, Public Opinion, and American and European Foreign Policy in the 21st Century.* Eds. Brigitte L. Nacos, Robert Y. Shapiro and Pierangelo Isernia, Robert M. Entman suggests that the predominant political actors in the U.S., which include the government, interest groups, perceived public opinion, and the press, influence framing. Robert W. Entman. 2000. 'Declarations of Independence: The Growth of Media Power after the Cold War.' *op cit* pp. ll–26. In relation to foreign policy issues, this approach suggests a stronger role for the press in the framing process during the post-Cold War era.

   Content-analytic-based *domestic prism* theory similarly suggests these multiple roles for the press, government, public opinion, and varied domestic actors, along with differing policy contexts. See Montague Kern. 1982. 'The Invasion of Afghanistan: Domestic vs. Foreign Stories.' In *Television Coverage of the Middle East.* Ed. William C. Adams. Norwood, New York: Ablex; Montague Kern, Ralph Levering and Patricia W. Levering. 1984. *The Kennedy Crises: The Press, the Presidency and Foreign Policy.* Chapel Hill: University of North Carolina Press.

30. For a discussion about the impact and limits of terrorism on public opinion see Christopher Hewitt. 1992. 'Public's Perspectives.' In *Terrorism and the Media.* Edited by David Paletz and Alex P. Schmid. Newbury Park, CA: Sage.

31. Thomas Patterson. 1993. *Out of Order.* New York: Knopf.

32. W. Lance Bennett. 1996. *News the Politics of Illusion,* 3rd Ed. White Plains, NY: Longman.

33. W. Russell Neuman, Marion Just, and Ann Crigler. 1992. *Common Knowledge: News and the Construction of Political Meaning.* Chicago: University of Chicago Press.

34. Hamid Mowlana. 1985. *International Flow of Information: Global Report and Analysis.* Paris: UNESCO; Hamid Mowlana. 1993. 'Towards a NWICO for the Twenty-First Century.' *Journal of International Affairs* 47(1): 59–72.

35. Pamela J Creedon. 1993. 'Framing Feminism—a Feminist Primer for the Mass Media.' *Media Studies Journal* 7(1): 68–81.

36. Shanto Iyengar. 1994. *Is Anyone Responsible? How Television Frames Political Issues.* Chicago: University of Chicago Press.

37. Thomas S. Kuhn. 1962. *The Structure of Scientific Revolutions.* Chicago: University of Chicago Press.

38. For example, in Northern Ireland, since at least the early 1970s, the 'terrorism' frame had long categorized 'friends' and 'enemies' of the democratic process, assigning legitimacy to reporting the viewpoints of certain groups, parties, and leaders, while delegitimizing others that resorted to violence. As discussed further in chapter 5, the peace process, culminating in the Good Friday agreement, radically altered the position of the major political actors, bringing the IRA far more firmly within the electoral arena of democratic politics, a process reinforced by their renunciation of political violence.

39. President George Bush. Address to Congress. *20 September 2001.*

PART I

Generating Terrorism Frames

CHAPTER 2

Terrorism, Censorship and the 1st Amendment: In Search of Policy Guidelines

DORIS A. GRABER

When important values clash in democracies, policy makers and publics face a typical trade-off dilemma. Which should prevail? The dilemma is starkest when the clashing values are national security threatened by terrorism or war, endangering the survival of large numbers of citizens, if not the nation itself, and freedom of the press, which is an indispensable ingredient of democracy. Arguments about whether a free press is actually essential to democracy are beyond the scope of this chapter. Many observers believe that it is and that press freedom is particularly vital in crisis periods because decisions made at that time are apt to produce profound consequences for the nation and its people.

In the post-World War II era, national security risks have appeared in a number of guises. Formal declarations of war have become less common while military confrontations involving terrorism, counter-terrorism, guerilla warfare, peacekeeping operations, and similar so-called 'low intensity conflicts' have increased. Government deliberations, like congressional hearings on the Anti-Terrorism Act of 2001, make it clear that public officials equate the dangers posed by such low-intensity operations with the dangers posed by open warfare.

Many such military missions are comparatively brief with little advance planning and require complete secrecy to succeed. They would be compromised by premature disclosure, especially since reporters are now able to send messages, including pictures, from remote locations at lightening speed. Hence it seems reasonable to consider the history of press restraints during anticipated or actual war as precedent for press freedom policies during periods of anticipated and actual terrorism and subsequent military operations. Periods of ideological onslaught, like the Cold War following World War II, also belong in this category of extreme dangers that generate calls for the suspension or dilution of constitutional guarantees.

The Patterns of Past Solutions

There are basically three approaches to the dilemma of reconciling the conflicting aspects of press freedom and survival security. The *'formal censorship'* approach has been most common. It involves legislation that sets forth what may or may not be published. Such laws vary in the terms and scope of the censorship operations and often stipulate severe penalties for violations. The press may still be allowed to decide what is publishable within the government's guidelines. Alternatively, the decision about what may be published may be in the hands of official censors who use their discretion about the sensitivity of particular information at a specific time. In either case, freedom of the press is in abeyance, as American constitutional lawyers generally interpret it, including the traditional reluctance of American courts to permit prior censorship of potentially harmful news reports (Silverberg 1991).

The opposite '*free press*' approach leaves journalists free to decide what is or is not safe to publish under the circumstances. Journalists may choose to follow guidelines provided by the government or respond to specific requests by public officials. But reporters make the ultimate decision free from formal pressure by public officials, although there are always ethical mandates to be risk-averse when national security is at stake.

The third approach, the '*informal censorship*' scheme, is an ingenious combination of the two: There are no censorship laws and the press is left officially free to decide what it does or does not wish to publish. But pronouncements by high-level government leaders constitute informal censorship because they create a coercive climate that forces the press into self-censorship in line with the wishes of public officials. Criticism of government policy is castigated as unpatriotic, flirting with treason. This form of pressure is often enhanced by a barrage of glowing reports about government progress in coping with the crisis. Self-censorship by the press is complemented by self-censorship by government officials who have been admonished by their leaders to keep their lips tightly sealed. Such "voluntary" constraints, as social scientists have documented, can be just as potent as official censorship laws (Aukofer and Lawrence 1995; Carter and Barringer 2001a).

In a 1987 speech at Hebrew University in Jerusalem, Associate U.S. Supreme Court Justice William J. Brennan Jr. reviewed what he called the "shabby treatment" that America's vaunted freedoms have received in times of war and threats to national security (Brennan 1987). He attributed these lapses to the crisis mentality that Americans develop when faced with danger intermittently, rather than living with it constantly. America's decision-makers have been inexperienced in assessing the severity of security threats and in devising measures to cope with them in ways that respect conflicting rights and liberties.

Brennan might also have added that the equally inexperienced American public has traditionally supported restraints on First Amendment rights and civil liberties when it has been polled during crises, especially if it feels militarily or ideologically threatened (Blendon et al. 2002; Fleischer 2001; Kinsley 2002; Pew 2001). For example, 53 percent of the respondents to a Pew poll reported in the press on November 29, 2001, in the aftermath of the September terrorist attack on U.S. sites, agreed that the government should be able to censor news that "it deems a threat to national security" (Pew 2001). The pollsters asked which was more important: the government's ability to censor or the media's ability to report what seemed in the national interest. Four percent of respondents volunteered that both were equally important.

It is important to note that the vote in favor of government censorship hardly constitutes overwhelming agreement. Besides, a bare majority (52 percent) indicated that the media should dig hard for the news rather than accept government refusals to release it, and 54 percent agreed that media's criticism of leaders keeps them from misbehaving. On balance, however, trust in government trumped trust in the media. Sixty-one percent of respondents expressed a fair amount of confidence that the government was giving the public an accurate picture about its response to terrorism, and 70 percent thought that public safety and protection of American military forces were the main reasons for censorship.

The 'Shabby' Record of Protecting Press Freedom

In a nutshell, press freedom has routinely succumbed to national security concerns on the home front as well as on foreign battlefields. Customarily, in the United States and other democracies with strong traditions of press independence from government, this has been accomplished through legislation or orders by the chief executive or administrative agencies. A quick journey through some of the relevant events in U.S. history is instructive. In democracies where the government owns or otherwise controls the press, wartime situations are more amenable to routine press management procedures (Sajó and Price 1996).

On the verge of war with France in 1798, Congress enacted the Alien and Sedition Acts, claiming that home front censorship was essential to forestall enemy espionage and sabotage. The Sedition Act made it unlawful to "write, print, utter or publish . . . any false, scandalous and malicious writing" against government officials intending "to bring them . . . into contempt or disrepute" (1798, 1 Stat. 570). There were 25 arrests, 15 indictments, and 10 convictions under the act, mostly involving newspaper editors and politicians from the party in opposition to the government. Legal challenges to the act were unsuccessful at the time. But when party fortunes changed, the convicted were pardoned, most fines were returned, and it was widely acknowledged that the laws had been an unnecessary aberration. The dangers had been exaggerated.

Still, when the Civil War presented a major test in 1861, the story was quite similar. As soon as armed conflict started, President Lincoln took drastic measures to neutralize disaffected citizens and potential traitors in the name of national security. Through executive orders, he blocked the distribution of dissenting newspapers and, during the latter part of the war, seized control of the telegraph lines that transmitted war news. The most drastic step was the suspension of habeas corpus. Thousands of people were arrested on suspicion of disloyalty and held in military custody, often without charges. Trials were before military tribunals that lacked the procedural safeguards available in civilian courts. Such steps were bound to intimidate reporters. The public, by and large, approved these actions and condemned judges who questioned their constitutionality.

Another example of censorship legislation comes from the First World War. Congress enacted the Espionage Act, making it a crime to utter, print, write, or publish any "disloyal, profane, scurrilous, or abusive language" or any language intended to bring the U.S. form of government or the Constitution or the flag "into contempt, scorn, contumely, or disrepute" (1918, 40 Stat. 553). More than 2000 individuals, including journalists, were prosecuted under the act. Convictions were mostly for criticizing U.S. participation in the war. In *Abrams v. United States* (1919, 250 U.S. 616) the U.S. Supreme Court upheld such convictions.

The constitutionality of the act was also indirectly sanctioned in the 1919 *Schenck v. United States* case. The Court supported the right of free speech except in case of "clear and present danger" of severe adverse consequences. Wars, in the mind of Justice Oliver Wendell Holmes, obviously constituted such a danger when national security concerns must take precedence over first amendment rights. "When a nation is at war many things that might be said in time of peace are such a hindrance to its effort that their utterance will not be endured so long as men fight" (1919, 242 U.S. 52). In 1943, in *Hirabayashi v. United States,* the Supreme Court clearly indicated that it is the president's prerogative to determine when a threat to national security exists. Internment of Japanese-Americans was appropriate "if those charged with the responsibility of our national defense have reasonable ground for believing that the threat is real" (1943, 320 U.S. 95). Decades later, in the Pentagon Papers case, the Supreme Court contrary to its earlier ruling refused to stop publication of the contents of a classified Defense Department study relating to the Vietnam War despite the administration's contention that the disclosure posed a grave, immediate danger to national security (*New York Times Co. v. United States,* 1971, 463 U.S. 713; Rudenstine 1996).

During the early years of the nation's history, when foreign policies were often highly controversial, the American government considered the media primarily as an obstacle to war that had to be kept under control through strict censorship legislation. That perception had changed by the time World War II started. Impressed by the successful use of propaganda by authoritarian governments, democratic governments had begun to appreciate the power of the press to rally mass publics. They now deemed it a potentially powerful ally in their struggle against the enemies of Western democracies.

The government wanted a policy that would yield ample favorable coverage of the war without risking adverse stories by roaming correspondents. This was to be accomplished by facilitating reporters' access to news about the war, including ongoing battles, but binding them to a gentleman's agreement that they would not reveal anything that might interfere with the military's mission.

Instead of the harsh censorship laws of the past, there would be voluntary cooperation. Most reporters knew and complied with the unstated terms of the compact because it gave them broad access to war information; they censored themselves to live within the terms (Thompson 1991; Thrall 2000). This was easy because, unlike the situation in earlier wars, the objectives of World War II were never controversial in the United States.

In addition to these unwritten understandings, there were more formal arrangements as well to provide guidance to reporters about the limits of safe reporting. On December 19, 1941, President Franklin D. Roosevelt established an Office of Censorship under the First War Powers Act, which operated with a staff of more than 10,000 censors as a home front security guardian until August 15, 1945. The office was authorized to censor mail, cables, newspapers, magazines, films, and radio broadcasts. It issued non-enforceable honor codes of acceptable wartime practices for print and broadcast media. Breaches required prior approval by the Office of Censorship. Compliance with these guidelines was excellent (Aukofer and Lawrence 1995; Thompson 1991). Military authorities in the war zones were authorized to conduct their own censorship operations, which tended to be more restrictive than the civilian censorship at home.

With the Korean War, which began in 1950, the country moved back to the conditions of earlier years when foreign policies had been controversial and civilian and military government leaders feared that hostile reporters might undermine the war effort. The controversial nature of the war made it difficult for the press to keep their stories supportive of the military action while also reflecting the political controversy. Military commanders complained that the system of voluntary self-censorship allowed news sources to publish stories that endangered the war effort. They therefore urged the Defense Department to provide compulsory guidelines. An official censorship code for war correspondents was issued shortly thereafter, in December 1950. Leaders from the journalism community and the military had agreed, following extensive discussions, that all future reports from Korea should first be cleared with Army headquarters. Stringent screening ensued that caused long delays in the transmission of news from the front and frustrated the press. As is usually the case, many provisions of the code were vague, such as the prohibition of stories that might "injure the morale" of American or Allied forces or stories that might 'embarrass' the United States, its Allies, or neutral countries. That made controversies over the administration of the codes inevitable.

By the time of the Vietnam War, the notion that news stories were likely to harm government efforts had regained full currency. Knowing that its policies in Vietnam would be highly controversial, the American government did not wish to alert the public to the extent of U.S. involvement or to the shortcomings of the South Vietnamese government, which it was supporting. Withholding of news so that it could not be published, exaggerating successes to make policies more palatable, and some outright falsifications of potentially damaging data, became accepted policy tools. News people and their reports would not be formally censored. Instead, correspondents would simply be kept in the dark or government sources would feed them carefully selected, and sometimes doctored, news morsels.

The government instructed the U.S. mission in Saigon to control information related to the war tightly by classifying documents and by keeping reporters away from military operations (Aukofer and Lawrence 1995; Thompson 1991). The U.S. mission also negotiated another code of voluntary restraint between the press and the military. Although the military favored a compulsory code in line with those used in earlier wars, none was instituted because of concerns that it might be unconstitutional absent a formal declaration of war. Overall, the self-censorship worked reasonably well; few serious security breaches occurred (Aukofer and Lawrence 1995; Thompson 1991). Of course, the codes did not prevent correspondents from reporting negative news.

To counterbalance unfavorable media stories, the Johnson administration engaged in large-scale press management. It supplied the press with favorable stories in hopes of gaining ample supportive news coverage. That approach backfired when military reverses presented a sharp contrast to earlier reports and appeared larger than they actually were because of the exaggerated optimism. Negative news provided by war correspondents was contradicted by positive reports from government sources, forcing home-front editors to choose between conflicting visions of the war. Initially, most stuck with the government's optimistic framing, but that changed later on. After the war, the military as well as many civilian analysts blamed negative news coverage for loss of public support for the war and the ultimate failure to accomplish U.S. objectives. That judgment poisoned subsequent relations between the military and the press.

During the mid-century Cold War years, Congress had passed laws to prevent spoken and written communications that might expose the country to the danger of a Communist takeover. These laws included the Smith Act, the Internal Security Act of 1950, and the Communist Control Act of 1954. The Smith Act, for example, made it a crime to advocate in a speech or in print the overthrow of the U.S. government by force (1940, 54 Stat. 671). There were many legal challenges to these laws at the time.

The clearest confrontation between the news media and the government's fight against communism occurred during and following a minor military venture in 1983 when the United States tried to avert a Marxist revolution in Grenada, a tiny Caribbean island nation. During the U.S. military invasion of the island, the media were at first kept out entirely and prevented from filing stories. When journalists were allowed to visit the island, military escorts accompanied them. It became clear after the fighting stopped that the operation had been seriously flawed and that the clumsy censorship had prevented disclosing mishaps to policy makers in the United States and to the American public. To avoid similar fiascoes, the chairman of the Joint Chiefs of Staff established a commission, headed by Major General Winant Sidle to study how relations between the press and the military could be handled better in the future. The commission was composed of experienced journalists as well as military and civilian press relations officers. The panel reported its recommendations in August of 1984. Unfortunately, its most novel recommendation—establishment of press pools for operations, which required limiting the number of reporters who cover the event—failed miserably in Panama in 1989 in a mission designed to oust Panamanian President Manuel Noriega.

Despite revisions, the pool concept did not work smoothly in the 1991 Gulf war. This brief conflict is a textbook example of government control over war news without resorting to formal censorship. The government took almost complete control of the war news supply. It used a handful of top-level military leaders to brief the press on all of the aspects of the war that it cared to disclose. When journalists were allowed to visit the front, military escorts accompanied them. The military also supplied excellent visuals of elegantly executed precision maneuvers for use by television reporters. A few journalists defied the constraints imposed by the military during the war and executives from major American media filed complaints with the Defense Department after the war about the efforts to control what reporters saw and about efforts to sanitize and delay the news. These complaints led to yet another revision of the pool system and new, albeit incomplete, rules designed to make it easier for reporters to cover the battlefronts without being leashed to officials.

The Statement of Principles—News Coverage of Combat, which was adopted in April 1992, failed to settle whose judgment prevails about what is publishable. Journalists and military personnel disagreed, and continue to disagree, about whether the military must have the final say on which stories must be submitted to it for security review and censorship. Multiple efforts to draft new ground rules have continued. But the problem may be insoluble (Department of Defense News 2001). The clashing objectives of the major players prevent permanent resolutions, despite a lot of good will and good faith on both sides.

During the conflict with Afghanistan that began in the winter of 2001, the familiar problems resurfaced (see chapters 3 and 7). The military initially restricted the media's access to the battle zones, claiming that complete secrecy was required to assure the success of the operation and the safety of the troops. Reporters were actually locked up in a warehouse to prevent coverage of one incident that involved injuries to U.S. troops from a U.S. bombing raid. The outburst of indignation that followed that episode led to a formal apology from the Defense Department and new rules to allow reporters greater access to the battlefronts. Access did improve subsequently, though many sites remained closed for a variety of hotly disputed reasons. As had been true in past wars, the courts sided with the military in censorship disputes brought before them. A federal district court, while agreeing that the First Amendment protects a limited right of access to foreign battle grounds, nonetheless refused to grant an injunction that would force the military to allow correspondents to accompany American troops in Afghanistan (*Flynt v. Rumsfeld,* 2002).

Terrorism and Censorship

In anticipation of a second Gulf War, the Pentagon announced in February, 2003 that this would be the best-covered military engagement in American history. The new plan is designed to produce battle front coverage from an American perspective to match coverage by foreign news venues like al Jazeera. Pentagon officials selected and trained a representative pool of approximately 600 print and broadcast war correspondents, including some from foreign countries, to accompany troops from all branches of the military. These 'embedded' journalists received elementary military training so that they would be fit to accompany their assigned units at all times. The journalists were required to sign an agreement on ground rules of coverage that obligated them to submit stories that the military deems sensitive to scrutiny by military censors. However, the Defense Department promised that most stories would remain uncensored. Journalists outside the embedded group were not to be subject to restrictive ground rules. But, in line with past history, freelancers had only very limited access to front-line operations.

It is far too early to assess whether this new plan will, indeed, lead to more extensive and informed coverage or whether it will become merely another form of government news management. It seems questionable whether journalists who are buddies with military folk will be able to retain their objectivity and skepticism when they share the troops' hardships, including combat and casualties on a daily basis. Being 'embedded,' as the term suggests, simply may amount to being 'in bed' with the military.

Post-9-11-01 Home Front Censorship

In the crisis following the September 11, 2001 attack, the main censorship problems on the home front have again involved strenuous government efforts to withhold information from the press, claiming that disclosures would endanger national security. These claims have been coupled with well-publicized appeals for self-censorship as a patriotic duty, adding the pressures springing from publicity to the request. Prominent examples of official secrecy are refusals to discuss war-related matters with reporters, withholding all information about people detained by the government, limiting reports about military activities in Afghanistan to reports by the Secretary of Defense and a few generals, and failure to produce the records of what the government knew prior to the 2001 attack that might have forestalled it (Steinhauer 2002).

The Justice Department has contended, albeit without providing evidence, that press inquiries about the detainees rounded up after September 11 could be denied on national security grounds because "public disclosure would undermine counter-terrorism efforts and put the detainees at risk of attack from angry Americans as well as terrorists" (Sachs 2002). Government lawyers have argued in cases that challenged the refusal to disclose the names of the detainees and the charges against them, that national security interests outweigh any public right to know who was detained for what reasons and for what length of time (Sachs 2002).

To throttle the circulation of war-related information, the government has followed the Gulf War pattern of allowing only a few top-level military and civilian officials to report about ongoing events and plans. Secretary of Defense Donald Rumsfeld, for example, has been very accessible to the media but extraordinarily circumspect in giving facts and making claims (Kilian 2002). Reporters have to accept his messages because most of the military activities are conducted by small groups of special operations forces who can be neither accompanied by journalists nor interviewed.

The Bush administration has also urged all high-level government officials to be extraordinarily, and probably excessively, tight-lipped. For example, Attorney General John Ashcroft declined to confirm information about the September 2001 terrorists that Prime Minister Tony Blair had given to the British House of Commons in open session. Ashcroft also issued a memorandum urging federal agencies to resist most Freedom of Information Act requests. As has been typical in these most recent examples of censorship, Ashcroft's request was framed as an act to protect cherished rights. Information disclosures, he argued, might endanger institutional, commercial and personal privacy interests. The Department of Health and Human Services has declined to disclose which antibiotics were used to treat anthrax in Florida when the disease became linked to terrorism threats. Following a leak of terrorism-related information to the press in early October 2001, President Bush announced that most members of Congress would henceforth be excluded from intelligence briefings. However, he relented when faced with strong political pressure to rescind the order.

One effort to suppress information concerned satellite images. It particularly riled the press because it damaged its ability to report the news. The U.S. government had bought exclusive rights to all satellite images of the bombing of Afghanistan available from the civilian satellite Ikonos. That purchase barred the press from seeing and publicizing these privately owned high-resolution images of damage caused by U.S. attacks in Afghanistan. At the time, the Pentagon already had its own, far sharper satellite images. The decision to buy came shortly after reports of heavy civilian casualties near the town of Darunta in Afghanistan. Critics saw it as a stealthy maneuver to hide a disaster.

Government clampdowns on access to video footage were especially damaging for television journalism. News media beyond the borders of the United States were able to feature pictures of the bombing damage in Afghanistan released by the pro-Arab media and framed to reflect anti-American views. There was no matching footage from U.S. sources for friends of the United States, who therefore chose to rely on the interesting footage provided by al Jazeera, the Arab-language satellite television network (see chapter 7).

The news about the purchase of Ikonos pictures was published in the Web issue of the *Guardian*, a British newspaper. Like many other stories about the war, it was unavailable from the American press because its usual sources of news had sealed their lips. American journalists conceded that some of the information circulating about this and other stories in the foreign press was false or distorted. But they also noted that the authenticity issue could not be debated properly if U.S. government officials refused to talk.

The government's policy of withholding news has been complemented by unusually strong appeals to the press for self-censorship. The debate about the propriety and scope of self-censorship escalated after National Security Advisor Condoleezza Rice phoned the chief executives of the major television networks on October 10, 2001, one month after the terrorist assault, asking them not to broadcast messages from Osama bin Laden, the alleged mastermind behind the terrorist assault on the United States. Rice warned that the taped broadcasts by bin Laden might contain encoded messages for terrorists. They could therefore stir up more violence against Americans and recruit more followers in countries like Malaysia where Muslims are in the majority. She urged broadcasters to edit bin Laden's messages before disseminating them.

Ari Fleischer, the president's press secretary, in an October 11 press briefing, denied charges that Rice's request amounted to censorship. He stressed that editorial decisions remained under complete control of media organizations. But he failed to acknowledge that journalists faced strong pressures to comply with White House requests in the wake of the horrific September 11 attacks. As commentator Michael Kinsley said in his *Washington Post* editorial on January 4, 2002, journalists found it exceedingly difficult to challenge the government because the September attack was such a monstrous crime. Journalists who might be inclined to dissent feared the wrath of their readers and their editors and publishers, possibly leading to loss of their job. Such social pressures transformed White House requests into commands.

Predictably, the news executives promised compliance with Condoleezza Rice's request. One network executive called it a "patriotic" decision. However, it was never entirely clear what compliance would entail. According to one news report, it meant that the networks would give the government control over what the public would hear by removing "language the government considers inflammatory" from future broadcast of bin Laden speeches (Carter and Barringer 2001). The executives also promised to put future broadcasts into appropriate context.

It is not unusual for the news media to censor their coverage when they deem it essential for security interests, especially when they agree with the government's objectives and face condemnation and economic penalties for voicing dissent. But self-censorship generally happens quietly behind the scenes to avoid the impression that the media are yielding to compulsion by the government. For example, Leonard Downie, the executive editor of the *Washington Post*, acknowledged that 'a handful of times' in the week's following the September 11 attacks, the *Post's* reporting had prompted calls from administration officials who raised concerns that a specific story or more often that certain facts in a certain story, would compromise national security. In response, Downie said, "In some instances we have kept out of certain stories certain facts that we agreed could be detrimental to national security and not instrumental to our readers, such as methods of intelligence collection" (Carter and Barringer 2001). Similarly, Clark Hoyt, the Washington editor of *Knight Ridder*, said that his organization had held back a report that "some small units of U.S. special operations forces had entered Afghanistan and were trying to locate bin Laden" within two weeks of the 9/11 attacks (Carter and Barringer 2001). Other examples of self-censorship have been reported that were not directly linked to government requests but were instead produced by an opinion climate that seems hostile to criticism of the government during war. For example, domestic criticism of President Bush abated. The Sierra Club removed the "W Watch" column from its website because it could be perceived as critical of Bush. It also stopped its phone solicitations and pulled ads from the air. The AFL-CIO, the Mobilization for Global Justice, Friends of the Earth, and many other groups canceled plans to protest at the annual meetings of the World Bank and the International Money Fund. According to the *New York Times*, "Some groups fear that if they are perceived as unpatriotic it will hurt them in the long run." The public is likely to judge protesters harshly (Pollack, 2001).

Cloaking Censorship with a 1st Amendment Mantle

A review of recent censorship practices in the United States makes it clear that when push comes to shove in reconciling wartime security and press freedom, the First Amendment is still forced to yield. The review also shows that American public officials, as well as the public, manage to cover censorship laws and admonitions with a cloak of First Amendment covers. The excuses that officials and others gave for censorship in the wake of the September 11, 2001, terrorist attacks, transformed censorship into a defense of First Amendment rights (Graber, forthcoming). This is quite typical behavior. America's wars have always been defended as a protection of essential democratic rights. The end—saving democracy—then justifies and hallows the means—self-censorship or censorship by government fiat. For example, a *St. Louis Post Dispatch* editorial on October 11, 2001, noted "Throughout our history, we [Americans] have been willing to trade freedom for safety during wartime."

In an address to the nation delivered on November 8, 2001, at Atlanta's World Congress Center, President George W. Bush justified censorship measures as necessary to protect the values Americans share. He contrasted Americans with their enemies:

> "We value life; the terrorists ruthlessly destroy it. We value education; the terrorists do not believe women should be educated. . . . We value the right to speak our minds; for the terrorists, free expression can be grounds for execution. We respect people of all faiths and welcome the free practice of religion; our enemy wants to dictate how to think and how to worship even to their fellow Muslims."

At the same time, people who question whether First Amendment and other civil rights are actually protected by government information policies are condemned as interfering with the war effort. At best, they are accused of lacking in patriotism; at worst they are called traitors willing to help the enemy and harm their fellow citizens. For instance, Attorney General Ashcroft tried to silence critics of censorship policies by suggesting that their pursuit of "phantoms of lost liberty" was unpatriotic, "giving ammunition to America's enemies and pause to America's friends" (*San Francisco Chronicle* 2001). All the while, Ashcroft continued to proclaim full support for civil liberties, saying that the United States had always met security challenges "in ways that preserved our fundamental freedoms and liberties." In meetings with the Senate Committee on the Judiciary on September 25, 2001, and again on September 28, he assured the committee that his office would not abuse the new authority that he requested to tap electronic messages. Surveillance would be conducted with "a total commitment to protect the rights and privacy of all Americans and the Constitutional protections we hold dear." These meetings were part of a series of Senate oversight hearings conducted under the title "DOJ [Department of Justice] Oversight: Preserving Our Freedoms While Defending Against Terrorism." Censorship was a weapon to preserve treasured freedoms, not an assault on them.

What Should be Done?

The recount of past and ongoing current events makes it clear that national security concerns have always trumped first amendment protections in periods of crisis. It also makes it clear that decisions made while the crisis mentality prevailed were later regretted when it became clear that curtailments of first amendment and other civil rights were excessive. Obviously, sound groundrules for appropriate behavior under crisis conditions are best forged in times of calm.

Is it possible to plan a proper balance of security and free press rights and then apply these rules in times of critical danger? The answer is "yes." Here the rich social-science literature on trade-offs is helpful because it shows how value conflicts in other types of situations are resolved when powerful stakeholders confront each other. How, for example, does one decide where the balance lies between the need to protect the environment and the need to protect the livelihoods of workers engaged in lumbering or oil production? When funding for medical research is limited, how do policy makers determine whether the demands of the AIDS epidemic should take precedence over the demands of the heart failure epidemic? Risk assessment studies and cost-benefit analyses tackle such perennial conundrums and have developed some guidelines, including policy manuals on the trade-off game.

The federal government, for example, has developed a step-by-step manual designed to facilitate trade-off decisions in the environmental policy realm (Decision Process Guidebook 1990). It presents a practical approach to decision-making in situations involving conflicts of vital interests. The Bureau of Reclamation in the Department of the Interior uses this manual for the countless trade-off decisions required for allocating the nation's limited water and hydro-electric resources fairly, efficiently, and cost-effectively to agricultural, municipal, industrial, tribal, and recreational activities in seventeen western states. The bureau must set priorities and mesh the interests of diverse stakeholders, such as states, cities, and local communities, as well as contractors, water and power customers, and representatives of Indian tribes. In the process, the bureau must heed complex environmental laws and regulations, accessibility and safety standards, and public employment diversity rules. The trade-off manual identifies a variety of typical situations, suggests the procedures that should be followed, and gives specific advice about building negotiating teams, identifying benefits to be reaped by individual stakeholders, and avoiding potentially disastrous political snags.

The principles set forth in the manual are relevant for conflicts about the balance between security censorship and press freedom. For instance, the manual stresses the crucial importance of determining who will make and be responsible for the ultimate trade-off decision. In situations involving wartime national security issues, the ultimate judge might be a joint body of media executives, Homeland Security personnel, and National Security Council staff members concerned with military intelligence.

The manual warns that planners who deliberate about trade-off procedures must first define the problem fully. That requires research of problems encountered in the past and how they were resolved or failed to be resolved. For example, as mentioned, we know why several versions of press pools have failed. The diverse characteristics of particular military engagements have made it clear that rules must vary accordingly. In fact, there must be multiple versions. For example, the mountainous terrain of Afghanistan, the presence of many hostile civilians, and the difficulty of communicating in unfamiliar local dialects precluded most journalists from striking out on their own, as would have been possible in Grenada or Panama.

Trade-off planners must agree on the ground rules for their deliberations and how these ground rules should be enforced. For example, they might agree to brainstorm about options without determining their viability initially. They could formulate the minimum standards that each option has to meet to be considered viable and they could establish evaluation criteria in advance of ranking the merits of options. Reaching agreement requires developing measurable indicators and mutual acceptance of the weighting system that will be used to assess each significant issue and to compare alternatives. When applied, the evaluation and weighting criteria should reveal which options have fatal flaws in conception or execution and need to be abandoned. The remaining options should then be ranked according to their numerical weights.

The trade-off manual also stresses that disagreements should be expected because there is never an ideal solution. It recommends focusing on the concerns of the parties who most strongly oppose the plans that enjoy the widest support. Judging from past negotiations about procedures, military leaders are likely to offer the firmest resistance. The goal should be to gain their grudging acceptance of the final policy. A compromise solution is the ultimate goal, after a thorough, dispassionate analysis of trade-offs among competing needs and solutions. Throughout, political considerations and influences and all known risk factors as well as overt and hidden agendas of all stakeholders should receive attention. All parties should realize that some of their goals are totally antagonistic but they should also realize that they must co-exist and it is to their advantage to do so as smoothly and productively as possible. Such a model of co-existence has been referred to as a system of "mutual exploitation" (O'Heffernan 1994).

In the end, the various trade-off options should be presented to the chosen decision-makers for final selection. In each case, the analysis should show how a particular option stacks up in terms of the agreed-upon evaluation criteria. The personnel involved in carrying out the policy should also be consulted to assure the technical feasibility of the plans.

The planning process need not end there. Limited pilot trials could ascertain that the accepted policy—or a fine-tuned version—works. This was done in the effort to iron out the practical problems encountered in operating rotating press pools for battlefront coverage. Once fully in force, implementation of the press policy must be continuously monitored. If needed, adjustments can then be made in line with the policy's guiding objective—a workable balance between press freedom and security needs that recognizes that both are equally essential.

Of course, outlining a trade-off process fails to capture how difficult implementation is in practice. Defining the issues, assigning weights, comparing the benefits and costs of alternatives will always be problematic. Risk assessment and cost effectiveness analyses are young, as yet inadequately developed, sciences. Nonetheless, given the urgency of replacing hastily improvised, flawed programs, cobbled together during times of crisis, with scientifically grounded plans, requires careful advance trade-off planning.

As for the ultimate trade-off, in situations when national security values and press freedom confront each other directly, history suggests that democracies are best served by balancing the scales in favor of a responsible free press. As the *Baltimore Sun* editorialized on October 15, 2001 about the War on Terrorism:

> "The United States is fighting this war in part to preserve democracy and freedom, neither of which can truly be achieved without an informed public. We need to keep the information flowing and work with each other to sort out what's true and what's not … there may be other instances in the next few months in which good judgment should inspire editors to hold back on information that could put the nation's troops or civilians in danger. *But editors, not government, must be the arbiters of what's fit to air or print.* [Italics added] For a free society that's fighting to retain its freedom and procure it for others around the world, no other alternative is acceptable."

References

Abrams v. U.S., 1919, 250 U.S. 616.

Administration's Draft Anti-Terrorism Act of 2001, *Hearing Before the Committee on the Judiciary, House of Representatives.* September 24, 2001. Serial No. 39. http://www.house.gov/judiciary.

Aukofer, Frank and William P. Lawrence. 1995. *America's Team: The Odd Couple, A Report on the Relationship Between the Media and the Military.* http://www.freedomforum.org/publications/first/media and the military.

Baltimore Sun Editorial. 2001. 'A High-tech Information War.' 10-15-2001.

Blendon, Robert J., Stephen R. Pelletier, and Marcus Rosenbaum. 2002. 'Extra-ordinary Measures: Who Wants Military Tribunals and Who Wants to Listen in when Suspects Consult their Lawyers?' May 17, 2002. Paper presented at the Annual meeting of the American Association of Public Opinion Research, St. Petersburg, FL.

Blodgett, John E. 1999. 'Environmental, Health, and Safety Tradeoffs: A Discussion of Policymaking Opportunities and Constraints.' *CRS Report for Congress*, RL30043.

Brennan, William J, Jr. 1987. 'The Quest to Develop a Jurisprudence of Civil Liberties in Times of Security Crises.' Speech, December 22, 1987, at the Law School of Hebrew University, Jerusalem, Israel.

Candea, George and Armando Fox. 2002. 'Making Sound Tradeoffs in State Management.' ACM SIGOPS [Association for Computing Machinery Special Interests Group Operating Systems] European Workshop, September 2002, Sintra, Portugal.

Carter, Bill and Felicity Barringer. 2001a. 'In Patriotic Time, Dissent is Muted.' *New York Times*, 9-28-2001.

Carter, Bill and Felicity Barringer. 2001b. 'Networks Agree to U.S. Request to Edit Future bin Laden Tapes.' *New York Times*, 10-11-2001.

Decision Process Guide Book, National Environmental Policy Act, 1990. http://www.usbr.gov/Decision-Process/execsum.htm.

Department of Defense. 2001. 'Seminar on Coverage of the War on Terrorism.' http://www.defenselink.mil/news/Nov2001/t11182001_t1108br.html, Statement by the *New York Daily News* reporter Tom DeFrank during the seminar, co-sponsored in November 2001 by the Department of Defense and the Brookings Institution.

Espionage Act, 1918, 40 Stat. 553, 1918.

Flynt v. Rumsfeld. Civ. No. 01=2399, DDC, Jan.8, 2002.

Graber, Doris A. 2002. 'Styles of Image Management: Justifying War Time Press Censorship.' *Discourse and Society,* forthcoming.

Hahn, Robert W. ed. 1996. *Risks, Costs and Lives Saved: Getting Better Results from Regulation,* Washington, DC: AEI Press.

Hirabayashi v. U.S., 1943, 320 U.S. 95.

Kilian, Michael. 2002. 'The Pentagon Puzzle.' *Chicago Tribune*, 1-7-02.

Kinsley, Michael. 2002. 'Listening to Our Inner Ashcrofts.' *Washington Post*, 1-4-02.

Luce, Mary Frances, James R. Bettman, and John W. Payne. 1997. 'Choice Processing in Emotionally Difficult Decisions.' *Journal of Experimental Psychology,* 23(1): 384–405.

National Research Council, Committee on Risk Characterization. 1996. *Understanding Risk: Informing Decisions in a Democratic Society.* Washington, DC: National Academy Press.

New York Times Co. v. United States, 1971, 463 U.S. 713.

Office of Censorship, 1941. EO 8985, 12-19-1941, established under First War Powers Act, 55 Stat. 840, 12-18-1941.

O'Heffernan, Patrick. 1994. 'A Mutual Exploitation Model of Media Influence in U.S. Foreign Policy.' pp. 231–249 in *Taken By Storm: The Media, Public Opinion, and U.S. Foreign Policy in the Gulf War,* eds. W. Lance Bennett and David L. Paletz, Chicago: University of Chicago Press.

Pew Research Center for the People and the Press, 2001. 'Terror Coverage Boosts News Media's Images But Military Censorship Backed.' http://people-press.org/reports/print.php3?PageID=14.

Pollack, Andrew. 2001. 'A Nation Challenged; The Advocates.' *New York Times,* 9-27-2001. Presidential/Congressional Commission on Risk Assessment and Risk Management, 1997. *Risk Assessment and Risk Management in Regulatory Decision-Making.* Washington, DC: Government Printing Office.

Rudenstine, David. 1996. *The Day the Presses Stopped: A History of the Pentagon Papers Case.* Berkeley: University of California Press.

Sachs, Susan. 2002. 'U.S. Defends Witholding Immigrants' Names.' *New York Times,* 5-21-02.

Sajó, András and Monroe Price, eds. 1996. *Rights of Access to the Media.* The Hague: Kluwer Law International.

San Francisco Chronicle Editorial, 2001. 'On Civil Liberties; Under Cloak of Security,' 12-9-2001.

Schenck v. U.S., 1919. 242 U.S. 52.

Sedition Act, 1798. 1 Stat. 570, 1798.

Shin, Michael and Michael D. Ward. 1999. 'Lost on Space: Political Geography and the Defense-Growth Trade-Off.' *Journal of Conflict Resolution,* 43(6): 793–817.

Silverberg, Marshall. 1991. 'Constitutional Concerns in Denying the Press Access to Military Operations.' pp. 165–175. In *Defense Beat: The Dilemmas of Defense Coverage,* Loren B. Thompson, Ed. New York: Lexington Books.

Smith Act, 1940, 54 Stat. 671.

St. Louis Post Dispatch, Editorial, 2001. 'The Power of Information.' 10-11-01.

Steinhauer, Jennifer. 2002. 'Records of 9/11 Response not for Public, City Says.' *New York Times,* July 23, 2002.

Thompson, Loren B. 1991. 'The Media Versus the Military: A Brief History of War Coverage in the United States.' pp. 3–56 in *Defense Beat: The Dilemmas of Defense Coverage,* Loren B. Thompson, ed. New York: Lexington Books, 1991.

Thrall, A. Trevor. 2000. *War in the Media Age.* Cresskill, NJ: Hampton Press.

CHAPTER 3

Clausewitz in the Age of CNN: Rethinking the Military-Media Relationship

ROBIN BROWN

In the months after September 11, 2001, the news media were dominated by the War on Terrorism and military operations in Afghanistan, the comments of politicians and pundits, as well as informed and not-so-informed speculation. This mass of coverage was accompanied by tensions between government, the military, and journalists. The media complained that they were denied access to the information needed to inform the public while military leadership fretted about security. In this respect the relationship between the military and the media appeared to fit a long running pattern of tensions between the two. This chapter argues that this conventional understanding of the relationship between media reporting and military activity actually obscures the extent to which, rather than simply reporting events happening "out there," the media have become part of the conflict. The growing pervasiveness of media coverage is reshaping the nature of the relationship between governments, publics, and the armed forces in a way that is not fully understood by any of the parties involved.

The argument of this chapter is that the relationship between government, military, and the media are increasingly intertwined as a result of long-term processes of political and technological change. These issues are explored via the work of Carl Von Clausewitz and his discussion of the relationship between the military and the political. Although Clausewitz has nothing to say about the press, he provides a way of placing the issue of government-military-media relations in wartime in a broader and more historical perspective. Clausewitz took the view that war was the continuation of politics and that war changed as politics and society altered. What are the implications of a world where politics is increasingly conducted via the mass media? This discussion suggests three major consequences. Firstly, national leaderships are becoming increasingly sensitive to how war is reported and the political consequences of that reporting. This leads them to exercise increasing degrees of direct control over field commanders out of fear of the consequences of this reporting. Secondly, efforts to actively shape media coverage will grow even as the expansion of the volume of reporting makes that task increasingly difficult. Thirdly, we can expect media coverage to have an influence on how the war is waged.

This chapter falls into four main parts. The first briefly reviews the development of the literature on the relationship of the media and international conflict. The second outlines Clausewitz's argument about the military-political relationship. The third examines some of the ways in which the changing social and technological environment over the past two centuries has affected this relationship. The final part of the chapter illustrates these themes with examples from the Kosovo Conflict and the War on Terrorism, drawing in particular on the case of British Task Force Jacana in the Afghanistan War to illustrate the changing dynamics of relationship between the press and the military.

The Military and the Media: From Vietnam to Bosnia

Over the past twenty-five years the paradigm for thinking about the relationship between the military, media, and public opinion has been set by the perceived lessons of the Vietnam War. This paradigm has shaped the approach of policymakers, academics, and the military. From the perspective of the military it has been argued that critical reporting undermined the U.S. war effort. That is, the media's focus on casualties and the lack of American success aided an antiwar movement and undermined public support. Despite criticism by analysts such as Daniel Hallin, who argued that media coverage was largely supportive of the war effort, this view had an impact on policy. The government and military in countries such as the United States, Britain, and Israel have been concerned to manage media coverage of conflict to ensure positive coverage (Wesmoreland 1976: 420, Hallin 1986, Thrall 2000).

The 1990–91 Gulf Crisis gave a new impetus to this debate but also introduced a new concern with the implications of twenty-four-hour global television in the form of CNN. While initial discussion was concerned with the impact of CNN as a diplomatic tool, by the mid-1990s this discussion evolved to ask whether television was actually shaping U.S. foreign policy in cases such as Kurdistan, Bosnia, and Somalia. It was argued that the impact of television pictures 'forced' policy makers into taking action whether it was to intervene in humanitarian crises or to pull out once intervention had actually occurred (e.g. Hoge 1994). As with the earlier conflict, an academic literature developed disputing the initial claims. This literature has demonstrated that it is difficult to find evidence for claims about the power of the media over policy (Livingston and Eachus 1995, Livingston 1997, Robinson 1999).

As with the earlier discussion about Vietnam, the "CNN effect" literature has tended to portray the media as something that influences the policy process through its impact on public opinion. This might be termed an "external" paradigm of government-media relations. In contrast, a growing body of work on domestic politics suggests the media should be seen as an integral part of contemporary governance. The media can be found deeply entrenched within the policy process by serving as a source of information for political actors, as a means of communication between them, and as an instrument of mobilization (e.g. Cook 1998, Kernell 1997). It has been argued that one of the reasons for the prominence of the media in the U.S. policy process is the decentralization of the American system of government compared with many other countries. Given the even more decentralized nature of the international system, there might be an even greater reliance on the media. Evidence to support this view can be found in the development of the modern apparatus of media management, the memoirs of political practitioners, and academic studies that draw on interviews, which almost uniformly give testimony (sometimes unintentionally) to the role of the media in the contemporary international political process.[1]

Clausewitz on War

Clausewitz observed that war is the continuation of politics with an admixture of other means—that is violence. This simple maxim conceals two ideas which underpin the discussion here. First, Clausewitz argues that war has changed over time. As the form of social organization changes so does the nature of war. The sources of conflict, the methods used, and the modes of thinking about it reflect the nature of the entities waging war (Clausewitz 1976: 586–93). Secondly, to understand what is going on in a conflict, military events must be put in a political context (Clausewitz 1976: 75–89). At a basic level, the scale of the political objective determines the type and scale of force that will be used. A conflict waged for national survival will generate very high levels of commitment and the use of extreme violence. Situations where the objectives are minor will suggest a lower level of political commitment and more limited use of force. Although this is the fundamental relationship, the interaction between war and politics is dynamic. As a conflict develops, events in the military and political spheres impact on each other. Because military activity was merely one aspect of a more complex whole, it follows that the narrower (military) instrument must be subordinated to the broader (political) perspective. Although politics is fundamental, military force it also has its own dynamic. As he puts it:

> Do political relations between people and between their governments stop when diplomatic notes are no longer exchanged? Is war not just another expression of their thoughts, another form of speech or writing? Its grammar, indeed may be its own, but not its logic. Military action has its own peculiar requirements. . . . [political] considerations do not determine the posting of guards or the employment of patrols. But they are the more influential in the planning of war, of the campaign and even of the battle. (Clausewitz 1976: 605–6)

Although Clausewitz does not make this point, the nature of this relationship was influenced by the relative difficulty of communication at the time. Clausewitz provides a metatheory of war—the political and social environment shapes war so this is always the most appropriate axis of analysis—and a specific theory of strategy for the early nineteenth century. The times have changed since then. How have the relationships between war and politics changed? How does the

Clausewitzian insight help to illuminate the relationship between media, government, and military?

Transformations

In the period since Clausewitz wrote, war has been transformed, along with contemporary society. Two dimensions of change in patterns of communication have particular resonance for the relationship between war and politics; first the emergence of a democratic mediated political space and second the impact of technology on the relationship between the political and military spheres.

Writing in the wake of the wars triggered by the French Revolution, Clausewitz was profoundly aware of the implications of the political and military consequences of democratization. Powerful political forces demanded greater political involvement while others resisted it. Throughout the nineteenth century, European political elites sought to restrict the impact of democratization on political military decision-making. But even as the old elites resisted change they came to recognize that popular sentiment was an important source of military power. Without the active involvement of large sections of the population, national military power would be limited. Thus the people came to be more involved in war. This increasing involvement led to total war. The First and Second World Wars reflected the Clausewitzian point that the day-to-day impact of politics declines as the scale of the conflict expands. Where two opponents aim at the total defeat of the other, the requirements of military operations, mobilization, and logistics push political influence into the background. Political debate shrank under the force of mass mobilization. The public sphere was dominated by a consensus that was actively encouraged by the machinery of the state, using the twin tools of propaganda and censorship (Carruthers 2000: chap. 2). Although the Allies had many political disagreements over strategy, there was a high degree of consensus over the need to destroy the Axis regimes.

In the post-1945 period, Western countries were involved in numerous conflicts, but because Cold War conflicts were designated as limited wars, the public sphere was less constrained by government publicity and censorship than during the World Wars. At the same time the more ambiguous nature of the conflicts, and the lower level of threat, meant that there was greater scope for political debate (Taylor 1997, Carruthers 2000). In the United States the aftermath of Vietnam further loosened the social and political pressures for consensus. The Gulf War added a new dimension to this opening of the public sphere with the emergence of twenty-four-hour television and a significant increase in the ability of media to gather and transmit news from around the world. Coverage could come from a broader range of locations, more quickly than before, and be beamed back across the world. In subsequent conflicts these changes in the media were even more marked. Some analysts have pointed to the development of media organizations whose behavior was marked by a combination of professional journalistic values, commercial considerations, and technological possibilities, rather than by national loyalties (MacGregor 1997, Entman 2000, Shaw 2000).

In terms of the military-political interface that so concerned Clausewitz, the changing media environment affects the political context of war in two ways. First, it changes the nature of the relationship between military operations and their environment; second, it changes the nature of the political discussion around warfare. The new media environment is marked by a vast increase in the flow of information from and to war zones via news organizations, NGOs, and individuals. Although the literature tends to place weight on the ability of military and governmental actors to shape the news media's access to information, it should be recognized that these efforts at management are happening in an environment where technology is working against that control. The consequences of technology were clearly seen during operations in Afghanistan (see Chapter 7). Although the U.S. media criticized the willingness of the government to provide access for journalists, the extent to which global media were able to report on a conflict in the interior of Afghanistan was striking (Hickey 2002). The widespread adoption of satellite phone technology allowed journalists to report back in real time with eyewitness reports and the views of local actors. In the period before the fall of Kabul, one impressive feature of media coverage (at least in the United Kingdom) was a running critique of coalition strategy from the Northern Alliance. As the Department of Defense briefed the media with their version of events, an alternative account was being beamed back from the interior of Afghanistan (e.g. Warren 2001, McCarthy and Meeks 2001).

The result of these information flows is potentially to change the nature of the political context of the conflict. As Schattschneider argued, to expand the scope of a conflict is to change who is involved and its outcome (Brown 2002a). As information flows out of the battle space more quickly, it becomes more feasible for external groups to exert influence through their political response to events. These external groups may be the American public, governments sympathetic or opposed to the cause, allied publics, and the Arab street. Reports are events in their own right. Comments are acts (Miller 2002). News about responses flows back to theater commanders and troops as well as to national command authorities. As the degree of scrutiny increases, the political consequences of minor activities have to be considered. Events that were so minor that they would not be known outside the immediate area may take great significance via the process of mediation. Isolated events come to stand as signifiers for a broader picture. Clausewitz understood that third parties could react to the events of warfare in ways that might have political or military consequences, but in his era those reactions were constrained by the difficulties of communication. In the twenty-first century more people learn about more events more quickly than ever before, and by doing so can react to them.

While this new media environment expands flows of information, it also affects the nature of the way in which conflict is discussed. Analysis of the impact of twenty-four-hour news has tended to focus on its significance in informational terms, but this phenomenon has also expanded the scope for comment, speculation, analysis, and explanation (MacGregor 1997).

Even where the news outlet is faced with a developing story—like a war—it is faced with the paradox that the coverage is much faster than the action that it covers. It takes only a few moments to report that a bombing raid is taking place but the flight to the target, the return, the planning, the evaluation all take hours or days. Twenty-four-hour news is confronted with the reality that war is boredom punctuated by fear. Much activity is routine. The result is that the media sphere is filled not with reporting—after all there are limits to how many times a piece of information can be repeated—but with commentary and speculation. It is this commentary which provides the perceptions of the progress of the war held by the public at large and much of the political community. Those actually running the war find themselves confronted by a running critique of the conduct of the conflict. It is a critique governed by the rules of the news cycle rather than by the reality of military and diplomatic activity. Given that the modern political class is highly sensitive to media commentary, there is recognition that shaping how war is presented and analyzed is an inescapable requirement.

These changes in the media environment obviously affect the relationship between the media and political leadership: These shifts need to be connected to technologically-driven changes in the relationship between political leadership and the military. Just as technology has transformed the ability of journalists to report, so has it transformed the ability of military organizations to communicate.

In the period after 1945 the United States actively sought to develop an integrated global system of command and control that provided decision-makers with the ability to communicate directly and in real time with military units around the world. The origins of such systems were partly technological and partly political. The fear of surprise nuclear attack and the risks of unauthorized use of nuclear weapons were major forces for the development of such systems. However, the development of the ability to communicate had political and organizational effects. They reinforced the sense of the world as a single space and encouraged a tendency to see isolated events as part of a single pattern (Bracken 1983).

While the ability to communicate is valuable, it was soon noticed that the existence of this capability had some negative consequences. The assumption underlying military organizations is that to function effectively lines of responsibility should be clearly defined and that patterns of communication should, in general, follow the chain of command. These conventions, in part, grew from the impossibility of doing anything else. The development of improved command-and-control systems created the temptation for the political leadership to exert direct control over subordinate units and for military commanders to breach the chain of command. It also, apparently, created the possibility for command to be exerted from greater distance literally, units could be commanded from vast distances, and figuratively, as a result command could be exercised by people with little understanding of what was happening on the scene. During the Vietnam War military commanders fumed at the way that President Johnson would insist on personally approving targets for attack in North Vietnam. In the field it was not unusual for platoon commanders to find generals hovering overhead and taking advantage of plentiful radio equipment to provide a running critique of their performance (Van Creveld 1985: chap. 7). In the succeeding decades the trajectory of technological evolution has only strengthened the ability of those in command to reach subordinates anywhere in the world.

What these developments suggest is a compression of the distance between political leadership, senior military commanders, and those on the ground. Information about events on the ground flows back more rapidly, in greater volume, and through a multiplicity of channels. Those in the field will have a greater awareness of the political requirements and situation and those in the rear will have a greater awareness of ongoing military events and their potential impact.

Bringing these transformations together we see a picture where decision-makers are more exposed to external criticism and debate. In the United States direct experience combined with the political folk memory of Vietnam leads to great sensitivity to the political consequences of military action. At the same time the military command, even in theater, are more tightly connected to the political context at home. As information flows out of the battlefield the military-political connections with the rest of the world become tighter. Because minor activities take on a greater visibility, their political consequences have to be considered: Politics may come to affect the posting of guards and the movements of patrols. The following hypotheses might apply.

- Field commanders will have declining autonomy: Because of the potential political significance of their actions their superiors will constantly monitor and seek to control these actions.
- As the diversity of media sources grow, managing the coverage of war will become more important: Leaders will need to shape coverage to attempt to maintain a consensus regarding the conflict, even as their ability to do this declines.
- Rather than the military-media relationship being simply a matter of how reporting affects public opinion, the media discourse comes to have an impact on how the war is waged.

To put it crudely, the separation between the political and the military as spheres of activity become blurred. The communicative elements of warfare have grown in importance.

Evidence from Kosovo and the Afghanistan War

The extent to which we can actually test these hypotheses in a systematic way will depend on further research and the availability of a more developed set of data; however, the available evidence from case studies gives a fair degree of plausibility to these suggestions.

Kosovo

While aspects of the Kosovo campaign remain obscure—in particular why Serbia finally conceded—it is clear that it was marked by high levels of concern over the public perception of the war (Clark 2001, Halberstam 2001, Daalder and O' Hanlon 2000). In his study of American decision-making over Vietnam, Leslie Gelb put forward the argument that the system worked perfectly—it produced a response that was the maximum politically feasible and the minimum militarily necessary (Gelb with Betts 1977). The problem was that this effort was insufficient to produce the desired result. The story of the NATO assault on Yugoslavia seems to have a similar logic. There was a minimal political consensus to launch an air campaign against the regime of Yugoslavian President Slobodan Milosevic, but no agreement about the military campaign that would defeat him. There was a distinctly improvised element to the campaign, based on an assumption that Belgrade would cave in after two or three days of bombing (Halberstam 2001: 425). When this did not happen the limits of the consensus became obvious. Some NATO members appear to have favored a bombing pause and negotiations; the British appear to have been the most aggressive in favoring a ground option; and NATO members favored a continuation of bombing with greater or lesser degrees of escalation. The key to being able to sustain the campaign was not military resources or casualties but the ability to sustain political support in the face of the uncertainties and contingencies of war: civilian casualties, targeting errors, the apparent ineffectiveness of air attacks in hitting Serbian units in Kosovo (Vickers 2000).

Those involved saw the public face of the conflict as being of extreme importance. Only by convincing Milosevic and his potential supporters of the inevitability of defeat could he be persuaded to back down. This could only happen by demonstrating allied resolve through the continuation of the campaign. Thus the presentation of the conflict became a key battlefield as NATO sought to maintain its minimal consensus. Trevor Thrall's view that the pressures for constraints on the media tend to come from the political authorities was strikingly illustrated when Alistair Campbell, Tony Blair's Director of Communication, imported media management techniques from domestic politics into NATO. The representation of the conflict was seen as part of the conflict. Both sides attempted to define the dominant narrative of the conflict (Vickers 2000, Brown 1999, Thrall 2000).

Shaping actions to minimize political risks led to arguments over which targets were legitimate and over the risks of collateral damage. Targets had to be approved at the highest political level. The arguments over bombing harked back to Lyndon Johnson's insistence on personal control over the bombing of North Vietnam and looked forward to George W. Bush's control over the air war against Afghanistan. Despite the critiques of the conduct of Rolling Thunder, the fact that the same practice endures reflects the changing political and technological environment of war rather than the idiosyncrasies of particular leaders (Clodfelter 1989: 84–8, Clark 2001: 201, Schmitt 2001: 4).

The availability of NATO's supreme allied commander, General Wesley Clark, at the end of a telephone or a videoconferencing link ensured that he was aware of practically every twist and turn of the policy debate in Washington and this led to a kind of management by nuance that would not be feasible in a less-wired age. His superiors judged his performance as much by his media appearances and reaction to them as by any military criteria. As an American officer, Clark was particularly exposed to the U.S. debate, but as a NATO commander, he was available to all the other member states (Clark 2001: 273).

The Afghanistan War

By the Afghanistan War, one might expect that the political and presentational concerns that marked the campaign in Kosovo would have disappeared. In Afghanistan, the United States, the greatest global power and the victim of a direct attack, was seeking to deal with its foes. But the war had many of the same characteristics as Kosovo. There was concern with the media consequences of actions and the importance of international public opinion. As in Kosovo there was the creation of an international news management mechanism (DeYoung 2001). We see the same insistence on the approval of targets at the highest levels. However it might be suggested that Kosovo and the War on Terrorism differed in that, while both demonstrate a high degree of sensitivity to media coverage, the levels of vulnerability were different. 'Sensitivity' can be treated as the degree to which coverage is a concern to be monitored, managed, and responded to. 'Vulnerability' can be thought of as the potential for coverage to bring about a change in policy either directly or through its impact on the members of a coalition or those who can exert pressure on them. Because Kosovo depended on a coalition whose leader, the United States, was only marginally committed to the war, the degree of vulnerability was high. In the Afghan case, the relatively high-level commitment by the United States serves to reduce the degree of vulnerability, if not sensitivity.[2]

Operations in Afghanistan provided further evidence of the increasing reach of command and control systems with their potential pathologies. At the Battle of Tora Bora, the most senior American officer present was reported to be a lieutenant colonel. The next highest level of command was at Central Command in Tampa, Florida. Critics of the way the operation was handled charge that the absence of more senior commanders meant that those on the ground did not have the clout to bring in additional coalition ground troops and prevent the escape of senior al Qaeda figures (Gellman and Ricks 2002). Similarly, cameras carried by troops or mounted on remote controlled aircraft allowed senior officers to watch troops in combat from a safe distance, with the result that in the view of one officer: "You get too focused on what you can see and neglect what you can't see." (Ricks 2002).

Task Force Jacana

By examining a British case study drawn from the operations in Afghanistan, in Task Force Jacana, it becomes clear that the developments that have been identified are not simply American. In the aftermath of September 11, Britain was the United States' most vocal supporter in the War on Terror. Once operations in Afghanistan began, it was widely assumed by the media, encouraged by government, that British ground forces would be deployed in combat operations. After the liberation of Kabul, Britain was quick to insert troops into Bagram Air Base as part of the International Security Assistance Force. But the lack of combat operations seems to have led to a degree of frustration both in the government and the media. Thus the announcement in March 2002 that a force of Royal Marine Commandos was to be deployed on combat operations in southern Afghanistan, in Task Force Jacana, caused some excitement in the British media. The developments that followed certainly provide prima facie evidence to support the view that ties between the political and military spheres are becoming ever closer, linked in large part by the news media.

The context for the deployment of Task Force Jacana was the aftermath of the Battle of Tora Bora in early-December 2002. It was widely believed that Osama bin Laden had been able to escape because of the unreliability of allied Afghan forces (Gellman and Ricks 2002). This view triggered a decision to commit coalition ground forces to similar operations. The most significant of these was Operation Anaconda in early March (Gordon 2002). In the wake of this operation the U.S. command requested the deployment of a British force. Largely composed of Royal Marine commandos from three commando brigades, Task Force Jacana was trained in mountain warfare and it seemed to be a logical reinforcement for the effort on the ground (Hoon 2002). The deployment of the task force was accompanied by extensive media coverage, assisted by the Ministry of Defence. The commander of the force, Brigadier Roger Lane, rapidly became a familiar face on UK television. The rhetoric around the force emphasized their capabilities, the dangers of the terrain, and the prospects of fighting and casualties (BBC 2002a). This rhetoric had a priming effect creating expectations for the media. These were not met. Having been dispatched to Bagram air base outside Kabul, the force was initially deployed on Operation Ptarmigan, a sweep through the mountains south of Tora Bora, in mid-April 2002. The British media filled with commentary emphasizing the dangers of the job and the inevitability of casualties. A skeptical voice was raised by a Conservative party spokesman who pointed out that valley had already been swept by allied forces (BBC 2002b). After days of patrolling the operation was terminated without contact with the enemy. In early May the task force was again sent to sweep mountainous territory in Operation Snipe. This failed to come into contact with enemy forces but it did discover a large quantity of ammunition which was found and blown up (literally and figuratively) with suitable publicity. The media described the explosion in hyperbolic terms. Almost immediately local leaders were disputing whether the munitions destroyed belonged to al Qaeda at all (BBC 2002c, BBC 2002d). After two operations without a contact, Brigadier Lane felt it necessary to downplay the situation, commenting that "the need for offensive operations is beginning to dwindle and they will be completed in a matter of weeks rather than months." When a reporter conveyed Lane's assessment to the U.S. Secretary of Defense, Donald Rumsfeld, he chose to rebut it (Gall 2002, Rumsfeld 2002). As the troops returned to their base at Bagram, members of the personnel of a British Army field hospital were diagnosed with a serious infection. At one point there was speculation that the illness was caused by a biological weapons attack, only for the UK media to wheel out public health specialists who attributed the probable cause to poor hygiene. There were comments about the poor living conditions of British forces versus those of the U.S. and German troops in the area (BBC 2002e). Rather than the force becoming evidence of British military prowess, it was becoming a joke. The British media were becoming frustrated with the lack of stories.

On Friday 17 of May Britain awoke to hear the voice of Brigadier Roger Lane announcing that "I can confirm that the coalition has made contact with the enemy and that some have been killed" (BBC 2002f). The marines were once again aboard their helicopters and moving to rescue a patrol of the soldiers from the Australian army who had been ambushed. The previous afternoon an Australian patrol had come under fire. A second patrol had moved to its aid under fire but with the support of US AC-130 gunships. Now it was clear that 'our boys' were going in as a quick reaction force to cover the extraction of the Australians and engage the enemy force. It was later reported that within a matter of minutes the Ministry of Defence in London had moved to deny Brigadier Lane's comments. The impression given that British troops were engaging the enemy was wrong (Rayment 2002). Across the following days the initial reports were undermined. It was reported that the men killed and injured by the American planes were locals engaged in a feud over access to woodlands, according to one source, or were firing into the air at a wedding, according to another (BBC 2002g, Bunting 2002). For the third time, the British commandos failed to make contact with the enemy.

The Sunday Telegraph carried a story citing an anonymous source in the MoD claiming that Brigadier Lane had lost the confidence of both the MoD and his subordinates. The story further suggested that Lane had pressed his American commander to allow his exhausted men to be sent to rescue the Australians rather than an American force.[3] In response the minister of defence, Geoff Hoon, rushed onto David Frost's Sunday morning television talk show to support Lane

(BBC 2002I). General Julian Thompson, who had commanded 3 Commando Brigade in the Falklands Conflict, popped up on Radio 4's *Broadcasting House* programme to support Brigadier Lane. His comments actually threw an unwanted sidelight on the narrative of the conflict by claiming that the failure of the enemy to engage was normal in this kind of "counter-insurgency operation." That was factually correct, but nobody in the coalition was using the language of counter-insurgency (BBC 2002h).

Hoon's support for Brigadier Lane was immediately undercut by the emergence of fact that the MoD had already decided to cut short Lane's tour of duty as commander of 3 Commando Brigade. The MoD then claimed that this decision had been made to free Lane for an important staff job. It then became clear that Lane in fact had no job to go to. The consequence was political criticism of Hoon and the government in general for hyping expectations of the operations, for damaging the morale of the troops, and for incompetence in not knowing the facts. The chief of the Defence staff appeared in public to take responsibility for the confusion (Norton-Taylor and Watt 2002a, Norton-Taylor and Watt 2002b, Smith 2002a). In the following days stories about difficult relations between the Coalition forces at Bagram and the British media emerged (Smith 2002b). These helped to explain the critical tone of some of the press coverage. "HUMILIATED" was the headline in the *Daily Mirror*. The men of 3 Brigade were reported to be hurt and angered by their coverage. As one marine was reported as saying "How can we be humiliated when we are out on patrol and al Qaeda won't dare to take us on?" (Smucker 2002). Subsequent reports claimed that the arguments over Brigadier Lane had damaged the morale of the forces and that criticisms had emerged from a struggle between the navy and the army (Smith 2002c, Chamberlain 2002).

There is nothing new in the saga of Brigadier Lane. Tensions between field commanders and their superiors, between the military and political leadership, between military and media, between allies are not unusual. What is striking here though is the relative seamlessness of the whole field. British and American figures commented on each others' statements, the distance between London and Bagram seemed insignificant, the journalists asked marines for responses to the day's press coverage, sources in London briefed against commanders in the field, local voices emerge to challenge the official account. Journalists were able to challenge the narrative of policy effectively in real time. People on the ground found that their performance is subject to media commentary and interpretation.

The British government found the credibility of their policy challenged as a result of these events. By the end of Operation Condor the media were treating Task Force Jacana as somewhere between a joke and activities of marginal significance (Jenkins 2002). While there were undoubtedly difficulties in the media-military relationship, most of the problems stemmed from the actions of the government and military. It was the government that created the expectations of combat that were not met. It was they who seemed to lack a clear view of what they wanted the journalists to do. The negative stories emerged from conflicts with the military command. Figures within the government were using the techniques of media politics to advance their own positions and attack their opponents. It was the military and political leadership that was unclear about both about the situation on the ground in Afghanistan and the overall policy context. It was the military and political leadership that effectively failed to develop an effective system to coordinate their message. The activities of Task Force Jacana provide example of Gould's words: "In a modern media environment, competence and good communications are inseparable: you cannot have one without the other" (Gould 1998: 334). If you are good at your job but you cannot communicate it effectively then the media will define you as a failure. Gould's maxim was coined in the context of British domestic politics, but it is increasingly true of international affairs.

Conclusions

The analysis presented here suggests that in times of conflict, the media, military, and government are interdependent to a degree that has yet to be recognized by the public, leaders, or scholars. The patterns of media reporting come to shape the political environment in which crises unfold. Politicians react to reports and comments of uncertain reliability. The media does not simply report events; instead the way that the media represents the crisis becomes an important part of the crisis. Media reporting does not simply affect domestic public opinion but forms the basis of reactions by third parties. For this reason government and the military increasingly seek to shape these representations even as their ability to do so declines.

Over the past decade as armed forces, particularly in the United States, have sought to come to terms with the impact of new information and communications technologies, it has come to be recognized that information is not just about computers but provides a way to link a number of military activities, including psychological operations, deception, truth projection, and public affairs. These ideas raise issues for the relationship between the media, government, and public. This was demonstrated in February 2002 when information was leaked to the press about the creation of an "Office of Strategic Influence" within the U.S. Department of Defense. This agency had a mandate to use the whole range of instruments of information operations to advance American interests, including deception via foreign media organizations. The initiative reflected the logical appreciation that briefing the media and black propaganda can influence an opponent. The result was a firestorm of media criticism that eventually resulted in the closure of the office. The furor that erupted around OSI followed precisely from a feeling that it broke the rules that govern the relations between government and media. This is true, but the emergence of the Information Operations doctrine and initiatives like OSI are a recognition that the information revolution is changing the extent to which communication can reach audiences and perhaps modify their information, attitudes, and behavior (Brown 2002b). The changing role of communication and information

recognized by the new military thinking requires citizens, politicians, and scholars to think more carefully about how the relationship between media and
government should operate.

This changing environment has implications for the media, for citizens,
and for governments. Perhaps most important, these changes have reduced the
ability of national governments to define events for their citizens. The ability of
the global communications system to gather and disseminate information has
vastly increased. These systems have the potential to change the scope of conflict
and of course change its outcomes. In such an environment it is no surprise that
the sensitivity of governments to the media increases. The consequence of a more
transparent and public environment is to force governments to engage with the
media and publics to tell their story. The effects of this will vary from case to case
(and from country to country), but it can only increase the interpenetration of
war, politics, and the media.

Notes

1.   For interview-based studies see (Cohen 1963, Davison 1974, Cohen 1986). The memoirs
      of press secretaries will of course emphasize the importance of the media but recent
      diplomatic memoirs contain much of interest about the way the media is used. For press
      officers see (Speakes 1988, Fitzwater 1995). For diplomats see for example (Schultz 1993;
      Bildt 1998; Holbrooke 1999).
2.   The distinction between vulnerability and sensitivity is taken from (Keohane and Nye
      1977). This distinction reworks the 'policy clarity' variable found in much writing in
      the CNN Effect (eg Robinson 2002). The issue is less one of having a clear policy but
      of the degree of commitment to it.
3.   (Rayment 2002). While Rayment's story makes this claim, an American account suggests
      that the available American quick reaction force was of only company strength and if it
      was believed (when the decision was made) that there was a sizeable enemy force it made
      sense to deploy the larger UK contingent (Anderson 2002). This story in *Stars and Stripes*
      was interpreted by one British opposition politician as an official American criticism
      of the Marines while another used it as a evidence of government incompetence (Press
      Association 2002).

References

Anderson, Jon R. 2002. 'British Marines Come up Empty Handed, US Troops Frus-
      trated as Backups.' *Stars and Stripes*. 20 May. www.estripes,com/article.asp?section+
      104&article=8110&archive=true [accessed 23 July 2002].
BBC. 2002a. 'Troops Ready for Bloody Campaign.' 16 April. http://news.bbc.co.uk/1/hi/world/
      south_asia/1932514.stm, [accessed 22 July 2002].
BBC. 2002b. 'UK Troops Start Afghan Action.' 16 April. http://news.bbc.co.uk/1/hi/world/
      south_asia/1932189.htm, [accessed 22 July 2002].
BBC. 2002c. 'I Saw Flames Leap a Hundred Feet.' 12 May. http://news.bbc.co.uk/1/hi/world/
      south_asia/1981399.stm, [accessed 22 July 2002].
BBC. 2002d. 'I Saw New Ammunition.' 15 May. http://news.bbc.co.uk/1/hi/world/south_asia/
      1989625.stm, [accessed 22 July 2002].
BBC. 2002e. 'Two UK Troops Seriously Ill.' 16 May. http://news.bbc.co.uk/i/uk/1989777.stm
      [accessed 23 July 2002].
BBC, 2002f. *The Today Programme*. Radio 4, 0700 17 May.
BBC, 2002g.'News Blackout on Afghan Battle.' 18 May. http://news.bbc.co.uk/1/hi/world/
      south_asia/1994496.stm [accessed 13 July 2002].
BBC. 2002h. *Broadcasting House,* Radio 4, 0900, 19 May.

BBC. 2002i. *Breakfast with Frost*, BBC1 Television, 1000, 19 May. Transcript of the interview at http://news.bbc.co.uk/1/hi/programmes/breakfast_with_frost/1996908.stm [Accessed 24 July 2002].

Bildt, Carl. 1998. *Peace Journey.* London: Weidenfeld and Nicolson.

Bracken, Paul. 1983. *The Command and Control of Nuclear Forces.* New Haven, CT: Yale.

Brown, Robin. 1999. *Campbell Over Kosovo: Mobilization and Media Management in British Foreign Policy,* paper presented at the British International Studies Association Conference, Brighton.

Brown, Robin. 2002a. 'The Contagiousness of Conflict: E. E. Schattschneider as a Theorist of the Information Age.' *Information, Commmunication and Society* 5 (2): 258–75.

Brown, Robin. 2002b. 'Information Operations, Public Diplomacy and Spin: The US and the Politics of Perception Management.' *Journal of Information Warfare* 1 (3): 40–50.

Bunting, Madeleine. 2002. 'This Futile Campaign.' *The Guardian,* 20 May: 17.

Carruthers, Susan L. 2000. *The Media at War: Communication and Conflict in the 20th Century.* Basingstoke: Macmillan.

Chamberlain. Gethin. 2002. 'Attack on Brigadier Damaged Marine's Morale.' *The Scotsman,* 12 August: 1.

Clark, Wesley K. 2001. *Waging Modern War: Bosnia, Kosovo and the Future of Combat.* New York: Public Affairs.

Clausewitz, Carl von. 1976. *On War,* trans. Michael Howard and Peter Paret. Princeton, NJ: Princeton University Press.

Clodfelter, Mark. 1989. *The Limits of Air Power: The American Bombing of North Vietnam.* New York: Free Press.

Cohen, Bernard C. 1963. *The Press and Foreign Policy.* Princeton, NJ: Princeton University Press.

Cohen, Yoel. 1986. *Media Diplomacy: The Foreign Office in the Mass Communications Age.* London: Frank Cass.

Cook Timothy E. 1998. *Governing With the News: The News Media as a Political Institution.* Chicago, Il: University of Chicago Press.

Davison, W. Philips. 1974. 'News Media and International Negotiation.' *Public Opinion Quarterly* 38, (2): 174–91.

DeYoung, Karen. 2001. 'US, Britain Step Up War for Public Opinion.' *Washington Post,* 1 November: A1.

Entman, Robert. 2000. 'Declarations of Independence: The Growth of Media Power after the Cold War.' In *Decisionmaking in a Glass House: Mass Media, Public Opinion and American and European Foreign Policy in the 21st Century* eds. Brigitte L. Nacos, Robert Y. Shapiro, and Pierangelo Isernia. Allanhead, NJ: Rowman and Littlefield.

Fitzwater, Marlin. 1995. *Call the Briefing.* New York: Times Books.

Gall, Carlotta. 2002. 'Afghan War is All But Over, Says Brigadier.' *The Times.* 9 May: 22.

Gelb, Leslie H. with Richard K. Betts. 1977. *The Irony of Vietnam: The System Worked.* Washington, DC: Brookings Institution.

Gellman Barton and Thomas E. Ricks. 2002. 'Bin Laden Escape in Battle Feared.' *International Herald Tribune.* 18 April: 1, 6.

Gordon, Michael R. 2002. 'This Time, US is determined to block escapes by Qaeda.' *International Herald Tribune.* 5 March: 4.

Gould, Philip. 1998. *The Unfinished Revolution: How the Modernisers Save the Labour Party.* London: Little Brown.

Halberstam, David. 2001. *War in a Time of Peace: Bush, Clinton and the Generals.* New York: Scribner.

Hallin, Daniel C. *The 'Uncensored War': The Media and Vietnam.* Berkeley, CA: University of California Press.

Hickey, Neil. 2002. 'Access Denied.' *Columbia Journalism Review.* January/February: 26–31.

Hoge Jr., James F. 1994. 'Media Pervasiveness.' *Foreign Affairs.* 73 (4): 136–44.

Holbrooke, Richard. 1999. *To End a War,* revised edition. New York: Modern Library.

Hoon, Geoff. 2002. Secretary of State for Defence's Statement in the Commons 18 March, at www.operations.mod.uk/veritas/statements/statement_18mar.htm [accessed 23 July 2002].

Jenkins, Simon. 2002. 'Mad Dogs and Our Men Go Out in the Afghan Sun.' *The Times,* 22 May: 20.

Keohane, Robert O. and Joseph S. Nye. 1977. *Power and Interdependence.* Boston, MA: Little, Brown.

Kernell, Samuel. 1997. *Going Public: New Strategies of Presidential Leadership,* third edition. Washington, DC: Congressional Quarterly Press.

Livingston, Steven. 1997. *Clarifying the CNN Effect,* Research Paper R-18. Cambridge, MA: Joan Shorenstein Center.

Livingston, Steven and Todd Eachus. 1995. 'Humanitarian Crises and US Foreign Policy: Somalia and the CNN Effect Reconsidered.' *Political Communication* 12 (4): 411–29.

MacGregor, Brent. 1997. *Live, Direct and Biased? Making Television, News in the Satellite Age* London: Edward Arnold.

McCarthy, Rory and James Meek, 2001. 'US Admits Raids Will Open Route for Rebels.' *The Guardian.* 23 October: 5.

Miller, Derek B. 2002. *Measuring Media Pressure on Security Policy Decision-Making in Liberal States: The Positioning Hypothesis.* Paper presented at the International Studies Association Convention, New Orleans, March.

Norton-Taylor, Richard and Nicholas Watt. 2002. 'Hoon Rallies to Aid of Marine Leader.' *The Guardian,* 20 May: 2.

Norton-Taylor, Richard and Nicholas Watt. 2002. 'Military Top Brass Rally to Defence of Beleaguered British Commander in Afghanistan.' *The Guardian.* 21 May: 3.

Press Association. 2002. 'Marines' Missions "Empty-Handed"—US Forces Magazine'. 20 May. available online at www.ananova.com/news/story/sm_591807.html [accessed 29 July 2002].

Rayment, Sean. 2002. 'Marine's Chief Under Fire for Afghan "Farce." ' *The Sunday Telegraph.* 19 May: 2.

Ricks, Thomas E. 2002. 'Keeping Eye on Combat.' *International Herald Tribune,* 27 March: 1, 4.

Robinson, Piers. 1999. 'The CNN Effect: Can the News Media Drive Foreign Policy.' *Review of International Studies* 25, (2): 301–9.

Robinson, Piers. 2002. *The CNN Effect: The Myth of News Foreign Policy and Intervention.* London: Routledge.

Rumsfeld, Donald R. 2002. 'DoD News Briefing—Secretary Rumsfeld' 8 May. www.defenselink.mil/news/May 2002/t05082002_50508sd.html [accessed 27 July 2002].

Schmitt, Eric. 2001. 'How Bush's War Team Works.' *International Heral Tribune.* 25 October: 4.

Schultz, George P. 1993. *Turmoil and Triumph.* New York: Simon and Schuster.

Shaw, Martin. 2000. 'Media and Public Sphere without Borders? News Coverage and Power from Kurdistan to Kosovo.' In *Decisionmaking in a Glass House: Mass Media, Public Opinion and American and European Foreign Policy in the 21st Century* eds. Brigitte L. Nacos, Robert Y. Shapiro, and Pierangelo Isernia. Allanhead, NJ: Rowman and Littlefield.

Smith, Michael. 2002a. 'Brigadier Put Troops Before Politics.' *Daily Telegraph,* On-Line Edition. 21 May. www.telegraph.co.uk [accessed 26 July 2002].

Smith, Michael. 2002b. 'Sorry, Sir. I Can't Answer That.' *The Daily Telegraph,* On-Line Edition. 24 May. www.telegraph.co.uk [accessed 26 July 2002].

Smith, Michael. 2002c. 'Top Job for "Sacked" Commander's Rival.' *The Daily Telegraph,* On-Line Edition. 27 July. www.telegraph.co.uk [accessed 29 July 2002].

Smucker, Philip. 2002c. 'Al-Qa'eda Rocket Attack Ignored as Marines Pull Out.' *The Daily Telegraph,* 23 May: 13.

Speakes, Larry. 1988. *Speaking Out: The Reagan Presidency From Inside the White House.* New York: Avon.

Taylor, Philip M. 1997. *Global Communications, International Affairs and the Media since 1945.* London: Routledge.

Thrall, A. Trevor. 2000. *War in the Media Age.* Cresskill, NJ: Hampton.

Van Creveld, Martin. 1985. *Command in War.* Cambridge, MA: Harvard.

Vickers, Rhiannon. 2000. 'Blair's Kosovo Campaign: Political Communications, The Battle for Public Opinion and Foreign Policy.' *Civil Wars* 3 (1): 55–70.

Warren, Marcus. 2001. 'US is Just Playing Around, Says Northern Alliance.' *The Daily Telegraph.* 18 October: 6.

Westmoreland, William C. 1976. *A Soldier Reports.* Garden City, NY: Doubleday.

CHAPTER 4

Framing the Palestinian-Israeli Conflict

TAMAR LIEBES
ANAT FIRST

Media and terrorism feed on each other. Terrorists need the media for amplifying their messages, and media need terrorists as a personification of the larger issue of conflict (Weimann 1994). But not all the forms of terrorism make equally good stories. Ongoing hijackings or hostage holding are more effective than suicide attackers, who leave reporters with only a messy aftermath of dead bodies.[1] And the story of terrorism, it should be remembered, is only one type of story that personifies conflict. There are other, no less important, forms of the personification of violence. One such sub-story is the killing and brutalization of children. This type of personalization has become central to the coverage of the Palestinian-Israeli conflict since its eruption in the fall of 2000.

ABC's evening news of October 1, 2000, opened with anchor Carol Simpson preparing her viewers for the exceptional power of the footage they were going to see. She recognized the potential of Muhammad Dura—a Palestinian boy, killed in his father's arms before the France 2 cameraman—to become a symbol for the larger story.[2] Viewers were going to see, Simpson said, "an image that would haunt everyone in this conflict in years to come." Two years after the start of the Second Intifada in September 2000, with more than 1,500 Palestinians and 700 Israelis dead, we can confirm that the Dura image, indeed the stuff that symbols are made of, has become the emblematic image of the Palestinian-Israeli struggle. For many viewers in the international television audience, viewing the conflict from the wings, the Dura image represents the essence of the human tragedy, the story that clinches the "larger narrative" of this bloody, distant, and everlasting struggle. As such, it became one more link in a chain of iconic images which (rightly or wrongly) signify historical events in public memory.[3] Icons represent emotionally evocative, self-explanatory, universally understood pictures. Once recognizable as identifying signposts, they are recycled everywhere, fixing the meaning of historic events long after much else is forgotten.

Dura's death became an important site for the struggle of the rival sides over international public opinion. As such, the image (rather than the fact) did "haunt everyone *in* this conflict." The horror and compassion invoked by the initial viewing gave way to the struggle over the image. The Palestinians promoted Dura into the most effective symbol of their suffering and the inhuman brutality of the Israeli military. Thus, logos in cyberspace sites feature a collage of the dying Dura with an Israeli soldier pointing a gun at his head.[4] The dying sequence was also recycled in lengthy clips on Arabic television channels featuring Dura as the emblem of martyrdom, his pictures interposed with tanks, funerals, and crying mothers, to the sound of long eulogies by popular singers, making him into the model for new heroes (in the form of suicide bombers).[5] Israeli journalists covered the Dura story no less than their colleagues elsewhere. On the Israeli side, the immediate focus of international attention on the killing of Muhammad Dura triggered an initially awkward but eventually thorough investigation by the Israeli army into the question of who was responsible for the killing. Israeli army chief of operations, Giora Eiland, said the internal investigation concluded: "The shots were apparently fired by Israeli soldiers from the outpost at Netzarim . . . This was a grave incident, an event we are all sorry about."[6] Eighteen months later, a fifty-five-minute-long investigative documentary by the German ARD television channel concluded that Muhammad Dura was most probably killed by Palestinian fire.[7] But the image, analogous to the images of Los Angeles police brutality in the Rodney King case, is here to stay. Bearing the authenticity and the (seemingly unmediated) "naturalness" of an anthropological fact, and evoking the kind of empathy for human suffering which crosses cultural boundaries, this image cannot be touched by considerations of facts or justice.

This chapter begins by pointing out why the global reporting of international news is increasingly important in the context of contemporary world order and the new media ecology. The argument is based on the dramatic transformation undergone in the last decade in the relationship between media, public opinion, and political leadership. The chapter analyzes two different cases on international television that originate on rival sides of the Palestinian Israeli conflict—the case of the shooting of Muhammad Dura and the case of the Ramallah lynching of two Israeli reservist soldiers. What makes certain distant images catch on whereas other (no less bloody) images attract far less public attention? The conclusion drawn from these cases raises the fundamental problem posed for journalists by the move to the electronic media, exacerbated by international news in situations of conflict over contested frames.

New Media Ecology, International Public Opinion and Local Wars

In the past two decades we have witnessed wars in which the media played only a marginal role, such as the intifada of the 1980s, the Gulf War of 1991, the Falklands War, and the Afghanistan war in 2002 (Gerbner 1992; Liebes 1997). These wars were relatively short, planned to achieve well-defined targets, and the movement of journalists was physically controlled by the government and the military, who regarded media and their potential to mobilize public opinion as an obstacle for achieving their goals (see chapters 2 and 3). The few exceptional cases did cause a rage in public opinion at home. This is exemplified by Peter

Arnett's reporting from the bunker in Baghdad during the Gulf War, generating a heated debate in the United States focused on the legitimacy of screening pictures which function as enemy propaganda. Another case is the telescopic lenses of a BBC camera that documented Israeli soldiers beating Palestinian prisoners in the intifada of the 1980s. In Israel, following the exposure of military brutality, a number of soldiers and officers were court-martialed for "deviant actions."

Unlike these tightly controlled wars, it has become impossible to keep the media out in cases of lengthy civil wars (such as in Kosovo or in the Palestinian-Israeli conflict), with no clearly defined target, where control by the warring sides is limited, and the boundaries (between front and rear) are unclear. In addition, in the present media environment the boundaries between domestic and international media are blurred. This phenomenon has been influenced by the rise of international news networks such as BBC World and CNN International during the 1990s. Cases of low-intensity local wars, where the United States or United Nations assume the role of global policeman and caretaker, have given new significance to the representation of local conflicts.

Traditionally, the claim that media plays an important role in foreign policy related to domestic coverage within the borders of the nation-state such as in the Vietnam War, in which the U.S. media sensed signals of change in American public opinion and reinforced this trend in news. (Alexander 1981). International news channels covering various conflict-ridden spots report not only to the public and also to political leaders, who in extreme cases may use television to legitimate intervention. One example of what has become known as "the CNN effect" is the potential power of images of large-scale suffering to influence public opinion and thereby push governments into humanitarian interventions (Freedman 2000). If the decision whether and how to intervene in civil wars is directly influenced by the images of conflict on television screens, the selection of these images takes on crucial importance.

For the news media, the representation of the Palestinian-Israeli conflict is a good story as a war in which neither side has a clear target in the field, neither side can win, the front is everywhere, the media cannot be kept out, and Western media have decided to focus on the conflict. Whether or not this focus is itself "biased," as Alan Dershowitz (2002) has eloquently argued, this conflict happens to fit the well-known rule of foreign news focusing on "the unexpected within the expected" (Galtung and Ruge 1970). As a place involved in a long struggle, Israel is a beat where the infrastructure of foreign correspondents is in place, and once the reporter is there, s/he sends stories. The centrality of Israel for Christians and Jews ensures its continuous relevance, and once a story enters the world's headlines it has a good chance of staying there. The connection made by Muslim terrorists between the United States and Israel may also play a part. Considering all this, points scored in international public opinion represent "victories" for Palestinians and for Israelis.

The Power of Distant Images

As in the case of the starving children in Somalia, or the refugees in Kosovo, television, as a medium, is in love with pictures of human suffering and human brutality (Boltanski, 1999). Boltanski, using Hanna Arendt's terms, argues that seeing distant conflicts in the form of personal suffering relates to the "politics of pity/empathy" rather than to the "politics of justice." The perception of justice demands that the suffering of the two sides is put to the test in a shared world, so that the just could be recognized. Empathy, on the other hand, in spite of the need to point to specific disasters for it to be aroused, sees the suffering as a mass. And the politics of empathy, especially when the sufferer is regarded as "victim," can at most compromise with justice within the boundaries of rhetoric. Who would dream of saying that the residents of a certain hunger-stricken country got what they deserved? The answer is always negative. According to the politics of empathy, the urgency of the action to bring about an end to the suffering overcomes considerations of justice. Justice will enforce its rights only in a world that has driven out suffering.

In the case of television news, in which the norms of journalism forever clash with the medium's technological and economic constraints, the compatability of images of suffering with the visual medium wins. If this is true for television news in general, it is much more so the case for foreign news where the bar of newsworthiness is set higher. Here, the need for effective, minimalist, touching, visual footage brings about the selection of dramatic images, transmitting emotional, empathy-arousing images, that can be simultaneously absorbed everywhere. These pictures are removed from the relevant sequence of events, as well as their political and historical context.

Out of the daily coverage of the Palestinian-Israeli violence, only a few images make it onto the international screens. Images judged to be capable of igniting viewers' empathy, and/or anxiety are the ones that can be turned into symbols. The power of these metonymic representations lies in their ability to tell a story without words. The images are adopted and recycled by the international channels. They expose immediately identifiable anguish, torture, and brutality. These are the cases in which pictures have a particular effect, even if there is room to doubt the validity of the cliche according to which 'one picture is worth a thousand words' (Schudson 1995).[8] And the understanding that these pictures deliver is particularly useful to viewers who are unfamiliar with the context from which they have been extracted.

The Cases of Muhammad Dura and Vadim Norzich

In the fall of 2000, two images competed for the status of the emblematic horror in the present eruption of violence, one from each side of the Palestinian Israeli divide. One was the killing of Muhammad Dura, a child caught in his father's arms in the midst of an exchange of fire between Palestinians and Israeli soldiers in Netzarim Junction, close to Gaza, on 30 September 2000. In spite of the live filming of this incident by Talal Abu Tahmeh, a Palestinian cameraman working for a French television station, questions about who shot Dura and what father and son were doing in Netzarim Junction remain open. The rival image was the lynching of Vadim Norzich, an Israeli soldier, by Palestinians in a local police station in Ramallah on 12 October 2000, two weeks later. The camera caught the beheaded body of Vadim Norzich as it was thrown out of the second floor window of the police station and a few seconds of the Palestinian mob in the courtyard below abusing the bodies, one lifting his bloody hands from the corpse to show them stained by the corpse's blood. Israeli helicopter gunships blasted the police station shortly afterward. Yet despite these two dramatic cases, the image of Muhammad Dura was the uncontestable winner in the U.S. network television news. Before addressing the reasons for this, we need to understand the initial framing of these events by domestic and distant media.

The itinerary of Dura's images from domestic to international television screens constitutes a powerful example of what happens to news when it travels. New stories on CNN International often have to distill events to their most succinct, universalistic, and unequivocal essence, as illustrated by CNN's anchor on October 3, 2000, "Let's now turn to the Middle East *for a moment.*" On September 30, 2000, Israeli television was concerned with deciphering the signs of the conflict and whether the outbreak of violence meant that the violence was moving into a new phase (Katz, 1989). For domestic news in Israel, Dura's killing happened in the Nezarim junction where control was divided between Israeli forces and Palestinian policemen. The event occurred one day into the outbreak of violence, in which the Oslo peace process, which held a hope for ending the struggle between Palestinians and Israelis, exploded in flames. Unlike the Palestinian uprising (the intifada) of 1987, in which protestors threw stones and Molotov cocktails and burned tires, this time armed Palestinian policemen of the newly established Palestinian Authority used their guns to shoot at the Israeli soldiers (Liebes 2002). These were the days in which the mechanism of Oslo collapsed regardless of whether the violence was spontaneous, whether it was provoked by Ariel Sharon who visited the compound of the Temple Mount/ el-Aqsa Mosque one day earlier, or whether it was planned by Yasser Arafat.

Following pictures of Palestinians shooting at an Israeli army post, Channel One's Shlomi Eldar reported:

> The Nezarim junction this morning looked like a battle field. All the characteristics from the times of the intifada are here: Inflamed youngsters, ambulances . . . and this time, an innovation—a lot of arms. The Palestinians tried to conquer the post. Pay attention to the screams of joy each time a Molotov cocktail hits the post head on. The post is in flames. A soldier inside is rather helpless. And the Palestinian police officers shoot. Note this policeman in jeans and a kallachnikov . . . The Palestinian cameramen documented him from every possible angle—here in the orange grove under cover, and there behind a lorry.

> Behind a brick wall, dozens of Palestinians are throwing stones, looking for ex-
> citement, otherwise it's difficult to understand what a father and son are doing
> here, behind a shelter, a father and son unlikely to happen incidentally in the
> field of battle. And this is how the camera documented it: Dozens of Palestinians
> around giving instructions to the father to take cover with his son. The child in
> panic, crying. The father pointing to the soldier's post. And here it ends. The
> child is hit and loses consciousness.

On that day, Israeli television and the Israeli military assumed (probably
wrongly) that the child was incidentally killed by Israeli crossfire. Channel One's
report by Shlomi Eldar ended with the army's expressing sorrow for the death.
On Israel's Channel Two, Yoram Binur quoted official Palestinian sources, who
said that Israeli soldiers did the killing. Both reporters questioned what father
and son were doing in the midst of the battle. The most common explanation
was that the boy went to take part in the stone throwing game, and his father
came to take him away. Binur told viewers that "today, these pictures from the
Nezarim junction in Gaza are causing a storm in the world." Thus, in domestic
Israeli news, Dura was one of an accumulating list of human tragedies in a
sudden, brutal, collapse into war, which took its toll, killing ordinary people on
all sides in those traumatic days of October 2000 with outbursts of violence in
Gaza, the West Bank, and in the villages of Israeli Arabs.

For many overseas observers, however, such as the French daily *Le Monde*,
Muhammad Dura was "Palestine's emblematic child" (October 2, 2000). Counting stories mentioning this event in the news does not provide an appropriate
test for the kind of icon that manages to remain in collective memory long
after, becoming recognizable as a public symbol for a war, a rebellion, or a
movement.[9] Clues to their resonance can be collected from an early recognition
of their staying power and their capacity to move among various genres and
a broad range of media. In Dura's case, recognition started immediately. On
October 3, the headline of *Agence France Presse* was, "World shocked at killing,"
citing reactions by leaders such as Mubarak, Clinton, and Albright, calling the
pictures "extremely shocking," "heartbreaking," "overwhelming." Italy's *La Re-
pubblica* called the images, "the most horrible we have ever seen." Dura, in the
words of *Agence France Presse* had become "a symbol comparable to the image
of a Vietnamese child running naked along a country road screaming in pain
from the napalm in her back, or that of a lone protestor defying tanks at Beijing's
Tiananmen Square." Two weeks after the event (October 13) on ABC's *Nightline*,
Ted Koppel, addressing American audiences, opened his show with "the power
of a single image . . . its power to reduce an entire conflict to a single image,"
confirming ABC's *World News* judgment of Dura (on September 30) as an image
that will remain in public memory.

Another way for assessing the lasting power of the image is by studying
the way in which the two sides in the conflict judged its potential to harm or
serve their case, and the actions they take. On the Palestinian side, the image

of Dura was used as a most effective propaganda tool to mobilize support. Two recent commemorations are Jordan's issuing stamps with Dura's icon, and the Iranian's renaming a street in Teheran after him (June 2001). The impact on Israel's side was the military's mobilizing for damage control by carrying out a lengthy investigation to establish issues such as the direction from where the bullets were fired and the type of bullets and guns. By the time the investigation was concluded, the icon had been fixated in public memory as the symbol of the brutality of conflict toward helpless victims (Wolfsfeld 2000). The icon of Dura broke through the confines of the news genre to a multiplicity of media and genres. The father became a star, traveling the world to give talks and interviews. The dead child became the ultimate shaheed on many Arab television and radio channels; his tragic fate is sung by Charles Anderlein, the Arab world's most popular singer. The producer of the France II channel in Israel wrote a book documenting the story, and became a popular lecturer on the subject. The icon, worked into news promotions, became familiar to television viewers and cyberspace surfers in many countries.

By contrast, considering its potential, the lynching of two Israeli part-time reservists in the Palestinian town of Ramallah was given far less attention by the international networks. The reason is partly explained by the belated arrival of cameramen at the police station and by the brutal means used to prevent photographs of the images. A British photographer working for the *Daily Telegraph*, Mark Seager, witnessed the lynching process.[10] His report describes how, while passing in Ramallah, he saw a big crowd of Palestinians shouting and running downhill from the police station dragging behind them the body of a man.

> The lower part of his body was on fire, and the upper part has been shot, and the head beaten so badly, it was a pulp, like red jelly . . . He was dead but they were still beating him, madly, kicking his head. They were like animals . . . I tried to get my film out but they were all grabbing me and one guy pulled the camera off me and smashed it to the floor. I knew that I had lost the chance of the photograph that would have made me famous and had lost my favorite lens that I'd used all over the world, but I didn' t care. I was scared for my life. . . . the crowd was getting angrier and angrier, shouting '*Allah akbar*,' dragging the dead man like a cat toying with a mouse . . . There was such unbelievable hatred and anger distorting their faces. It was the most horrible thing I have ever seen and I have reported from Kongo, Kosovo, many bad places . . . there was such unbelievable hatred distorting their faces.

The camera of an Italian RAI television crew also documented a few seconds of the killing of the second reservist, Vadim Norzich, whose body was thrown out of the police station's window (Barne'a 2000).

In some international news media both stories were given equal weight in an attempt to provide balanced coverage of both sides of the Palestinian-Israeli conflict. Hence in a special thirty-minute program, broadcast on 18 November 2000 by the BBC World Service, focusing on the consequences for the Oslo peace settlement, entitled "When Peace Died," the events surrounding the death of Vadim Norzich were given ten minutes coverage, exactly equal time to the events surrounding the death of Muhammed Dura.[11] The events were described in the commentary as the "Ramallah lynching." By contrast on American television evening news broadcast by CNN, CBS, NBC, and ABC on October 12, 2000, there were brief glimpses of the falling body and the crowd in the police court-yard as part of the framing to the story of Israel's retaliatory helicopter attack on terrorist targets in Gaza. The term "lynching" was absent in the reports of the four American networks and instead the verbs used were "attack," "killing," and "murder," while the word "mob" appears only once (on NBC).[12] Thus, the lynching had passed without leaving much impact on American news moni-toring events. Dura's story, on the other hand, became a journalistic scoop in the international news. The Israeli government's frustration can be seen in the decision to send Nachman Shay, the government public relations adviser, to the Sharm el-Sheikh meeting chaired by President Clinton five days later to show the RAI tapes to American journalists. By then, however, it was old news, and none of the foreign correspondents present was interested.

A number of reasons emerge for the success of the Dura image. First, his killing was documented by the eye of the camera as a complete and coherent sequence of events, exposing, without the need for any words (or so it seems), the essence of human tragedy. Photographic images have two advantages over other types of reporting when crossing national boundaries. Documentation by the camera seems like a piece of unmediated reality unlike the story of a witness or an account by the studio anchor, which is mediated by definition. This gives images the status of objectivity, and at the same time, presents a live drama, creating instant emotional involvement among viewers. In his illuminating description of the way in which the "truthfulness" of photographs is conceived, Roland Barthes (1980) has argued that the mechanical mediation of the camera, with its analogic representation is perceived as a guarantee of factualness, authenticity, and "naturalness." These are the qualities that provide camera reporting with its journalistic legitimacy. But, as Barthes points out, this perception is a dangerous illusion. All that the image does is to draw out the boundaries into which meaning can be injected, thereby facilitating the investigation into the essence of the ("signified") object through a process of signification. In other words, a photograph selects the spontaneous (sometimes "managed") reality on which we should focus our attention.

To this we add that in the case of media images, once the photographer has defined the boundaries of the field, the creation of the context from which the meaning is derived remains in the hands of two players—the professionals and their audiences. From the field, television's reporters fill-in the information gaps, and anchors in the studio inject the meaning by reframing the pictures with words (Scannell 1996). At the receiving end, audiences bring their expe-rience to the decoding of texts, including their pre-existing knowledge about the event and about television practices (Livingstone 1998; Liebes 1997). In the case of consensual television, reporters make sure to fit the story to their viewers. In the terms of literary analysts, the 'author in the text' (i.e., the editors) ensures that the text's 'implied reader' corresponds to the community of 'real readers'.

True, at a first look, the Dura story told by the camera—that of a father and son caught in the midst of battle, with the scared father trying to protect his crying son, and the boy being shot and killed in front of the viewers' eyes— is coming as close as possible to a story that needs no telling. A second look, however, reveals that the story lacks the central facts needed to make sense of "who did what, when, where," and (especially) "why" (Mannoff and Schudson 1986). Whereas, as we have argued, the power of the Dura pictures lies in its exposure of inhuman brutality, its weakness lies in failing to provide the answer for the two main questions: Why did the two happen onto the battle field? And, more important, who shot and killed the child? More information is needed to answer these questions. This information, critical to the decoding of the photograph, is provided via linguistic mediation in the words of the reporter and the anchor.

The ABC *World News* coverage of the Dura event on 30 September 2000 lacks the crucial facts needed for making sense of the story. The answer to the question of who the killer/killers are, crucial for making sense of the story, was spoken in a casual, taken for granted, manner. The following is the opening sentence to the story: "It happened yesterday in Gaza. A man and his injured son are trapped under *Israeli* fire" (our italics). The sequence of photographs that construct the story is characterized by a careful guiding of viewers. Concluding an overview of the day's bloody clashes between Palestinians and Israelis, the anchor, turning to the Dura story, signals that what comes next deserves special attention. "And we warn you that some of the images are disturbing." In television's familiar code, such an offer to refrain from watching, reads as a loud "stay with us" for the shocking pictures coming up. Rising above the day's events, anchor Simpson makes a historical observation, opening with: "Four days of fighting, dozens of martyrs, and an image that would haunt everyone in this conflict in years to come." This pre-framing from the studio contextualizes the photographs as a representation of the conflict between armed soldiers and helpless victims (with "shaheeds," a term used to describe suicide bombers, translated as "martyrs"). ABC's crowning the photographs as valuable evidence that would remain in the world's memory as a symbol of the conflict takes place on two levels. One is pointing to the meaning of the event from the perspective of the emotional effect on viewers; the second highlights the significance of its documentation by the camera for its becoming a primary source for the historiography of the larger context.

Playing with the tension between two times—when the event happened in the past, and its showing in real time—the voice over, and narrating the Dura sequence moves in the direction of "live" presentation, "as if" we are watching an event that is happening now (Bourdon 2000; Blum-Kulka and Liebes 2002):

> It happened yesterday in Gaza. A man and his injured son are trapped under Israeli fire. The boy is terrified. "My son is dying" the man yells, and then the shots come in lower. Twelve-year-old Muhammad Dura was buried as a Palestinian hero last night.

At the end of the newscast, in a regular supplement entitled "The Reporters' Corner," another layer in the construction of Dura as a symbol played out. This time audiences are positioned for what Barthes (1975) calls "a second reading" of the text. What characterizes the reading of a familiar text is that this time we are no longer motivated by the dramatic tension that arises from not knowing how it all would end. Once the end is known the reader can concentrate on the "how," rather than the "what." On this second round, the viewing directions for how to view the pictures were given by the ultimate authority—Talal Abu Rachma, the Palestinian photographer who photographed the event for France II. Invited to the ABC studio to accompany the item by his own words, he could not provide any new information concerning the two questions which are critical for understanding the event, the ones not answered by the photographs, namely, why they were there and who killed them. What he added was the credibility and emotional weight of the personal experience of witnessing, of "being there." Once it is established that the anchor and photographer do not fulfill the role of commentators, it should be asked what role they play in the mediation of the story. It seems that the two play the role that cinema theory terms as "suture" (an idea first introduced by Daniel Dayan (1983) in his analysis of the classic Western *Stagecoach*). In films, the 'suture' is a secondary character who provides the 'seams' that tie viewers to the screen by directing their involvement with leading characters, in the center of the picture. The suture's mediation is carried out by the way he/she looks at the hero (always a male) from the wings. The admiration, pity, or horror in the suture's gaze act as guidance for the viewer's look at the hero.

In the Dura case, the presence of the photographer on screen, in the studio, makes a formal division between the on-screen-guide and the on-screen-heroes, providing viewers with a frame within a frame. The photographer, whose pictures constitute evidence to the factuality of the information, contributes to the reinforcement of the viewers' emotional experience. And indeed, both anchor and photographer play their part in leading the audiences' response. At high moments their voices are choked with tears, signaling that even tough professionals well trained in neutral and polished reporting, for whom showing gory atrocities is routine, are capable of breaking the conventions and allowing their humanity to take over. What we share as human beings—pity toward human suffering, and rage toward whomever is responsible—are stronger than any commitment to the conventions of news reporting.

Analysis of this item reveals that what was perceived as an event of authenticity, truthfulness and lack of mediation, is in fact an ideological construction on three levels: the selection of reality materials (by pulling out one event, tragic as it may be, from the chaotic and bleeding reality of October 2000), the camera angle (directed at the boy and his father and not searching for the killers), and the interpretation of the pictures in the studio (which draws on the overall way in which the conflict is understood). On all three levels, professionals make sure to adapt the story to the viewers, that is, to guide the way in which the pictures are perceived, thus reinforcing once again the existing image of the viewers, telling them what they already know (Carey 1989).

All this brings us back to Barthes's rejection (1977) of the possibility that analogic representations can be a source for creating symbolic systems and to his conclusion that the image can only demarcate the boundaries within which a true investigation of the object we are looking at should be conducted. Especially in the case of international news, the problem with much contemporary commercial television—evermore constrained by the need for immediate transmission and "good" pictures—is that it turns in one of two directions: either moving into the breaking news mode or, on routine news, devoting only a few seconds to each item. In both cases, it has no time for, nor any interest in, getting into this process of investigation. This is one reason for seeking, in advance, an image which would be as "closed" and "clear" as possible, one that (on its face) does not require any process of interpretation. The Dura icon is exemplary.

The impact of the story drew the attention of a television documentary maker, Esther Shapira, working for the German ARD channel. Her fifty-five-minute investigative report entitled *Das Rote Quadrat: Drei Kugeln und ein Totes Kind,* shown in Germany on March 18, 2002, long after the original broadcast, considered the questions that remained open. She conducted an investigation in the field and came to a conclusion which contradicted the intuitive perception adopted by television news editors and the internal investigation conducted by the Israeli military at the time. Shapira's report concluded that Muhammad Dura was killed by Palestinian fire, based on interviews with participants and witnesses on both sides. This included the Palestinian local commander ("We did not conduct an investigation since the identity of the killers was obvious"), the three Israeli soldiers who were positioned at the nearby post (at the angle from which they aimed their guns it was not possible to hit Muhammad and his father), and the Palestinians who described the massive Palestinian fire in the direction in which the two were located.

Why Television Neglected the Vadim Norzich Case

As we have shown, the Dura image turned into a massive journalistic scoop. The lynching of the two Israeli soldiers, an image regarded by Israel as an "answer" to the Dura image, attracted far less attention. First, the victims in this case were reservist soldiers who are perceived as a legitimate target in civil war, although any killings are contrary to all existing conventions. In terms of its immediate appeal to viewers, the Dura story provided a complete, coherent sequence of visual images encapsulating the tragedy. What the camera offered of the lynching was a series of scant segmented and blurred images from which the lynching had to be reconstructed. Moreover, Israel's release of the lynching footage was delayed. The Israeli military, still not fully aware of the relative importance of the respective battles on screen and on the ground, hastened to avenge the soldiers' killing by destroying the Ramallah police station, leaving only a narrow "window of opportunity" for the lynching pictures to penetrate global screens. Footage of the reprisal—the bombing of Gaza—took over before the lynching had time to sink in.

Nevertheless, the lynching could have caught more attention in the news media. Although the camera caught short flashes of the lynching, the evocative power of such images is not necessarily any less strong. What these images lacked in coherence and continuity they compensated for by showing the deed via the eyes of the ecstatic mob, including the symbolic gesture of immersing one's hands in the blood. Unlike the killing of Dura, these pictures make it clear that this is no accident, that there is an intention behind the action. Second, the relative ambiguity and the lack of closure in terms of what is seen of the actual killing may be more effective in envoking horror than the photographer's unraveling of the lynching before the viewers in all its horrible details (Kampf, 2003). The latter type of press photography, so goes the argument (Barthes 1980), may not create a sense of horror at the deed, as the photographer has done all the work himself and left his viewers with the shock of seeing the picture rather than the trauma of the event. As McLuhan before him, Barthes believes that involvement needs active participation. The power of the lynching, according to this argument, lies exactly in its hinting at the story, in leaving it as unfinished business. Thus pictures such as that of a man looking down at the mob from the second floor window with dark characters seen hovering in the back of the room, alluded to the threatening uncertainty about what was to happen. Reconstructing the sequence in their mind should cause viewers to invest creative powers to complete the picture, generating involvement.[13]

Why then, in spite of the evidence of a cruel, intentional mob killing, followed by a macabre celebration, did the story of the lynching not enter more fully into the world's consciousness? Here, we have to return to the deeper, structural reasons. International pubic opinion, in many ways understandably, sees the Palestinians as victims. The Ramallah lynching was done by the weaker side. And the term "lynching," as Toni Morison has convincingly argued, often describes an action by a stronger group against a weaker one (Morison 1992). Lynching typically describes white men "restoring order" following the rape of a white woman by a black man. The very same action when done by an oppresed group may be regarded as a legitimate action.

In addition to these reasons there are others, which have to do with the vulnerability of foreign correspondents. Viewers and researchers may exercise their own judgment regarding the inherent power of the various images. However, they are only partially aware of the battle over rival images conducted behind the scenes. The framing of Muhammad Dura's death was challenged by Israeli officials who responded by accusing the Palestinians of "sending children to the front to enable cynical exploitation of their death for propaganda purposes." It may have been a poor defense, but its validity could be assessed and challenged accordingly. Palestinian attempts to contain the lynching damage were conducted behind the scenes, before the images were ever aired. In seeking to prevent the airing of scenes not to their liking, Palestinians intimidated professional reporters and photographers doing their job, even threatening their lives. Nahum Barnea and Uzi Benziman (*Ha'ayin Hashvi'it* 2000), two of Israel's leading journalists, reported that the pictures of the lynching were aired only due to the insistence of an Israeli producer, working for the Italian RAI channel. RAI's editors' reluctance to air the lynching stemmed from fear of Palestinian revenge, as well as Italian public opinion's overwhelming support for the Palestinian cause. It should be noted, then, that the RAI example raises questions about global images on TV. It demonstrates that behind the airing of what appear to be authentic, human images, ostensibly speaking for themselves, there may be a process of selection, editing, and framing that has little to do with professional decisions. In regard to domestic audiences, as we have shown, reporters have to take into account the expectation of their viewers and their editors, engendering reluctance to admit any dissonant notes.

As a recent study shows, foreign correspondents working in the Middle East seem to internalize the rules of non-democratic host countries and are not disturbed by the lack of transparency about the conditions in which they work (el-Nawawi and Kelly 2001) and which directly affect their work. Interviews with Western correspondents in Egypt show that reporters complained mostly about the inefficiency of the government official who served as their source, rather than about the constraint of being allowed to talk to only one person, with an absolute prohibition on crosschecking information with any other sources. In Israel, however, correspondents took for granted the freedom of cross-checking information with any official they choose to speak to and were highly critical about the sources' suspect professionalism.

Conclusions

These two cases are good examples of how television images can be used for framing conflict. In deeply divided plural societies any conflict becomes more complicated and reporting becomes more controversial as there are at least two contrasting definitions of the larger truth. The story of the chain of events that made Muhammad Dura into a symbol and of the investigation conducted long after the fact acutely raises the problematics of news broadcasting based on individual icons and on a process of selectivity that recycles identical scripts, which are reconfirmed by each additional news story. It is the dark side of James Carey's description (1989) of news as the same old stories we tell ourselves about ourselves, in different variations each morning. Images turned into symbols, recorded in some corner of the globe, are viewed by audiences in different countries watching a shared story, most of whom are uninformed of the complexities of the larger context. Telling stories for such disparate audiences means that the one remaining criterion is the universalistic effectiveness of a story, that *needs no* context, preferably no words.

It may be argued that it is legitimate for newsmakers to create visual images that are representative of the larger truth about the conflict, even if the example chosen has not occurred quite according to the script that it is chosen to represent. But the dangers inherent in journalistic practices on television almost prevent the introduction of information that contradicts, or even cracks, existing preconceptions. This means that all hints for a change in the larger process or of an alternative story are lost. Therefore there is no choice but to return to the conservative position according to which, even if the image seems to fit with what is seen as the "truth" of the larger context, the facts behind the camera image have to be carefully verified and cross-checked. If the examination raises inconsistencies and question marks, these should be put upfront, even at the cost of "destroying" the image. Precisely because it is more difficult to call them to account, international television channels have a particular responsibility to reject "good" images as illegitimate and unprofessional journalism when they "show" an unsubstantiated story. If we do not join the assumption that the factual basis of iconic frames *does* matter, the slippery slope toward circular, "closed" representations will continue, and television news will lose its status, credibility, and authority.

Notes

1. September 11 was an exception because of its magnitude, its symbolic power, and the unresolved mystery about the motive and identity of the perpetrators.
2. The victim is known as Muhammad Dura or as Mohammad al-Durrah.
3. Such as the frightened Jewish child, with his arms raised, in a concentration camp; the Vietnamese girl, naked, fleeing from her burning village, following an American bombing; the American student, abhorred by the police shooting at her friends in an anti-Vietnam demonstration; the Cormorant emerging from the oil drenched water, in Iraq, during the Gulf War; or the Israeli soldier reaching the Wailing Wall in Jerusalem, in the Six Day War.
4. For examples of rhetoric see for example, *Palestine-info.com/index.htm, a2zegypt.com/ isr/heaven1.swf, Israel defenseforce.org*. Note the very different rhetoric on television channels and cyberspace sites addressing Arab supporters versus English language channels addressing Western audiences.
5. Such as El Mannar (the Hizballa channel transmitting from South Lebanon), Syrian television, Palestinian television (from Gaza), al Jazeera (from Kattar) and Abu Dhabi.
6. BBC Online News Tuesday, 3 October, 2000, 16:34 GMT 'Israel 'sorry' for killing boy.' http://news.bbc.co.uk/1/hi/world/middle_east/954703.stm.
7. After conducting interviews with all concerned, ARD's reporter Esther Shapira in her film entitled *Drei Kugeln und ein Totes Kind*, 23.4.2002, concluded that Dura was

probably shot by Palestinian fire. The conclusions are based on examining the height and the angle from which the Israeli soldiers could shoot from the post in which they stood, their professionalism (Dura and father were in the same place for a whole hour before the killing, giving enough time for the soldiers to shoot them), and the type of bullets used (seen by the depth of the holes in the wall on which Dura and his father leaned) which fitted the type of guns and ammunition used by the Palestinians). The Palestinian officer in charge, interviewed by Shapira, claimed that the Palestinians did not investigate the killing, as they assumed that the Israeli soldiers were responsible.

8. Michael Schudson (1995) argues that when words contradict the visuals, viewers interpret the visuals in terms of what they hear (and not the other way round). In the case of images of distant suffering the attitude of the reporter is (by definition) that of horrified empathy. Suffering cannot be contradicted.

9. And methodologically, counting frequencies on the evening news is an outdated measure as CNN-ization means that the same item can be repeated every 30 minutes (or less) in one day. One way to trace the impact of such images is to test their recognition by people situated in various degrees of distance to the events represented by the images.

10. Mark Seager. 2000. **"I'll have nightmares for the rest of my life."** 15 October. http://dailytelegraph.co.uk.

11. http://news.bbc.co.uk/hi/english/static/audio_video/programmes/correspondent/transcripts/1026340.txt.

12. The verb used for the lynching, CNN: Palestinians 'attack,' (1), 'killing' (2), CBS: 'murder' (2), 'killing'(2), NBC; murder (1), 'mob,' ABC: 'killed by' (1). The item in all 4 channels is 'balanced' by Israel's 'retaliation'—helicopters shooting/terrorists' sites.

13. For a discussion of types of viewer involvement, see Liebes and Katz, (1993) pp. 128–29, 144–45, 152–54.

References

Alexander, Jeffrey. 1981. 'The Mass News Media in Systemic, Historic and Comparative Perspective.' In *Mass Media and Social Change*. Eds. E. Katz and T. Szecsko. Beverly Hills, CA: Sage.

Barne'a Nahum. 2000. 'Interview with Esther Vizelteer.' *Haayin Hashvi'it*. November.

Barthes, Roland. 1977. 'The Rhetoric of the Image.' In *Image, Music, Text* (trans. By S. Heath). Glasgow: Fontana.

Barthes, Roland. 1975. *The Pleasures of the Text*. New York: Hill and Wang.

Barthes, Roland. 1980. *La Chamber Claire*. Le Seuil: Edition de l'Etoile, Gallimard.

Boltanski, L. 1999. *Distant Suffering: Morality, media and politics*. Translated by Graham Burchell, Cambridge University Press.

Bourdon, Jerome. 2000. 'Live Television is Still Alive: On Television as an Unfulfilled Promise.' *Media, Culture and Society* 22(5): 531–556.

Carey, James. 1989. *Communication as Culture*. Boston: Unwin Hyman.

Dayan, Daniel. 1983. *Western Graffiti*. Paris: Edition Clancier-Guenaud.

Dershowitz, Alan, M. 2002. 'A challenge to House Master Hanson.' A lecture at the Harvard Law School, September 30.

El-Nawawy, M. and J. Kelly. 2001. 'Between the Government and the Press: the Role of Western Correspondents and Government Public Relations in Middle East Coverage.' *Press/Politics*, 16(3): 90–109.

Freedman, Lawrence. 2000. 'Victims and Victors: Reflections of the Kosovo War.' *Review of International Studies* 26(3): 335–358.

Galtung, Johan and Mary Ruge. 1970. The Structure of Foreign News. In *Media Sociology*. Ed. J. Tunstall. London: Constable.

Gerbner, George. 1992. The triumph of the image: *The Media War in the Persian Gulf—A global perspective*. Boulder: Westview Press.

Goffman, Erving. 1981. *Forms of Talk*. Philadelphia: University of Philadelphia Press: 124–159.

Ignatious, David. 2000. 'Keeping the Media Out.' *Herald Tribune*, December 11.

Kampf, Zohar. 2003. 'Crime and Punishment: The icon of the Ramallah lynch from the perspective of Israeli viewers.' *Panim* 23, Febuary (in Hebrew).

Katz, Elihu. 1989. 'Journalists as scientists.' *American Behavioral Scientist* 33(2): 238–246.

Liebes, Tamar. 1997. *Reporting the Arab Israeli Conflict: How hegemony works.* London and New York: Routledge.

Liebes, Tamar, and Katz, Elihu. 1993. *The Export of Meaning.* Cambridge, Britain: Polity Press.

Livingstone, S. 1998. 'Relationships between media and audiences.' In *Media, Ritual and Identity.* Eds. T. Liebes and J. Curran. London and New York: Routledge.

Manoff, Robert K. and Michael Schudson. 1986. *Reading the News.* New York: Pantheon Books.

Morrison, Toni. 1992. *Playing in the Dark: Whiteness and the Literary Imagination.* Cambridge, MA: Harvard University Press.

Scannell, P. *Radio, Television and Modern Life.* Cambridge, Mass: Blackwell Publishers.

Schudson, Michael. 1995. *The Power of News* (chapter 5: Trout or hamburger). Cambridge: Harvard University Press): 113–124.

Sontag, Susan. 2002. 'Looking at a War: Photography's view of devastation and death.' *The New Yorker* (December 9).

Weimann, Gabriel. 1994. *The Theatre of Terror; Mass Media and International Journalism.* New York: Longman.

Wolfsfeld, Gadi. 2000. 'Political Waves and Democratic Discourse: terrorism waves during the Oslo peace process.' In *Mediated Politics.* Eds. L. Bennet and R. Entman. New York: Cambridge University Press.

CHAPTER 5

Paramilitaries and the Press in Northern Ireland

TIM COOKE

The reporting of sustained conflict poses particular challenges for news organizations and journalists in the search for truth, objectivity, accuracy, balance, independence, and responsibility. For news media most closely linked to the arena of conflict, the challenges are unique. While international or foreign media often go largely unaccountable to the society about which they report, indigenous news organizations must wrestle daily with both the short- and longer-term consequences of their judgments and actions. The very proximity of news organizations rooted in broadcasting or publishing to a society affected by conflict, and in particular by political violence, makes them important players in the battle for hearts and minds in a war of weapons and words, of politics and pictures. The Middle East, South Africa, and Northern Ireland have all offered examples of how the news practices of indigenous journalism can be heavily conditioned by political violence. They also offer case studies of how news organizations used to reporting conflict have responded to the fresh challenge of reporting a society attempting the transition to peace. What role does the news media play in such a transition and how do news programs, newspapers, and the journalists who frame our daily window on the world assess what we should see when we look through it? This examination of the role of news organizations in Northern Ireland in reporting the paramilitary groups responsible for thirty years of headlines, at home and abroad, as they have moved into the political arena, attempts to offer insight into this interactive process in one divided society.

Context

After decades of conflict, Northern Ireland has been riding the roller coaster of constitutional change. The Good Friday Agreement of 1998 placed the province firmly in the center of a political vortex that proffered the most fundamental transformation in governance since the foundation of the state in 1921—more far-reaching than the abolition of the unionist-dominated Stormont Parliament and the imposition by the British Government of direct rule from Westminster in 1972. One of the key reasons the conditions for such change existed was that many of the people who sustained and directed the political violence of the last quarter century and more had agreed to silence their guns and emphasize politics rather than paramilitarism. Encouraged in latter years by changes in the policies of both the British and Irish Governments, most of the key paramilitary groups involved in three decades of violence finally had a political party which represented their thinking. On the republican side the Provisional IRA (Irish Republican Army) was represented by Sinn Fein. On the loyalist side the UDA/UFF (Ulster Defense Association/Ulster Freedom Fighters) was represented by the UDP (Ulster Democratic Party), and the Ulster Volunteer Force (UVF) was represented by the PUP (Progressive Unionist Party). These three paramilitary groups, the IRA, UDA/UFF, and UVF were responsible for most of the 3,500 deaths in Northern Ireland since 1969—the IRA for some 1,600 deaths and the two loyalist groups for almost 1,000. One of the key elements of government policy aimed at encouraging a transition to politics was the devising of an election in May 1996 which helped even the smallest of these political parties (the UDP) achieve representation at the multi-party talks sponsored by the British and Irish governments, which ended on April 10, 1998, with a new cross-community agreement on future governance. All this had a profound effect in and on the media in Northern Ireland. After years of reporting a catalog of horror, grief, and destruction within a paradigm which condemned acts of terrorism as illegitimate and irrational, new questions emerged as to whom government and the media viewed as legitimate actors in the political sphere. The transmutation of violent protagonists into politicians and brokers of peace was a process that the media had both facilitated and wrestled with. A news media proficient in reporting the paramilitaries in conflict appeared less prepared for the consequences of the paramilitary role in peace making. Journalists were still adjusting to a changing situation that was giving the paramilitaries a new role in the press, public, and political arenas. The purpose of this chapter is to examine how journalists and news organizations in Northern Ireland dealt with the questions of legitimacy and voice in a period of transition and to discuss the influences that affected their framing and treatment of paramilitary groups inside and outside the peace process.

The role of the news media in the process of political communication has been of particular importance in Northern Ireland. In a society with many traditional religious divisions in education, housing, employment, sport, and culture and where previous attempts to build political institutions with cross-community consensus failed, the media had been a primary arena for communication between and within the Catholic and Protestant communities. A notable factor here is that Northern Ireland did not fall victim to one of the difficulties apparent in some other divided societies—that of a media divided by language and speaking to only one side in the conflict. The mainstream news organizations in Northern Ireland are English language and most of the population experienced exposure to more than one news source. Thus, while the two morning newspapers published in Belfast catered to particular constituencies, the *Irish News* to Catholics and the *News Letter* to Protestants, the newspaper with the largest circulation, the *Belfast Telegraph* (29 percent market share) was sold to Catholics and Protestants. The news services provided by BBC Northern

Ireland and Ulster Television were also aimed at the whole community. This study draws mainly on material from these five news organizations. Between them, the *Belfast Telegraph, Irish News,* and *News Letter* accounted for some 47 percent of market share. The daily television news programs discussed here, Ulster Television's *UTV Live* at 6pm and BBC *Northern Ireland's Newsline 6:30* a half-an-hour later accounted for a combined share of around 70 percent.

Of course not all the paramilitary groups active in Northern Ireland were involved in the transition into the political process—and even those on ceasefire had been judged in varying degrees to have infringed upon the principles of nonviolence to which they were required to subscribe as a precondition for participation in the talks process. Both the UDP and Sinn Fein were suspended temporarily from the talks for varying periods during the first three months of 1998. Furthermore the IRA ceasefire, which allowed Sinn Fein to take part in the talks, was viewed by some Irish republicans as at best ill-advised, and, at worst, a treacherous betrayal. Hence we saw the emergence of the Continuity IRA which had bombed a number of town centers in Northern Ireland in the first months of 1998. On the loyalist side the emergence of the LVF (Loyalist Volunteer Force) was a challenge to the analysis of the established pro-British paramilitary groups the UDA and the UVF. At the beginning of 1998 the LVF carried out a series of killings of Catholics after another small republican group not on ceasefire, the INLA (Irish National Liberation Army), killed the LVF leader Billy Wright inside the Maze Prison. Against this complex web of violence and ceasefire, infringement and observation, the emergence of groups more radical than the established extremists, and the background of the multi-party talks, the media was confronted with irregular patterns and conflicting messages, reporting both paramilitaries in pursuit of peace and others in pursuit of violence.

This chapter examines the media's dilemma. First, concentrating on the methods of communication between the paramilitaries and the media, I discuss the extent to which news organizations tried to differentiate between propaganda and news. Key issues here were the way in which the rules about what makes news gave stories about paramilitaries and their actions a journalistic appeal. At the same time, news organizations also see themselves as representatives of society's anti-terrorist stance. Second, I discuss the transition of actors, who were viewed from within an anti-terrorist paradigm, onto the public stage and into the political sphere. In the case of Northern Ireland, this meant that the same people who had been involved in specific acts of violence in what the media generally viewed as a "terrorist" campaign were accorded a public role as politicians and negotiators. The changing portrayal of individuals and movements in transition would appear a necessary condition for wider social and political change. With journalists, it would seem, old habits die hard and the ambivalence of paramilitary groups (including threats to return to violence and actual bombings and killings) continued to foster suspicion and cynicism toward paramilitaries. That does not mean however that change did not take place within the media. In fact there was significant movement over time in both the public role and the portrayal of paramilitary-related politicians. But as the pace of political change accelerated, news organizations found themselves caught in a dichotomy—in the vanguard of reflecting the dynamics, consequences, and potential of change, while at the same time allowing the inheritance of past experience to weigh more heavily on their decisions and outlook than was apparent with some other actors. It does not follow that such a cautious approach was harmful toward positive transition. Rather, the converse may have been true. The rewards offered by the news media to those embracing peace seemed ultimately to be more highly prized by the paramilitaries than the publicity benefits of violence.

Propaganda and News

The actions of paramilitary groups had a dominant place in the news agenda in Northern Ireland and frequently made headlines around the world. A town center devastated by a car bomb explosion, an indiscriminate sectarian gun attack on a public house, the killing of a prominent politician, an assault on a British army barracks were all events which registered firmly with reporters, producers, editors, audiences, readers, and government. The publicity which inevitably followed violent action was part of the paramilitary calculation, sending a message of political determination, technical ability and military will. It was a message directed toward enemies *and* supporters. While the paramilitaries had, through violence, the ability to generate publicity, the character of that publicity was not in their control. Reportage of their actions routinely brought with it the condemnation of politicians and community leaders, the stories and grief of the victims, the reaction of government and of paramilitary groups on the opposing side. Within the output of the Northern Ireland media (newspapers and broadcast news programs), the negative response to paramilitary violence was ritual and overt, reflecting the disapproval of the community (a large majority of Protestants and Catholics viewed the violence of the paramilitaries as politically, legally, and morally wrong) and of government.

That disapproval was reflected in news narratives and in the practices of newsrooms. Reportage had generally, although not exclusively,[1] characterized the activities of paramilitary groups as "terrorist," offering a negative representation of the groups and their methods. News organizations had also been aware that they were targets of paramilitary propaganda. Against the background of societal and governmental disapproval of paramilitary activity, they tried to avoid overt manipulation of the content of reports and of their news agendas. Apart from the broadcasting ban imposed by the British Government between October 1988 and September 1994, this effort was self-regulated. It has also been variable, depending on the decisions of individual journalists, photographers, producers, and editors, although the BBC published its own guidelines to staff. The paramilitaries, discontent with a pattern of coverage and condemnation which portrayed them as evil, psychopathic, and often irrational, took their battle to another front, attempting to explain, justify, and legitimize themselves through media under their own control and through a public relations strategy that sought to achieve greater portrayal of their chosen image of themselves. Understanding the way in which the paramilitary organizations viewed themselves is crucial to understanding the image they sought to portray through the wider media. Insight into their self-perception was available through the media they had under their direct control. Here I briefly discuss five key idioms—*statements, briefings, staged events, publications,* and *murals.* The first four played a pivotal role in the patterns of communication from paramilitaries to journalists while the fifth provided paramilitaries with direct communication to local communities. The way in which these idioms filtered into and through the editorial and production chain and the extent to which the self-styled symbolism, imagery and terminology translated into the narrative of news is instructive as to how journalists in Northern Ireland sought to balance propaganda and news.

Statements

Statements from paramilitary groups were a well-established news source in Northern Ireland and were frequently telephoned to newsrooms in Belfast and Dublin. They were usually accompanied by a code word which certain journalists recognized and which authenticated the source. These statements were used by the paramilitaries for a variety of purposes—for example, to warn of explosive devices which they had left in a particular place where they were not seeking to achieve casualties, to admit responsibility for killings or other attacks in order to achieve association in the public mind with the event, or to set out their current political analysis at a time they assessed to be useful in sending a message to the government or supporters. The terminology indicated that the groups saw themselves as legitimate armies with military structures and ranks. The IRA had an "Army Council," while the various loyalist groups had a "Combined Loyalist Military Command." The Ulster Defense Association had an "Inner Council." The statements spoke of "brigades," "battalions," "companies," and "active service units." Members held ranks and identifiable positions such as "commander," "brigadier," "quartermaster," or "volunteer." They described members who were serving sentences in prison for violent acts as "POWs" or as "political prisoners." Statements were a common source of information about the paramilitaries and their activities and often had an immediate news value. In the aftermath of its attacks on police or army personnel, or following a bomb attack on a town centre, it was common practice for the IRA to contact a journalist and claim responsibility. Such claims, when believed to be genuine, were regularly reported by news organizations. Information, warnings or claims judged authentic usually found their way quickly onto air or into print. While the statements often had an undeniable news value and aided understanding or interpretation of events, the terminology used in them was often rephrased or ignored by journalists, although there was no universal set of rules or guidelines adopted by news organizations.

Briefings

One-on-one briefings, sometimes at the request of journalists and other times offered by the paramilitaries, were another source of information about the groups and the historical and political context in which they saw themselves. Depending on timing and content, these briefings could result in lead story treatment by one news organization with the subject matter then being picked up by others. From the paramilitary perspective it could be an effective way of influencing news agendas or getting a message across at a chosen time, particularly when it was a message which news organizations deemed to be politically significant. For example, following bomb attacks in Moira on February 20, 1998, and Portadown, February 23, 1998, the IRA briefed the BBC in Belfast with the message that it was not responsible, that its cessation of violence was intact and that there was no split in the organization. That briefing was of value to Sinn Fein in its efforts to stay involved in the talks and turned suspicion more directly toward the Continuity IRA. The briefing resulted in a lead story on *BBC Newsline 6:30* (February 24) and was picked up and reported by all the other news organizations in Northern Ireland. In addition, information and views gleaned in briefings—either directly from paramilitary figures or from someone considered close to their thinking—often found its way into background analysis, explanation, or context given by reporters as to the current thinking within paramilitary groups.

Staged Events

On occasion paramilitary groups staged events in order to send a message to government, to the "other side" or to a faction on their own side. They might organize their own publicity, distributing photographs or video footage to the media. At other times, they might specifically invite journalists and cameras to meet them at the corner of a certain street at a certain time of night. On arrival masked men with guns would emerge and parade around as if on patrol. There had also been cases of journalists being blindfolded and taken by car to a secret rendezvous where a photo opportunity had been arranged. In 1993, when the IRA was having particular success with a so-called "barrack buster" mortar device used mostly against RUC bases in rural towns, a video appeared in television newsrooms showing masked men in combat gear training with the device. The instructor featured in the video could be heard explaining that the device was similar to what had been used by the IRA in an attack on 10 Downing Street, an attack the IRA regarded as a major military and propaganda coup. Parts of the video were used occasionally by television news programs in Northern Ireland in the context of analyzing the IRA's activity or political position. The reporting of staged events was problematic. Journalists were not excluded from the provisions of the Prevention of Terrorism Act under which it was a criminal offense to withhold information about terrorist activities. Beyond that however there were editorial considerations with some organizations taking the view that they would not respond to invitations from illegal groups involved in violence to meet and film or record them. Others did find themselves, at times knowingly and at other times without design, at staged events and they broadcast or published the material they gathered. It was a question of judgment and practice—and both varied among journalists and news organizations. When Billy Wright, leader of the Loyalist Volunteer Force, was shot dead by INLA inmates inside the Maze Prison in December 1997 and his body returned to his home in Portadown, a photograph was issued to the media showing him lying in an open coffin, flanked by four hooded men in uniform, three of them with handguns. What was a journalist or editor to make of this? Was it macabre bad taste to publish the photograph? Was it offensive? Did it glorify a dead terrorist? Did it glamorize a group which murdered innocent Catholics? What was the LVF's intended message in staging the photograph? The media could choose to publish or not. Both decisions were made. The *News Letter* (December 29, 1997) published the photograph alongside a story headlined "FEAR AND FURY" with a caption "Shot dead: loyalist gunmen guard the body of LVF leader Billy Wright." The *Belfast Telegraph* on the same date also published the photograph, but neither the *Irish News* nor the BBC used it.

Publications

The most sophisticated and regular publication offering insight into the affairs and analysis of the largest paramilitary group, the IRA, was *An Phoblacht/Republican News*, published as a weekly newspaper in Dublin and on the web. It carried statements from and interviews with the IRA and embraced the organization's imagery and terminology. It was designed to advance the Irish republican agenda and to communicate within the movement. It promoted Sinn Fein, giving prominence to party policy and representatives. Emphasis was given to the republican analysis, the welfare of republican prisoners, a negative portrayal of what were termed "crown forces" (*i.e.*, the British Army and RUC). At times, *An Phoblacht/Republican News* was a news source for journalists, particularly when it quoted directly from the IRA in relation to policy position. However, the terminology and rhetoric inherent in the editorial narrative did not normally carry over into mainstream or dominant news narrative. Publications associated with loyalist groups—the UDA's *Defender* and the UVF's *Combat*—had limited circulation and were only rarely featured as news sources.

Murals

The urban ghettoes of Northern Ireland are often awash with color—from the bunting strung between the street lights to the red, white, and blue or green, white, and gold painted sidewalks which mark out territory as Protestant or Catholic. Beyond this lies another more arresting landscape, the paramilitary murals which adorn the gable walls. These five or six meter high brick canvases depict masked men with automatic weapons as heroes devoted to a cause which is politically, religiously, and morally legitimate. They frequently invoke history, God, and the use of rocket launchers or automatic rifles. Flags, emblems, armed and hooded figures acting as guardians or defenders, rolls of honor commemorating members who have been killed, celebrations of local sub-divisions within the group's structure are common. In his study of Northern Irish murals, Bill Rolston says that for both loyalists and republicans, murals were an important form of political mobilization, sending a message to the "converted" and acting as a potential source of "conversion" of others:

> Although also fought out at the society and international levels, it is at the local level that the battle for state legitimacy is waged daily. In the midst of that battle, murals are not just folk artifacts but a crucial factor in the politicization of the community. Politically articulate murals simultaneously become expressions of and creators of community solidarity. Although it would be too far-fetched to argue that the propaganda war is won or lost at the local level, there can be no denying the role the murals play as crucial weapons in that war.[2]

Television, of course, demands pictures and many of the reports dealing with paramilitary groups were limited in the range of pictures available. Television journalists embraced the paramilitary mural as an additional picture source. In the race against the clock, where a television journalist was balancing concern over video of a mural which proclaims the heroism of the UVF or IRA with a demand for pictures over which to explain a development affecting a paramilitary organization, production demands could influence the result. The murals are colorful, graphic, and clear and will not defame anyone. They are also part of the urban landscape and can be seen in reality by anyone daily. While judgments were made in television newsrooms about frequency of use and context, murals painted by the paramilitaries and designed to glorify their cause did find their way onto television screens in Northern Ireland regularly. Thus the murals could achieve a prominence or send a message more widely than originally intended, although the growing professionalism and technical ability displayed in more recent examples suggested that those who conceived them were alive to this possibility.

News Production, Judgment and Legitimacy

It is clear that while the paramilitaries were a vital news source, their access to newsprint and airwaves was not unfettered. Apart from the period of the broadcasting ban there was no legislation in force which directly prevented journalists reporting what paramilitaries said or even publishing or broadcasting interviews with them. Nevertheless news organizations in Northern Ireland rarely sought on-the-record interviews with paramilitaries for publication or broadcast, evidence of reluctance to give airtime and column space to the analysis of groups which had been killing people on a weekly and sometimes daily basis.

Yet most individual journalistic decisions were heavily influenced by judgments over news value and by production demands. The need to illustrate or visualize a story deemed important while the clock ticked toward broadcast time could be more powerful than any notion of a model for reporting on paramilitaries. This could result in different judgments at different times in balancing the overlap between news and what could be argued to be propaganda advantage for paramilitaries. Such judgments might also have been affected by other factors including a current level of violence or the state of public opinion. In an effort to achieve consistency of approach, the BBC published its own guidelines for staff on coverage of Northern Ireland. The guidelines cautioned against according "spurious respectability" to paramilitaries.[3] They counseled staff to "avoid anything which would glamorize the terrorist, or give an impression of legitimacy" and said statements can be "paraphrased to avoid the military titles and pomp."[4] While news organizations saw the paramilitaries as an important news source and accorded their activities a major role in the news agenda, there were varying attempts to remove or dilute the most obvious propaganda and report activities in a context of disapproval. News organizations therefore, while acknowledging the paramilitaries as a central player on the political and media stages, did not accord them the overt recognition and legitimacy they believed they deserved from the public, the politicians and the press. We now turn to the process of how that axis of legitimacy in terms of political involvement and news coverage can change.

Paramilitaries and Politics

It was evident in reading or watching reports by news organizations in Northern Ireland in the mid to late 1990s that political parties such as Sinn Fein, the PUP, and the UDP were woven into the tapestry of daily news. Representatives were given voice routinely, commenting with their latest analysis or calling for movement in line with their policy. The news report in which they appeared could well have been about a meeting with the British prime minister, contact with the White House, or their participation in discussing or implementing political change in Northern Ireland alongside what had been traditionally described as the "constitutional parties," i.e., against the use of violence. It was remarkable how far events and the place of Sinn Fein, the PUP, and UDP in the media had moved. Five years earlier Sinn Fein President Gerry Adams was refused meetings with even the most junior British Government Minister, the United States refused to grant him an entry visa, and his voice was largely banned from being heard on British and Irish airwaves. The change came about through a complex political process in which the news media played an important role. Many factors contributed to this evolutionary process, among them the emergence of Sinn Fein into the electorally successful political wing of the IRA.

The Provisional IRA is an illegal organization and membership is a criminal offense in the United Kingdom and in the Republic of Ireland. For legal reasons alone it was not possible for an identifiable individual to appear publicly as someone speaking directly for the IRA. But the "Republican Movement" was made up of both a military wing, the IRA, and a political wing, Sinn Fein. Sinn Fein is a legal political party which, since the early 1980s, has been developing an electoral strategy. In the May 1997 election in Northern Ireland (Local Government Election), the party gained 16.9 percent of the vote, the third highest percentage of all the parties, giving it seventy four of the 582 seats across the twenty six local councils.

The electoral impact of political parties representing the loyalist paramilitary groups was a later development. The UDP was formed at the end of 1989, although it evolved from the earlier electorally unsuccessful Ulster Loyalist Democratic Party. The PUP had been active on a small scale since 1979. But both parties only emerged in the mid 1990s with a cohesive public profile which translated into electoral support in the elections of 1996 and 1997. In the election to the Northern Ireland Forum in May 1996, a qualifying election for participation in the talks on the future of Northern Ireland, the UDP and PUP between them won 5.6 percent of the vote—they had previously never managed to exceed a 1 percent share. In the Local Government Election of May 1997 they won 3.2 percent between them, yielding a total of ten seats compared to two in the 1987 election. This small but significant breakthrough for the loyalist parties reflected a peace dividend and a higher media profile following the announcement of a ceasefire by the Combined Loyalist Military Command (CLMC) in October 1994, a group which represented all the loyalist paramilitary organizations. In the run-up to that announcement and in its aftermath, new, articulate, media-friendly voices emerged onto the public stage.

The republican and loyalist ceasefires announced in 1994 were a crucial factor in creating conditions which allowed for the beginning of a process of "normalization of relations" between parties such as Sinn Fein and the British and Irish Governments. Both Governments had previously refused to meet Sinn Fein representatives at a ministerial level. Initially the Irish government under Albert Reynolds moved with greater speed and enthusiasm to embrace Sinn Fein as a legitimate player on the political stage. Under John Major's premiership, the British government was much more cautious in its response, so cautious that republicans became disillusioned and the IRA ended its ceasefire in February 1996. The election of the Labor Party under Tony Blair as the new British Government in May 1997 generated new impetus, so much so that the IRA ceasefire was restored in July 1997. Before the year was out Sinn Fein was participating in the Talks at Stormont and in discussions with Prime Minister Blair at 10 Downing Street. Crucially though, under the Major premiership, an election was organized in Northern Ireland to determine who would take part in the talks process. The system of election all but guaranteed that the political representatives of the paramilitaries would qualify as participants. The formula was specifically designed to include the loyalist parties (the PUP and UDP), which had limited electoral support. All this was a lengthy and tortuous process affected by many variables, among them the level of violence, the impact of particular bomb explosions and shootings, and the broadcasting ban imposed by the Thatcher government. It was also a process characterized by a media challenge, in interviews and opinion columns, to the ultimate commitment of parties with paramilitary connections to democratic ideals. Ed Moloney discussed many of these variables in his essay on the broadcasting ban, in which he highlights some of the features of the axis between journalists and Sinn Fein in the late 1980s:

> Over time though legitimate journalistic interest in the conflicts between Sinn Fein politics and the IRA's violence developed into something of a preoccupation, not to say obsession for some. Sinn Fein interviews and press conferences became almost exclusively contests between defensive Sinn Feiners and reporters trying to get a revealing and damaging response to the latest IRA disaster... Some reporters began to see this essentially confrontational approach as the only way in which the IRA could or should be covered and when the media ban was announced voices were raised complaining it would no longer be possible.[5]

The media's difficulty with accepting the democratic credentials of elected Sinn Fein representatives while IRA violence ran hot was a reproduction of both governmental and societal disapproval. In terms of Irish history, 1990 is not long ago, but at that time journalist and commentator David McKittrick was writing:

> From the republican point of view, Sinn Fein, the political wing of the IRA, provides a useful political and propaganda adjunct to the terrorist campaign. Its presence in political life is a standing embarrassment to the authorities and a continuing affront to Unionists who continue to lobby for the banning of the party.... The government is uncomfortable with Sinn Fein. On one level it is a legal political party, standing for elections and representing its voters. But on another it is clearly attached to the IRA and is, to most intents and purposes, subordinate to it. The government has not sought to ban Sinn Fein (which was legalized in 1974), and civil service departments routinely deal with its members. At the same time, however, ministers will not meet Sinn Fein personnel, and its representatives are, in general, banned from appearing on television and radio.[6]

The broadcasting ban, which was in effect for almost six years, was an attempt by the Thatcher government to penalize Sinn Fein, particularly for its association with the IRA. The electoral success of the party and the emergence to prominence of capable media performers caused offense to the unionist population and to the British government. In an effort to deny access to airwaves, the British Home Office introduced restrictions controlling the circumstances in which representatives of a series of organizations including the IRA, Sinn Fein, the UDA, and UFF could be heard speaking on television and radio. Thatcher took the view that BBC and Independent programs were too lax, allowing groups running a dual military and political campaign to have the best of both worlds— the publicity impact and political leverage of bomb attacks and shootings and access to television and radio to promote their political analysis in the wake of such events. Announcing the ban in the House of Commons the then Home Secretary Douglas Hurd said:

> For some time broadcast coverage of events in Northern Ireland has included the occasional appearance of representatives of paramilitary organizations and their political wings, who have used these opportunities as an attempt to justify their criminal activities. Such appearances have caused widespread offense to viewers and listeners throughout the United Kingdom, particularly in the aftermath of a terrorist outrage. The terrorists themselves draw support and sustenance from having access to radio and television and from addressing their views more directly to the population at large than is possible through the press. The government has decided that the time has now come to deny this easy platform to those who use it to propagate terrorism.[7]

So, for example, when Gerry Adams was a member of Parliament for West Belfast while the ban was in force, he could appear on television in his capacity as MP and have his voice heard speaking about housing, roads, or schools; but when it came to speaking on political matters on behalf of Sinn Fein, he could be seen and his views reported but his voice could not be broadcast. Nevertheless, the fact that the broadcasting ban was introduced at all clearly suggests that news organizations were ascribing more legitimacy to Sinn Fein in particular than the British government of the time. Sinn Fein had already demonstrated significant and sustained electoral support before the ban was introduced—a fact which news organizations could scarcely ignore even if they did continue to challenge Sinn Fein on its support of "armed struggle" and its association with the IRA. Despite the British Government's stated unwillingness to meet with or talk to Gerry Adams at the time, news organizations continued to give him voice as president of Sinn Fein and as MP for West Belfast between 1983 and 1992 (he lost the seat to the SDLP in 1992, regaining it in 1997). The political landscape against which the broadcasting ban was first imposed changed markedly (it was lifted by John Major shortly after the IRA ceasefire announcement of August 1994), as did the media landscape in which Sinn Fein, the PUP, and UDP became prominent features.

Observation of this transitional process over the course of two decades enables us to identify the key components that impacted the changing media relationship with the paramilitaries, who sought progressive involvement in the political process. The key components which influenced a changing media relationship in Northern Ireland included *politicization, electoral participation, electoral success,* the subsequent *holding of official positions,* the *emergence of celebrities* onto the media stage, the *halting of violence,* an *inclusive political initiative,* and the *emergence of new extremists.*

The election of IRA prisoner Bobby Sands as an MP—as he lay dying on hunger strike inside the Maze Prison in 1981—was a powerful demonstration of the republican movement's potential to harness electoral support. At Sinn

Fein's ardfheis (annual conference) in the same year one of the party's leaders, Danny Morrison, spoke of republicans taking power "with an Armalite in one hand and a ballot paper in the other." This was the public evidence of an increasing emphasis on *politicization* and the efforts of Sinn Fein to mobilize urban and rural support behind its objectives and its strategy. Although there was nothing new in the political nature of republican objectives, it did signify a broadening of the means of achieving them beyond the military arena. That politicization created dynamics of policy debate within the movement, and it at least offered the media the potential to broaden its coverage beyond events with which republicans were connected—acts of violence, public rallies—into an examination and discussion of ideology, analysis, methods, and goals. It also contributed markedly to the emergence of the peace strategy within Sinn Fein.

Electoral participation in itself confers legitimacy and adds credibility to actors who receive media attention and, in the case of Northern Ireland, a legal entitlement to due and fair coverage under the Representation of the People Act, the legislation regulating election publicity. This means, for example, that parties of any background are legally entitled to make party election broadcasts on the BBC and Independent television. This provides a guarantee of coverage in a formal setting, in which the parties themselves have control of what they say and how they present themselves, within a given time frame.

Electoral success brings further rewards through public demonstration of the strength of support and the subsequent *holding of official positions*, the acquisition of titles (in local government, say, councillor, chairperson of committee, appointment to a health or education board, or chair of one of Northern Ireland's district councils). This results in views being quoted more widely, additional credibility via status, and at times automatic involvement in news by virtue of position.

The emergence of celebrities into the public sphere—figures who become prominent in representing a particular cause—was another feature accelerated by electoral validation. Election to public office reinforces the role of individuals as well as of parties. Another issue in the emergence of media personalities is the role of journalistic resonance, an unscientific process whereby the media repeatedly seek out and give voice to actors who bring one or more particular qualities to the news arena. These may include novelty, power of articulation, rationality, drama, charisma, and availability. This may or may not be associated with electoral success but it can certainly be intensified by voter support. Organizations can influence this process themselves by giving people titles or positions with names which translate more widely and carry overtones of authority, i.e., president, leader, chairman.

The halting of violence was pivotal, allowing governments that had previously vowed not to talk to those engaged in violence to devise an *inclusive political initiative* in which the paramilitary groups are fully represented. Within the paramilitary organizations and the parties associated with them, the inclusive nature of the process justified the halting of their campaigns and the emphasis on politics. It also provided them with the public recognition and legitimacy they had long desired. The end of the campaigns of violence had also allowed the media more freedom to reflect and explore the analysis of the parties associated with paramilitary groups. Their involvement in a formal political dialogue sponsored by the London and Dublin administrations also made them valid media players, right on a par with other participants. It was also significant that the political initiative was official in nature. When the then leader of the largest nationalist party in Northern Ireland, John Hume of the SDLP (Social Democratic and Labour Party), embarked on a series of talks with Sinn Fein President Gerry Adams in 1993, in what became known as the Hume-Adams initiative, he faced widespread criticism for engaging in such dialogue in the absence of an IRA ceasefire. There can be little doubt, however, that this dialogue was a decisive factor in creating the circumstances which led to the IRA ceasefire of August 1994.

The *emergence of new extremists* was a further factor that began to affect the media role of Sinn Fein, the PUP, and the UDP. After the IRA, UDA, and UVF announced their ceasefires, new paramilitary groups emerged—the Continuity IRA on the republican side, which was responsible for a series of bomb attacks, and the LVF on the loyalist side, which killed ordinary members of the Catholic population in random sectarian attacks. There were also tensions within the paramilitary groups on ceasefire and violent events involving some of their members. The result was that Sinn Fein, the UDP, and the PUP positioned themselves as the moderates, expressing commitment to peaceful methods, to dialogue and to agreement. For example, in response to an attempt by the Continuity IRA to bomb a bank in Londonderry, Gerry Adams issued a statement calling for an end to all paramilitary violence. "We think this very unique opportunity for peace should be consolidated and I would call on anyone engaged in armed actions, from right across the spectrum, to cease," said Adams (*Belfast Telegraph* March 20, 1998). Loyalists formerly involved in violence also portrayed themselves as moderates. Following the murder of a Catholic man by the LVF in Belfast, the PUP leader David Ervine said his death had been caused by "some obscure group of head cases" (*News Letter* January 12, 1998). As the UDP returned to the talks after an expulsion because the paramilitary group associated with them (the UFF) had killed people, the *Irish News* (February 24, 1998) under the headline "UDP rejoins peace talks" reported: "The Ulster Democratic Party has said efforts must be redoubled inside the political talks and loyalists should not be provoked into reacting to the Portadown and Moira bombings." Many of the elements discussed are interrelated and some are more important at particular times. They are the pivots around which media interaction has evolved with political change involving the paramilitaries in Northern Ireland over twenty years.

Discussion

This analysis has focussed primarily on an intense period of transition in the run-up to the conclusion of the Good Friday Agreement in Belfast in April 1998. Events since then have served to support its findings.

The election of a new Northern Ireland Assembly at Stormont in June 1998 changed the political landscape. For example, Sinn Fein won 18 out of the 108 seats, entitling the party to two ministerial positions. The party's chief negotiator Martin McGuinness, who had been widely regarded as a leading IRA figure, was appointed Education Minister. The news media, as expected, accorded the new political institutions and office-holders full legitimacy, reinforcing their role and authority. On the loyalist side the UDP, party representing the UDA, failed to win a seat. The party was subsequently dissolved after the UDA, adopted an anti-agreement and returned to violence.

The legitimacy of the elected representatives formerly associated with violence was further reinforced by fresh violence from new extremists. In August 1998 a group calling itself the Real IRA detonated a car bomb in Omagh—leading to the largest loss of life in any single incident in Northern Ireland since 1969. The Real IRA viewed Sinn Fein's participation in the Northern Ireland Assembly as a betrayal of true republican principles and disagreed with the IRA's ceasefire.

The bulk of the early releases of both republican and loyalist prisoners as part of the agreement was completed within a two-year timescale. This issue was a subject of intense media focus, displaying the tension between the emotive and moral issues on one hand and the *realpolitik* approach on the other, viewing the early releases as a necessary evil—the price of paramilitary complicity in peace.

Another area of public debate and media attention has been the question of decommissioning illegal paramilitary weapons. Two acts of decommissioning by the IRA and one by the LVF had taken place by April 2002, under the auspices of the Independent International Commission on Decommissioning.

The collapse of the Northern Ireland Assembly in the Fall of 2002 over alleged IRA activities led to a further round of talks in early 2003 and projections of fresh elections in the summer of 2003.

Amid these developments and for the foreseeable future, Northern Ireland will continue to offer a field of study of the way in which a news media rooted in the community, conditioned by conflict, interacts with wider political change. No one elects journalists to their public role and yet they make decisions on behalf of society as to who gets to speak, when they speak, and how the messenger or message is framed. Apart from legal constraints, many of those decisions are independently made against a prevailing and variable notion of a correct balance between freedom and responsibility. The notion of that responsibility clearly weighs heavily in a divided and violent society. News organizations in Northern Ireland continue to face the question of how that responsibility is to be defined in a society tentatively edging toward peace.

Notes

1.   The *Irish News* decided in the early 1990s to specifically drop the use of the word "terrorist," taking the view that there were differences in the types of incidents happening and that overtly labeling violent acts as "terrorist" was stereotypical. In its editorials, in common with other newspapers, the *Irish News* was overt in its denunciation of paramilitary violence.

2.   Bill Rolston. 1991. *Politics and Painting: Murals and Conflict in Northern Ireland.* London, Rutherford: Fairleigh Dickinson University Press.

3.   BBC *Style Guide* 1993 Section 15. London: BBC Publications.

4.   BBC *Guidelines For Factual Programs.* 1989. Section 80.

5.   Ed Moloney. "Closing Down the Airwaves: The Story of the Broadcasting Ban," in Bill Rolston, ed. *The Media and Northern Ireland* (London: Macmillan, 1991).

6.   David McKittrick. *Endgame.* Belfast: Blackstaff Press. 1994.

7.   Statement by the British Home Secretary Douglas Hurd. October 19, 1988.

PART II

Comparing Terrorism Frames

Framing the US Embassy Bombings and September 11 Attacks in African and US Newspapers

TODD M. SCHAEFER

Frames are likely to come into sharpest focus when we can compare similar news stories through contrasting media contexts, whether different types of media such as television news, newspaper reports, magazine feature stories, and internet websites; different subcultures such as coverage by the *New York Times,* the *Miami Herald,* the *Chicago Sun-Times,* and the *San Francisco Chronicle;* or reporting in different countries and regions of the world. This section of the book focuses on these sorts of comparisons, exploring how far the same acts of terrorism are framed through similar or distinctive cultural lenses, for example whether reporting the events of 9/11, coverage of Palestinian-Israeli conflict, or the war in Afghanistan.

In particular, this chapter examines local-versus-foreign coverage of two sets of terrorist attacks—the 1998 United States Embassy bombings in Nairobi, Kenya, and in Dar es Salaam, Tanzania, as well as the September 2001 attacks in New York and Washington, DC. The research design compares coverage of these events provided by the major national newspapers headquartered in the cities where the attacks took place: the *New York Times, Washington Post,* Nairobi *Daily Nation,* and the Dar es Salaam *Daily News.* The study assumes that terrorist attacks are inherently newsworthy, as accounts of human drama, tragedy, and perseverance (Johnpoll 1977), but also that the amount of news coverage is typically determined by factors such as type of attack, the group(s) involved, and of course the sheer magnitude of the act. Like all news events, we explore how far the proximity of the media is also a key variable. The study examines whether media organizations cover attacks closer to home differently from those occurring on the other side of the globe and also how far coverage is influenced by cultural frames, both professional and societal. The chapter concludes that geographic proximity and the "local angle" influenced the prominence and amount of coverage of the terrorist events under comparison; that cultural influences played a modest role in how these events are reported; and that, most important, national worldviews derived from the international system greatly shaped the interpretation and framing of the causes of the terrorist attacks.

The Comparative Framework

In any 'most-similar' comparative study, it is crucial that the cases are similar enough across relevant variables to draw valid conclusions. When analyzing media coverage, comparative case studies help illuminate the inevitable biases, framing, or other news judgments journalists use in constructing a narrative (Entman 1991). As Entman notes, these cases do not have to be identical but merely have "comparable journalistic potential" (1989: 40).

This study focuses on two events. On August 7, 1998, truck bombs exploded minutes apart from each other outside the American embassies in Nairobi, Kenya, and Dar es Salaam, Tanzania. In the Kenya attack, over 200 died (11 Americans and the rest, Kenyans) and 1800 were injured, whereas in Dar es Salaam, nine were killed and over fifty were injured. On the morning of September 11, 2001, four hijacked U.S. airliners were turned into missiles aimed at major U.S. landmarks: two struck the World Trade Center in New York City, while two others were aimed at Washington, DC—with one striking the Pentagon and the other crashing in Pennsylvania after passengers staged a revolt. All told, many thousands were injured or died, the vast majority in the New York attacks.

The circumstances of these two events are quite close: Both were double-attacks, carried out almost simultaneously in similar fashion. Indeed, even the culprits were the same: Although no one claimed responsibility at the time, both attacks were eventually linked to Saudi dissident Osama bin Laden and more directly, members of his al Qaeda terrorist network. The targets and method of attack were different, but comparable. The major differences were that one was an attack on American targets abroad, while the other was aimed at the United States itself; and the U.S. attacks caused much greater damage, death, and psychological impact. While these differences certainly should affect the coverage the events received, nevertheless their similarities should provide a reasonable basis for comparison.

For practical reasons, newspapers were selected as the medium of study. While television is the most widely used source of news for Americans and radio plays a similar role for Africans, comparing two disparate media would be difficult, and archives of African broadcast media are almost impossible to obtain. Newspapers are both accessible and provide a common format for analysis. The newspapers used in the analysis were selected primarily because they are major national media outlets as well as local ones, making them roughly comparable on this dimension. Furthermore, newspapers tend to have more in-depth content than many other media. The *New York Times* and the *Washington Post* are two of the premier newspapers in the United States, read by the nation's elite and outside their immediate communities. While they are not the largest papers in terms of circulation within the country, their elite status and audience make them more influential than the pure numbers of readers dictates (Cf. Paletz 2002: 72).

The *Daily Nation* and the *Daily News* are two of the leading English-language newspapers in Kenya and Tanzania, respectively. Their language of publication necessarily gives them a smaller readership than papers published in Swahili, the most common African language of the region, at the same time they are significant in ways analogous to the elite status of the *New York Times* and *Washington Post* in the United States.[1] The Nairobi *Daily Nation* is one of the oldest, and largest, independent papers in Kenya.[2] Started in 1960 by the Aga Khan, head of the Bohra Ismaili Community, expressly to give an independent, African (as opposed to European or colonial settler) perspective on public affairs, the paper has grown in size and stature. Most observers attribute its success to journalistic professionalism either unknown or unparalleled in sub-Saharan Africa (Opiyo 1994: 79). The *Daily News* of Dar es Salaam, Tanzania was formed in 1972 by the ruling party TANU (Tanganyka African National Union), as a mainstream, hard-news counterpart to the Swahili *Uhuru;* together they accounted for almost all of the circulation in the country until 1993 (Lederbogen 1992). "*Uhuru* and its sister *Mzalendo* were party publications aiming at the Tanzanian citizen. On the contrary, . . . the *Daily News* and the *Sunday News* were the property of the government, intended to satisfy the needs of the educated elite and moreover, to ensure Tanzania's presence on the international newspaper market" (Sturmer 1996: 138).[3]

Both sets of papers, conveniently located in cities where the attacks took place, thus have local concerns and markets to go with the national focus they have developed. In addition, their elite status also means that international news plays a significant role in their coverage in the case of attacks on foreign soil. The analysis examines most news coverage of the four newspapers, along with editorial, op-ed, and commentary pieces, for a two-week span following each attack. While arbitrary, this period was chosen as enough time to account for the attacks' ramifications, while not so long as to have faded off the radar screen of news organizations (especially those for whom the respective attacks were foreign stories). Content of all four papers, for both events, was analyzed both quantitatively and qualitatively in different ways depending on the issue, or hypothetical influence (see below) involved. These included the amount, prominence and nature of the coverage of each event in each newspaper. In particular, editorial, commentary, and op-ed pieces were examined as measures of interpretations of the terrorist attacks, their aftermath and retaliation.

Potential Influences on Coverage

1. *International vs. Local Nature of the Story*

One major influence on the nature, type, and amount of coverage an attack receives from a particular media outlet could depend on its location, especially how close it is to home. Greater prominence and volume of coverage is expected to be devoted to attacks occurring in the paper's own country and especially hometown—where ease of reporting, journalist resources, access to sources and information, and audience interest would be greatest, as opposed to an event in a land thousands of miles away. Weimann and Winn examined which terrorist events were reported in the *New York Times* and the three major U.S. networks from 1972 to 1980, and they found that the location of the event and the nationality of the victims were both significant, especially for television news. The regional bias meant that the *New York Times* devoted most attention to terrorist events occurring in the Middle East, Asia, and North America and least to similar events occurring in Africa (Weimann and Winn 1994: 78). Therefore, when an attack is "local," we expect the newspaper in question to devote more attention and importance to it; to focus more on the "criminal disaster" side of the story, such as the rescue efforts, victims, and investigation and prosecution of the act; and to have more coverage of public reactions. When the attack occurs on foreign soil, however, there should be greater focus on the causes of the attacks and more weight given to the implications for politics and international relations, as physical distance provides less material and a more detached perspective.

2. Cultural and Journalistic Norms

Cultural and journalistic values and ways of seeing (or perhaps more accurately—*national* culture as well as professional or journalistic culture) are also expected to influence how the attacks are reported. As mentioned earlier, the cultural traditions of both the society within which the journalist operates and their own professional class, can lead to potentially different presentations of reality. As Ellis (2000: 221) puts it: "[o]n any given day, newspapers and radio and television stations in the United States, Britain, and France are likely to choose dissimilar stories for their lead news items. Even if they were to pick the same story . . . they are likely to approach it differently, according to what they presume to be the interests of their audiences." Lipset (1996) suggests that American cultural values place a high emphasis on the values of individualism, freedom, democracy, and capitalism and that the media arguably reflect these values (Shoemaker and Reese 1996: 222). Conversely, traditional African social values stressed group orientation, continuity, harmony, and balance, which "required the individual to negotiate personal needs into the framework of the group" (Bourgault 1995: 4–5).

Furthermore, Western press traditions derive from an emphasis on facts, in the sense of empirically-verified events. The U.S. news media, in particular, is generally seen as operating under a creed of professionalism and objectivity, within the larger context of American culture. "American journalists are generally more rigorous than their European counterparts in considering reporting as the assembly of carefully corroborated facts" (Ellis 2000: 222). In the view of Bennett (2001), the practice of objectivity consists of a set of shared norms of journalistic behavior, including balance, the journalist as "neutral adversary," a descriptive narration story format, and the practice of editorial review.

African media, while influenced by Western traditions, nevertheless retain their own character. Bourgault notes that Africans' main modes of discourse did not develop along the same lines as the West, which in turn influenced their journalism:

> The printed word was introduced during the colonial period on peoples whose . . . societies had not evolved communication norms typical of commercial capitalism. They had not, for example, evolved a discourse tradition clearly separating subjective and objective categories . . . Although the press in Black Africa *appears* [emphasis in the original] in printed form, it has inherited little of the reasoned discourse associated with the printed tradition of post-Reformation Europe. Rather, the press in Africa displays "pre-empirical" stylistics typical of oral discourse (Bourgault 1995: 181).

African journalism puts less emphasis on facts and mere description and on the separation of fact and opinion. It includes oral-narrative story forms more akin to fiction and reporting of sensational or supernatural "events" such as ornate conspiracy theories or miracles. "Even courageous and skillfully produced African papers often contain stories that to a Western reader appear shocking, bizarre, or simply incomprehensible," but nevertheless they "presume certain values commonly held by the population, just as the *Daily Telegraph* or the *New York Times* do in their own way" (Ellis 2000: 225).

These forays into cultural effects on reporting and journalists lead to some expectations about how these events will be reported by the respective nations' media. One would expect coverage in the American papers to be more "professional," objective, and descriptive in style, while that in the African outlets to be more personal, interpretive, sensational, and stylistically akin to oral communication. In terms of national culture, it is difficult to conjecture how value differences might be reflected in terrorism coverage. Possibly, one might expect American coverage to focus on the individual motives and the effects of terrorist attacks, as well as bolstering support for American values; whereas African journalists might instead frame them based on larger group concerns and their effects on the community (both local and global).

3. North-South/Structural Contexts and Ideological Biases

The structural context, as employed here, refers to the position of the respective paper's country in the global political-economic order. In related fashion, ideological biases are predispositions toward viewing events derived (in part) from that position. It is useful to distinguish between the concepts of culture and ideology. In terms of communication theory, culture is a common pattern of meaning expressed through symbols, enabling individuals to communicate with one another and share their experiences, conceptions, and beliefs. Ideology is more of a worldview or an integrated set of frames for interpreting which draws on cultural themes in order to resonate with audiences. While culture and ideology are both concerned with meaning, ideology is meaning tied to specific political or social interests, or *meaning in the service of power* (Shoemaker and Reese 1996: 222). Thus, although likely entwined with cultural norms, the larger structural position of a nation, accompanied by the characteristics that place it there and the interests that flow from it, surely influences the way in which journalists portray events. The conceptual framework most applicable to the cases analyzed here is the North-South distinction.

The United States is a Western, advanced post-industrial democratic nation with the most powerful military in the world. It is the preeminent (if not dominant) actor in world affairs, the "last remaining superpower." According to a number of observers, these attributes (along with audience concerns, history, and other factors) have led the media in the United States to have an *ethnocentric, nationalistic* bias in covering foreign affairs (Hallin 1986, Page and Shapiro 1992). This means the American media tend to focus on international issues of greatest concern to the United States, devote more coverage to countries geographically or economically closer, and portray American allies in a more favorable light than enemies. Therefore, the expectation is that the American newspapers will focus far more on U.S. domestic and international concerns arising from the attacks. For example, we would expect that they will give greater weight to implications of the attacks for American domestic and international politics, will focus more on American sources for their information, and in the case of the African bombings, may devote more attention to the American than African victims.

Kenya and Tanzania, like almost all other African countries, are members of the "Third World" of economically underdeveloped nations. They are poor, to one degree or another economically and politically dependent, and weak actors in the international system. Given the realities of their societies, journalists in these countries are presumed to interpret events through these lenses. Therefore, one would expect more internationalism than in the American media, yet with biases toward their own and developing nations' concerns.

Comparing Coverage
Proximity; Local vs. Foreign Milieu

Not surprisingly, the results reveal substantial coverage differences depending on the location where the attacks occurred—with greater emphases and particular biases in the local instances. But, these differences actually reflect similarities in the newspapers' coverage orientations. All of the papers showed a preference toward covering stories in their own back yard, and even the nature of their coverage was not that different.

First, when one looks at the sheer number of news stories it is obvious that proximity to the event is a major determinant.[4] When the four papers are cross-indexed with the four locations where the attacks occurred, not only were there more stories on attacks in their own continent, there were more stories on attacks in their hometown than those of the other city (See Table 6.1).[5] In other words, there were far more stories on the American attacks in the American papers, as well as stories on African attacks in the African papers.

Table 6.1   The Number and Percent of News Stories, by Paper and Event

	NAIROBI BOMBING	DAR BOMBING	NYC ATTACK	DC ATTACK
New York Times	18	6	94	13
	(75%)	(25%)	(88%)	(12%)
Washington Post	21	8	28	32
	(72%)	(28%)	(47%)	(53%)
Nairobi Daily Nation	56	5	21	16
	(91%)	(9%)	(57%)	(43%)
D.E.S. Daily News	9	13	6	4
	(40%)	(60%)	(60%)	(40%)

Additionally, there was substantially more coverage on their own locale, even when the "objective reality" of the attacks in terms of potential newsworthiness is taken into account. For example, the *Daily News* carried more stories on the Dar embassy bombing, and the *Washington Post* more on the Washington, DC, attacks—in absolute and relative terms—than their continental counterparts, despite the fact that more people died and there was greater destruction in the Nairobi and New York attacks, respectively.

Indeed, an interesting parallel emerges when one looks at the relative distribution of the stories across continental and municipal boundaries. The American papers both focused about 75 percent of their coverage on the Nairobi attacks, and the African papers, about 60 percent on the New York attacks. Furthermore, both the *New York Times* and *Daily Nation* overwhelmingly focused on attacks in their own cities than in those of their sister cities.

A similar conclusion can be drawn when prominence of coverage is examined. Prominence is of interest because placement of stories signal importance to readers, a key component in agenda-setting. Here, prominence is measured in three ways: the number of stories concerning the attack and its aftermath on the front page; the number of days (length of time) such stories appeared on the front page; and lastly, how often during the period these types of stories appeared as the lead (e.g., largest headline, top story) of the day (see Tables 6.2 and 6.3). In a nutshell, the American attacks were given far more importance in the American media, and the African attacks in the African media, than the reverse. It should also be noted that the greater number of stories in the American papers in part reflect layout differences, meaning that the American papers contain more stories on their front page.

Comparing and contrasting the nature of coverage—in terms of the types of stories emphasized—presents a more complex picture. First, front-section news stories were examined and separated into relevant categories of emphasis.[6] Since terrorism stories fall into particular patterns—and are a combination

Table 6.2 The Prominence of African Attacks in News Stories

	FRONT PAGE (THE NUMBER OF STORIES CONCERNING THE ATTACK ON THE FRONT PAGE)	DURATION (THE NUMBER OF DAYS SUCH STORIES APPEARED ON THE FRONT PAGE)	LEAD (THE NUMBER OF DAYS THE STORY WAS THE LEAD STORY ON THE FRONT PAGE)
New York Times	16	11	5
Washington Post	20	11	6
Nairobi Daily Nation	21	14	13
D.E.S. Daily News	24	13	9

Note: The amount of coverage during the two-week period following each event.

of disaster, crime, and political or war reporting—a common classification scheme was created. The categories included: *disaster* elements (the attack/event itself, rescue efforts, stories about or concerning victims); *criminal* aspects (the investigation and prosecution of culprits); *political* or "war" elements (the effects of the attacks, retaliation, leaders, politics, and international relations deriving from the event); *domestic public reactions* (marches, vigils, interviews, polls); and *miscellaneous*. The stories were then tabulated and relative percentages calculated (see Figs. 6.1 and 6.2).

We expected earlier that there would be more on the disaster (the attacks, victims, rescue, and investigation) angle of the story in the domestic cases than the foreign ones. Looking at relative amounts of coverage, surprisingly this is not the case, with coverage of the two events being more dissimilar than the news outlets themselves. Indeed, the amount of disaster coverage appears the same regardless of whether the attack is "local" or not. These stories account for 30 to 40 percent of the coverage of all four papers in the African embassy bombings

Table 6.3 The Prominence of American Attacks in News Stories

	FRONT PAGE (THE NUMBER OF STORIES CONCERNING THE ATTACK ON THE FRONT PAGE)	DURATION (THE NUMBER OF DAYS SUCH STORIES APPEARED ON THE FRONT PAGE)	LEAD (THE NUMBER OF DAYS THE STORY WAS THE LEAD STORY ON THE FRONT PAGE)
New York Times	82	14	14
Washington Post	89	14	14
Nairobi Daily Nation	13	13	11
D.E.S. Daily News	19	14	3

Note: The amount of coverage during the two-week period following each event.

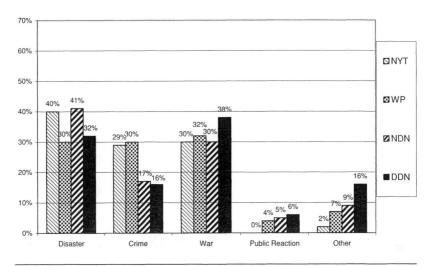

Fig. 6.1 The proportion of news stories, on African attacks by subject, in each newspaper.

and about 25 percent for the American and 15 percent for the African papers in the September 11 attacks. Oddly, then, given their smaller size, the African attacks were portrayed as more of a disaster story than those on September 11 by reporters from both continents.

The amount of coverage of the criminal side of the attacks—the investigation and prosecution of the perpetrators—also reflected this pattern, contrary to the expectation that it would receive greater coverage in the local cases. The African

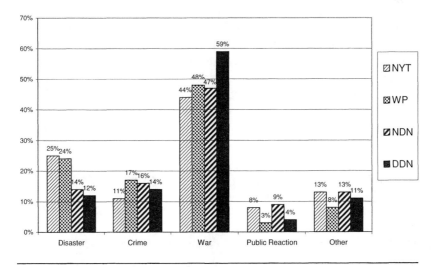

Fig. 6.2 The proportion of news stories, on US attacks by subject, in each newspaper.

news media devoted almost exactly the same amount of coverage to this angle in both attacks. The American papers in fact devoted relatively more coverage to it in the African case. This finding may be due to the fact that discovering the culprits is equally newsworthy no matter the locale or perhaps that American investigators were primarily involved in both cases. As for the American media, the heightened role of American investigators in Kenya and Tanzania may have increased the relative importance of the investigation, whereas judging from the relative amounts of coverage to this topic, the September 11 attacks appear more as an act of war than an act of crime.

More coverage in all outlets was devoted to the effects of, and retaliation for, the September 11 attacks than the embassy bombings, and more coverage was devoted to public officials, politics, and international relations. Again, this reflects the "reality" of the greater scope of this event but also that its ramifications were more far-reaching and akin to a major military action. Not surprisingly, greater amounts of coverage were devoted to public reactions when the attack was local, in all outlets. African newspapers devoted more to American reaction than vice-versa, probably due to the availability and salience of poll results in the U.S. case.

Therefore, while local considerations do play a role, the circumstances of the event itself also influenced coverage. September 11 was seen by all the newspapers under comparison as more of a political and war story than a disaster, probably due to the event's unprecedented nature and size.

Despite the lack of complete compelling evidence for a "local" bias in the distribution of story types, there were nonetheless some clear qualitative impacts on coverage that arose from physical location. The first is what Robert Entman terms *event context*: namely, what else is going on in the news at the time which affects a story's relative importance (Entman 1989: 52). In the case of terrorism in faraway foreign lands, the story must inevitably compete with other domestic events that the public—or media—may also be concerned with. Indeed, after its shock effect, it may be relegated to the foreign news section. Conversely, when the attack happens in the paper's hometown, it drives all other news off the front pages, or at the very least, it remains at the top of the news agenda. This dynamic is one reason for the reduced prominence of the foreign attacks. For example, on September 12, 2001, the Dar *Daily News* ran a piece on upcoming foreign investment as its lead story, though the American attacks were prominently displayed below. During the period of the African attacks, the Monica Lewinsky scandal was in full bloom in the United States, sharing front-page coverage with terrorism news. President Clinton's admission of sexual relations replaced the bombing story as the lead in both American papers on August 14. Likewise, Kenya was in the throws of a ruling-party struggle over presidential succession, and that story replaced the September 11 attacks as the lead story in the *Daily Nation* after five days, continuing to receive prominent coverage thereafter.

Second is the prevalence of local angles in what otherwise was a national and international tragedy. Both the *Washington Post* and *Daily Nation* ran news and commentary pieces about municipal and national (as the capital) disaster preparedness, or the lack thereof, and the need for a better system for future emergencies. The *Daily Nation* covered the effects of the bombing on an impending banking strike. The *New York Times* focused more heavily than the other papers on the performance of Wall Street, the delayed mayoral primary election, and the issue of the newly-heroic Mayor Rudolph Giuliani's impending term limitation. The latter was covered to a lesser extent in the *Washington Post* and not at all in the African papers. The *Washington Post* covered the closure and uncertain re-opening of Reagan National Airport and the postponement of the IMF meetings more extensively and prominently than the other papers, as both of which are more of a concern to residents of Washington.

Cultural Influences: Reporting Style and Content

Some differences in coverage between the African and American newspapers are probably attributable to the cultural differences mentioned earlier. The African papers tended to have more dramatic headlines, such as "*Bomb Terror,*" "*Terror Rocks U.S.,*" and "*Unprecedented Kamikaze Plane Attacks Hit U.S.,*" for the lead stories on the attacks themselves; or "*Alive From Blast Tomb,*" describing miraculous survivors rescued from the rubble, a headline actually used by the *Daily Nation* in both attacks. Such headlines obviously are written mainly to sell papers—and might not be any different than many American papers of lesser pedigree (or presumption) than the *New York Times* and *Washington Post*. And in any event, the stories underneath these headlines were written little differently than similar ones in the American papers.

Within stories there were some examples of reporting appearing in the African papers that (at least in form) wouldn't appear in the *New York Times*. These might be termed "I was there" stories as opposed to the "you were there" reporting of American journalism. For example, after the Nairobi bombing the *Daily Nation* ran first-hand accounts of staffers with titles such as "*Tragedy Through the Eyes of an Editor*" and "*We're Both Alive for Declining Tea Offer,*" a first-person account of a reporter whose polite refusal to have tea with the U.S. Ambassador, so he could file his story, led him to miss being in the blast by minutes.[7] Similarly, "*The Last Words of a Very Brave Victim,*" literally began with, "Thank you so much for helping me, *lakini bahati mbaya* (but it is unfortunate). Now I have to leave you people—goodbye," as if the victim were speaking to the reader.[8] Sometimes these stylistic differences were lodged within stories rather than the focus of them, as seen in this account of a Tanzanian reporter accompanying their vice-president on a tour of the destruction the day after the attack:

> A woman was rummaging in her destroyed house near the embassy looking disheartened and desperate. She was away from her house when the blast occurred and when she came to see the dilapilated [sic] house she could not believe her

eyes. She started throwing her belongings from inside the house, but security men went to her and asked to postpone her shifting until the security of the place could be assured. She could not take heed to the plea but continued shifting her clothes. The tragedy had made her moody.[9]

This type of reporting occurred almost exclusively in the "homeland" terrorism case of the embassy bombings rather than the September 11 attacks, obviously due to its first-hand nature.

But for the most part, these are the exception rather than the rule—stories in the African newspapers looked and were written similar to those in the United States. Indeed, the U.S. papers likewise contained personal accounts of victims and witnesses to add color to their coverage.[10] So when it comes to the terrorism genre, at least based on the cases examined here, the idea that there would be differences in American and African reporting due to journalistic norms appears unfounded. More likely, these forces impact story selection or story genres rather than being expressed within stories that journalists from both countries would find newsworthy. Also, Africans may well have adopted Western styles of reporting, even in domestic terrorist attacks.

Most differences and similarities in content, however, likely come from production and resource differences. At the same time, the relative similarity between American and African reporting on September 11 probably arises from the African reliance on Western wire services (usually Reuters, not Associated Press). These undoubtedly reflect the African papers' smaller budgets and resource bases, as the American papers can afford to have support staff and foreign bureaus or reporters stationed abroad (granted, in some cases merely stringers). Again, though, perhaps cultural influences are limited by the nature of terrorism stories themselves, which contain universal human concerns like drama, tragedy, fear, heroism, and survival.

North-South/Structural Influences; Ideology and Political-Economic Frames

Whether coverage was influenced by national cultural differences such as societal norms and values is more difficult to discern. Again, the nature of terrorist attacks drew universal reactions muting such differences. To discern the effect of paradigmatic frames on coverage, one must compare coverage of the same attack by different national media. First, to determine if American media as predicted concentrated on the "American angle," we examine in particular U.S. coverage of the African attacks.

On the surface, it does appear that U.S. news coverage of the embassy bombings did in fact "favor" American victims in terms of the amount of coverage and focus of stories. For example, both the *New York Times* and the *Washington Post* ran individual portraits of the victims. With the exception of miraculous survivor Sammy Nganga—who, after being dug out from the rubble after thirty-six hours, received prominent coverage in both American and Kenyan media—Africans were only mentioned as supporting parts in stories. Only two stories out of seventeen in the *New York Times,* and three out of ten in the *Washington*

Post, were specifically about African victims. Even in stories on the victims more generally, Americans were given more prominent treatment in terms of placement and space, despite the fact that more Africans were killed. Similarly, while both African papers mentioned that American Ambassador Prudence Bushnell as well as Kenyan Trade Minister Joseph Kamotho (who had been in a meeting together) were injured, only the *Washington Post* did so (in two stories the day after, and only one line in each).

Both African papers also gave front-page treatment, with accompanying wire-service photos, of the arrival of U.S. victims at Andrews Air Force base for a tearful ceremony with President Clinton. In contrast, there was little on African ceremonies in the American papers, and visuals merely showed pictures of Kenyans lying on the floor of a makeshift morgue with mourners filing by to identify them, and/or pictures of wailing African women. In fairness, each paper ran a front-page story on the impact of the African victims' deaths on their families.

Also, the U.S. media relied more heavily on American sources in their stories. As expected, President Moi of Kenya and President Mkapa of Tanzania were mentioned much less often than President Clinton. Given that American lives were lost, that could be expected, but Clinton was a major actor in, or subject of, eleven stories in each of the two papers, while Moi was in only two and Mkapa not at all. All told, the names of the African presidents appeared in a total of five stories in the *Post* and four in the *Times.*

If one looks to editorial and commentary pieces as an indication of how the attacks were interpreted, an even stronger picture emerges. The American papers focused exclusively on how the event affected the United States, what to do in the future to prevent recurrences, and how best to respond. The African countries were treated as unfortunate, if honorable, bystanders (which, although true, still slighted them). These especially emphasized the lack of security at the embassies and better ways to both protect against, and fight, terrorism. There was also more discussion of potential responses and the eventual retaliation against Sudan and Afghanistan than there was about Kenya and Tanzania.[11]

The most telling example of the clash between U.S.-centric and Afro-centric frames concerns claims of American "insensitivity" and "arrogance" toward Africans in the aftermath of the Nairobi blast. Soon after the attack, criticism was leveled at U.S. officials in Kenya for their handling of the crisis and for putting "America first." This began with charges that American marines guarding the embassy kept Africans at bay and impeded ordinary rescuers at the scene, and went on to include comments attributed to Ambassador Bushnell that they were trying to prevent looting; the quick airlifting of injured Americans to European hospitals; and even President Clinton's slighting of the loss of African lives in his first public statement. On top of this was a U.S. decision (later quickly rescinded) to issue a travel advisory to its citizens, thus damaging Kenyan tourism, a major industry. In fact, Secretary of State Madeleine Albright was dispatched to the two East African countries, and Clinton issued a televised statement of apology.

Needless to say, this issue was a major point of contention in the *Daily Nation*.[12] It ran several pieces on the entire affair, from the actions of the marines, to the travel warning and effects on tourism, to Albright's apologetic visit. It also ran a large, two-page "news analysis" feature article entitled, "What Kenyans Think: This was not our war. Why then were the Americans so insensitive?"—complete with a menacing photo of a rifle-toting U.S. marine (see Fig. 6.3). Though not entirely anti-American (at the end, it rejected an Iranian assertion that the United States brought it on itself, arguing no nation "deserved this"), it began, "Kenyans used to think their police were unfeeling buffoons. But that was before they met the American marine, and had a first-hand peep at the American sense of priorities, their view of friendship, and like we say here, being mindful of each others' welfare." It then went on to review the entire affair.

'This was not our war. Why then were Americans so insensitive?'

A US marine shoos off bystanders: "In the first outpourings of emotion, a lot of Kenyans felt America was the victim. After the events of the past week, no one is so sure any more."

Fig. 6.3 *DAILY NATION* story on "American Insensitivity."

Admittedly, both U.S. papers covered the issue of the diplomatic controversy, though one was from the perspective of the ambassador. But there were only three stories total, and these were on the inside pages. They listed (as did the Kenyan media) the U.S. response that the marines were trying to protect further casualties and/or the integrity of the crime scene.

The Kenyans refrained from outright editorial criticism, though they did voice some hope for American aid for the victims, especially since Kenyan insurance companies would not cover losses to terrorism. Albright's visit was seen as portent of that aid, which apparently never came. Poignantly, one op-ed piece told Kenyans to stop expecting handouts, especially from the self-interested, egocentric Americans and that they should instead rely on themselves, as this excerpt shows:

> Americans . . . are only interested in what affects them individually. This would be seen here as selfishness and indeed it could be, but that is simply the American way. . . . Secondly, Americans neither know nor care much about the rest of the world. It might be difficult for Kenyans to understand that very few Americans who have heard about Kenya cares about it. Thirdly, Americans see themselves as the ultimate country and nobody else matters. The Americans' media do not help and this might explain the gung ho attitude that is seen, especially among U.S. marines, that other people loath so much."[13]

Interestingly, the American media made almost no comment on the entire affair, nor did it even cover Albright's trip on the news pages. The closest they came to addressing this issue was the last line of a *Washington Post* masthead editorial entitled "Source of Terrorism," which concluded, "In Kenya, a similar American impulse to preserve unimpaired access to evidence in the debris has apparently caused some friction with Kenyan authorities, who have not had prior occasion to become experienced in American counter-terrorist ways. The Kenyans have suffered harshly. Their cooperation is vital, and surely can be worked out."[14]

Examining African coverage of the September 11 attacks, however, one also sees evidence that they viewed it and its aftermath through their own eyes. Most of the news stories in both African dailies directly detailing events in the United States were wire service reports, and thus differed little from comparable stories in the American papers. Even here, however, African papers put their own spin on it, especially building up the dramatic, ominous signs of U.S. retaliation. For example, a Reuters story on Bush calling up American reserves and meeting with his advisers to discuss military options—something that was seen as a largely understandable action to increase security in the United States—was labeled by the *Daily Nation* as "50,000 Troops Called Up as US Prepares for War." One article headlined "Bush Vows Revenge" contained one line quoting Bush, "We are engaged in a monumental struggle against evil," but was otherwise a descriptive account of rescue efforts and the like, even quoting Secretary of State Colin Powell as saying no military action had been planned.

The *Nation* and the *News* thus also demonstrated a degree of Afro-centrism in their coverage. They frequently mentioned the 1998 attacks and also drew on African sources for reaction. These included stories about their own leaders' statements and views. For example, the *Daily News* lead story for September 13 was "Mkapa Hits at Terrorism," detailing their president's position and reporting his delivery of a message of condolence and condemnation to the American ambassador. The *Daily Nation* ran a story on the Kenyan Foreign Minister's view of the Middle East, including a statement of Kenyan support for a Palestinian state. There was also a "people in the street" story on Kenyans with personal memories of the 1998 attacks, which "offered sympathy but also urged Americans to understand why U.S. Middle East policy makes them targets." It quoted a Kenyan woman injured in the Nairobi attacks as saying, " 'Maybe the Americans will get a taste of what we went through,' " and " 'It will be interesting to see how they treat their own people, compared with the way they treated us,' " referring again to the demands for U.S. compensation.[15] Similarly, the coverage of the victims and investigation also carried an African tint. The *Daily Nation* ran front-page stories on the sole Kenyan killed in the World Trade Center attack, complete with tearful comments from his mother, and on the son of a Kenyan Member of Parliament who was arrested in an FBI sweep; the *Daily News* ran a front-page story on how no Tanzanians had been killed in the attacks. Alongside official government support for the United States was also debate over whether Kenya should or would play a role as a staging ground for American retaliation. In some ways, perhaps this is again merely an attempt by the media to find a "local angle" to the story.

In the opinion sections, African papers also framed the incident in African terms, distinctly different from that of the American papers. These pieces focused on two main areas: the cause of the attacks and the proper response to them. But a common theme ran through all: U.S. culpability and the need to take others' views into account.

To African editorial writers, though horrible and unjustifiable, the cause of the September 11 attacks were rooted in the swaggering manner in which America carried out its global leadership role. Almost unanimously, they saw America's self-interested Middle East policies, coupled with global inequities, to be the root cause. Africans often identified surrogate causes in America's unilateral foreign policy under Bush, citing as examples the rejecting of the Kyoto global warming treaty, the ABM treaty (Bush's missile defense plans), and the Durban, South Africa, conference on racism, which the U.S. boycotted because of its denunciation of Israel. "To many observers, it is America's smug, arrogant, isolationism that has begotten this disaster. Is America humble enough to admit it has been wrong in its dealings with the world and must change in the interests of world peace?"[16] Another stated, "the any number of unacceptable, unilateral, not to mention illegal (under international law) violations by the U.S. in the Arab world, certainly underlie the motivation behind the terrorist attacks."[17]

The Africans also recognized, like American opinion writers, the end of American innocence and the shocking vulnerability revealed by the attacks, perhaps in awe that someone could deal such a blow to the United States. "The American nation appears not only immensely distressed and angry about the bombings, but surprised too. It cannot understand why anyone should be moved to such hatred against it. Insulated from the rest of us by the isolationism of most of its political representatives and its media, it has little understanding of the events swirling around it."[18] Unlike the Americans, however, who mourned for the past or called for a new realism, Africans in a sense responded by saying "now they know how we feel." "Now Americans, together with the rest of the world, mourn the senseless waste of life just as do Iraqis and Palestinians. Americans will bury people, just as thousands do every day in Africa."[19]

Incidentally, little was said about the causes of terrorism beyond the Middle East dimension in the American editorial pages, which focused instead on the aftermath and potential responses. While there was some allusion to Bush's support for missile defense, it usually was in the context of its proven irrelevance or need to broaden his foreign policy outlook to encompass the new global politics of terrorism. Only one piece, and then in passing (about Yasser Arafat), mentioned the Durban conference on racism, unlike the African media.

In terms of the proper response, African opinion pieces were uniformly in favor of slow, multilateral, and international action. "The entire world must co-operate with the America people and President Bush in pursuit of the culprits . . . Whatever the case, terrorism must be dealt with collectively to maintain international peace and security."[20] They often linked this to the above point about American ("don't give a damn about the rest of the world") foreign policy mentioned earlier. "The U.S. must get its foreign policy acts together and stop living in the ivory tower of politics, where it listens only to itself or its blue-chip equals. The time has come for it to sit down with its enemies . . . It is not money, military might, or a well-funded Pentagon or CIA that will save America. Only thoughtfulness and a respect for humanity."[21] While certainly there were opinions in the American press along these lines, there were also ones supporting decisive U.S. action. Perhaps most notably, the vast majority of commentary pieces were written by Africans, with little from outside the continent. The *Daily News* only ran two stories by Americans—one, a piece by a U.S. reporter who feared his countrymen's bloodlust and called for restraint and the other, by international relations historian Paul Kennedy, explaining the limits of American power.

Therefore, as seen in their coverage of the other, both American and African media reflect a degree of self-centeredness. Although it is difficult to say with any certainty, one interpretation is that these differences may be due to national cultural values. Perhaps the African frame that the United States should help African victims in the embassy attacks and that the United States should be more internationalist and responsible in the world following September 11, derives instead from their more "collectivist" culture. The American media's neglect of the African victims' plights (because it was not "America's fault" and each country should be responsible for its own), and its more U.S.-centric and unilateralist stances after the U.S. attacks may reflect its more "individualistic" culture. This process may also be affected by the reporters' different perspectives derived from their nations' position in the larger world political-economic system, of which they are a part. American journalists may thus frame the politics of terrorism from their own First World perspective, just as African journalists do from their Third World one. While one might argue this is natural, nevertheless it is a framing bias, and not "reality."

Conclusion

Terrorism news, like other genres, is colored and framed with a local tint. As seen here, while geographic parochialism may not be the dominant force in shaping the amount and nature of news coverage, even when stories are officially "foreign" they often contain local components. Furthermore, when events abroad are interpreted and framed, they often carry with them the domestic perceptions of those events.

It also appears that cultural influences—both journalistic and national—are not as important as other factors in shaping coverage. Perhaps this is because terrorism news itself leads to similarities greater than any differences, with the inherent and universal shock, horror, sympathy, and unity such attacks bring. Even so, while media in every society rally the public together following domestic attacks, they tend to portray themselves as "special" and they may thereby miss their larger commonalities with all peoples.

Yet there were notable differences in reporting. In covering the embassy bombings, the American media in a sense confirmed the Africans' charges of insensitivity, since while they did cover some of how Americans were perceived and Africans felt, their focus concerned the meaning of the attacks for the United States and what the United States should do in response; they ignored the others' perceptions. There were no American editorials calling for aid to the African victims, for example. Similarly, in conveying the September 11 attacks, the African media showed American viewpoints through news coverage of government officials and to some extent, average U.S. victims, but when it came to editorial interpretations, they were almost uniformly African voices less predisposed toward American worldviews. Where they did provide American or Western opinions, these were in line with African views (America needs to say it is sorry, should not lash out, and so on).

Because journalists searched for local angles and reflect the biases in their societies, American and African newspapers were ethnocentric in putting their own concerns and structural frames first and not challenging what they already thought about the other. It remains to be seen whether these findings are typical, and if, for example, media coverage of terrorist incidents in other nations is similar to that found here. But rather than confirming that cultural differences are at work, differences in terrorism coverage instead may be simply a reflection of mindsets rooted in the larger international system. Just as terrorism may be in part caused by peoples' perceptions of the global political-economic power structure, the message of terrorist attacks appears to be mediated to diverse publics around the globe through frames crafted by that very same system.

Acknowledgements

I would like to thank the Central Washington University Office of Graduate Studies and Research for a summer research leave that made this possible; the librarians at the CWU library and Northwestern University's periodicals and Africana collection for their helpful assistance; and my wife Kathy who provided lots of moral and a little research support. I also pay solemn homage to the victims of these horrible attacks, fully realizing that whatever knowledge is gained from studying these incidents cannot come close to equaling that which has been lost.

Notes

1. Though each in a sense has a Swahili version as well: The Nation Group also publishes *Taifa Leo* (the Nation Today) and *Taifa Jumapili* (Sunday Nation), and in Tanzania, the ruling party publishes *Uhuru* (Freedom) on weekdays and *Mzalendo* (the Patriot) on Sunday, which to some extent parallels the *Daily News*. The author, who has some knowledge of (albeit not complete fluency in) Swahili, examined the Wednesday and Sunday editions of these papers and found they appeared to be roughly the same, though the Kenyan papers' editions more closely mirrored their English-language counterparts.
2. Opiyo (1994) reports that circulation of the entire Nation Group was 165,000 copies in 1993, which accounted for 50% of the newspaper market; the media profile at www.newafrica.com lists its current circulation at 170,000.
3. Sturmer (1996) lists the circulation (or at least, print run) of the *Daily News* at 50,000 and the *Sunday News* at 60,000, though the data at www.newafrica.com list it at a mere 15,000.
4. Editorial and opinion pieces were excluded. Furthermore, for a more accurate comparison, only stories appearing in the first, main news section were counted—e.g., Section 1, or A, etc., in the case of the *Times* and the *Post;* any special features sections of the *Daily Nation,* and to a lesser degree the *Daily News* (which really doesn't have any—each page of its ten-to-twelve sheets focuses on a different type of news). Specialty feature sections, such as local ("Metro") or style, etc., were excluded for obvious reasons, though undoubtedly would simply add to the amount of "local" stories.
5. Stories were double-counted for location if they spent a substantial amount of attention on both attacks, but not if they were scarcely mentioned.
6. The headline and lead paragraph were used to determine which category a story fit into; if it appeared ambiguous, it was placed in all relevant categories, a relatively rare occurrence.
7. Both are from *Daily Nation,* August 8, 1998, p. 5.
8. *Daily Nation,* August 9, 1998, p. 11.
9. *Daily News,* 'Death Toll Now Nine.' August 9, 1998, p. 1.
10. For example: 'A Day of Terror: The Voices—Personal Accounts of a Morning Rush That Became the Unthinkable,' *New York Times* September 12, 2001, p. A10; 'September 11, 2001; Steve Miller Ate a Scone, Sheila Moody Did Paperwork, Edmund Glazer Boarded a Plane: Portrait of a Day That Began in Routine and Ended in Ashes,' *Washington Post,* September 16, 2001, p. A1.
11. Obviously, some of these differences could be due to the fact that American targets were involved in each case (just one on foreign soil) and that accounts for the parochialism of the American coverage. Indeed, different results might well be found if one examined a completely African domestic attack. Of course, if there had been a terrorist attack in Africa, directed at an African government or historic landmark, it is unlikely the American media would pay much attention at all.

12. Interestingly, the *Daily News* carried nothing at all about the entire Kenyan-U.S. flap, nor anything about how the Americans had responded to their attack. The front-page story on Albright's visit was celebratory and positive. This omission and portrayal may have been due to the Tanzanian government's control over the paper, and perhaps their desire not to anger the United States, or impair their own hopes at aid. But this is only speculation.
13. Mutahi Kagwe. 'Pleas Fail to Grasp American Psyche.' *Daily Nation.* August 20, 1998, p. 6.
14. *Washington Post,* August 11, 1998, p. A20.
15. 'Kenyans Express Mixed Reactions to US Assaults.' *Daily Nation.* September 12, 2001, p. 2.
16. David Makali. 'Lessons from the Humiliation.' *Daily Nation.* September 15, 2001, p. 6.
17. L. Wanyeki Muthoni. 'Examining the Historical Background,' *Daily Nation.* September 16, 2001, p. 9.
18. 'America's Isolationism Cost It Dearly,' *Daily Nation.* September 14, 2001, p. 9.
19. Betty Caplan. 'Apocalypse Now: Another Vietnam?' *Daily Nation.* September 19, 2001, p. 9.
20. *Daily News.* September 13, 2001, p. 1.
21. John Kamau. 'Why the US Must No Longer Come First.' *Daily Nation.* September 18, 2001, p. 9.

References

Altheide, David L. 1987. 'Format and Symbols in TV Coverage of Terrorism in the United States and Great Britain.' *International Studies Quarterly* 31: 161–76.
Bennett, W. Lance. 2001. *News: The Politics of Illusion.* 4th ed. New York: Longman.
Bourgault, Louise M. 1995. *Mass Media in Sub-Saharan Africa.* Bloomington: Indiana U. Press.
Diamond, Matthew. 2002. 'No Laughing Matter: Post-September 11 Political Cartoons in Arab/Muslim Newspapers.' *Political Communication* 19(2): 251–272.
Ellis, Stephen. 2000. 'Reporting Africa,' *Current History.* May: 221–26.
Entman, Robert M. 1989. *Democracy Without Citizens: Media and the Decay of American Politics.* New York: Oxford.
Entman, Robert M. 1991. 'Framing US Coverage of International News: Contrasts in Narratives of the KAL and Iran Air Incidents.' *Journal of Communication* 41(4): 6–27.
Graber, Doris. 1993. *Mass Media and American Politics.* 3rd Ed. Washington, DC: CQ Press.
Hallin, Dan. 1986. *The 'Uncensored' War: The Media and Vietnam.* Berkeley: U. California Press.
Johnpoll, Bernard. 1977. 'Terrorism and Mass Media in the United States.' In *Terrorism: Interdisciplinary Perspectives* Ed. Yonah Alexander and Seymour Maxwell Finger. New York: John Jay.
Lipset, Seymour Martin. 1996. *American Exceptionalism.* New York: W.W. Norton.
Lederbogen, Utz. 1992. *Watchdog or Missionary? A Portrait of African Newspeople and their Work.* NY: Peter Lang.
Opiyo, Baruck. 1994. *The Press and Kenyan Politics: A Study of Newsmaking in a Newly Democratic State.* Ph.D. Dissertation, Mass Communications, University of Iowa. Iowa City.
Nacos, Brigitte L. 1994. *Terrorism and the Media.* New York: Columbia U. Press.
Page, Benjamin, and Robert Shapiro. 1992. *The Rational Public: Fifty Years of Trends in Americans' Policy Preferences.* Chicago: U. Chicago Press.
Paletz, David L. 2002. *The Media in American Politics.* New York: Longman.
Paletz, David L, and Alex P. Schmid, eds. 1992. *Terrorism and the Media.* Newbury Park, CA: Sage.
Patterson, Thomas. 1998. 'Political Roles of the Journalist.' In Doris Graber, et al., eds., *The Politics of News, the News of Politics.* Washington, DC: CQ Press.
Semetko, Holli, et al. 1991. *The Formation of Campaign Agendas: A Comparative Analysis of Party and Media Roles in Recent American and British Elections.* Hillsdale, NJ: Lawrence Erlbaum.
Shoemaker, Pamela J., and Stephen D. Reese. 1996. *Mediating the Message: Theories of Influence on Mass Media Content.* Second Ed. New York: Longman.
Sturmer, Martin. 1996. *The Media History of Tanzania.* Salzburg: Afro-Asiatisches Institut Salzburg.

CHAPTER 7

CNN and al Jazeera's Media Coverage of America's War in Afghanistan

AMY E. JASPERSON

MANSOUR O. EL-KIKHIA

From the vantage point of the United States, it seems that one unified reaction swelled in the hearts of the public, politicians, and media in the aftermath of the September 11 attack on America. The American public saw horrific scenes of the Twin Towers collapsing and smoldering wreckage from the Pentagon, followed by painful images of celebration by anti-American protesters in many countries in the Middle East. As American policy makers decided on a course of action in response to these attacks, the selling of the plan unfolded in the American media, including in CNN television coverage. Simultaneously, the U.S. military response was broadcast to the Arab world through a variety of Middle Eastern media sources, including al Jazeera television.

This chapter focuses on the framing of wartime news coverage from both regions of the conflict in the Afghanistan war. Typically, past research on international crises has often focused primarily on 'one-sided' perspectives, commonly in American media coverage. This study seeks to extend this work by comparing 'two-sided' media perspectives, contrasting coverage of the war in Afghanistan in CNN America and in al Jazeera, the Arab television media outlet, which emerged as an important primary source of news from the frontlines within Afghanistan. How did CNN and al Jazeera frame the discourse about the war? Further, how did CNN use news reports presented by al Jazeera and what consequences did this footage have for the range of information available in the U.S. information environment? We focus on comparing three types of frames in each outlet: governance frames, military frames, and humanitarian frames. By examining news footage of the war in Afghanistan provided in al Jazeera and in CNN we can illuminate the range of ideas present across cultures, giving us a better understanding of the debate in different regions, and the similarities and differences in how these media influenced perceptions of the war in Afghanistan.

Comparing Frames

As discussed throughout this book, media framing, also known as the "second level of agenda setting" (McCombs 1992), is a mechanism of influence in which journalists employ a frame of interpretation in presenting an issue to the public. In other words, media coverage is characterized by an active construction, selection, and structuring of information to organize a particular reality in a meaningful manner for the public (Gamson 1992; Goffman 1974). Framing occurs when media make some aspects of a particular issue more salient in order to promote "a certain problem definition, causal interpretation, moral evaluation, and/or treatment recommendation" (Entman 1993: 52).

The selection of particular attributes of a story gives important information about the perspective of the media source. These perspectives can make selected attitudes salient and shape public opinion differently in political contexts with varying coverage. A limited set of media messages can lead to a narrow range of activated attitudes in the collective public opinion. Past research has analyzed a variety of types of frames (Gamson 1992, Iyengar 1991, Jasperson et al. 1996, Patterson 1994). In the Persian Gulf War, researchers argued that the technical and military language framed the war in a way that made dissent more difficult and discouraged democratic debate (Allen et al. 1994). The language of war and coverage of dissent reinforced the suppression of opposition views. Patriotic themes were repeated and euphemisms and metaphors were used by experts and reporters alike to characterize the military operations. Use of this language allowed citizens to process events of the Persian Gulf War without experiencing the true realities of war (Cohn 1991). "The language of clean technology directs us to evaluate the war's success in terms of the technological precision of weapons, rather than in terms of other values, including loss of life, environmental damage, or even U.S. policy objectives" (Allen et al. 1994: 280). We expect to see similar framing in American media coverage of the war in Afghanistan since these antiseptic portrayals allow Americans to cope with the consequences of war.

Media framing can also influence opinion through the choice of news sources. Sources differ in credibility and those that are seen as more credible can be more persuasive in influencing opinion (Page et al. 1987, Garramone 1984, Tinkham and Weaver-Lariscy 1993). During the Persian Gulf War, access to information was strictly controlled and few sources of news existed outside of the Pentagon's version of events (Allen et al. 1994). "Of the top 15 experts most often mentioned on television, five men account for 36 percent (545 of 1531) of the quotations and other discussions" (278). The most highly quoted expert was Admiral William Crowe, former chair of the Joint Chiefs of Staff, with a total of 280 quotes in print or on television (Dennis et al. 1991: 43). Further, war reporters were hindered by the pool system of press reporting. According to Guy Gugliotta of the *Washington Post,* access to the story was more of a problem than outright censorship by the administration (Dennis et al. 1991: 29). Still, media experts claim that the U.S. military's Joint Information Bureau was highly effective in controlling media's portrayal of the Persian Gulf War (Dennis et al. 1991: 30; also see Allen et al.: 270–1). The Gannett Report quoted Lawrence Grossman, former president of NBC News and PBS and a former fellow at the

Gannet Foundation Media Center, as saying that the press was held captive by the Pentagon. Another reporter claimed that the administration's control over information was much like that of a political convention (Dennis et al. 1991: 30).

During the war in Afghanistan, however, the Pentagon has been less successful at limiting the information that made its way to the public (see chapters 2 and 3). While the Bush administration and Pentagon tried to control the information getting out to American media sources and the Taliban attempted to control the information getting out of Afghanistan, al Jazeera emerged as an alternative source of information from behind the battle lines. al Jazeera was one of the only sources inside Afghanistan to have unhindered access to the al Qaeda and Taliban leadership (Lidster and Rose 2001). Immediately after the September 11 attack on the World Trade Center and the Pentagon, the al Jazeera television network began to set the visual agenda for American news coverage of the war by supplying images of unfolding events in Afghanistan. On September 11, Peter Jennings from ABC News reported that there were explosions in Kabul, Afghanistan and that pictures were being supplied by al Jazeera, the Middle East broadcasting company in the Persian Gulf. As another reporter questioned Secretary of Defense Donald Rumsfeld, it became clear that the questions resulted from news emanating from visuals supplied by al Jazeera to CNN in the United States. "Mr. Secretary, we are getting reports of . . . from CNN rather, that there are bombs exploding in Kabul, Afghanistan. Are we at the moment striking back and if so, is the target Osama bin Laden and his organization?" According to Rumsfeld, "in no way is the United States government connected to those explosions." (ABC News Special Report: America Under Attack, 11 September 2001). American media would not have known to ask these questions without the reports from these Middle Eastern sources and, in particular, from al Jazeera.

This context raises some important questions that provide insights into how cultural factors shape coverage of the same event in two regions of the world. In particular, how did CNN America frame its coverage of the war in Afghanistan and how did this coverage differ from al Jazeera, a media source from the Middle East? Moreover how did CNN regard this station and was it treated as a credible source of information? Was al Jazeera able to provide an alternative frame to the discourse in the American press? This chapter compares the ways in which CNN and al Jazeera framed their war coverage, in the expectation that significant differences will emerge. While certain frames of war may be common, different cultural contexts should shape the tone and balance of frames present in political discourse from different cultural perspectives.

Comparative Research Design

We analyzed television news coverage from CNN, selected as the American news network that first established its reputation with its coverage of breaking news during the Persian Gulf War in 1991. Further, it often served as the source of information for the other major networks. As reported by the Gannett Foundation, many journalists claimed that CNN received favored status in reporting on the Persian Gulf War in terms of access to U.S., Saudi, and Iraqi military (Dennis et al. 1991: 33). CNN also seemed to achieve this status again in the war in Afghanistan given its access to information from the ground in Afghanistan from Middle Eastern news sources, such as al Jazeera. Since this analysis is largely an extension of the Allen et al. (1994) study, as the first author of this chapter was a part of that research team, this chapter uses parallel coding categories.

Through the NEXIS database, we selected television transcripts from CNN news programming. We searched for stories with the key words "war" and "Afghanistan" from September 11, 2001, through July 2002. Due to the incredibly large number of stories produced by the search per day, we included stories that utilized frames identified in the earlier study by Allen et al. (1994: 270–284). We focused on comparison of governance, military, and humanitarian frames. "*Governance*" frames refered to news frames concerning support for the government and political leaders in each country, including issues of national unity and public support for the government. "*Military*" frames included depictions of the strategy used by each side in the Afghan war and particularly the use of the technology of war. "*Humanitarian*" frames included images of the victims of the conflict, notably the suffering and damage caused by war. We also included stories that mentioned the words "al Jazeera," discarding simple mentions. Similarly, brief mentions of the war in Afghanistan or transcript records with minimal details were discarded. A total of 164 stories were analyzed. Two researchers coded each story. We also acquired television footage provided by al Jazeera in Arabic. Given the difficulty of conducting content analysis in Arabic, one coder analyzed forty-two stories from al Jazeera from September 30, 2001, to May 5, 2002.

Within this news coverage, we examined the comparative use of frames by CNN and al Jazeera in stories about the war in Afghanistan. How did reporters on CNN and on al Jazeera television frame the war on Afghanistan from their unique perspectives? What similarities and differences are seen in the nature and number of frames used by each media outlet in the stories analyzed? Certainly, we cannot claim that the examples we discuss are completely exhaustive; CNN and al Jazeera are simply two television news outlets and the stories used in the analysis were selections from the overall output. In this chapter, our approach to understanding frames is primarily qualitative, deconstructing the meaning of the stories, rather than quantitative. Yet, given that our goal is primarily comparative and thematic, we argue that this selection of stories and our use of frames provide reasonable evidence of the variation in war coverage in these two channels.

CNN America's Coverage
Governance Frames

The governance frame concerns how far the news media reported either consensual support or critical dissent with political leaders. Where national leaders are united in agreement against a perceived external threat to the country, then we would expect that the news media's coverage would generate and reinforce support for the administration and its security policies, providing positive frames of government. Generally, in times of international crisis, the American public supports its political leaders and military actions taken in these contexts. As Mueller (1973) argues, it is natural for the public to exhibit a "rally-round-the-flag" response, uniting behind the president. This support is seen in terms of public approval from political elites as well. According to Brody (1989), since the White House controls information during an international crisis, members of the opposition party will suppress their disagreement with the president in public, thereby creating the appearance of an elite consensus.

As the literature on "rally-round-the-flag" effects predicts, when President George W. Bush went on television to comfort and unify the American public and announce decisive action in the war on terrorism, his approval ratings soared. "On my orders, the United States military has begun strikes against the al Qaeda terrorist training camps and military installations of the Taliban regime in Afghanistan. These carefully targeted actions are designed to disrupt the uses of Afghanistan as a terrorist base of operations and to attack the military capability of the Taliban regime" (Bush 2001). "We are beginning another front in our war against terrorism, so freedom can prevail over fear." (White House Briefing Room 7 October 2001). CNN placed the speeches in the context of the September 11 terrorist attack by stating, "Bush is not letting up on the quest for justice" (CNN 7 October 2001). According to Gallup poll results, Bush's approval in handling foreign affairs rose from 54 percent in July 10–11, 2001 to 81 percent in early October. By late October, approval for the war had risen to 88 percent (Frank 31 October 2001). When the strikes on Afghanistan were announced at the Atlanta football stadium, the crowd began to chant "USA. USA." As one reporter remarked, "I suspect that was something heard in football stadiums around the country on this Sunday" (CNN 7 October 2001).

Bush's message was echoed as well in media outlets by various political elites from around the world. The first reaction was reported from an interview with Shimon Peres, Israel's foreign minister. "I don't have the slightest doubt that the decision that was taken by the President of the United States is the right one, the just one, and you are going and we are going to win it for the simple reason, not just because you have the technological supremacy, you have the moral supremacy." France and Canada agreed. (CNN Breaking News 7 October 2001).

When CNN reporter Judy Woodruff interviewed Javier Solana, EU Defense Minister, he communicated a message of the legitimacy of the Western actions against Afghanistan. "Well, we think that this operation is fully legitimate, according to the U.N. Security Council and the European Union has all the solidarity with the United States in these operations. The fight against terrorism is our fight, and together we are going to win it." He also emphasized the fact that it is a unified action and that it will be an extensive, long involvement. "We have full confidence that the United States and Great Britain and other countries of the European Union . . . that it will be done as a targeted operation, with their objective to defeat terrorism . . . So, this is a battle in which we are all engaged" (CNN, 7 October 2001). In addition, on Capitol Hill, "a strong unified statement" from the congressional leadership read:

> We strongly support the operation President Bush ordered our military forces to carry out today. The administration has properly made it clear that today's action and any future action are directed against those who perpetrated the heinous acts on the United States on September 11, not against Islam or the people of Afghanistan. We stand united with the President, and with our troops and will continue to work together to do what is necessary to bring justice to these terrorists and those who harbor them (CNN 7 October 2001).

Even reporters acknowledged in candid self-reflection that their humanity caused them to support America's president. As Howard Kurtz noted, "Journalists, believe it or not, are human beings, and they're spooked by what's going on. They want a strong leader so their own emotions made you lean toward giving the guy the benefit of the doubt" (CNN 13 October 2001).

As these examples indicate, the rhetoric of a range of political elites mirrored the President's words and repeated themes of targeting selected "evil-doers," not innocent Afghans, and that this battle against them could take an extended effort. As one reporter noted, even Afghanis recognized that they were not the targets of American operations in Afghanistan. "I think more and more people are beginning to understand that the war is not going to be directed against Afghanistan's civilian population, and they're now willing to take their chances by going back to the cities" (CNN 6 October 2001). This dominance of a discourse of elite consensus has important consequences of solidifying unwavering support behind President Bush and his actions, as it unified support behind his father during the Persian Gulf War in 1991.

When opposition to actions in Afghanistan was shown, protesters were portrayed as not fully engaged in their opposition to the U.S. effort. Dissent was reported as under control and better than expected, rendering a more optimistic picture of the reaction of the world to our actions. "Obviously if there is (sic) civilian casualties, well, then those inflame people's passions. But so far, all of the protests, not only in Pakistan but elsewhere around the Islamic world, have been for the most part peaceful, although loud and noisy, but controlled." (CNN Live Event 13 October 2001). In another example, Gerald Post, a government Professor at George Washington University, reflected, "We have seen anti-American protests, and the pictures are stunning . . . the demonstrations themselves. But when you count and put them in a context, perhaps not as great as many had anticipated" (CNN Tonight 13 October 2001).

Military Frames

As seen in the Persian Gulf War, the rhetoric of the war in Afghanistan also reflected a focus on the technology of the battle in approximately 38 percent of the CNN stories analyzed. A larger percentage (62 percent) of stories focused on general military activity. A focus on military capabilities, precision technology, "clean language" and euphemism by military experts and media allowed Western audiences to remove any idea that lives were being lost in the battles. According to Defense Secretary Donald Rumsfeld, one of the goals was to "soften up" the enemy so that U.S. ground troops could eventually go in. CNN highlighted new concepts in the "vocabulary" of the war, such as tank plinking as tanks were "picked off in various locations" (CNN 22 October 2001). On another occasion, reporters discuss the 15,000 pound daisy cutter, "known as the commando vault." "The BLU-82 is 17 feet long and weights as much as three SUVs. It's dropped from an MC 130—the only aircraft big enough to carry this huge bomb" (CNN Live This Morning 7 November 2001). This focus on munitions and their descriptive characteristics distracts the public from their lethal impact.

In one segment, General David Grange, Retired, CNN military analyst, discusses the Pentagon's term of "long stick bombing" vs. "carpet bombing."

> Carpet bombing does lead you to believe that it's just munitions thrown out there in an area, and that's not the case. Usually, it's a strip of targeted land and positions longer than it is wide. It's very detailed in this location. And it's very accurate, even though it looks like it takes very large area of explosions, it is very accurate . . . So the "carpet bombing" does lead you to believe it's not accurate but, in fact, it is . . . It's mainly to eliminate personnel; to take out enemy personnel and soft targets (CNN Live This Morning 1 November 2001).

This characterization illustrates the painstaking effort by military personnel to frame the American military effort as accurate, precise, and an abstraction. The euphemisms of personnel and "soft targets" keep us processing the information using a military mindset versus a humanistic understanding of soft targets as human beings.

Further, while American and coalition forces had superior military technology, the weapons of our enemies were lacking. According to Major General Don Sheppard, Retired U.S. Air Force, the Taliban's aircraft were "not very good. They've got old MIG-21s, a couple dozen of them. They're short of pilots. They're short of spare parts. It's no match for the United States Air Force" (CNN 8 October 2002).

These discussions served to focus attention on a clean, antiseptic, and controllable version of events. If those who disagreed with the U.S. efforts were covered, they were discussed as weaker than expected. These types of frames were prevalent in media coverage, particularly during the first two to three months which provided the heaviest amount of war coverage.

Reporters also accepted criticism from former military experts when they did not use precise language to reflect the Bush administration's mission. As General Wesley Clark scolded in an interview with a CNN reporter,

> I think we ought to be very clear to our viewers that the United States has said it's not attacking Afghanistan. It is attacking the Taliban and the al Qaeda network, and we're certainly not attacking cities, but may be attacking facilities in or near those cities with very precise weaponry. And so, I think the clarity of this is extremely important, particularly since we've seen how Osama bin Laden on his side wants to escalate the rhetoric and mischaracterize the operation (CNN 8 October 2001).

Reporter Aaron Brown responded, "I take that as a gentle admonition. We need to be as precise in our language in some cases as these weapons are in their ability to do the function they're created to do. We talk about attacks on a city. In fact, it would be more accurate to say they are trying to hit an airport, or they are trying to hit an oil or munitions place" (Brown CNN 8 October 2001). While, indeed, precision in the language of military goals reflects the theoretical objectives, it distracts viewers from the underlying mission and potential consequences of such actions on the population of the country.

Humanitarian Frames

Another frame that was present to a lesser degree, in approximately 17 percent of the CNN stories analyzed, was a "humanitarian" frame. This frame was rarely present in Persian Gulf War coverage because of the media's general lack of access to ground zero of the military battle. Any humanitarian discussion focused on the atrocities committed by the Iraqi military and administration against their own people. In CNN's coverage on the war in Afghanistan, an equal number of stories covered deaths or humanitarian problems caused by Americans or the Taliban/al Qaeda. Much of this coverage was available only through the cooperation of al Jazeera since the station provided visual images of damage on the ground. Al Jazeera provided a new perspective not present in American media during the 1991 Persian Gulf War. Because CNN had access to its coverage, al Jazeera and its reporters served as eyewitness sources for CNN, oftentimes providing video images along with an alternative view of events than the Pentagon. In one segment common of the use of such CNN footage, al Jazeera's reporter Taysseer Allooni, describes attacks that he has seen directly on buildings, radar antennae, and the home of a civilian near a military site (CNN 8 October 2001).

In another report from 9 October, al Jazeera reports, "As you have seen, the American missiles have actually hit a humanitarian aid building and a poor populated area was completely destroyed. But it seems that the fighting concentrates on airports and the air defense installations." "There were pictures from the hospital inside Kabul, which showed some injuries, showed some children, women and men who the Taliban claim have been injured in the previous night's attack. Reports of fear from ordinary civilians." (CNN LIVE 13 October 2001).

In addition, al Jazeera helped to shape the discourse on strategy covered by CNN. In an exchange on CNN Breaking News, CNN Senior White House correspondent John King, along with other correspondents, discussed the role that inside coverage had on their ability to get the U.S. administration to give details about the operations in Afghanistan. According to King, "We will ask the Pentagon and the White House, although we should tell you, the Pentagon and the White House both have been very reluctant to discuss any details of any of the military activities. At first the Pentagon did not even acknowledge at all that one of its spy planes was missing about two weeks ago, finally the defense secretary, Donald Rumsfeld, did acknowledge it was missing." Another reporter adds, "And John, we're seeing that video. You just saw the video that we ran moments ago. Do you think, because we did bring pictures about that the Pentagon will have to respond? And what do you think about those pictures? Is this something that we definitely should believe in?" King responds by adding, "Well, the Pentagon will have to respond to our questions. Very reluctant to discuss any operational details" (CNN 6 October 2001). Jamie McIntyre, CNN military affairs correspondent, noted that there is no way for reporters to really know what is going on inside Afghanistan because there is no access to soldiers, even after missions are completed. "It took al Jazeera to tell Americans that a helicopter had a problem" (CNN Tonight 23 October 2001).

In November 2001, CNN ran a segment claiming that the United States was behind in the "war of words" because of Osama bin Laden's frequent use of media relative to Rumsfeld's lack of desire to deal with media on a daily basis. One reporter noted that the United States had not responded to previous statements by bin Laden, "[b]ut the United States is definitely changing its strategy, because almost immediately after the al Jazeera network broadcast in full Osama bin Laden's statement, the U.S. was on the same airwaves with somewhat of a response." This example reflects the strategy frame that Western reporters employ. "So, a new strategy here; the administration trying to respond quickly to counter any statements coming from bin Laden and the Taliban, after many analysts believe that the administration has fallen behind the Taliban and Osama bin Laden in the so-called propaganda war." (CNN Saturday 3 November 2001). This coverage provides further evidence of the impact of al Jazeera and its perspective on the framing of CNN stories.

The presence of al Jazeera in CNN coverage of the war in Afghanistan provided a different picture of war than Americans had seen during the Persian Gulf conflict in 1991. This picture of reality undoubtedly had an impact on the opinion of the American public. Despite the overwhelming support for Bush and the Afghan war effort, less than half of Americans thought that the United States was winning the war against terrorism. On 31 October 2001, only 4 in 10 Americans thought that it was likely that we would succeed in removing the Taliban from power. Only one fourth of Americans in a CBS/New York Times poll felt that the war was going very well (Newport 31 October 2001). Yet, the American public was still committed to the general approval of Bush and some sort of military action against terrorism.

Al Jazeera's Coverage

In order to understand coverage of the war in Afghanistan in other countries, including those in the Middle East region, it is necessary to consider the context within which this conflict was taking place. The Arab street was already furious at the Bush administration for its unconditional support of Israel's Prime Minister Sharon, who was viewed by Arabs not as a "man of peace" as President Bush referred to him, but as a "war criminal." Moreover, daily doses of Arab satellite television footage showing the brutal repression of Palestinians in the occupied territories of the West Bank and Gaza led the majority of Arabs to look at U.S. policies with suspicion. Writing for the *New York Times*, Mark Rodenbeck maintained:

> Never, in a half a century of Middle Eastern conflict, have ordinary Arab so identified with the Palestinian tragedy as they do today. As network coverage of Vietnam shocked Americans with the immediacy of far-off war, satellite television's insistent graphic imagery of the intifada has taken its bloody drama into millions of Arab households (Rodenbeck *New York Times* 17 April 2002).

The initial response of most Middle Eastern regimes was to openly sympathize with the United States immediately after 9/11. Most of these regimes had already felt the sting of radical Islam within their individual societies and hence, were genuinely sympathetic to the calamity that befell the United States on September 11. Yet in the summer of 2002, a poll conducted by the Pew Research Center in many Muslim countries confirmed that the initial sympathy for the United States in the aftermath of September 11, 2002, has dissipated as a result of perceived U.S. anti-Muslim, anti-Arab, pro-Zionist policies (Pew Research Center 2002). Al Jazeera may have had an important impact on shaping these views by reporting on events in the occupied territories of Palestine and other Muslim areas around the world, as well as on the intense hostility manifested by some anti-Arab and anti-Muslim Americans (Watson BBC 29 December 2002).

The United States' response to September 11 further aggravated what little support it had even among Arab regimes. These regimes were forced to distance themselves from the United States when the U.S. classified Iraq and Iran as part of the "Axis of Evil," further reviving in the minds of many Arabs the images of the Christian crusades. And, for the first time since establishing relations with Saudi Arabia, the United States openly criticized the conservative kingdom and accused Saudi Wahabism of being the root of terror in the Islamic world. Regimes of the Gulf States felt confident enough within their societies to permit their media a degree of freedom to do what they as regimes could not do, namely criticize U.S. policies as well as Arab regimes without naming specific countries. In doing that, these regimes were able to placate their citizens by venting the extreme anger and frustration resulting from their apparent paralysis in the Palestinian-Israeli conflict. The Saudis, Libyans, and Iraqis felt less secure and thus placed more restrictions on their local media. These organs continued with their normal coverage. The Saudis reduced their usual dose of religious programming emphasizing the "huge" gap between them and bin Laden's radicalism, and the Libyan and Iraqi media increased their endless glorification of their respective dictators as peacemakers and secularists. Their deliberate attempts at distancing themselves from both the September 11 disaster and the Afghan-U.S. conflict were clear. Syria and Lebanon focused on Palestine and the Palestinians, not on Afghanistan (BBC 12 July 2002).

The Egyptian government-owned Nile television gave full coverage to both the New York and Kabul events but emphasized the intellectual debate on both conflicts. Egypt's state-owned media was very careful not to antagonize the United States, its benefactor, or the average Egyptian who had already displayed his or her anger at Mubarak's government for its unwillingness to confront Israeli and U.S. policy in the region. Also, as a security blanket, the Egyptian regime imprisoned individuals it classified as part of the Muslim Brotherhood. Many of those imprisoned did not necessarily belong to radical Muslim organizations, but served to assure the Bush Administration and the U.S. Congress that Egypt was cracking down on religious elements within Egyptian society and hence was an ally in the war against terror. Egypt was also eying a comparable $300 million grant to Israel by the Bush administration to fight terror. There is no denying that Egyptian government came out financially ahead in the 1991 Gulf War against Saddam Hussein, and President Mubarak's regime was certainly not going to permit an anti-American media blitz to take place in Egypt attacking the U.S. invasion of Afghanistan.

This environment provided two newcomers, the United Arab Emirates (UAE) and Qatar, with a golden opportunity to put their mark on television broadcasting in the Arab world. At the heart of this was an effort to influence Arab perception and thinking about world events. Both countries took the plunge into the world of satellite transmission in the Arab world when it became apparent that there was little that regimes in the region could do to prevent their citizens from receiving direct satellite transmission. Both of these countries made the decision to participate in the process and hence not only stakeout a claim in the new technology, but also influence the dissemination of news in the Arabic language throughout the world. Abu Dhabi and Dubai are two excellent, high quality, free news and entertainment services transmitted from the Middle East to Arab speakers everywhere. Qatar's al Jazeera, on the other hand, is a subscription service through ART pay network and is also disseminated throughout the world. Initially, viewership for al Jazeera was minuscule but rapidly increased after the network began to take on controversial topics that included conducting interviews with opponents to a number of Arab regimes. Al Jazeera is much more liberal than any other Arab broadcasting network. Until the advent of al Jazeera, Abu Dhabi, and Dubai, satellite broadcasting was dominated by the London-based, Saudi-owned Middle East Broadcasting Corporation. The Saudis also dominated the Arabic print media industry. The Saudi daily al Sharq al Awsat was the most widely read paper in the Arab world (Sakr 1999).

For these stations, the second Intifada in the occupied Palestinian territories, and the Afghan campaign was an opportunity. Both events were turning points in media history in the Middle East. Indeed, both events were just as important as the Vietnam War and Persian Gulf War were to America's media coverage. It was an opportunity for these services to thrust themselves into the twenty-first century media scene with a huge splash. Thus they spared no effort or cost in acquiring the latest technological equipment, along with very able correspondents throughout the world.

Understandably, there was nothing in al Jazeera's or most of the Arab media's coverage to indicate support or sympathy for bin Laden or the al Qaeda organization. Expectedly, the media was not pro-U.S. either, but in the zero-sum environment, imposed by the Bush administration, any country not supporting the US was classified by most of America's media as anti-U.S. America's understandable animosity toward Arabs and Muslims in the aftermath of September 11 was apparent to many Arabs, and al Jazeera was instrumental in conveying that message. It was also instrumental in providing a forum for American policy makers to address the Arab world. Senior members of the Bush administration realized that dismissing these new Arab stations as censored and hence irrelevant was detrimental to U.S. interests in the region. Hence, they went out of their way to give interviews during the Afghan campaign and in its aftermath, to explain America's reasoning and position on the Arabs and Islam.

The Afghan war was the first real war to be covered by any Arab network and al Jazeera was lucky enough to have had a monopoly on some of the coverage of that conflict. Yet, unlike many other networks, the Arab stations that took part in the coverage were in the process of learning how to cover a war, what to look for, and most important of all what they can get away with saying or showing without antagonizing the sensibilities of their state governments. What was evident was that these three stations headed by al Jazeera had a great deal of latitude to report the news, yet they imposed on themselves a certain amount of self-censorship. Covering the Afghan war from a humanitarian perspective was the safest venue, until they acquired more familiarity with their milieus. The Afghan experiment convinced these stations that their conservative owners are more tolerant than they had assumed and that was manifested itself in the free rein they acquired. Their budgets have grown and activities increased. The topics they discuss are more controversial than ever before, and their viewers have increased several fold. What is also interesting is the fact that the conservative owners have discovered that freedom of the press can be beneficial, legitimate, and also profitable (*Agence France-Presse* 24 June 2002). It is also interesting to note that this experiment with a free press structure is increasing the ire of neighboring states whose press is not so free. In an interview with Abu Dhabi television on August 19, 2002, Ahmad Zaki Yamani, the former Saudi Arabian oil minister, stated that al Jazeera started a media revolution in the Middle East but felt it is also becoming a dangerous threat to the region.

Al Jazeera was the only network with staff inside of Taliban-controlled Afghanistan and prior to the September 11 attacks it had an estimated viewership of twenty to twenty-five million people (NPR, 8 October 2001). As Howard Kurtz noted, "It's very controversial, but at the same time very popular, because it tells all sides—in other words, it may cover the Palestinian uprising very intensely, but also allows access to Israeli officials. It gets the videotape of Osama bin Laden that every network in the universe, including CNN, has now aired many times, but it also puts Tony Blair on the air to give the Western view" (CNN 10 October 2001).

For example, Ahmad Sheikh, duty editor for al Jazeera, describes how the network discusses the concept of terrorism. "When it is an American official or someone is saying it, we keep it as terrorism, right? But when we are quoting one of them, we say "What he called terrorism." We do not use the word ourselves because, you know, this is controversial. Can we agree, first of all, on a definition of what a terrorist act is? Some people may—it's too wide a definition" (NPR 8 October 2001). Part of this effort to show all sides included broadcasting the message of Osama bin Laden and al Qaeda directly to the international public. On October 7, an al Qaeda spokesperson delivered a speech via al Jazeera television. Osama bin Laden delivered several speeches on videotape via al Jazeera with the assistance of a translator. For one speech, al Jazeera brought in three people to comment on it, a cleric from Kuwait, an ex-French diplomat, and an advisor to the U.S. State Department, to put it in context.

In many instances in the war in Afghanistan, it was very difficult for an independent observer to discern whether the Arab media and the U.S. media were covering the same events in spite of the fact that the coverage might have come from the same dates. The U.S. media appeared to be primarily interested in how the U.S. military was conducting the war against the Taliban and al Qaeda. To that end, U.S. coverage was mostly limited to pictures and analysis of U.S. bombs falling on various areas of Afghanistan where Taliban and al Qaeda forces were thought to be located. On the other hand, original al Jazeera footage, and by extension other Arab media outlets, were primarily interested in the impact of the war on the ordinary Afghan as well as on the perceived ineptness and paralysis of Arab regimes in influencing events on the ground. Hence much of the coverage focused on the havoc U.S. bombing had on Afghanistan's people, cities, and already dilapidated infrastructure. The forty-two stories provided by the al Jazeera's network revealed that while there was an overarching humanitarian theme in all of them, they also reflected some of the same frames present in CNN war coverage.

Governance Frames

Al Jazeera was careful to distance itself from Osama bin Laden and the Taliban, and it tried to play the role of the impartial source of information in that area of the conflict. Yet, the media outlet still applied a different cultural lens to the American military efforts in Afghanistan. Ten stories (almost 24 percent of coverage) focused on rallying Arab and Muslim masses and leadership to confront what was portrayed as the United States' "arrogance" and "disproportional" response to the September 11 terrorist attack. In a report on 2 December 2002, al Jazeera's footage showed the impact of U.S. bombing on mosques in Afghanistan. The footage depicted destroyed mosques and pictures of torn Qurans laying amidst the rubble. These images meant little to the average American viewer, who unless told that they were images of mosques would have no idea that they were places of worship. However, the Arab or Muslim viewer recognized the images without the need for any commentary. Taysseer Allooni, al Jazeera's correspondent in Kabul on more than one occasion after viewing the havoc caused by U.S. bombing raids lamented that "Afghans are looking towards brothers of faith for support, but will they find support in the hurried attempts by the Arabs and Muslims to satisfy America's arrogance?" (al Jazeera 5 January 2002). In a broadcast from Tora Bora in the White Mountains, another al Jazeera correspondent answered Allooni's question when he asked: "Why doesn't the Arab League or Arab countries provide a third alternative to either surrender or death and hence remove off them the charge of collaboration with the United States" (al Jazeera 12 March 2002).

It was precisely this type of coverage that appeared to have angered the US government and military establishment and ultimately lead to the "mistaken" bombing of al Jazeera's offices in Kabul. The meaning of these messages signified that Arab opposition to the war was in large part not against America's invasion of Afghanistan but rather against America's invasion of the Middle East. This media framing reinforced the popular perception among Arabs that the war in Afghanistan was not against the Taliban per se but rather against Islam and Arabs. These reports were an attempt to rally the Arab street against Arab regimes. In none of the ten segments did al Jazeera's reporters mention a specific country, but merely referred to the "Arab League," "Arabs," or "Muslims," but as Taysseer Allooni's reports indicate, Arabs were unable to confront the will of the "arrogant" United States in Afghanistan as they have been unable to confront it in the Middle East. This impotence has led to "disastrous" consequences for the region in general and the Palestinians in particular. This second message put many Arab regimes on the defensive and some ordered the closing of al Jazeera's offices in their countries.

Military Frames

Al Jazeera's military coverage was unlike typical CNN coverage in that it did not concentrate as much attention on military and strategic issues. But the fourteen stories (33 percent of the footage) that employed military frames proved to be far more graphic than anything shown on CNN. They emphasized the "collateral damage" that resulted from U.S. bombing on the buildings and infrastructure. Images comparing the Taliban's antiquated arms with the modern military of the United States provided a vivid image of a forgone conclusion that it was going to be a one-sided war that will end with the decimation of the Taliban. During the Northern Alliance's campaign to occupy the northern city of Mazar-i-Sharif, al Jazeera emphasized the strategic importance of the city to the United States war effort and covered the liberation of the city from the Taliban. Simultaneously, the Arab network also covered the bombing of the city and conducted interviews with retreating Taliban fighters.

In the framing of military conflict, al Jazeera coverage was similar to that of CNN. Yet the frames of technological precision and euphemism used by CNN were largely supplanted in al Jazeera by a humanitarian perspective. In a report from Kandahar during the sixth day of the War, al Jazeera dealt with a number of issues, most prominent among them was the newness of America's weapons and the infallibility of American military technology. The report also surveyed the damage caused by the bombing of schools, homes, mosques, as well as the airport and the loss of innocent Afghani life "that had nothing to do with the bin Laden or the Taliban." Interviews with survivors were characterized by the labeling of the United States and Americans as "infidels."

In another report from Kabul, al Jazeera aired video footage of the destruction of radio transmitters' antennas, burning Red Cross depots' housing grain and other food supplies, as well as many dead and wounded civilians. Interviews with victims centered on the "fallacy of U.S. beliefs in human rights" and the unifying impact that U.S. attacks on civilian targets had on Afghanis. Interestingly, al Jazeera chose to air a long interview with Afghanis that compared the U.S. campaign to the one launched by the former Soviet Union in which more than one million Afghanis lost their lives. Another recurring theme centered on the question: "Why is the U.S. targeting civilians who have nothing to do with al Qaeda or bin Laden?" After interviewing bomb victims during the first few days of the campaign at a Kabul hospital, reporter Allooni laments, "All this damage and the second phase of the war didn't even start yet." The video footage portrayed America's military campaign with a negative tone, emphasizing vengeance on the part of the U.S. While the primary framing of the military efforts examined the decimation of infrastructure and the strategic unfolding of the military campaign, the civilian toll was certainly a focus of al Jazeera's coverage.

Humanitarian Frames

Most of al Jazeera's coverage framed the war in terms of the human toll and the personal suffering of Afghanis. On the first night of the War, al Jazeera's correspondent reporting from Kabul set the tone for the coming battle when he said, "If the United States prepared its citizens and citizens of the world with a long campaign, the Afghan had nothing to prepare him except his patience, his poverty, and his faith, factors that have distinguished him throughout history." Yet it seems that none of these factors prepared the Afghan for the terrible emotion of al Jazeera's visual images. Graphic video footage of death and destruction had a profound affect on Arab audiences. Unlike the U.S. media, al Jazeera did not acquiesce to the Bush administration requests to sanitize its Afghan footage. There was a concerted effort by al Jazeera not to gloss over the Afghan campaign in the same way U.S. and global media glossed over the Persian Gulf War that claimed more lives and caused more infrastructure damage. To that end, al Jazeera's correspondents documented the impact of U.S. bombing on Afghan civilians.

The video footage presented images of dead civilians within Kabul and other Afghan cities as well as pictures of whole villages decimated by U.S. carpet-bombing. Al Jazeera's reporters conducted interviews with surviving wounded children who has lost all their families. In the village of Tche Agha, seventy houses were destroyed by the bombing, resulting in the death of 120 of the village's 500 inhabitants. Similar scenes were seen from the village of Ismarzi where 200 of its 1500 inhabitants died. The dead had to be interned in mass graves and the remaining inhabitants had to leave and seek shelter because no structure remained standing in the village. Other villages that met a similar fate were al Gandhab and al Ranjan. Yet perhaps some of the most disturbing videos of the campaign were those that specifically dealt with the personal lives of Afghanis that lost loved ones or were facing hardship looking for food or in moments of grief. One such image was presented of an Afghani who had lost fifteen members of his family in a bombed building in Kabul. He did not need to elaborate on his calamity with actions or words. Video footage showing the man searching for his relatives in the rubble was enough to make viewers empathize with his pain.

Presenting these images for the world to see did not sit well with the Bush administration and the American Secretary of Defense Rumsfeld. However, as a result of its coverage in Afghanistan, al Jazeera earned the reputation as one of the very few mediums "bearing witness" to social and political injustice in the region. According to Nic Gowing, a presenter on BBC, al Jazeera's offices in Kabul were deliberately bombed by the United States because "it was 'bearing witness' to events the U.S. would rather it did not see" (Wells 16 November 2001). A month before this report, the United States government made the unprecedented request of the United States' "five major TV networks and the nation's newspaper not to broadcast live or print unedited communiqués from Public Enemy No. 1" (Adler 15 October 2001).

Discussion and Conclusions

As Fouad Ajami said,

> In the next phase there will be a great deal of soul searching and a great deal of reckoning about how this story has been covered. Al Jazeera was on the ground. It had the advantages of being on the ground, and it had access—let's face it, it had access to Osama bin Laden, and these were advantages it brought to this particular story, and we had to basically take pretty much what al Jazeera gave

us. And what we see now in the aftermath of the sacking of the Taliban will be a bit of the truth of Afghani society, and I think it will be an important lesson for us all." (NPR *Talk of the Nation* 13 November 2001).

Our analysis reveals that the commentary above has some elements of truth. In some ways, the Pentagon was predictably in control of the information disseminated from Western media sources, including CNN. CNN stories followed the format of typical international crisis stories, similar to the Persian Gulf War, with frames of consensus, a focus on strategy, technological precision, and a euphemistic description of events. From a different cultural perspective, al Jazeera's international coverage also rallied its viewers by calling for unification of the Arab world in international issues. Further, it mimicked some of the same frames of American technological superiority. But the primary contrast in news coverage and framing is that al Jazeera did not gloss over a humanistic portrayal of the consequences of war.

This humanistic viewpoint, and al Jazeera's availability to Western media outlets such as CNN, provided an alternative viewpoint not present to the same degree in the Persian Gulf War ten years earlier. Al Jazeera's pictures and ground-zero reports from within Afghanistan provided the impetus for CNN reporters, as representatives of the American media, to question information from official Bush administration sources. Still, even though the perspective of al Jazeera was present in CNN coverage, the American media frames contextualized its humanistic approach.

Further research also reveals that media coverage of events in the Middle East, since the U.S. War in Afghanistan, has changed dramatically. The al Jazeera and Abu Dhabi networks, in particular, have succeeded in making U.S. and European media services take notice. When it comes to covering Middle East affairs, U.S. broadcasters have developed a more balanced reporting of events. The U.S. government has seen the need "to spend $500 million to launch a satellite channel that would compete with al Jazeera and aimed at younger Muslims who are seen as anti-American" (Campbell 23 November 2001). CNN is also in the process of creating a new U.S. Arab network to compete with others in providing the Arab world of its positions on various global issues (Rath 7 February 2002).

What does this mean for the future of Middle Eastern politics? Simply stated, thanks to these new Arab networks it is quite possible to now see the beginning of a common Arab consensus on some global issues. Political talk and call-in shows have enabled many Arabs from different parts of the world to interact and discuss issues that were denied them in the past. Mr. Yamani was quite correct in his assertion that al Jazeera created a revolution in the Middle East. In revolutions, the unexpected usually happens and one of the unexpected results is the ability of many Arabs to compare standards of living, freedom, and future potential. No one is more aware of this than the Arab regimes that have been unable to stem the communications tide and are constantly faced with having to deal with criticism of their policies on such outlets as al Jazeera. In 2002, Kuwait closed the network's offices in its country and Jordan did the same in Amman after withdrawing its Ambassador from Qatar, the owner of al Jazeera (Habib 2002). Earlier in July of the same year, Saudi Arabia threatened to also close the offices of the network in response to a program that was seen by the Saudis as an affront to the royal family (*Agence France-Press* 29 September 2002). Libya also threatened to sever its relations with Qatar. In Libya's case, Colonel Gaddafi was angered by an al Jazeera interview of a number of Libyan dissidents who criticized his dictatorial policies. Bahrain also banned al Jazeera, accusing it of bias toward Israel. Further, the Arab League was irked by al Jazeera's interviews of Israeli politicians and drafted a resolution banning Arab media from becoming a forum for Israeli officials (*Agence France-Press* 19 June 2002).

Regardless, Qatar refused to pressure al Jazeera to change its reporting methods. Even the U.S. was angered by al Jazeera's unrestricted reporting, accusing it of fomented anti-Americanism in the Arab and Islamic world (Fisk 11 October 2001; also see Garfield 13 October 2001). Al Jazeera had already accused the United States of deliberately bombing its Kabul office (Wells 17 November 2001). There are no hard statistics to prove the following assertion, yet Arab media observers believe that few citizens in both these countries view their local television networks anymore. Satellite technology has provided Middle Easterners with the means to access an array of international and regional transmissions. This fact combined with their growing ability to access the Internet has dramatically changed the social and cultural scenes in the region (Ayad 2000; also see Amin 2000).

Coverage of the war in Afghanistan, with little competition from domestic Middle Eastern media outlets, provided al Jazeera with the opportunity to hone many of the skills needed to successfully operate in the international arena. The coverage of the war in Afghanistan might have been a small event in the development of the Arab media, yet it did remove the shackles that had until then hampered its development. How far media freedom will continue to grow will depend on how much the political powers that be in the Arab World feel threatened by its action. Until then most Arab experts hope that those few relatively free media outlets in the Arab world continue to grow in power and influence to resist any future attempts to censor them or their coverage.

Yet, despite these conclusions, it is important to note that al Jazeera is an anomaly at this time. All activity the network has taken thus far has been novel for the region. Al Jazeera is never sure of its position and is constantly playing a balancing act over an edge of a sword. It is still in the learning phase and is acquiring legitimacy. No Arab media outlet in the past has covered any war using its own correspondents or resources. And, since most didn't even know what to say or what to cover, they relied on the BBC or other western media outlets for news feeds. Few if any had any popular legitimacy or independence. Their coverage of wars was purely from a humanitarian perspective and al Jazeera began its coverage along those lines. Its success and growth have earned it both legitimacy and viewers along with confidence to approach conflict and war from different perspectives. Also, what makes its coverage so potent is the fact that the only limit its owners placed upon it is over reporting in Qatar. The rest of the world is open territory for it to experiment in and as evident by the success of its experimentation, it is forcing a change on not only other media outlets in the region but also on non-Arab media covering Arab issues. It is much too early to tell how other Arab media outlets will cover future wars, but thanks to al Jazeera, it will certainly be radically different from past coverage.

References

ABC News Special Report: America Under Attack. 11 September, 2001.
Adler, Belle. 2001. "D.C.'s Request to Media is Unprecedented." *Newsday* 15 October.
Agence France-Presse. "Israeli TV Ban." 19 June 2002.
Agence France-Presse. "Al Jazeera Thrives on Afghan and Bin Laden Business." 24 June, 2002.
Agence France-Presse. "Saudi Arabia recalls envoy to Qatar amid spat over al Jazeera." 29 September 2002.
Al Jazeera Network. Qatar. Raw video footage, 30 September, 2001-5 May, 2002.
Allen, Barbara, and Paula O'Loughlin, Amy Jasperson, and John L. Sullivan. 1994. 'The Media and the Gulf War: Framing, Priming and the Spiral of Silence,' *Polity,* 27, 2, 255–84.
Amin, Hussein. 2000. "The Current Situation of Broadcasting in the Middle East." *TBS Archives* 5, Fall/Winter. (http://www.tbsjournal.com).
Ayad, Christopher. 2002. "Middle East: Media Pluralism Via Satellite." *UNESCO Courier,* January. (http://www.unesco.org/courier/2000_01/uk/connex/txt1.htm).
BBC Worldwide Monitoring. "Director says al Jazeera TV meets Arab's "thirst for democracy." Published by Belgian newspaper De Standaard web site on 10 September, 2001. 11 September, 2002.
Brody, Richard. 1991. *Assessing the president: The media, elite opinion, and public support.* Stanford, CA: Stanford University Press.
Brody, Richard and C. Shapiro. 1989. "Policy failure and policy support: The Iran-Contra Affair and Public Assessments of President Reagan." *Political Behavior,* 11, 353–69.
Bush, George W. Speech to the Nation, reported on CNN, 7 October, 2001.
Campbell, Duncan. 2001. "U.S. Plans TV Station to Rival al Jazeera." *The Guardian,* 23 November.
CNN, 6 October, 2001.
CNN, 7 October, 2001.
CNN Breaking News, 7 October, 2001.
CNN, Aaron Brown reporting, 8 October, 2001.
CNN, 10 October, 2001.
CNN Newsroom, 11 October, 2001.
CNN, 3 October, 2001.
CNN Live Event, 13 October, 2001.
CNN Tonight, 13 October, 2001.
CNN, 22 October, 2001.
CNN Live This Morning, 1 November, 2001.
CNN Saturday, 3 November, 2001.
CNN Live This Morning, 7 November, 2001.
Cohn, Carol. 1991. 'The Language of the Gulf War,' *Center Review: Publication of the Center for Psychological Studies in the Nuclear Age,* 5. Cambridge: Harvard Medical School, 14–15.
Dennis, Everette E., David Stebenne, John Pavlik, Mark Thalhimer, Craig LaMay, Dirk Smillie, Martha FitzSimon, Shirley Gazsi, and Seth Rachlin. 1991. *The Media at War:*

The Press and the Persian Gulf Conflict. New York: Gannett Foundation at Columbia University.

El-Nawawy, Mohammed and Adel Iskandar. 2002. *Al Jazeera: How the Free Arab News Network Scooped the World and Changed the Middle East.* Boulder CO. Westview; Perseus.

Entman, Robert M. 1973. 'Framing: Toward clarification of a fractured paradigm.' *Journal of Communication.* 43 (4): 51–8.

Feuilherade, Peter. 2002. "Changing Trends in Middle East Media since 11 September," BBC Worldwide Monitoring 12 July.

Fisk, Robert. 2001. "A Bold and Original TV Station that America Wants to Censor." *The Independent,* 11 October.

Gamson, William. 1992. *Talking Politics.* Cambridge, England: Cambridge University Press.

Garfield, Bob. 2001. "Al Jazeera." *On the Media,* 13 October.

Garramone, Gina. 1984. "Voter responses to negative political ads." *Journalism Quarterly,* 61 (summer): 250–9.

Goffman, E. 1974. *Frame Analysis.* Boston: New England University Press.

Habib, Randa. 2002. "Political row brewing up between Jordan and Qatar over al Jazeera TV." *Agence France-Presse* 8 August.

Iyengar, Shanto. 1991. *Is Anyone Responsible? How Television Frames Political Issues.* Chicago: University of Chicago Press.

Jasperson, Amy, and Dhavan Shah, Mark Watts, Ron Faber, and Fan David. 1998. "Framing and the Public Agenda: Media Effects on the Importance of the Federal Budget Deficit." *Political Communication,* 15 (2) 205–24.

Jones, J. M. 2002. "Most Bush Ratings Retreating from Post-Sept. 11 Highs." Gallup News Service Poll Analyses, 31 July. (http://www.gallup.com/poll/releases/pr020731.asp?Version=p).

Lidster, Suzanne and Mike Rose. 2001. "Al Jazeera Goes It Alone," *BBC Newscast,* 8 October.

McCombs, Maxwell. 1992. 'Explorers and surveyors: Expanding strategies for agenda-setting research,' *Journalism Quarterly,* 69 (4), Winter, 813–24.

Mueller, John E. 1973. *War, presidents and public opinion.* New York: John Wiley.

National Public Radio, 8 October, 2001.

NBC Nightly News, 18 March, 2002.

Newport, Frank. 2001. "Public Opinion of the War in Afghanistan," Gallup News Service Poll Analyses, 31 October. (http://www.gallup.com/poll/Releases/Pr011031e.asp).

Page, Benjamin, Shapiro, Robert and Glenn R. Dempsey. 1987. "What moves public opinion?" *American Political Science Review,* 81, March, 23–43.

Patterson, Thomas. 1994. *Out of Order.* New York: Random House.

The Pew Research Center For The People & The Press. 2002. *How Global Publics View: Their Lives, Their Countries, The World, America* Washington, DC, 2002. (http://www.people-press.org).

Rath Tiare, 2002. "Al Jazeera in English? CNN in Arabic?" *The Daily Star* (Beirut), 7 February.

Rodenbeck, Mark. 2002. "Broadcasting the War." *The New York Times,* 17 April.

Sakr, Naomi. 1999. "Satellite Television and Development in the Middle East." Middle East Report. Spring. (http://www.merip.org/mer/mer210/210_sakr.html).

Tinkham, S. F. & Weaver-Lariscy, R. A. 1993. 'A diagnostic approach to assessing the impact of negative political television commercials,' *Journal of Broadcasting and Electronic Media,* fall, 377–99.

White House briefing room, 7 October, 2001.

Wells, Matt. 2001. "Al Jazeera Accuses U.S. of Bombing Its Kabul Office." *The Guardian,* 17 November.

Wells, Matt. 2001. "How Smart was this Bomb?" 2001. *The Guardian,* 19 November.

CHAPTER 8

Framing Muslim-Americans Before and After 9/11

BRIGITTE L. NACOS
OSCAR TORRES-REYNA

Previous chapters have compared framing of the same events by the news media in different countries, including newspaper coverage of the U.S. Embassy bombings and 9/11 in African and U.S. elite newspapers, and reporting of the war in Afghanistan broadcast by CNN and al Jazeera. But important insights into the framing process can also be illuminated by studying changes over time within one culture, particularly how minority groups are routinely framed and depicted by the U.S. news media. This chapter presents such an analysis, focusing on coverage of Muslim-Americans before and after the events of September 11. We undertook this study to examine whether American news was biased against Muslim-Americans and if so, in what ways. The focus was on the following basic questions: Was the framing of Muslim-Americans in the U.S. news mostly negative and stereotypical? Did the terrorism of 9/11 affect U.S. news framing of the Muslim American minority and if so, how did changes manifest themselves? And did the local news in New York City, with its rather large Muslim population, differ from the national coverage in the rest of the United States?

When a powerful bomb destroyed the Alfred P. Murrah Federal Building in Oklahoma City on April 19, 1995, news organizations were quick to identify Middle Easterners as suspects and reported that the FBI was specifically looking for two men with dark hair and beards. Within hours, Arab- and Muslim-Americans became the targets of physical and verbal assaults. As it turned out, an American with European ancestors, Timothy McVeigh, committed what was said at the time to be the most deadly terrorist deed on American soil. When the twin towers of the World Trade Center crumbled into a nuclear-winterlike cityscape and part of the Pentagon outside of Washington, DC in flames on September 11, 2001, news organizations reported soon thereafter, this time correctly, that the perpetrators were Arabs and Muslims. And once again, perfectly peaceful Arab- and Muslim-Americans as well as persons "looking like them" became the victims of hate crimes and of the stereotypical image of Muslims and Arabs as perpetrators of violence and terrorists.

The preponderance of cliches to characterize and demonize Muslims and Arabs has been documented well (Shaheen 1996, 2001; Simon 1989). "The reason why many Arab- and Muslim-Americans are discriminated [against]," wrote one Amazon.com customer-reviewer shortly after the events of 9/11, "is because many people probably think of the 'TV-Arab' image (i.e., suicide bomber, fanatics, lazy, etc.)."[1] Although Hollywood movies, television shows, and popular fiction have long dwelled on stereotypical portrayals of Arabs and Muslims, one would not necessarily expect similar typecasting and cliches in the news. However, popular culture and news reporting do not operate in a vacuum but seem to feed on each other. Drawing on the depiction of Middle Easterners in crime fiction, Reeva Simon concluded that "authors know that today, after watching the evening news and reports of bombed American embassies, kidnapped or killed diplomats, and the latest exploits of religious fanatics, the public will readily read about Middle Eastern conspirators and that books about the area will sell." (Simon 1989: 140).

Years ago, with the Iranian Hostage Crisis fresh in mind, Edward Said wrote about the failure of the American media and U.S. experts to understand and explain the Arab and Muslim world. In particular, he argued that "Muslims and Arabs are essentially covered, discussed, apprehended either as suppliers of oil or as potential terrorists. Very little of the detail, the human density, the passion of Arab-Muslim life has entered the awareness of even those people whose profession it is to report the Islamic world." (Said 1981: 26).

Muslim-Americans have long been convinced that the news about them is colored by negative biases. This was clearly expressed by Muslim New Yorkers who participated in focus groups well before the events of 9/11. Muslim women especially mentioned the media's tendency to stereotype Muslim males as violent and Muslim women as submissive.[2] This belief in a widespread anti-Muslim news slant among American Muslims and Arabs did not weaken after 9/11. On the contrary, less than a month after the attacks of 9/11, teenage students in a Muslim school in Brooklyn, for example, expressed the conviction that "Muslims are the victims of a prejudiced news media." As one 16-year-old girl put it, "[a] lot of newspapers write negative things, and we get so upset."[3] In the spring and summer of 2002 some Arab merchants in Brooklyn tried to organize a boycott of the New York Post to dramatize their opposition to what they believed was an anti-Arab and anti-Muslim stance and a consistently pro-Jewish/pro-Israel coverage of the tabloid. The goal was to convince Arab-American merchants to keep the Post off their newspaper shelves. According to flyers in English and Arabic that were distributed to vendors, the New York Post "is not only pro-Zionist, but it hates everything called Islamic or Arabic."[4] Complaints about negative mass-mediated stereotypes were not peculiar to Muslims in New York City before and after September 11, 2001, but shared by Muslims across the United States. According to the "American Muslim Poll" that questioned Muslims in the United States in October and November 2001, more than two in three (68%) respondents said that the news media were not fair in their portrayal of Muslims and Islam (better than three of four or 77% thought that Hollywood was not fair in this respect).[5] The key question explored in this chapter is whether these criticisms of news coverage of Muslim-Americans are indeed justified, and how this coverage was affected by 9/11.

Framing the News and the "Pictures in Our Heads"

Some 55 years ago, before the advent of television, Walter Lippmann observed that what people know about the world around them is mostly the result of second-hand knowledge received through the press and that the "pictures in our heads" are the result of a pseudo-reality reflected in the news (Lippmann 1946). In today's mass societies people are even more dependent on the news because they have "nowhere else to turn for information about public affairs and for cues on how to frame and interpret that information" (Neuman, Just, and Crigler 1992:11).

As discussed throughout this book, the media tend to report the news along explanatory frames that cue the reader, listener, and viewer to put events, issues, and political actors into contextual frameworks of reference. Framing can and does affect the news in many ways, for example, in the choice of topics, sources, language, and photographs. According to Entman, "a frame operates to select and highlight some features of reality and obscure others in a way that tells a consistent story about problems, their causes, moral implications, and remedies" (Entman 1996, 77, 78). Accordingly, reporters, editors, producers, and others in the news media make decisions constantly about what and whom to present in the news and how; such choices are influenced by their organizations' standard operating procedures. Bennett, for example, suggests that "sources and viewpoints are 'indexed' (admitted through the news gates) according to the magnitude and content of conflicts among key government decision-makers or other players with the power (as perceived by journalistic insiders) to affect the development of a story" (Bennett 1996: 377). Whether the press covers the critical voices and viewpoints of more or less established interests depends on the particular positions of authoritative sources, especially government insiders. Because "indexing" has proven to be most potent in foreign news, one wonders whether it affects the coverage of Muslim-Americans in the face of the perennial "Middle East problem" between Israelis and Palestinians and the U.S. government's traditional support for Israel. It has been suggested that foreign news "has two dimensions: the foreign story that deals with events abroad and the domestic story that concentrates on the United States's role and reaction to world events" (Kern 1981:106). Similarly, domestic coverage may have two dimensions as well: one that concentrates on ethnic and religious minorities in America (i.e., Muslim-Americans and Arab-Americans) and another that concentrates on their ties to their regions of origin (i.e., the Middle East).

Some framing patterns seem especially important in terrorism news and in the perceptions and reaction of news consumers. Iyengar found that network television coverage of terrorism in the 1980s was overwhelmingly episodic or narrowly focused rather than thematic or contextual. His research demonstrated that narrowly focused coverage influenced audiences to hold the individual perpetrators responsible, while thematic reporting was more likely to assign responsibility to societal conditions and public policies. Moreover, when exposed to episodic framing of terrorism, people were more inclined to support punitive measures against individuals, when watching thematically framed terrorism news, audience members tended to be more in favor of policies attacking the root causes of terror (Iyengar 1991:26–45).

Of Stereotypes and "Symbol Handlers"

We know more of the portrayal of African-Americans in the news than about the coverage patterns with respect to other minorities. Research has pointed to one persistent problem in the way the news reports about black Americans, namely the tendency to highlight the extraordinary at the expense of what is the routine of everyday life in black communities. As a result, non-black Americans—especially whites—think of black America in terms of stereotypes—positive in regard to African-American superstars in sports and entertainment and negative as to black males as criminals and black females as welfare queens (Campbell 1995, Entman and Rojecki 2000, Nacos and Hritzuk 2000). Researchers found that few whites are aware of this hero or villain syndrome that seems especially prevalent in TV-news (Entman and Rojecki 2000: 207).

It seems that reporting on other minorities is equally spotty and stereotypical. With respect to Latinos in the United States, for example, one study found that Hispanics in six southwestern cities were mostly covered in the context of sports and otherwise in terms of soft news (Greenberg 1986). And the report of President Clinton's Advisory Board on Race noted under the heading "Media and Stereotyping" that apart from African-Americans "a major problem still remains regarding the representation, coverage, and portrayal of minorities on the news." One board member, former New Jersey Governor Thomas Kean, reported that "[a]lmost every group we have gone to has said that the media is a problem that has to be addressed" (Advisory Board 1998: 97). Presumably, Muslim-Americans represented one of those groups.

By framing the news along the lines of the traditional attitudes and prejudices of society's predominant groups, the news media convey stereotypes that affect a broad range of public perceptions, among them how people think about race, ethnicity, and religion. According to Gitlin, media frames are "persistent patterns . . . , by which symbol handlers routinely organize discourse, whether verbal or visual" (Gitlin 1980: 7). "Symbol handlers" are still most and foremost members of the white majority and their news judgments are increasingly affected by the profit imperatives of the large media corporations, but day-to-day decisions in the newsrooms are also influenced by deep-seated prejudices in the dominant white culture. A generation ago, Gans found that "the news reflects the white male social order" (Gans 1979, 61). While contemporary newsrooms are more diverse than twenty-five years ago, entrenched prejudices and stereotypical perceptions have not disappeared. One experienced newsman observed recently that "Newsrooms are not hermetically sealed against the prejudices that play perniciously just beneath the surface of American life" (Shiper 1998: 28); and according to another expert in the field, "Journalism helps shape how racially diverse people think of each other and how public policy on race-related issues is formulated." (Gissler 1994: 123). It seems equally true that the media affect how religiously diverse people view each other. Referring to the predominant visual images of black Americans in the media's depiction of poverty in America, Martin Gilen concluded that "subconscious stereotypes" guide newsroom decisions. Similarly, overtly rejected stereotypes may affect subconsciously the judgments concerning the news about American Muslims and Arabs.[6]

Muslim-Americans and Arab-Americans

Given the persistent complaints about media bias by American Muslims and their organizations and the growth of this minority, our research aimed at shedding light on the way the news media report on Muslim-Americans in New York City and across the United States.[7] Since the U.S. government is prohibited from collecting census data on people's religious affiliations, there is no official data on the total number of Muslims in the United States. Estimates range from one to seven million—with the real number somewhere in the middle and, according to Muslim organizations, closer to the higher end of these assumptions.[8] According to a recent religious survey, the proportion of Muslims in the United States population may be 1% but experts among American Muslims believe 2% to be more realistic.[9] As for New York City, researchers at Columbia University, who canvassed the city's five boroughs to locate Muslims and their communities, have estimated that about 600,000 Muslims live in the five boroughs.[10] Assuming that this is a sound number and considering that New York City has a total population of just over eight million according to the 2000 census, Muslims represent about 7.5% of the city's population and thus a sizeable religious minority.

We are aware that not all Arabs in the United States (or abroad) are Muslims and that only about one in four Arab-Americans are said to be Muslims. We have nevertheless included "Arab-Americans" in this study because the news media tend to report on Muslims and Arabs at home and abroad in the same stories and, more important, seem to use the terms frequently as if they were interchangeable. We did code non-Muslim Arab-Americans as separate source identification but found few references to them.

Research Methodology

The stereotypes that depict Muslims and Arabs as perpetrators of violence and terrorism were magnified by a long series of spectacular anti-American acts of terror that span from the long-lasting Iranian Hostage Crisis (1979–81) to the suicide attack on the USS *Cole* in 2000. All of these incidents in the 1980s and 1990s (including the first World Trade Center bombing in 1993) were widely reported, indeed over-reported, as the news media dwelt on shocking images of death, destruction, and the victims of this sort of political violence (Nacos, 1996). But because none of the previous strikes came even close to what happened on September 11, 2001, there was reason to investigate whether this unprecedented event triggered changes in the news with respect to American Muslims. For this reason we compared the news coverage of Muslim-Americans and Arab-Americans before and after 9/11.

For our newspaper analysis we selected the three largest daily U.S. newspapers that are published in Manhattan, the *New York Times, New York Post,* and the *Daily News.* While the *Times* has a sizeable national circulation besides its local and regional readership, the *Post* and the *Daily News* are mostly read within the New York metropolitan area. We also chose *USA Today* because of its national focus and readership. Recognizing early on that the quantity of news about the Muslim and Arab minority was significantly larger after the events of September 11, 2001, than before, we selected the twelve months preceding 9/11 and the six months thereafter for our main comparisons. By extending the duration of the pre-attack period, we avoided possible distortions caused by the limited number of cases in the six months before 9/11. For example, in the six months before 9/11 the *New York Post* reported about, quoted, or referred to the Nation of Islam, African-American Muslims, and Black Muslims so frequently that members of these groups represented 20% of all sources in such stories. But this prominence in the selection of sources was not at all representative for the news that the *Post* published over a longer period of time.[11] Still, whenever there was an opportunity to perhaps add to the understanding of the twelve months versus six months comparison, we contrasted the shorter pre-9/11 period with the post-9/11 period of equal length.

We kept track of the placement of articles (front pages, inside pages), the type of the news (straight reporting, news analysis, editorial, column, letters-to-the-editor), the geographical context (New York City, domestic, international topics), news sources, themes or topics addressed in each news item, and positions/policy preferences expressed by or attributed to news sources. Coders also evaluated whether a news story's full content depicted American Muslims/Arabs in a positive, negative, or neutral light.[12] Finally, articles were categorized according to their framing modes—narrow or episodic, broader or thematic, or equally both, following a coding scheme used in an earlier research project (Iyengar 1991) mentioned above. We met several times with our coders, six undergraduate and graduate students, explained and discussed the various coding categories, conducted joint practice sessions, and asked each of the students to individually code several sets of articles in order to check coding reliability. Once a satisfactory degree of inter-coding reliability was established, the six students began the task of analyzing the content of all retrieved articles.[13]

We coded all news items that reported on or made reference to Muslim-Americans and Arab-Americans, regardless of whether the context was local/regional, national, or international. As long as "Muslim-Americans" or

"Arab-Americans" were the topics of these articles or were simply cited or mentioned, we deemed the news relevant for our study.[14] But in order to trace possible differences in the reporting patterns of local, national, and international news that referred directly to Muslim-Americans and Arab-Americans, we kept track of articles in those three "geographical context" categories. Altogether we analyzed a total of 867 newspaper articles.

We also examined the pertinent stories televised on the CBS program *The Early Show* and the *Evening News* with Dan Rather using the same time periods and coding categories. Since earlier research has demonstrated that the news broadcasts of the major TV-networks have very similar content (Altheide 1982), we restricted our analysis to one of the networks.

Comparing Coverage

Frequency of Coverage, Placement, and Types of Stories

Not surprisingly, significantly more news reported about or mentioned Muslim-Americans and Arab-Americans in the half-a-year period after 9/11 than in the six months before those horrific events. However, we had not expected that the four newspapers combined published nearly eleven times as many such news items in the six months after 9/11 as in the six months before and three times as many as in the twelve months before the terror attacks. Each of the four publications reported far more frequently on Muslim-Americans and Arab-Americans in the six months after than in the six months before the terror attacks. At first sight, however, it seemed surprising that the *New York Post*, unlike the *New York Times* and *USA Today,* published more stories with references to Muslim-Americans and Arab-Americans in the twelve months before than in the six months after 9/11 and that the increase of coverage in the six months following the terror attacks was quite modest in the *Daily News* (see table 8.1). This was the result of the two tabloids' (*Post* and *Daily News*) extensive reporting on campaign donations that Hillary Clinton had received from American Muslim

Table 8.1   The Amount of News Coverage of Muslim-Americans and Arab-Americans before and after September 11, 2001

	SEPT. 11, 2000 TO MARCH 11, 2001 (6 MONTHS) (N)	MARCH 12, 2001 TO SEPT. 11, 2001 (6 MONTHS) (N)	SEPT. 12, 2001 TO MARCH 11, 2002 (6 MONTHS) (N)
New York Times	37	17	376
New York Post	58	15	50
Daily News (NY)	52	21	99
USA Today	8	6	128
Total:	155	59	653

Notes: N = Number of news segments/articles mentioning the search words 'Muslim-Americans' or 'Arab-Americans'.
Source: Muslim Communities in New York Project.

Table 8.2 The Amount of News Coverage of Muslims, Arabs, and Islam before and after September 11, 2001

	MUSLIMS		ARABS		ISLAM	
	BEFORE (N)	AFTER (N)	BEFORE (N)	AFTER (N)	BEFORE (N)	AFTER (N)
ABC News	31	163	11	99	1	31
CBS News	32	144	27	117	1	27
NBC News	9	98	5	90	–	18
CNN	23	203	43	200	1	31
Fox News	1	100	2	64	1	46
NY Times	345	1,468	345	1,272	216	1,190
NPR	54	217	53	182	10	84

Notes: N = Number of news segments/articles mentioning the search words 'Muslim', 'Arab', and 'Islam'. Before = six months before the terrorist attacks of September 11, 2001; After = six months after the attacks of 9/11. Source: Muslim Communities in New York Project.

organizations in her race for a New York seat in the U.S. Senate in the fall of 2000, their spacious coverage of controversial issues raised about the endorsement of candidates by Muslim groups during New York City's municipal primaries a year later, and of similar partisan disputes in the New York metropolitan area during this period. Still, the more appropriate comparisons of the six months before and after 9/11 leave no doubt about the increased frequency of stories on American Muslims and Arabs after the terrorist attacks. According to one observer, this was no coincidence but rather the result of the news media's efforts in "reaching out [to] Muslim civic leaders, visiting mosques, and in general providing opportunities to American Muslims to 'speak their minds.'"[15]

Just as the news paid far more attention to American Muslims and Arabs following 9/11, they also covered Muslims, Arabs, and Islam in general far more frequently as well (see table 8.2). One comprehensive content analysis of religious news in ten American daily newspapers, nine newsmagazines, and one wire service (the Associated Press) found that stories on Islam and Muslims dominated this coverage in the weeks following the events of 9/11. Indeed, 70 percent of the stories fully devoted to religion concerned Islam and Muslims and the remaining 30% dealt with Christianity and Christians, multi-faith, Judaism and Jews, non-denominational, and Buddhism and Buddhists.[16]

This surge was a natural reaction to the attacks that killed more than 3,000 Americans and were perpetrated by Muslim and Arab followers of America's most wanted terrorist leader, Osama bin Laden. But the sudden media attention to the Muslim and Arab world and the religion of Islam also happened to satisfy terrorists' perennial need for publicity (Nacos 2002).

Muslim-Americans and Arab-Americans rarely made the front pages in the year before 9/11, faring best in the New York Times where 5 percent of these stories were placed on page one, and worst in the *Post* and *USA Today* with no front-page placements. In the six months after September 11, the *New York Times* placed 10 percent of the news stories mentioning Muslim-Americans and Arab-Americans on the front page, *USA Today* 7 percent, the *New York Post* 2 percent, and the *Daily News* 1 percent. The changes were more conspicuous with respect to the six months before and after 9/11: In the pre-event period none of these stories were published on the front pages of the four newspapers; in the post-period 7 percent were given this prominent placement.

In all four newspapers the proportion of straight news articles that covered, mentioned, or quoted American Muslims and American Arabs declined after 9/11 (both in comparison to the six months and twelve months prior to the terror attacks). But apart from the proportion of straight news articles there was no across-the-board uniformity with respect to other types of news: In the *Times* and *Daily News*, news analyses took a significantly higher share in the post-9/11 period than during the previous year (and six months). The *Post* and *USA Today* carried a larger proportion of opinion columns that addressed one or the other aspect of American Muslims and Arabs; and in *USA Today* the share of letters-to-the-editor and editorials increased. Taken together, the newspapers devoted a significantly larger proportion of their total news about American Muslims to analytical perspectives, elite opinion, and the sentiments of readers at a time when the American public tried to make sense of the attacks and their aftermath.

After 9/11: More Muslim-American Voices in the News

TV correspondents who cover presidential election campaigns amass significantly more air-time than the candidates themselves, a situation common in television news in general (Kerbel 1994). The print media, too, rely a great deal on journalistic descriptions and background information (Nacos 1990). In the twelve months before 9/11, what some have come to call "Black Tuesday," 19 percent of all the sources quoted or mentioned (18 percent in the six months before the terror attacks) in the relevant text of the four newspapers were journalists, reporters, and correspondents describing news events, problems, and issues, or providing background information; in the six months thereafter, the proportion of journalistic sources shrank to a combined 12 percent. While the *Daily News* and *Times* used clearly less journalistic sources in the post-9/11 period, *USA Today* retained the same ratio, and the *Post* used actually more journalistic descriptions in post-9/11 articles that covered or referred to Muslim-Americans, Arab-Americans, or both. Still, after 9/11 some editors and perhaps reporters themselves seemed less inclined to rely on journalistic descriptions and explanations and were more open to let Muslim-Americans and Arab-Americans express their views and sentiments. Media sources expressing explicitly their opinion (i.e., editorials, op-ed columns) increased their share from 2 percent of all sources in these kinds of stories before 9/11 to 3 percent thereafter.

American Muslim and Arab sources captured a significantly larger share of the total news sources after the events of 9/11. In the twelve months before

"Black Tuesday," 25 percent of all sources in the relevant news were identified as Muslim or Arab U.S. citizens or residents versus 41 percent in the following six months. (The source ratio for American Muslims and Arabs was 34 percent in the six months before 9/11 and thus higher than in the twelve-month period before the attacks of September 11, 2001.) All three New York newspapers used these sources more frequently after "Black Tuesday" than in the year before. The increase was especially striking in the *Times* in that the share of Muslim-American and Arab-American sources increased from 24 percent in the year before 9/11 to 46 percent afterward. In the *Post* the proportion of Muslim- and Arab-American sources increased from 20 percent to 23 percent, in the *Daily News* from 29 percent to 35 percent. The exception was *USA Today* where the share of Muslim- and Arab-American sources declined actually from 32 percent before 9/11 to 28 percent thereafter. But in *USA Today* the proportion of American Muslim and Arab sources before 9/11 was greater than in the other three newspapers and remained high in the post-9/11 period.

The big "losers" in terms of news sources were non-Muslim local politicians in New York City, who constituted 16 percent of all sources in stories related to Muslim-Americans and Arab-Americans in the year before 9/11, but plunged to a tiny share of 1 percent in the 6 months thereafter and thus became nearly invisible in the news about Muslim and Arab New Yorkers. This steep decline occurred in all three New York newspapers (*Times* from 19 percent to 1 percent; *Post* from 18 percent to 4 percent; *Daily News* from 17 percent to 5 percent); the shrinkage was not quite as pronounced when we compared the six months before and after 9/11. National public officials and politicians, who provided 13 percent of the total number of sources in this sort of news before 9/11, were less affected than their local colleagues holding on to a 10 percent share of the four newspapers' total pool of sources in the months after 9/11. While "indexing" worked in favor of authoritative sources in the news about Muslim-Americans before the terrorist attacks, it nearly disappeared after 9/11 with respect to local politicians and merely weakened concerning national public officials. In news stories that mentioned Muslim-Americans, the U.S. public in general (i.e., by citing the results of polls) and (non-Muslim) members thereof were more often cited as sources after 9/11. In the twelve months before that date, 13 percent of all sources fell into this category, in the six months thereafter 19 percent.

From Partisan Controversies to Civil Liberties and Civil Rights Issues

Before September 11, 2001, the predominant news themes that related to American Muslims and American Arabs were taken from local, domestic, and international politics. Typically, this sort of news focused on partisan controversies, especially during election campaigns, and concerned one or the other candidate's relationships with American Muslim and/or Arab individuals or groups with alleged sympathies for or ties to terrorists and terrorist organizations in the Middle East. This became a prominent issue in the fall of 2000, when published reports revealed that the Republican presidential candidate, George W. Bush, had received $1,000 and the Democratic candidate in the New York race for the U.S. Senate, Hillary Clinton, $50,000 for their respective campaigns from American Muslim groups. Because of New York City's large bloc of Jewish and pro-Israel voters, this was of particular interest in the city. When the *Daily News* reported in the last stage of the New York race that the First Lady's campaign had benefited from a fundraiser thrown by an American Muslim organization, the newspaper provided Clinton's opponent Rick Lazio and the New York State Republican Party with ammunition to attack her as pro-terrorist and anti-Israel. While literally all news organizations in New York City (as well as the media elsewhere) reported on what became quickly the central campaign issue, the *New York Post* was especially relentless in bashing Mrs. Clinton for her alleged ties to terrorist-friendly circles. The following lines were quite typical for the *Post's* tirades:

> "Do you believe that Israel has a right to exist? Do you believe that America needs a dependable, democratically in the strategically vital, oil-rich Middle East? Then Hillary's record should really give you pause."

> "Before becoming first Lady, Hillary chaired the New World Foundation—an organization that funded groups controlled by the Palestinian Liberation Organization. And this was back when even liberals considered the PLO a terrorist group."

> "Over the years, she's befriended Arab- and Muslim-American organizations that refuse to denounce—and often defend—terrorist groups." "And just last month, frequent White House guest Nihad Awad, of the Council on American-Islamic Relations, railed against the notion of Arab coexistence with Israel, preaching instead the virtues of violence—and of Arab plans to reclaim 'all Palestine.' Hillary's response? None to speak of."[17]

While American Muslims were mostly mentioned in the news in the context of what the *Daily News* called Mrs. Clinton's "Mideast problem," they did not get a great deal of access to the media to speak for themselves on the issue. An article in the *Daily News* was among the exceptions in that it reported on Dr. Ahmad Jaber, an American Muslim and New York City resident, who voted for Democrats in the past but said he would vote for Republicans this time around. According to the newspaper, "New York Muslims yesterday seemed more upset with Hillary Clinton over the donation issue [and for returning the donations] even though it was Clinton's GOP opponent, Rick Lazio, who called the funds "blood money."[18] According to this article, Muslim-Americans were less upset about the fact that presidential candidate George Bush sent back $1,000 to an American Muslim organization than about Mrs. Clinton doing the same.

But, as the *New York Times* put it, Clinton and Lazio "battled intensely ... over each other's loyalty to Israel, signaling the extraordinary emphasis on Jewish voters in the final days of their race."[19]

A year later, the issue of American Muslims and their connections to terrorist groups abroad made the headlines once again, when it entered into the Democratic primary races in New York City. A coalition of American Muslim groups that had endorsed one of the mayoral candidates, Mark Green, and three candidates for borough presidencies, withdrew its endorsements after a State assemblyman had gone public with the accusation that members of the coalition had links to terrorist groups in the Middle East. In the midst of the ensuing controversy, the coalition withdrew its endorsements hoping not to damage the changes of the candidates of its choice. In a departure from the news that dwelled on this immediate campaign issue, *New York Times* reporter Jennifer Steinhauer addressed the broader problem of American Muslims trying to participate in the city's political process, when she wrote:

> The inability for any candidate to do business with Muslim groups without taking heat raises questions about whether Muslims, who have gained some political power in places like Detroit, will ever be able to get a foothold in New York.[20]

The dominance of these topics and themes involving the roles, interests, or positions of Muslim- and Arab-Americans in American body politics diminished after the events of 9/11. In the four newspapers a combined 43 percent of the pertinent news addressed these sorts of topics in the twelve months before 9/11 but only twelve percent in the six months thereafter. While the three New York newspapers reported heavily on local and regional news that often involved partisan clashes before 9/11, *USA Today* focused on domestic and international politics as they related to the interests of American Muslims and Arabs. The similarities in the four newspapers were striking: In the year before 9/11 these themes comprised the lion's share of each newspaper's topics in the Muslim- and Arab-American context (42 percent in the *Times*, 49 percent in the *Post*, 43 percent in the *Daily News*, 31 percent in *USA Today*); after 9/11 the proportion of these news themes decreased drastically (in the *Times* to 12 percent, in the *Post* to 11 percent, in the *Daily News* to 7 percent, and in *USA Today* to 17 percent). Moreover, after 9/11 there was little discussion of Muslim-Americans' political participation; instead news articles were likely to quote members of this minority on issues such as military action against al Qaeda and the Taliban in Afghanistan and the war on terrorism in general.

The private and family life of American Muslims, their customs, and the observance of their religious holidays received far more media attention before September 11, 2001, than afterward. In the twelve months leading up to the attacks, 14 percent of all themes in these sorts of stories were about private lives, customs, and religious practices compared to only 6 percent in the following six months.

In the months following the events of 9/11, the most often covered topics about Muslim and Arab citizens and residents concerned their civil liberties and civil rights as well as immigration issues. Before the terror attacks on the World Trade Center and the Pentagon these topics were not particularly prominent, comprising only 6 percent of the total themes in the combined coverage of the four newspapers. After 9/11, civil rights/civil liberties issues and the violation of those rights—including physical attacks on members of these groups—were by far the most frequently addressed topics: The four newspapers combined devoted 30 percent of all pertinent themes to these themes compared to only 6 percent in the previous year. This drastic change occurred in each of the publications: in the *Times* from 13 percent before September 11 to 31 percent thereafter, in the *Post* from 4 percent to 22 percent, in the *Daily News* from 0 percent to 26 percent, in *USA Today* from 0 percent to 33 percent.

Not surprisingly, the devastating terror attacks of September 11 were often the theme of stories that reported on or referred to American Muslims and Arabs. There was a wave of reports that highlighted the patriotism of American Muslims and Arabs and downplayed the stereotype that members of these groups support terrorism. Headlines such as "Muslims in B'klyn call for peace." (*NY Post,* Sept.17, 2001); "City Arabs & Muslims back U.S." (*NY Daily News,* Oct. 8, 2001); "Public Lives: A daughter of Islam, and an enemy of terror." (*NY Times,* Oct. 25, 2001) were quite common in the weeks and months after 9/11. In all, 9 percent of all discernible themes in this sort of news dealt directly with the terror of 9/11 and its aftermath.

There was also a surge in topics that dealt with the difficult life circumstances and identity problems of some American Muslims (an increase from 1 percent of all themes before 9/11 to 7 percent in the months thereafter). The *New York Times,* for example, devoted several articles to this topic and, in some cases, managed to educate non-Muslim-Americans about their Muslim fellow-citizens. Thus, a 21-year-old woman in Bridgeview, Illinois, told the *Times,* "I love Islam and I love anything in this country." But because her apparel identified her as a Muslim, "she also admitted that she is sad and fearful in the wake of 9/11."[21] But these stories also intensified the uneasy feelings in some non-Muslim Americans. Reporting on high school students in a private Islamic Academy in Brooklyn, Susan Sachs wrote: "They are Americans who feel duty-bound by Islam to obey American laws. But some of them say that if their country called them to war against a Muslim army, they might refuse to fight." And: "Some of the students, for example, said they would support any leader who they decided was fighting for Islam."[22] Another story in the *Times* contained a quote by a female college student who said: "In high school I was asking myself, am I more Pakistani or more American. Being Muslim answers that question." Her friend was even more specific when she said: "I am Muslim first, not even American Muslim. Because so much of the American culture is directly in conflict with my values as a Muslim, I can't identify solely as an American, or even as an American

Muslim."[23] The question of whether the views of some of these teenagers were representative among young American Muslims was not discussed in these kinds of articles that reflected typically an understanding for the plight of American Muslims but raised troubling questions in the minds of some, perhaps many, readers. Thus, the *Times* published a letter to the editor that described one of these stories as "one of the more frightening you have published in memory" and continued, "Though raised in our free society, some might not fight for America against fellow Muslims. Imagine what we would think of Christian students who refused to fight Germany in World War II because Germans were Christians." The letter closed with this sentence: "If the views of these young Muslim-Americans are at all typical, we are in trouble."[24]

Support for the Civil Liberties of American Muslims and Arabs

We mentioned above that civil liberties and civil rights of American Muslims and Arabs were the predominant topics in the months after 9/11. But the fact that a theme is more frequently covered than other topics does not tell us what views and opinions are expressed in the mass-mediated debate, whether in straight news articles, letters-to-the-editor, editorials or op-ed articles. The following excerpts illustrate the range of viewpoints in the news on the civil liberties/civil rights theme:

One day after 9/11 the *New York Times* published a letter to the editor in which the reader pleaded: "The inevitable temptation to change fundamentally the nature of our society, by attacking the civil rights and civil liberties of any individual or group, must be resisted."[25]

Addressing the controversy over racial/ethnic profiling of people "with Middle Eastern looks." Stanley Crouch wrote in the *Daily News*:

> We have had war declared on us by a spider at the center of a web of terrorist cells. Followers of that spider are hiding in the Arab-American community. No one doubts this. No one. In fact, it should bother all of us that a moratorium was not declared on immigration from the Middle East after the 1993 attack on the twin towers, especially since most of those identified with Sept. 11 arrived here after that time. If more Americans are murdered by people who are part of the terrorist web from the Middle East and successfully hiding out in a certain community, the response is going to have less to do with any kind of bigotry than with the icy nature of war.[26]

And while attacks on Arabs and Muslims were increasingly reported in the news, one commentator in the *New York Post* praised "the breathtaking paucity of violence against Muslims and Arabs."[27] This was a stunning assessment at a time when President George W. Bush, during a visit to the Islamic Center in Washington, DC, denounced violence against Muslim- and Arab-Americans, saying,

> Those who feel like they can intimidate our fellow citizens to take out their anger don't represent the best of America, they represent the worst of humankind, and they should be ashamed of that kind of behavior.[28]

Those who defended the civil liberties and civil rights of American Muslims and Arabs after the events of 9/11 expressed their views more frequently in the mass-mediated debate than those who advocated curbing those freedoms: Of all positions mentioned in the news about Muslim and Arab citizens and residents, 15 percent were in support of unfettered civil liberties and civil rights for these minorities, 5 percent against protecting these freedoms for American Muslims and Arabs. Before 9/11, such issues were not frequently discussed in the media counting for only 2 percent of all positions expressed in the news—1 percent for and 1 percent against protecting these rights for the Muslim and Arab minority. While differing in degree, the debate on civil liberties and civil rights of American Muslims and Arabs was substantially tilted in favor of those who spoke out in support of American Muslims' and Arabs' freedoms. In the *Times,* the share of supporting positions increased from 2 percent of all mentioned viewpoints in the pre-9/11 crisis to 17 percent thereafter, in the *Post* from less than 1 percent to 4 percent, in the *Daily News* from 0 percent to 11 percent, and in *USA Today* from 3 percent to 15 percent. While the calls for curbing American Muslims' and Arabs' civil liberties and equal rights increased in the six months after 9/11 in comparison the previous twelve months as well, these gains paled in comparison to increases for the opposing viewpoint.[29]

Of all views expressed in the pertinent news of the four publications during the twelve-month long pre-9/11 period, 8 percent stated expressly or implied that American Muslims and Arabs support terrorists, 4 percent rejected such accusations. In the following six months the numbers flip-flopped in that 4 percent associated Muslim and Arab-Americans with terrorism while 8 percent rejected the proposition.

Also, stories about American Muslims and Arabs or those mentioning them were far more likely to contain expressed opinions on Israel in the context of the Middle East conflict before rather than after 9/11. In the twelve months before the terror attacks 9 percent of all policy positions mentioned in the news were pro-Israel and 7 percent anti-Israel. In the six-months post-9/11 period, only 2 percent of these viewpoints concerned Israel with 1 percent expressing anti-Israel and 1 percent pro-Israel sentiments.

More Positive Depiction of Muslim-Americans after "Black Tuesday"

Surprisingly, the depiction of American Muslims and Arab Americans in the news was more positive and less negative in the wake of the terrorist events of 9/11 than in the previous year. Twenty-five percent of the pertinent articles in the four newspapers were categorized by our coders as positive/supportive or probably positive/supportive before the pre-9/11 period compared to 43 percent afterward; and whereas 31 percent of the stories depicted these minorities in a negative or probably negative light before the terror attacks, only 22 percent conveyed this impression in the post-9/11 period (see, table 8.3). In the *Times* and *Post* the share of positive stories grew significantly after 9/11, in the *Daily News* there was a modest increase on this count. And while negative depictions

Table 8.3   Depiction of Muslim-Americans and Arab-Americans in the News before and after 9/11

	12 MONTHS BEFORE 9/11 (%)	6 MONTHS AFTER 9/11 (%)	CHANGE (%)
Positive or supportive	9	17	+8
Probably positive or supportive	16	26	+10
Neutral/ambiguous/does not apply	44	36	−6
Probably negative or critical	21	14	−7
Negative or critical	10	8	−2
Total:	100	100	

Source: Muslim Communities in New York Project.

of American Muslims and Arabs decreased after "Black Tuesday" in the *Times* and *Post,* the share of negative stories went up in the *Daily News* and *USA Today.* These differences are probably best explained by the negligible percentage of negative stories and the high share of positive articles in *USA Today* before the terror strikes. In the *Daily News,* too, the proportion of stories that our coders perceived as negative was significantly lower before 9/11 than in the *Times* and *Post.* Regardless of these differences, three of the newspapers (*Times, Post* and *USA Today)* depicted American Muslims and Arabs more favorable than unfavorable after 9/11, and the fourth newspaper (*Daily News*) carried an equal share of positive and negative articles in this respect.

The Rise of Thematic News

As mentioned above, television news in particular is overwhelmingly episodic and narrowly focused on specific events, issues, or developments at the expense of thematic approaches that report more extensively on the larger context (Iyengar 1991). In the age of sound bites, there is less opportunity for thematic reporting. Increasingly, newspapers, too, opt for short, snappy news and episodic frames. Following the terrorism of September 11, the news about American Muslims and Arabs in the four newspapers combined changed from overwhelmingly episodic to mostly thematic. The ratio in the twelve months before 9/11 was 60 percent to 30 percent in favor of episodic stories with 10 percent equally episodic and thematic. In contrast, after the terror attacks on U.S. soil 49 percent of the stories were framed overwhelmingly thematic, 39 percent mostly episodic, and 12 percent were a mixture of the two. Three newspapers, the *New York Times, Daily News,* and *Post* published less episodic and more thematic stories after 9/11 than in the previous year. While these changes were most pronounced in the reporting of the *Times* and *Daily News,* the *Post,* too, decreased the ratio of episodic stories and increased the share of thematically framed articles. *USA Today* marched to its own drummer, switching from more thematically framed stories before 9/11 to slightly more episodic articles thereafter.[30] Because *USA Today* comes closest to a printed version of television news, we did not expect to find more stories with thematic than episodic frames in either of the time periods we studied. The perhaps best explanation is that the more thematic framing mode in the pre-9/11 months was an aberration, the result of a relatively small number of stories about Muslim-Americans that typically described interesting aspects of this minority and were best told in thematic or contextual frames. After the attacks of 9/11, American Muslims and Arabs were far more frequently covered and mentioned in this newspaper—often in short and typically episodically framed news items or paragraphs. But except for *USA Today*, thematic framing increased and episodic framing decreased in the newspapers we examined.

Metropolitan New York News and National Coverage

We discussed our research findings for the pertinent local New York City coverage and the national news combined because the similarities were striking and the differences minor. Thus, in both geographical settings local and national politicians were the dominant sources before 9/11 followed by Muslim-Americans and media-based sources. But in New York City with a far more significant Muslim population than in the nation as a whole, Muslim-Americans' share of the total sources was larger before and after 9/11 than in the national coverage. Not surprisingly, local politicians were cited more often in the New York metropolitan context, members of the administration and Congress more often in the national news coverage.

Local, state, national, and international politics and policies that referred to American Muslims in one way or the other were by far the most covered topics in both the New York City and the nationwide context in the twelve months before September 11, 2001, while civil liberties/civil rights issues affecting the Muslim and Arab minorities were the most often covered themes in the six months after 9/11 in the local and national news. The only difference with respect to positions and opinions expressed by sources was one of degree only: Before 9/11, pro-Israel and anti-Israel voices were more frequently mentioned in the local New York City news than in the national coverage; after 9/11 support for protecting the civil liberties of American Muslims and Arabs was more often expressed in the national than in the local news.

In both local and national news there was a shift from overwhelmingly episodic coverage before 9/11 to a mostly thematic framing pattern after 9/11. It is noteworthy, however, that this change was more pronounced in the local news that was far more episodic (68 percent of all pertinent stories) than the national news (54 percent) in the months before 9/11.

Finally, there were differences with respect to the perceived portrayal of Muslim- and Arab-Americans in that before 9/11 the negative or probably negative stories were more numerous in the local New York City news than those perceived as positive or probably positive by our coders. In contrast, pertinent stories in the national news were perceived to be more positive or probably positive (29 percent) than negative or probably negative (23 percent). After 9/11, these differences diminished with positive stories outscoring negative stories in the local news 41 percent to 24 percent and in the national media 43 percent to 21 percent.

More Similarities than Differences in Television News

In the twelve months before 9/11 the CBS-TV "Early Show" and the "Evening News with Dan Rather" aired only seven stories mentioning Muslim and Arab-Americans compared to 51 such stories in the six months after the terror in New York and Washington, DC. Thus, a comparison between the pre-9/11 and post-9/11 coverage seems not very meaningful. Yet, our analysis demonstrated that television news changed mostly in the same directions as newspaper content after 9/11. One of the exceptions was the dominance of journalistic sources before and after 9/11 that was far more pronounced than in the print press— a tendency observed with respect to television coverage in general.[31] But the share of media-based sources shrank in CBS's news from 53 percent before to 35 percent after 9/11. In the sparse coverage before 9/11 local and national politicians made up 10 percent of all sources while no Muslim-American source was mentioned in the relevant CBS news; after 9/11, however, 23 percent of the total sources were members of this minority while politicians remained at 10 percent with the share of local officials plummeting and that of national public officials increasing.

Local, state and international politics referring to Muslim- and Arab-Americans along with aspects of these minorities' family life and religious customs were mostly covered by CBS before 9/11, but like the print media, the network focused mostly on issues surrounding violations of Muslim- and Arab-Americans' civil liberties and civil rights after 9/11, when 38 percent of all pertinent stories were devoted to these themes. Contrary to the newspaper coverage that strongly favored voices that rejected curbs on Muslim- and Arab-Americans' civil liberties and rights, there was a much less pronounced advantage of these positions (11 percent of all expressed views) in comparison to those who advocated such curbs (7 percent).

Just as in the print press there was a decline of episodic stories in CBS newscasts after 9/11 and an increase in thematic stories. The result was that the same number of overwhelmingly episodic and thematic stories were aired (49 percent of all stories for each and 2 percent evenly split by the two framing modes).

Discussion and Conclusions

The terrorism attacks of 9/11 changed the ways newspapers and television news reported about American Muslims and Arab-Americans. The results of our comprehensive text analysis demonstrate that there was a shift from a fairly limited and stereotypical coverage in the pre-9/11 period to a more comprehensive, inclusive, and less stereotypical news presentation. Besides covering and referring to Muslim- and Arab-Americans more frequently and placing pertinent stories more prominently in the post-9/11 period, reporters and editors selected American Muslims and Arabs more frequently as sources after the catastrophic attack on New York and Washington than in the months before. Or, to put it differently, the "indexing" patterns in favor of officialdom and authoritative sources weakened as a result of the 9/11 disaster in stories that reported on these minorities. Moreover, in the wake of the terrorist nightmare, the print media were more inclined to publish news analyses, columns, and letters-to-the-editor concerning Muslim- and Arab-Americans and thereby contributed or even initiated mass-mediated debates on their pages and elsewhere.

The probably most important change occurred in the choice of news topics and how they were reported. Before 9/11 by far the most prominent news theme concerned Muslim and Arab-Americans who participated in the political process, or tried to, especially during election campaigns and were accused of sympathizing or supporting terrorists in the Middle East. We are not suggesting that the press should have ignored such matters but that the news we examined failed to cover other aspects of American Muslims as frequently and extensively. As it was, the two-dimensional perspective that Kern traced in foreign news reporting manifested itself in the pre-9/11 coverage of Muslim- and Arab-Americans in that the foreign story colored the domestic story (Kern 1981) in stereotypical ways. While this did not disappear in the post-9/11 period, the more frequent use of Muslim- and Arab-Americans as sources resulted in a more balanced presentation of the news.

After 9/11, the predominant themes, namely the status of civil liberties and civil rights of American Muslims and Arabs, were hardly less problematic with respect to reinforcing the stereotypical image of these minorities. After all, these issues arose in the aftermath of an unprecedented terrorism attack that was perpetrated by Arab Muslims. But the newspapers also pleaded for a better understanding between Muslims and non-Muslims in the United States, more assurances that most Muslims have nothing to do with terrorism, and that Islam does not preach violence. Just as important, as mentioned above, there was significantly more support to protect the civil liberties and rights of American Muslims and Arabs than calls to curb their freedoms in the mass-mediated discourse. Large parts of the post-9/11 news topics that concerned or touched on the interests of Muslim- and Arab-Americans was devoted to the domestic rather than the foreign story.

Another positive change was the increase in thematic and the decrease of episodic news frames in the months after September 11. When stories provide readers with more than bare-bone facts and explain news events in a larger context, news consumers get more comprehensive information and are able to make their evaluation of individuals and groups on a more informed and educated basis.

Taken together, these changes may well explain the move to significantly more positive and less negative media depictions of American Muslims and Arabs that our coding team recognized after the events of 9/11. Since most Americans get most or all of their information about Muslim-Americans from the news, we wondered whether the different news content affected the way they viewed the American Muslim minority in the post-September 11 months. As table 8.4 shows, surveys reveal that the American public in general viewed Muslim-Americans more favorable after September 11, 2001, than before. Interestingly, after a significant increase in the volume of coverage after 9/11, fewer survey respondents said that they had never heard of Muslim-Americans or could not rate their attitude toward them.

On the other hand, the public expressed doubts about Muslim-Americans' loyalty to their country. In April 2002, 44 percent of the public believed that American Muslims were not doing enough to help the authorities to track down terrorist cells inside the United States, 32 percent were not sure, and only 24 percent thought that Muslim-Americans cooperated in this respect.[32]

When Americans are faced with grave national crisis, racial and ethnic prejudice and fear tend to sweep away support for the constitutionally guaranteed civil liberties of whole groups whose loyalty was questioned. This was especially true for Japanese-Americans in World War II. As one observer concluded more than twenty years before 9/11,

> The racism that led to the internment of Japanese-Americans during World War II was created partly by the motion picture industry, which for years typecast Orientals as villains, and partly by the press, especially the newspapers of William Randolph Hearst ... The "yellow peril" hysteria and the stereotyping which helped produce that myth have retreated into history. The Arab has now become the latest victim of media stereotyping (Shaheen 1981, 89).

After 9/11 and following the news of physical and verbal attacks on Muslim-Americans and people wrongly thought to be Muslims, the media reported how Japanese-Americans recalled the persecution during World War II. The explicit or implicit message here was to not repeat the mistakes of the past. In the six months after 9/11, the U.S. newspapers and wire services represented in the Lexis-Nexis archive published a total of 109 stories, ABC News, CBS News, NBC News, CNN, and NPR combined aired nine segments that recalled the treatment of Japanese Americans in the context of Muslim- and Arab-Americans' post-9/11 predicament. One day after 9/11, for example, John Donovan said in his report on ABC-TV's *World News Tonight,*

> Any common American will tell you immigrants from Middle-Eastern countries are as law abiding as anyone. They have unusually strong family values. They mostly vote Republican. But Oklahoma City happened in 1995 and they all felt like suspects. Now the World Trade Center, and they feel like it's happening again. The principal at work here is guilt by association.[33]

Table 8.4 The U.S. Public's Attitude Toward Muslim-Americans

	VERY FAVORABLE (%)	MOSTLY FAVORABLE (%)	MOSTLY UNFAVORABLE (%)	VERY UNFAVORABLE (%)	NEVER HEARD OF (%)	CAN'T RATE (%)
Aug./Sept. 2000	11	39	13	8	2	27
March 2001	7	38	16	8	4	27
November 2001	15	44	12	5	1	23
Feb./March 2002	8	46	14	8	2	22

Source: Pew Center for the People & the Press & Pew Forum on *Religion and Public Life.*

And the *Seattle Post-Intelligencer's* Joshunda Sanders mentioned in a story about the painful memories of Japanese-Americans,

> Like Arab-Americans and Muslims who have been the targets of anger and vi-
> olence during the last week, Japanese-Americans—particularly those who sur-
> vived the internment camps of World War II—remember the same treatment.
> They, too, were targeted and punished because of their heritage. (Sanders 2001)

The media reported also that leaders like President Bush and New York's Mayor Rudi Giuliani urged Americans not to direct their anger toward ethnic and religious minorities. It seems that these reports did not erase the public's doubts about Muslim- and Arab-Americans' patriotism.

As discussed in the previous section, there were far more similarities between the pertinent local and national coverage in the four newspapers we examined, and between those newspapers and television news, based on our analysis of the CBS morning and early evening broadcasts.

The events of 9/11 forced the media's hand to cover the Muslim and Arab minorities more frequently. This also caused the press to present news consumers with a more comprehensive picture of these groups. One result was that the news media granted Muslim-Americans more access after 9/11, and members of this minority made themselves available to the media. The limited news about Muslim- and Arab-Americans, the prevalent topics, and the more episodic than thematic framing patterns before 9/11 added up to more negative and stereotypical associations than the more frequent reporting, the different topics, and the dominance of thematic frames in the post-9/11 months. As one expert in the field has pointed out, the cultures and peoples of the Middle East "are not easily explained in quick two-minute network news stories" (Shaheen 1981: 104). The same holds true for episodically-framed stories in the print media. Our research shows that the news about Muslim-Americans after 9/11 was less negative and stereotypical than before that memorable date. What we do not know yet, however, is whether the changes we found were temporary or will turn out to be permanent.

Notes

The study described here was conducted in the first phase of an ongoing research project on the news media and Muslim-Americans and part of the comprehensive 'Muslim Communities in New York Project' at Columbia University that is funded by the Ford Foundation. We are grateful to Peter Awn, Ester Fuchs, and Reeva Simon for recognizing the need to understand how the news media report on Muslim-Americans in New York City and in the United States, and to Louis Abdellatif Cristillo for managing the coding process with skill and patience. We also thank the members of our excellent coding team Daniel Berghoff, Ayesha Hasan, Seyfi Kenan, Leslie Orderman, Anindita Dutta Roy, and Emilio Spadola.
1. The reviewer was Adil Sohail Qureshi, and the comment concerned Jack Shaheen's book *Reel Bad Arabs: How Hollywood Vilifies a People.* See, http://www.amazon.com/exdec/obidos/ASIN/1566563887/ref=pd_sim . . . /002-929853-184886, retrieved 10/22/2001.
2. The focus groups were conducted for the 'Muslim Communities in New York Project' by researchers at Columbia University.

3. For more on the sentiments of Muslim high school students at the Al Noor School see Susan Sachs, 'The 2 worlds of Muslim-American teenagers.' *New York Times,* October 9, 2001.

4. The quote is from Ben McGrath, 'Brooklyn Boycott.' *The New Yorker,* July 22, 2002, p. 24. Although it was not clear whether and to what extent the initiative was successful and affected the *Post's* circulation, people at the newspaper were concerned enough to dispatch marketing and promotion people to meet with boycott leaders.

5. The first ever systematic poll of American Muslims was conducted for Project MAP: Muslims in American Public Square by Zogby International. See http://www. projectmap.com/PMReport.htm.

6. We do not know how many Muslim- and Arab-Americans work in the non-ethnic press in the United States because professional journalism organizations keep track only of the number of Black, Hispanic, and Asian Americans in the news media; but we suspect that the number of Muslim- and Arab-Americans in the newsrooms is rather small.

7. Although part of the 'Muslim Communities in New York Project,' this study examines both the news about Muslim-Americans in New York and across the United States assuming that the perceptions of Muslim and non-Muslim New Yorkers are not only affected by local news but by national reporting as well. Indeed, in a forthcoming part of this project we will analyze photographs in newspapers and newsmagazines and TV visuals of Muslims abroad because we are convinced that such images (as well as spoken and written words about non-American Muslims) also affect what Muslim and non-Muslim Americans think about each other and about news reporting bias in this respect.

8. See, for example, Dr. Barry A. Kosmin and Dr. Egon Mayer, 'Profile of the U.S. Muslim Population.' ARIS Report No. 2, October 2001, The Graduate Center of the City University of New York.

9. Interview with Louis Abdellatif Cristillo, Columbia University, July 25, 2002.

10. The research was part of the ongoing 'Muslim Communities in New York Project' at Columbia University. The canvassing was conducted between 1998 and 1999.

11. We retrieved the articles from the Lexis-Nexis online archives using the search words "Muslim American" and "American Muslim," "Arab American" and "American Arab," "black Muslim," "Nation of Islam," and "Muslim convert." In many instances, these search words produced the same article two times or more often, but we coded only one of the texts.

12. The actual coding choices were positive/supportive, probably positive/supportive, neutral/ not clear/ not applicable, probably negative/ critical of, negative/critical of.

13. In our first test coding rounds, our coders did not achieve a high degree of reliability in the coding of sources, themes or topics, and policy positions with the best inter-coding correlation (gamma) of .75 for sources, .59 for themes, and .61 for policy preferences. But when we collapsed similar sources (i.e., Muslim American, South East Asian Muslim American, etc.) into larger categories, the results were far better (.92). Similarly, some of the policy preferences with respect to civil liberty issues were so specific that it was difficult for coders to make fine distinction. When we bundled very similar positions together in our reliability tests, the results went up to .93. With respect to themes, coders tended to identify not simply one or two predominant themes or topics per story but half a dozen or more. When the focus was on the overriding theme of a story, the reliability was nearly perfect (.99). Because we had a very diverse group of coders in terms of ethnic and religious background, we expected that agreement between them on the depiction of Muslim- and Arab-Americans, Muslims and Arabs in general, and the framing modes would be very unlikely. Indeed, we asked the coders to use their initial sentiments to code these categories. Our goal here was simply to get input from the diverse group members in order to compare their subjective evaluations in the months before and after 9/11. That is precisely how readers of different backgrounds react to the news day-in and day-out. As it happened, in their evaluations of how Muslim- and Arab-Americans were depicted, the coding reliability was surprisingly high (.75) but it was very low with respect to Muslims and Arabs in general (.18) and quite low with respect to the framing modes (.35).

14. We are in the process of examining thousands of photographs depicting Muslim- and Arab-Americans as well as Muslims and Arabs abroad that appeared in the four newspapers and in *TIME* and *Newsweek.* While our focus was on the news as it relates

to Muslims and Arabs in the U.S., we assumed that the American public's perceptions and those of the American and Arab minorities are not simply affected by the news about Muslims and Arabs in the United States, but by those living abroad as well. For this reason, we will include visuals of non-American Arabs and Muslims in part of our ongoing study. In addition, we are analyzing transcripts and tapes of the *CBS Evening News* and of local news programs of WCBS-TV in New York City.

15. Stephen Kaufman, "American Natural Museum of Natural History stages events about Islam." http://usinfo.state.gov/usa/islam/a013002a.htm.

16. "A spiritual Awakening: Religion in the Media, Dec 2000–Nov. 2001." Study prepared by Douglas Gould & Co. for the Ford Foundation.

17. "Hillary's World." *New York Post,* October 26, 2000, p. 44.

18. Leslie Casimir. "Anger among N.Y. Muslims: React to Hillary return of money." *Daily News,* October 30, 2000, p. 6.

19. Randal C. Archibold and Adam Nagourney. "Lazio and Clinton swap charges." *New York Times,* November 4, 2000, p. 1.

20. Jennifer Steinhauer, "Political Memo: On the road to endorsements by ethnic groups, mayoral hopefuls fall into potholes." *New York Times,* August 10, 2001, p. B3.

21. John W. Fountain. "Sadness and fear as they feel doubly vulnerable." *New York Times,* October 2001.

22. Susan Sachs. "The 2 Worlds of Muslim-American teenagers." *New York Times,* Oct. 7, 2001.

23. Laurie Goldstein. "A nation challenged: Islamic Traditions; Muslims nurture sense of self on campus." *New York Times,* November 3, 2001, p. B1.

24. America at War: Voices in a nation on edge. Roles of religion." *New York Times,* October 9, 2001, p. A24.

25. The letter was written by John S. Koppel on September 11, 2001 and published in the *New York Times* of September 12, 2001, p. A26.

26. Stanley Crouch. "Drawing the line on racial profiling." *Daily News,* October 4, 2001, p. 41.

27. John Podhoretz. "Our fellow Americans—the friends within." *New York Post,* September 17, 2001, p. 41.

28. The President was quoted in Tamar Lewin and Gustav Niebuhr, A Nation Challenged: Violence; Attacks and Harassment Continue on Middle Eastern people and mosques." *New York Times,* September 18, 2001, p. B5.

29. In the *Times* the share of positions in favor of curbing the civil liberties and civil rights of American Muslims and Arabs increased from 1 percent before 9/11 to 4 percent thereafter, in the *Post* from 1 percent to 2 percent, in the *Daily News* from 0 percent to 3 percent, in *USA Today* from 0 percent to 8 percent. But in none of the publications was the increase larger than the jump in expressions in support of protecting the freedoms of these minorities.

30. The ratio in the *Times* was 60 percent to 33 percent in favor of episodic stories before 9/11 and 51 percent to 33 percent in favor of thematic articles thereafter with the rest of the stories equally thematic and episodic. In the *Post* the pre-9/11 ratio was 57 percent to 32 percent in favor of episodically framed stories, 52 percent to 42 percent in favor of episodically framed articles afterward. In the *Daily News* 67 percent of the stories were episodic and 28 percent thematic before 9/11, 51 percent thematic and 41 percent episodic in the post-9/11 period. In sharp contrast, *USA Today* changed from a more thematic coverage (50 percent of the pertinent stories were mostly thematic and 36 percent episodic) before 9/11 to more episodic framing (48 percent episodic, 44 percent thematic) after the terror attacks.

31. During the 2000 presidential election campaign, for example, reporters received 74 percent of the pertinent air time on the three broadcast networks ABC, CBS, and NBC, while the candidates themselves were granted only 12 percent according to the Center for Media and Public Policy. See, "Campaign 2000 Final." *Media Monitor* XIV (6) (November/December 2000): 1–5.

32. Conducted by *Fox News,* April 2–3, 2002. People were asked: "Do you think American Muslims are doing enough to help U.S. authorities track down terrorist cell members here in the United States?"

33. Donovan's report was aired on ABC's *World News Tonight* on September 12, 2001.

References

Adams, William C. 1981. *Television Coverage of the Middle East.* Norwood NJ: Ablex Publishing. 1981.

Altheide, David L. 'Three-in-one news: Network coverage of Iran.' *Journalism Quarterly* 59: 482–86.

Bennett, W. Lance. 'An Introduction to Journalism Norms and Representations of Politics.' *Political Communication* 13(4): 373–384.

Campbell, Christopher P. 1995. *Race, Myth, and the News.* Thousand Oaks, CA: Sage.

Entman, Robert M. and Andrew Rojecki. 2000. *The Black Image in the White Mind.* Chicago, IL: University of Chicago Press.

Entman, Robert M. 1996. 'Reporting Environmental Policy Debate: The Real Media Biases.' *Harvard International Journal of Press/Politics* 1(3): 77–92.

Gans, Herbert. 1979. *Deciding What's News.* New York NY: Vintage Books.

Gitlin, Todd. 1980. *The Whole World is Watching.* Berkeley, CA.: University of California Press.

Gissler, Sig. 1994. 'Newspapers' Quest for Racial Candor.' *Media Studies Journal* 8(3): 123–132.

Greenberg, Bradley S. 1986. 'Minorities and the Mass Media.' In *Perspectives on Media Effects,* eds. Jennings Bryant and Dolf Zillmann, Hillsdale, NJ: Lawrence Erlbaum.

Iyengar, Shanto. 1991. *Is Anyone Responsible?* Chicago, IL: University of Chicago Press.

Kerbel, Matthew Robert. 1994, *Edited for Television.* Boulder, CO: Westview.

Kern, Montague. 1981. 'The Invasion of Afghanistan: Domestic vs. Foreign Stories.' In *Television Coverage of the Middle East,* ed. William C. Adams. Norwood, NJ: Ablex Publishing.

Lippmann, Walter. 1946. *Public Opinion.* New York, NY: Free Press.

Nacos, Brigitte L. 2002. *Mass-Mediated Terrorism.* Lanham, MD: Rowman & Littlefield.

Nacos, Brigitte L. 1990. *The Press, Presidents, and Crises.* New York, NY: Columbia University Press.

Nacos, Brigitte L. and Natasha Hritzuk, 2000. 'The Portrayal of Black America in the Mass Media.' In *Black and Multicultural Politics in America,* eds. M. Alex Assensoh and Lawrence Hanks. New York, NY: New York University Press.

Nacos, Brigitte L. 1996. *Terrorism and the Media: From the Iran Hostage Crisis to the Oklahoma City Bombing.* New York, NY: Columbia University Press.

Nacos, Brigitte L. 1990. *The Press, Presidents, and Crises.* New York, NY: Columbia University Press.

Neuman, Russel W. et al. 1992. *Common Knowledge.* Chicago, IL: University of Chicago Press.

Norris, Pippa, ed. 1997. *Women, Media, and Politics.* New York, NY: Oxford.

Sanders, Joshunda. 'Japanese Americans see similarities to WW II conditions.' *Seattle Post-Intelligencer,* September 18, 2001, p. A7.

Shaheen, Jack. 1997. *Arab and Muslim Stereotypes in American Popular Culture.* Washington, D.C.: Center for Muslim-Christian Understanding.

Shaheen, Jack. 2001. *Reel Bad Arabs: How Hollywood Vilifies a People.* Northampton, MA: Interlink Publishing Group.

Shaheen, Jack. 1981. 'Images of Saudis and Palestinians: A Review of Major Documentaries.' In *Television Coverage of the Middle East,* ed. William C. Adams. Norwood, NJ: Ablex Publishing.

Shipler, David K. 1998. 'Blacks in the Newsroom.' *Columbia Journalism Review* (May/June): 26–32.

Simon, Reeva. 1989. *The Middle East in Crime Fiction.* New York, NY: Lilian Barber Press.

CHAPTER 9

Framing World Opinion in the Elite Press

FRANK LOUIS RUSCIANO

As previous chapters have demonstrated, framing is often best understood through comparisons, whether temporal or spatial, where the same events are depicted through different journalistic lenses. This study contributes toward this approach by exploring the events of 9/11 and depictions of terrorism and the United States through several elite newspapers in countries ranging from Nigeria, Israel, and China to Russia, Argentina, and India, as well as the United States and UK. In the aftermath of the attacks of September 11, 2001, an editorial writer stated in the *International Herald Tribune* that the events heralded the first blow in a "clash of civilizations"—Western versus Muslim. At the same time, he also asserted that the events were an affront to world opinion and the international community.[1] Inadvertently, he was employing two perspectives that contradict each other, implying different discourse conventions, meanings, and ultimately, actions as a consequence of their words.

The "clash of civilizations" refers to Huntington's assertion that in the post-Cold War era, the major conflicts were to occur between different "civilizations," or primordial groupings based around the complex of ethnicity, religion, and culture. Huntington dismisses the "international community" as a "euphemistic collective noun (replacing 'the Free World') to give global legitimacy to actions reflecting the interests of the United States and other Western powers."[2] Further, he rejects the notion of "world opinion" as based upon "argument[s] that a universal culture or civilization is now emerging . . . none of which withstands even passing scrutiny."[3]

"Global opinion theory," by contrast, argues that nations advance interpretations of "world opinion" whose structure and content are favorable to their interests and values. A process of negotiation then ensues among the involved nations to resolve these interpretations. Nations that violate any resulting consensus risk isolation from the "international community." World opinion is defined as *the moral judgments of observers which actors must heed in the international arena, or risk isolation as a nation.* This approach combines my previous studies of world opinion with notions of "international society" derived from the English school of international relations.[4] Global opinion theory shares with the English school the notion of shared opinions supporting the origins of the nation-state, and of the nations of the world constituting some unit like a society.

Regarding the first, Mayall notes how a general consensus had to undergird even the existence of the nation-state, since "if sovereign authorities are to conclude agreements, they must recognise one another as sovereign."[5] Similarly, global opinion theory notes how "the first genuine 'world opinion' may have been the consensus among countries that nation-states were legitimate groupings for the organization of human activities."[6] Regarding the second, Mayall notes:

> Anyone who has ever tried to discuss the general context of international relations has been forced, sooner or later, to *use some collective noun*. Some have opted for the community of mankind, others for the society of states, yet others for a states-system, or world society, or a series of international regimes.[7]

Global opinion theory similarly includes the notion of the "world as a unit" deriving such phrases as "world community," "world public," or "civilized nations"[8] as synonyms in its analyses.

The theories depart, however, in that global opinion theory stresses the influences of *communication* and *world opinion* in the creation and maintenance of international society, rather than power and the imposition of values by one set of nations (such as Europe). Hence, an international community defined by world opinion "tends to appear when the 'imagined community' of nations, constructed from common linguistic usages, becomes integral to the administration of scarce resources beyond the nation-state."[9]

This chapter tests the applicability of the "global opinion" and "clash of civilizations" theories following the attacks of September 11 by analyzing how several international newspapers conceptualize world opinion toward the United States and these events. The newspapers were categorized to represent the major "civilizational" groups that Huntington describes. They include the *New York Times, London Times,* and Israel's *Ha'aretz Daily* (Western civilization), the *Arab News* (Islamic civilization),[10] *China Daily* (Sinic civilization), *Times of India* (Hindu civilization), the Argentinean *Nacion* (Latin American civilization), the Nigerian *Guardian* (African civilization), and *Pravda* (Slavic-Orthodox civilization). The *International Herald Tribune* was added as a newspaper that aspires to an international perspective. All the newspapers are independently published, with the exceptions of the *China Daily* and the *Arab News,* both of which are government controled. The analysis was done in English, using translated versions of the newspapers where needed, except for the *Nacion,* which was analyzed in the original Spanish edition.

With the exception of "Western civilization," all of the other regions are represented by only one newspaper. The former included three newspapers because it was appropriate to use an Israeli newspaper, given the relevance of the Middle East to the issue, and because it was also useful to include a newspaper not published in or from the United States. It is, of course, debatable whether the *Arab News* is a valid "representative" of "Muslim civilization." Huntington's analysis begs that classification, however, since the "clash of civilizations" thesis assumes implicitly a great degree of issue coherence within, but not between, the regions he defines.[11]

These media analyses follow Herman and Chomsky's assumption that newspaper framing tends to reflect the dominant ideological and regime interests of the nation of origin.[12] While the newspaper's national origin does not *determine* its discourse, it does provide clues to how certain issues are discussed and framed. A limited sample of ten elite newspapers cannot actually measure world opinion, or even elite opinion for that matter. Different newspapers within the same country, state, or region often adopt contrasting editorial positions. However, as chapter six notes, analyzing the main newspapers of record or the elite press does give some general guidance about elite perceptions of world opinion. Moreover, because this study examines changes in perceptions of world opinion over time, it demonstrates how these perceptions change as global events change. Since these are influential publications, the shifts they record can be interpreted as both *reflecting,* and *affecting,* world opinion to some extent.

The Agenda for World Opinion Following September 11, 2001

In the seven weeks of the study, 287 references to "world opinion" on the attacks appeared in the ten newspapers. Consistent with its goal of being "the world's newspaper," the *International Herald Tribune* contained the most references, comprising 25% of the total (72 references), or more than twice that of the nearest proportion from the Nigerian *Guardian* (12%, or 34 references). The rest followed with 11% (*Ha'aretz*), 11% (the *New York Times*), 9% (*Nacion*), 8% (the *Arab news*), 8% (*Pravda*), 7% (*London Times*), 5% (*China Daily*), and 5% (*Times of India*).

In the sample, 67% of the references appeared in editorials, with the rest appearing in reports. Finally, "world opinion" was more likely to be referenced implicitly (91% of cases) rather than explicitly. Explicit references include the phrase "world opinion" or some equivalent such as "international opinion," "world public opinion," "international public opinion," and so on. Implicit references refer to some judgment or reaction being attributed to the world, such as "worldwide shock," "world outrage," and a "complete political and ideological isolation of terrorists through international cooperation." Other implicit references attribute actual expressions of opinion to the world or the international community, noting for instance how "the world had ignored" support for terrorism, "the world will not forget" the United Nations, and "the world was appalled" by the attacks.[13]

Does "The World" Hate the United States?

From discussions of opinions on "the Arab street" to American news magazine covers asking "Why Does the World Hate Us So Much?," the attacks of September 11, 2001, have stimulated interest about how the world thinks of the United States, or how *world opinion* regards the country. Raising the

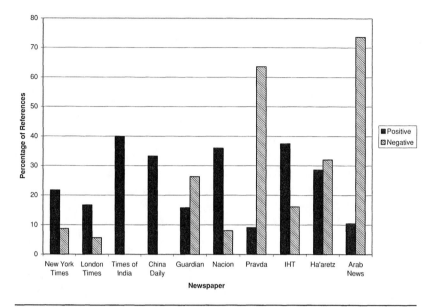

Fig. 9.1 Positive and negative references to world opinion on the United States, by newspaper. Note: The analysis included 213 stories. For the classification of newspapers, see Table 9.1.

latter question refocuses our attention toward whether "the world" does indeed "hate" the United States, or more generally, how the rest of the world perceives the nation. Beyond certain anecdotal evidence, however, this issue has been difficult to address. Polls that deal with responsibility for the attacks in the narrow sense of the term do not really capture the meaning of this question for Americans.

Perceptions of "how the world feels about the United States" are as diverse as the newspapers and regions of the world studied. Contrary to critics of the United States, positive evaluations of the nation outweighed negative ones by a margin of 27% to 23%.[14] As Figure 9.1 indicates, however, these assessments varied somewhat according to newspaper—the Nigerian *Guardian*, Russian *Pravda*, and, surprisingly, both the *Arab News* and Israeli *Ha'aretz* all showed negative evaluations of world opinion outweighing positive evaluations for the United States. Positive evaluations outweighed negative evaluations in the other six newspapers.[15]

These findings are reflected in the reactions of leaders abroad. Two weeks after the attacks, a former German minister of economic affairs stated that "the United States enjoys a wave of sympathy and friendship around the world." Similarly, the Gulf Cooperation Council representing six Arab Persian Gulf nations stated it was "willing to enter an alliance that enjoys the support of

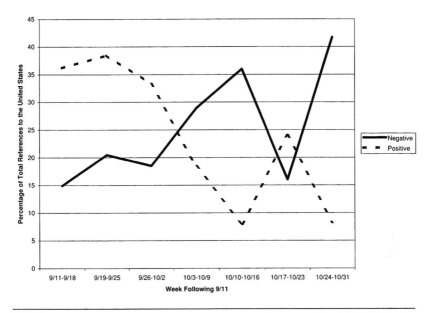

Fig. 9.2   Positive and negative evaluations of world opinion on the United States, by week. Note: The analysis included 213 stories. For the classification of newspapers, see Table 9.1.

the international community to fight international terrorism and to punish its perpetrators," despite the Saudi paper's negative evaluations of world opinion. It is notable that the Israeli *Ha'aretz* and the Saudi *Arab News* both perceived negative evaluations of the United States as outweighing positive ones. Upon examination of the stories, however, these results occurred for different reasons. The Israeli paper generally held the position that after the attack, the United States, like Israel, understood how it felt to be under siege and surrounded by a hostile world. The Saudi paper took a different perspective, indicating that the attack on the United States was, in part, in response to world opinion about our country's foreign policy, notably toward Israel and the Palestinians. In the first case, the negative evaluations of world opinion were an expression of empathy and fellow-feeling; in the second case, they were a criticism of American policies.

These results do not tell the entire story, however. As Figure 9.2 illustrates, perceptions of world opinion toward the United States shifted in the newspapers during the period under study. In the weeks up to October 3, positive evaluations of world opinion far outweighed negative evaluations. But in the following week, negative evaluations outweighed positive ones, and while the findings reverse themselves again in the week starting October 17, the high levels of international support do not repeat themselves. Indeed, the trend reverses itself again in the final week of the study, when the negative evaluations of world opinion on the United States outweigh the positive in the foreign press studied.

The likely reason for this shift was the American and British bombing campaign against Afghanistan, which began on October 7. When the United States took military action in response to the attacks, its international image probably shifted from injured party to aggressor in certain foreign newspapers. Compare, for instance, these two quotations from the Nigerian *Guardian*, published September 13 and October 16, 2001, respectively:

> Tuesday's terrorist attack on the United States of America must be condemned by the whole world (9/13/2001).
> Strained by heavy bombardment of Afghanistan, which entered its second week on Sunday, global support for the Anglo-American air strikes against the host of prime suspect in September 11 terrorist attack on World Trade Centre and Pentagon is under the threat of snapping (10/16/2001).

The problem goes beyond the retaliation taken by the United States against the Taliban. The very nature of the subject for world opinion makes efforts at creating an international consensus on the subject difficult.

Terrorism and International Reaction

In the newspapers' references to world opinion, "terrorism" was routinely condemned by all the nations studied. But problems arose regarding how to define "terrorism" beyond the horrible examples in New York and Washington, DC. Because terrorism is a *method,* rather than an ideology, a nation, or a leader, it is a difficult subject for world opinion; one may "know it when they see it," but generating a general description for all or even most nations to accept has proven elusive. If "terrorism" can be defined to include unintended civilian casualties in a military campaign, for instance, along with the intentional targeting of civilian populations, it becomes very difficult to reach an international consensus on the term's meaning or legitimate responses to it.

In order to understand how this problem impacts upon potential world opinion processes, one must examine the terminology used in the newspapers more closely. Previous research has revealed a consistent terminology for world opinion across several international newspapers.[16] This terminology includes the following basic components:

- the *moral component,* which refers to values shared by all nations in their judgments of *world* opinion;
- the *pragmatic component,* which refers to interests shared by all nations in their judgments of world opinion;
- the *power* of world opinion, which refers to its apparent influence on world events and nations' behaviors;
- the *nation's image,* or reputation, in world opinion, as it is perceived by itself and other nations;

- the *world considered as a unit,* such as an international community, which may judge and respond to other nations' behaviors; and
- the *threat of international isolation,* which operates as a potential punishment for nations which do not heed the dictates of world opinion.

The newspapers' discourse defines a *process* of world opinion involving these components. The *moral component* provides value-driven justification for condemning a given nation or action; the *pragmatic component* contributes to the *power* of world opinion to influence events, by convincing nations that what is moral is often also consistent with the common interest. At stake for the subject country is the *nation's image,* or its reputation in world opinion; indeed, citizens tend to integrate their nation's international image in their construction of national identity.[17] Finally, errant nations or leaders are threatened, or punished, by *international isolation* from the world community, or some other entity that defines the *world as a unit.* One may summarize the global opinion process in a preliminary definition of world opinion: *"World opinion* refers to the moral judgments of observers which actors must heed in the international arena, or risk isolation as a nation."[18]

In past studies of world opinion, the moral component tended to be more common and more important than the pragmatic component.[19] The moral component partially explained the influence of world opinion over international affairs; indeed, morality tended to be central to the discussion of the international opinion's power to influence events, leaders, or nations' actions. In this study, however, the moral component appeared in slightly fewer cases (42.2%) than the pragmatic component (44.3%). Further, the moral component was not correlated with the power or influence world opinion was assumed to have regarding the crisis ($r = 0.038$, significance $= 0.521$); by contrast, the presence of the pragmatic component was correlated with the power of world opinion ($r = 0.164$, significance $= 0.005$).

Given the difficulties involved with defining "terrorism," it appears that the judgments rendered regarding world opinion were more driven by the *interests* nations were perceived to share. Put another way, the newspapers generally acknowledged that even without a moral consensus regarding value judgments, attacks such as those on September 11 threatened the peace and security of all nations. This perspective is reflected in a number of newspaper reports and editorials where the attacks were interpreted not just solely as being against the United States, but as an assault on the very notions of "civilization" or "civilized society." As General Assembly President Han Seung-soo of South Korea stated at the United Nations, "terrorism is not a weapon wielded by one civilization against another, but rather an instrument of destruction through which small bands of criminals seek to undermine civilization itself" (*China Daily* 10 April 2001).

This view also appears affected by the United States's response to the attacks in the week of October 3 through October 9. As shown in Figure 9.3, the percentages

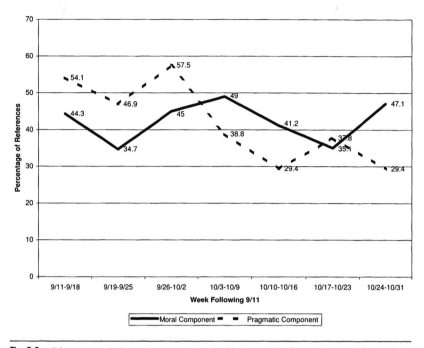

Fig. 9.3 References to moral and pragmatic components of world opinion, by week. Note: The analysis included 287 stories. For the classification of newspapers, see Table 9.1.

of references to the moral component of world opinion are fairly consistent over time during the study; at no time do they include a majority of the citations, instead varying between 34.7% and 49% of the references to world opinion. By contrast, the pragmatic component is more evident in the first three weeks of the crisis, appearing in a majority of cases in two out of the three weeks. This pattern shifts sharply after October 3, when the percentage of pragmatic citations drops below that of the moral citations; as with the positive references to the United States, the pattern recovers somewhat in the week of October 17, only to fall below the moral component's references in the final week of the study.

It seems reasonable that the patterns of positive references to the United States and of citations of the pragmatic component should appear so similar. Other nations could find common cause and a common interest with our country while the United States was viewed as a victim of these attacks; all countries could identify with the threat such actions pose to world order. Once the United States took aggressive action in response, though, certain newspapers perceived that world opinion no longer reflected interests shared internationally and instead focused on the implications of the seemingly unilateral action by the United States and Great Britain.

The changes in perceptions of world opinion over time do not appear to have been lost on the Bush administration. Prompted in part by the British, the administration released partial evidence linking bin Laden to the attacks on the United States and providing the basis for their suspicion that Afghanistan was harboring him. This effort continued past the dates included in this study, with the release of videotapes of bin Laden discussing the attacks and rejoicing over the resulting loss of life. Given the apparent importance of events to media perspectives on world opinion, it remains the province of future research to test whether this new evidence affected opinion toward the United States's actions in a more positive direction.

Reconsidering the Results: A Clash of Civilizations or a Process of Global Opinion?

For the purposes of comparing the usefulness of the global opinion model versus the civilizations model, the newspapers were combined into three groups. Since the "clash of civilizations" argument posits a conflict between the Western and Muslim civilizations in the aftermath of September 11, 2001, it was deemed appropriate to classify the nations in the following manner for purposes of comparison. The categories include the West (*New York Times, London Times,* Israel's *Ha'aretz Daily,* and *International Herald Tribune*); Muslim civilization (*The Arab News*)[20]; and the other civilizations (the *China Daily* representing Sinic civilization, the *Times of India* representing Hindu civilization, the Argentinean *Nacion* representing Latin American civilization, the Nigerian *Guardian* representing African civilization, and *Pravda* representing Slavic-Orthodox civilization).

Figure 9.4 shows the timing of references to world opinion broken down into these three groups. Two results stand out. First, the timing of references between the Western and other civilizations' newspapers are strikingly similar; indeed, the eta value for the relationship between dates for the two groups barely registers at .024. By contrast, the eta values for the relationships between the Western and Muslim newspapers (.167), and the other civilizations' and Muslim newspapers (.223) both indicate significant differences. Past research on media content regarding world opinion suggests that when the dates of references on a given issue *converge* among two or more media outlets, there is an apparent *consensus* on the agenda for world opinion in those media.[21] Conversely, when the dates of references to world opinion *diverge,* it suggests an apparent *disagreement* on the agenda for world opinion in those media. If the clash of civilizations thesis were correct, one would expect perceptions of the agenda to differ for the West and the Muslim newspapers; however, one would not expect the rest of the newspapers to correspond with the Western perception of this agenda.[22]

There are also significant differences when one compares the evaluations of world opinion toward the United States across these categories. If the clash were primarily between civilizations, one would expect little or no correspondence

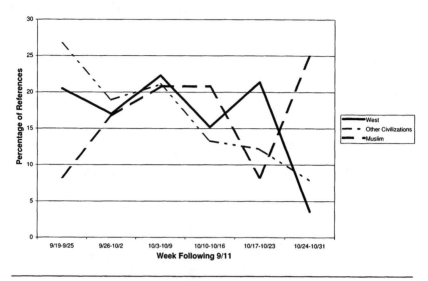

Fig. 9.4 References to world opinion, by Western, Muslim, and other newspapers. Note: The analysis included 287 stories. For the classification of newspapers, see Table 9.1.

between the content of world opinion from nations not involved in the conflict and the content of those who were. However, that is not the case. As Figure 9.5 shows, the percentages of positive and negative references to world opinion on the United States in the Western and other civilizations' groups are virtually the same. Positive references outweigh negative ones by 29.6% to 16.8% in the West, and by 26.1% to 20.3% in the other nations, respectively. In the Muslim newspaper, however, negative references outweigh positive ones by 73.7% to 10.5%. Further, a multiple range analysis indicates significant differences occur between mean evaluations in all the Western and Muslim newspapers, and in all the other civilizations' and Muslim newspapers[23]; by contrast, the Western and other civilizations' newspapers show significant differences in only one case other than the *Arab News.*

When one examines the timing of positive and negative references to the United States, however, a surprisingly different pattern emerges. Figure 9.6 shows the mean evaluations of the United States in each group's newspapers, derived by coding positive references as 1, neutral references as 0, and negative references as –1, and adding and averaging the results. Two findings stand out. First, the *Arab News*'s mean evaluations of world opinion on the United States are much lower than the other groups' evaluations. But a second critical pattern also emerges. The peaks and valleys of evaluations co-vary over time between the Muslim newspaper's evaluations and the other civilizations' newspapers.

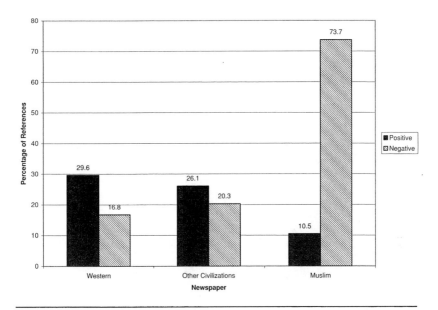

Fig. 9.5   Positive and negative references to world opinion on the United States, by newspapers. Note: The analysis included 213 stories. For the classification of newspapers, see Table 9.1.

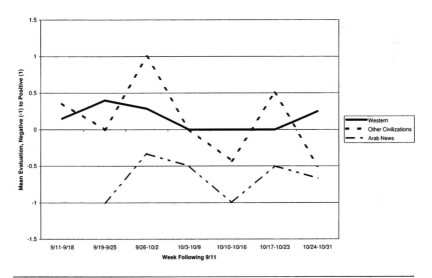

Fig. 9.6   Mean evaluations of world opinion on the United States, by week and civilization. Note: The analysis included 213 stories. For the classification of newspapers, see Table 9.1.

When the *Arab News*'s evaluations become more positive, the other civilizations' evaluations also become more positive; when the *Arab News*'s evaluations become more negative, the other civilizations' evaluations also become more negative. The Western newspapers did not follow this model over time, but rather defined a comparably flat pattern over time, with values ranging from 0 to around .4. As a result, the timing of references shows a weak negative correlation between the Western newspapers and other civilizations' newspapers (tau-b = -0.138, $p = 0.037$); a weak positive correlation between the Western newspapers and the Arab newspaper (tau-b = 0.138, $p = 0.042$); and a strong positive correlation between the rest of the civilizations' newspapers and the Arab newspaper (tau-b = 0.482, $p = 0.000$).[24]

While the previous findings may appear contradictory, they actually define a possible insight into the process of world opinion. When a nation or group of nations is the object of negative world opinion, they generally do not tend to evaluate the ebb and flow of that opinion. When one looks at the general pattern of world opinion in this study, one finds that it is primarily sympathetic to the Western perspective; the general convergence of Western newspapers' evaluations and other civilizations' newspapers for all references to world opinion suggests this conclusion. However, when one focuses primarily on the evaluations of the United States as a specific topic, there is an apparent co-variance between the rise and fall of these evaluations in the Saudi and other civilizations' newspapers over time. As the object of world opinion changes, then, the object nations' newspapers may not perceive the ebb and flow of world opinion, even as other newspapers around the world appear to do so. A closer examination of the manner in which these three groups construct world opinion helps to explain this process further.

Disaggregating the Components of World Opinion in the Three Groups

World opinion functions best when it is focused on a particular nation, leader, or action taken by some participant on the "world stage." Hence, while it was possible to condemn the Taliban regime in Afghanistan for harboring terrorists, it was far more difficult to pinpoint other possible targets against whom there would be an international consensus regarding responsibility for September 11. An example of this problem can be seen in an article in the *Arab News* from October 9, 2001. On the one hand, the reporter notes that after the attacks on Afghanistan:

> Bin Laden and his Taleban (sic) protectors vowed revenge and a holy war. But they looked *increasingly isolated* as most Arab and Muslim states remained circumspect—only Iraq and Iran openly denounced the US-led military action' (10/9/2001; emphasis added).

On the other hand, the choice of new targets was condemned in the paper's perception of world opinion:

Table 9.1 Factor Analyses of Components of World Opinion by Type of Newspaper

		FACTOR 1		FACTOR 2		FACTOR 3
Western newspapers						
	Moral	.711	Isolation	.806	Unit	.768
	Pragmatic	.768	Image	.603		
Arab newspaper						
	Moral	.917	Unit	.682		
	Pragmatic	−.758	Isolation	−.787[26]		
Other newspapers						
	Pragmatic	.761	Isolation	.787	Image	.845
	Power	.763	Unit	−.663	Moral	.616

Notes: *Western newspapers* include the *New York Times,* the *London Times,* and Israel's *Ha'aretz Daily.*
Arab newspapers include *The Arab News.*
Other newspapers include *The China Daily, The Times of India,* the Argentinean *Nacion,* the Nigerian *Guardian,*
Pravda and *The International Herald Tribune.*

> European diplomats said any attempt to extend the campaign by targeting Iraq,
> as some US officials have suggested, *would blow apart the global coalition against
> terrorism,* and alienate not only Arab and Muslim states but also key European
> partners including Russia (*ibid.*; emphases added).

In such an atmosphere, the most visible actors involved in the conflict—in this
case, the United States—became a natural focus for world opinion, both positive
and negative. It is natural that American and Western newspapers in general
might miss this focus; it is equally natural that newspapers from other regions
of the world, Muslim and non-Muslim, focused upon it.

In order to analyze the effects of the problems of defining terrorism, a factor analysis was performed to compare the ways in which the three groups of
newspapers constructed the concept following September 11. This analysis is
designed to reduce the references to the six components of world opinion that
generally compose the different newspapers' perspectives on world opinion.
From these factors one may interpret the values and interests each group of
newspapers reflects as it constructs its perception of world opinion. The results,
presented in Table 9.1, indicate that the different groups constructed their usages
and discourse on world opinion from its components in different ways.

The Western newspapers' factors were defined in the following manner:

- *Opinion Consensus Factor*—consisting of the moral and pragmatic
  components, both with positive loadings. This factor illustrates that
  the Western newspapers perceived a close alliance between the value
  issues and the interest issues of all the nations in the world on terrorism
  in this instance.

- *Image Projection Factor*—consisting of the threat of isolation and the nation's image, both with positive loadings. This factor illustrates how the Western newspapers perceived that their very identities and images in world opinion were tied to the unambiguous stance against terrorism as they wished to define it, since those who disagreed risked the threat of international isolation.
- *Unit Definition Factor*—consisting of just the world as a unit, with a positive loading. This factor indicates the role of the international community in the Western newspapers' perceptions in enforcing this consensus.

Taken together, these three factors define a region whose perception of world opinion requires them to link their very identities and images to the international community's condemnation of their definition of terrorism, and support for the actions they deem necessary to combat it. These roles are articulated in terms of the international status they create in an article in the *International Herald Tribune:*

> Parallel to the United States' campaign in Afghanistan against terrorism, Europe's leading countries—Britain, Germany, France. . .—are using their engagement in the American-led coalition *to strengthen their status in the world's hierarchy of power.*
>
> In the case of France, the stakes involve sustaining rather than widening a first-rank role in the strategic equation . . . For Britain, the goal was described as taking a new handhold on leadership in Europe . . . In German terms, Chancellor Gerhard Schroeder's pledge of willingness to take full military risks in combating terrorism beyond NATO's borders represented a gesture of emancipation from the limited international role the country has played since the defeat of Hitler . . . Germany . . . could feel free to move gradually toward a level of global political influence corresponding to its vast economic capacity (10/12/2001; emphases added).

Not surprisingly, the *Arab News* perceived the role of world opinion differently. Its references portrayed an awareness of the dangers of a Western scramble for international status in world opinion on this issue, as shown in the factors derived:

- *Opinion Ambiguity Factor*—consisting of the moral component with a positive loading and the pragmatic component with a negative loading. This configuration is common in cases where a nation's newspaper perceives a conflict between the interests and the values shared by the world. In this case, the Arab newspaper perceives that while it shares the values of fighting terrorism, it might not share the interests of other countries in how to go about this task.
- *Community Ambiguity Factor I*—consisting of the world as a unit with a positive loading and the threat of international isolation with a negative

loading. This configuration reflects the desire to be part of a global community, while not wishing to be threatened with international isolation if the conflict attached a stigma to Muslim nations.

In essence, the *Arab News* recognized the moral issue of terrorism, but is generally suspicious of the methods that might be used to combat it, and any resulting condemnation that might be directed toward Saudi Arabia or other Muslim nations as a result. This conflict is evident in a statement by the Imam of the Grand Mosque in Makkah, who called upon world leaders not to resort to violence in response to the terror attacks against the United States on September 11, "We should exercise restraint and look at things very deeply, we should give priority to public interests and promote world peace and security." Saudis warned Muslims "not to mix up the concepts of real terrorism and legitimate jihad (holy war)," which he said was governed by clear rules and ethics. "[Those who practice terrorism] do not consider the grave dangers to the future of Islam and Muslims, especially Muslim minorities around the world," the Imam said. "*Officials in Islamic countries have voiced concern over an anti-Muslim backlash in the West after the September 11 attacks*" (9/29/2001; emphases added).

The ambiguity of the value issues when trying to define terrorism versus "legitimate jihad" creates a situation in which the interests of Muslim nations and those of the West risked divergence. Hence, the Arab newspaper perceived world opinion to be more ambiguous than the Western newspapers, and more likely to threaten Islamic nations if allowed to isolate actors or dictate other punishments by the "international community."

The other civilizations' newspapers perceive world opinion as having influence in two ways, through the power of the interests it defines for all nations, and through the importance of taking a moral stance against terrorism for the nations' images. However, these newspapers also expressed mistrust about the threat of international isolation by the world community:

- *Interest Protection Factor*—consisting of the pragmatic component to world opinion and the power of world opinion, both with positive loadings. This configuration indicates that the other civilizations' newspapers perceived the common interests in fighting terrorism as constituting the influence world opinion had over their actions.
- *Community Ambiguity Factor II*—a factor similar to the factor in the Arab newspaper, except that in this case, isolation has a positive factor loading and the world as a unit has a negative factor loading. This result indicates some mistrust, perhaps of the Western interpretations of world opinion regarding terrorism, and the possible direction the threat of isolation might take.
- *Image Protection Factor*—consisting of the nation's image and the moral component of world opinion, both with positive loadings. This configuration indicates the need these nations' newspapers feel to make a

statement condemning terrorism, as a means of protecting their images and identities.

One can see in these results the power which world opinion has due to the interests nations share in combating terrorism, and the fear of not condemning the attacks and putting one's own nation's image at risk. As an editorial in the Nigerian *Guardian* stated:

> When a thing like this happens, it is impossible for people to take a neutral position. It is either you support what has been done or you are against it. And we have seen the outpouring of sympathy from all over the world that has greeted this tragedy.
> There are several reasons why some people may choose to jubilate at the misfortune that has hit America ... These are arguments which will make for scoring impressive points if one is writing a term paper at a university. However, the tragedy that took place last Tuesday was not an academic exercise. It is for real. (9/16/2001).

The editorial states the necessity of making a clear statement of where one stands on this issue, and the genuine interests of all people at stake that give the problem its prominence and power to influence world opinion. As Soh Chang Rok, a South Korean specialist in international relations was quoted as saying in the *International Herald Tribune,* "There's enormous international pressure to help out the U. S. So we have to keep silent" about the buildup of Japanese forces in their participation in retaliating against terrorism (9/28/2001). Rhuslan Khasbulatov argued in an editorial in *Pravda* that one must address the unequal divisions of wealth and power in the world, which

> reflect the colossal accumulation of inner antagonism between the different parts of this world community. They take account of the variety of opinions not only in the countries of "the enlightened West," but also in the developing world, where the concentration of world poverty happens; as well as the "Islamic sector" of the world community (10/26/2001).

There is evident mistrust of any notion of a "world community" that does not work to treat all nations as part of a "single, integral organism" (*ibid.*). This mistrust is reflected in the conflict between international isolation as a threat and the world being considered as a unit.

From these analyses, one can hypothesize about how the different constructions of world opinion fit to reflect a process. For the Western newspapers, there is no ambiguity about the moral or interest issues involved in the fight against terrorism, and these nations endeavor to project their image as leaders as a means of gaining international status. For the Arab newspaper, there was considerable mistrust in the opinion leadership being offered by the Western nations, and a fear that it might be directed toward the interests of Muslim countries. The rest of the civilizations' newspapers fall somewhere in between—

aware of the interests they share in fighting terrorism, and protective of their images leading them to condemn such actions, yet wary of Western leadership that might potentially define the international community in a manner that threatens them. The center position of the other civilizations' newspapers helps to explain why their references to world opinion in general follow those of the West. But it also explains why, when the issue is focused upon the United States and its leadership, their references to world opinion tend to correspond to the Arab newspaper's references over time and in content.

Conclusions

It is natural for American citizens to react to a trauma like the attacks on September 11 by feeling under siege from a hostile world. It is also natural for Americans to seek to partition the world into allies and enemies, those "for us" and those "against us." Absent the Berlin Wall, the borders—however loosely defined—of clashing civilizations that harbor either good will or bad will toward us could provide a comfortable means of ordering and framing our understanding of the world and its dangers.

The preceding analysis suggests that these reactions oversimplify the way other nations view the world's intentions toward the United States. World opinion about the United States, or any subject for that matter, is an ongoing process that potentially affects international images, and shifts it in response to events. An international consensus might arise through a negotiation among the different perspectives on world opinion. The evidence here suggests that such a consensus eluded American efforts, at least through October 31, 2001. This however does not herald an ongoing or impending "clash of civilizations," however. Indeed, several newspapers from different civilizations explicitly reject this interpretation of the attacks. Consider this statement from the *Arab News*:

> The specter of the "Clash of Cultures" as predicted by Samuel Huntington should be treated like the work of a fortuneteller. His thesis is no more than Armageddon dressed up as social science (9/28/2001).

The Israeli *Ha-aretz* expressed a similar sentiment within a week of the Arab newspaper:

> Public debate was ushered down the wrong lane immediately after the attacks in the United States, the moment formulations such as ... "clash of civilizations" took hegemonic hold. Thanks to these bin Laden notched up a major triumph: a terrorist gang that does nothing to help the population in the name of which it purportedly murders was transformed by the West and anointed the representative of a billion people (10/4/2001).

The problem was acute enough for Arab officials to meet in Cairo on October 29, 2001, "to discuss the threat of a 'conflict of civilizations' following the September 11 attacks on the United States." This effort was justified by the concern from delegates that "Today the world is burning" and their desire "to pour a little water on the fire" (*Arab News*, 10/29/2001).

If potentially opposing sides in the conflict do not wish to have the attacks interpreted as a "clash of civilizations," and the process of world opinion in the major newspapers here suggests otherwise, why does this danger persist? Huntington stated in a CNN broadcast that:

> The events of Black Tuesday do not reflect the clash of civilizations he spoke about. The reason for this is the speedy condemnation of the events by all Muslim countries. But the events themselves are very dangerous... and could lead to a clash of civilizations if the zealous on both sides chose confrontation (*Arab News*, 10/9/2001).

The critical deciding point, then, appears to be the interpretations of the actors involved and the rest of the world that observes their actions. As David McDowell stated, "There is only a clash of civilizations if that is the way people wish to interpret recent events" (*ibid.*).

When all is said and done, interpreting the meaning of the September 11 attacks is a matter of choice and consensus internationally—that is, decisions to be rendered in *world opinion*. World opinion is the key factor determining the manner in which we construct the emerging global configuration; considerations such as a "clash of civilizations" or other interpretations become secondary to this force, and therein lies the danger when dealing with the issue of terrorism.

This analysis suggests that an international consensus on terrorism had, until at least October 31, 2001, eluded nations in the world community for two reasons. A clear definition of terrorism must precede its condemnation, and such a definition has not been reached. In a related fashion, even the general condemnation of terrorism is directed against a *method*, not a nation, leader, or some other actor on the international stage. One must recall here our working definition of world opinion: *the moral judgments of observers which actors must heed in the international arena, or risk isolation as a nation.* When the actors are not clearly associated with any nation, and the definition of the method becomes problematic, the influence of world opinion is likely to be limited. To interpret the attacks as a "clash of civilizations" by default is equivalent to a cry of despair.

The tragic events of September 11, 2001, and the subsequent continuation of terror as a weapon, suggests that resolving the underlying problem of definition demands the full attention of world opinion and the international community. Secretary General Kofi Annan, in a speech to the United Nations General Assembly on the September 11 attacks, stated:

> Terrorism will be defeated if the international community summons the will to unite in a broad coalition... Terrorism is not an issue that divides humanity but unites it. We are in a moral struggle to fight an evil that is anathema to all faiths... This was an attack on humanity, and humanity must respond to it as one.[25]

World opinion can bridge the boundaries of supposed civilizations, for they are relevant only if we make them so. That general self-knowledge is clearly necessary to build a consensus on defining and denouncing terror as a weapon; whether it is sufficient to reach this end remains an open question.

Notes

1. John Vinocur. "The New World Order is a Clash of Civilizations." *The International Herald Tribune.* 13 September 2001. P. 1
2. Samuel P. Huntington. *The Clash of Civilizations and the Remaking of World Order.* New York: Simon and Schuster, 1996. P. 39.
3. Samuel P. Huntington. "The Clash of Civilizations?" *Foreign Affairs.* Summer 1993. P. 191.
4. See, for instance, Frank Louis Rusciano. 1998. *World Opinion and the Emerging International Order.* Westport: Praeger; Hedley Bull and Adam Watson. 1984. *The Expansion of International Society.* Oxford: Clarendon Press.
5. Mayall. *Nationalism and International Society.* P. 19.
6. Frank Louis Rusciano, et. al. *World Opinion and the Emerging International Order.* Westport: Praeger, 1998. P. 164.
7. Mayall. P. 7. Emphasis added.
8. Rusciano. *World Opinion.* P. 24.
9. Rusciano. *World Opinion.* P. 156.
10. Due to archival problems, the first week after September 11, 2001 was unfortunately not included in the analysis of the *Arab News.* All subsequent analysis thus does not include this newspaper's results for the first week.
11. It will be useful, no doubt, for some future project to include a number of Muslim newspapers, but availability, and time and language constraints limited the present study to one paper. The Nigerian *Guardian* is also published in a nation with a pre-dominantly Muslim population. It is not included within the "Islamic civilization" newspapers, though, for two reasons. First, Nigeria is placed within "African civilization" in Huntington's typology; second, the *Guardian* was chosen specifically because it is a secular newspaper from Nigeria. Certainly, there are newspapers in that nation written from the Islamic perspective, but they were not chosen for that reason and because they are not generally newspapers of record like the *Guardian.*
12. Edward S. Herman, and Noam Chomsky. 1988. *Manufacturing Consent: The Political Economy of Mass Media.* New York: Random House.
13. In order to assure inter-coder reliability on these items, all results were reviewed, first in the research group, and then by the principal investigator, for consistency of interpretation.
14. The remaining 50% of the references were neutral. Only those stories that evaluated the United States were included in this portion of the analysis, for a total of 213.
15. The eta value for these results was .410.
16. See Frank Louis Rusciano and Roberta Fiske-Rusciano. "Towards a Notion of 'World Opinion.'" *International Journal of Public Opinion Research.* 2 (1990): 305–322.
17. See Frank Louis Rusciano and Bosah Ebo. "National Consciousness, International Image, and the Construction of Identity." In Frank Louis Rusciano. *World Opinion and the Emerging International Order.* Chapter 3.
18. Frank Louis Rusciano and Fiske-Rusciano, Roberta. "Towards a Notion of World Opinion." In Rusciano, Frank Louis. *World Opinion and the Emerging International Order.* Chapter 1.
19. See, for instance, Frank Louis Rusciano and Roberta Fiske-Rusciano. "Towards a Notion of 'World Opinion.'" *International Journal of Public Opinion Research.* 2 (1990): 305–322.
20. Due to archival problems, the first week after September 11, 2001 was unfortunately not included in the analysis of the *Arab News.* All subsequent analysis thus does not include this newspaper's results for the first week.

21. See Frank Louis Rusciano. "Media Perspectives on 'World Opinion' During the Kuwaiti Crisis." In *Media and the Persian Gulf War*, Robert E. Denton, ed. (Westport: Praeger, 1993): 71–87.
22. Unfortunately, it is impossible to test whether the dates of references to world opinion converge on the attacks in the first week, since that week is missing from the archival data for the *Arab News*. Anecdotal evidence suggests it is likely they did converge for the Western civilization's and other civilizations' newspapers; it is more difficult to predict the results for the *Arab News*. The important point here is the divergence that occurs between the Muslim newspapers and the others following September 19, 2001.
23. Tukey HSD was used in the ANOVA analysis for these comparisons. When one examined the differences among the individual "civilizations" in the "other" category, the results were remarkably the same. The Western newspapers differed significantly in evaluating world opinion on the United States only from the *Arab News* and *Pravda*. By contrast, the *Arab News*, besides differing significantly from the Western newspapers, also differed significantly from the Indian, Chinese, and Argentinean newspapers; only the Nigerian *Guardian* and *Pravda* did not show significant differences there.
24. The analysis excludes the first week of the study, where archival problems interfered with results from the *Arab News;* also, cases were weighted by the total number of cases per week for the three groups.
25. Kofi Annan. Address to the United Nations General Assembly. October 1, 2001.

References

Avinieri, Shlomo. 1991. *Proceedings of the Conference on Europe in the New World Order.* Georgetown University. Washington, DC.
Barber, Benjamin R. 1995. *Jihad vs. McWorld.* New York: Random House.
Bartley, R. L. 1993. "The Case for Optimism: The West Should Believe in Itself." *Foreign Affairs.* September/October: 15–17.
Bogart, Leo. 1966. "Is There a World Opinion?" *Polls.* 1:1–9.
Bull, Hedley and Adam Watson. 1984. *The Expansion of International Society.* Oxford: Clarendon Press.
Davison, W. Phillips. 1973. "International and Public Opinion." In *Handbook of Communication.* Eds. Ithiel del Sola Pool, et al. Chicago: Rand McNally.
Doty, R. L. 1993. "Foreign Policy as a Social Construction: A Post-Positivist Analysis of U.S. Counter-insurgency Policy in the Philippines." *International Studies Quarterly.* 37:297–320.
Grader, Sheila. 1988. "The English School of International Relations: Evidence and Evaluation." *Review of International Studies.* 14: 29–44.
Herman, Edward S. and Chomsky, Noam. 1988. *Manufacturing Consent: The Political Economy of Mass Media.* New York, NY: Random House.
Hill, Christopher J. 1996. "World Opinion and the Empire of Circumstance." *International Affairs:* 109–131.
Hinckley, Ron. 1991. "World public opinion and the Persian Gulf crisis." *Proceedings of the American Association for Public Opinion Research.* Phoenix, Arizona.
Huntington, Samuel P. 1993. "The Clash of Civilizations?" *Foreign Affairs.* Summer: 22–49.
Huntington, Samuel P.1993. "If Not Civilizations, What?" In *The Clash of Civilizations? The Debate: A Foreign Affairs Reader.* New York: Council on Foreign Relations.
Huntington, Samuel P. 1996. *The Clash of Civilizations and the Remaking of World Order.* New York: Simon and Schuster.
Inglehart, Ronald. 1977. *The Silent Revolution: Changing Values and Political Styles Among Western Publics.* Princeton: Princeton University Press.
Jones, Roy E. 1981. "The English School of International Relations: A Case for Closure." *Review of International Studies.* 7: 1–12.
Knudson, Tonny Brems. "International Society and International Solidarity: Recapturing the Solidarist Origins of the English School." Paper presented at the workshop *International Relations in Europe: Concepts, Schools and Institutions.* 28th Joint Sessions of the European Consortium for Political Research. 14–19 April, 2000. Copenhagen, Denmark.

Mayall, James. 1990. *Nationalism and International Society.* New York: Cambridge University Press.

Morgenthau, Hans J. "Is World Public Opinion a Myth?" *The New York Times Magazine.* 25 March 1962. p. 23.

Obasanjo, O. 1991. *Proceedings of the Conference on Europe in the New World Order.* Georgetown University. Washington, DC.

Rusciano, Frank Louis. 1997. "First and Third World Newspapers on World Opinion: 'Imagined Communities' in the Cold War and Post-Cold War Eras." *Political Communication.* 14(2):171–190.

Rusciano, Frank Louis. 1996. "Media Observations on World Opinion during the Kuwaiti Crisis: Political Communication and the Emerging International Order." *Southeastern Political Review.* 24(3):505–530.

Rusciano, Frank Louis. 1998. *World Opinion and the Emerging International Order.* Westport: Praeger.

Rusciano, Frank Louis. 2000. "Die Neuaushandlung der deutschen Nationalidentaet nach 1989." In *Deutsche Umbrueche im 20. Jahrhundert.* Koln: Boehlau Verlag GmbH & Cie.

Rusciano, Frank Louis. 2001. "A World Beyond Civilizations? New Directions in Research on World Opinion." *International Journal of Public Opinion Research.* 13: 10–24.

Rusciano, Frank Louis and Fiske-Rusciano, Roberta. 1990. "Towards a Notion of World Opinion." *International Journal of Public Opinion Research.* 2: 305–322.

Rusciano, Frank Louis and John Crothers Pollock. 2000. "World Opinion During Times of Crisis." In Doris Graber, ed. *Media Power and Politics, 4th ed.* Washington, DC: Congressional Quarterly Press.

Rusciano, Frank Louis, and John Crothers Pollock. 1997. "Media Perspectives on World Opinion During the Recent Bosnian Crisis." *Current World Leaders: International Issues.* 40 (2):56–72.

Rusciano, Frank Louis, Fiske-Rusciano, Roberta; and Wang, Minmin. 1997. "The Impact of 'World Opinion' on National Identity." *Harvard International Journal of Press/Politics.* 2(3):71–92.

Wilcox, Clyde; Tanaka, Aiji; and Allsop, Dee. 1993. "World Opinion in the Gulf Crisis." *Journal of Conflict Resolution.* 37(1):69–93.

CHAPTER 10

Explaining 9/11*

MICHAEL W. TRAUGOTT
TED BRADER

As discussed in the introduction, acts of terrorism do not require extensive media coverage to satisfy all of the goals of those who perpetrate them. Nonetheless, the news media and their coverage can be "considered modern tools of terrorists" (Picard 1993: 6) as they magnify the size of the audience for a terrorist act. This section of the book focuses on the impact of news frames on the public, including how far news framing of 9/11 influenced what the American public understood about these events (in this chapter), whether exposure to news about terrorism reinforced American anxieties (Chapter 13), and whether it weakened or strengthened confidence in U.S. government officials and institutions (chapter 12).[1]

As illustrated by the previous section of the book, much analyses of the coverage of terrorism has been comparative, typically focusing on whether and how events get framed (Weimann and Brosius 1991; Enders and Sandler 2002). An earlier review suggests that overseas terrorist activity goes largely unreported in US news outlets, even in papers of record like the *New York Times* (Kelly and Mitchell 1981). The coverage of terrorism during the 1970s and 1980s in the *New York Times* and the *Times* of London occupied less than half of one percent of the available space (Crelisten 1987). When coverage does occur, conventional media models of selection and prominence tend to explain the form it takes. The standard criteria of newsworthiness are thought to apply to a news story about terrorism, including timeliness, proximity, impact, conflict, sensationalism, and novelty (Gans 1979). Because of this, studies have found few differences between US news organizations covering the same events (Altheide 1982; Atwater 1987). Given the violent nature of terrorist actions, "deviance" has often been used as the term to describe the confluence of impact, conflict, sensationalism and novelty that makes them newsworthy (Shoemaker et al. 1987). The

*This analysis is based on data collected with support from the Institute for Social Research, the Russell Sage Foundation, and the Howard R. Marsh Center for the Study of Journalistic Performance in the Department of Communication Studies at the University of Michigan. The analyses are the sole responsibility of the authors. This paper benefited from conversations with our colleagues Paul Huth and Doug Lemke and the comments of participants in the symposium "Restless Searchlight: Terrorism, the Media, and Public Life," held at Harvard University, August 28, 2002. We gratefully acknowledge the research assistance of Eric Groenendyk and Heather Colleen Schaar.

prominence of the coverage, its extensiveness, and duration are related to the number of fatalities or injuries involved in an incident, especially of a proximate population.

Coverage tends to focus on events and details, often from the perspective of the government under attack (Paletz et al. 1985). Studies of how perpetrators are labeled (e.g., as "guerillas," "terrorists," or "insurgents") suggest the selective use of these terms by journalists in ways that correspond to the interests of the government (Epstein 1977). Picard (1988) describes a three-stage process of coverage of extended terrorist actions that begins with an initial emphasis on the details of the incident, lasting about two days, followed by an emphasis on government-initiated reports of how they are responding, with an eventual third phase in which background reporting may focus on "explaining" the event. In general, the coverage of motives, goals, or explanations gets short shrift. Paletz (1985) found that less than 6 percent of newspaper coverage of selected terrorist activities was devoted to explicit explanations, and the vast majority of coverage (almost 75 percent) ignored discussion of causes or objectives altogether. Atwater (1987) found that less than 3 percent of network television coverage was devoted to these kinds of explanations.

The inability to produce stories that contain extended analysis or explanation of the causes of actions can be frustrating to correspondents as well. In the case of the September 11 attacks, there was press criticism of journalists' use of airtime for attempts to explain why al Qaeda targeted the United States. As foreign correspondent Christiane Amanpour (2002) describes it:

> We tried to answer a question that Americans were asking and that is, why do they hate us? What is going on over there? It was roundly criticized, and very few people for the first few weeks dared to put in their newspapers or on their televisions any kind of analysis or background reasoning, context for some of those negative feelings that go on about the United States.

These concerns about characteristic patterns of coverage and the nature of news content are important because of the perceived impact on the public exposed to such news frames. These potential effects range from the formation of attitudes about the perpetrators of terrorist acts or their cause, support for government security policies, and reactions such as anxiety and perceived threat to personal safety. In the typical instance of terrorism, the vast majority of individuals are not exposed directly to events as they unfold but instead receive their information through the mass media. A number of factors can explain how individuals understand such mediated information, including their general ability to process and integrate new information with prior knowledge and opinions (Converse 1964) and their level of political knowledge that can help to interpret and organize the new content (Price and Zaller 1993). Few studies have looked closely at the effects of terrorism coverage on the beliefs and opinions of citizens, but there is a growing set of studies, including later chapters in this book, which indicate that anxiety can be induced by exposure to terrorism (Slone 2000, Lerner et al. 2002).

In particular, in this chapter we are interested in whether or not elements of the media coverage of the terrorist attacks are related to the ability of American citizens to explain what happened on September 11. We had two primary questions: To what extent did the American coverage provide information about explanations for the attacks? And did exposure to media content help Americans explain about why the attacks occurred? Few Americans had any personal acquaintance with Muslim fundamentalists or had heard of Osama bin Laden, al Qaeda, or even the Taliban before September 11. Yet the novelty and enormity of the event and the level of fatalities may have forced many citizens to search for an explanation about why the attacks happened. Would news consumers be able to use such information, in addition to the value of personal resources such as education and political knowledge, to construct a story to explain why the attacks took place?

Research Design

The analysis presented here is based on two data collections that attempt to capture how the US national news covered the events of September 11, 2001, and how Americans responded to those events. As an initial assessment of coverage, we conducted a content analysis of all issues of *U.S. News & World Report* that appeared between September 10, 2001, and April 17, 2002. This involved twenty-eight regular weekly issues of the magazine as well as two special issues devoted to the attacks, for a total of thirty issues across this time period.[2] The purpose was to construct a national time-series of coverage of the attacks and their aftermath in a way that could be analyzed in conjunction with the survey data measuring public reactions and specifically how Americans understood or explained the events. The survey was conducted first to uncover citizen responses in the immediate wake of the attacks; the coding of news coverage followed in the summer of 2002. A set of codes had been developed to correspond to the answers survey respondents gave when asked about the "reasons for the attacks." Each news article was later coded for references to explanations or motivations for the attacks using the same coding scheme as had been applied to the survey data.[3]

The survey, carried out as a project entitled *"How Americans Respond"* (HAR), was conducted in two waves. Data from the initial survey were collected from a national probability sample of the adult population of the United States residing in telephone households that was interviewed between September 17 and October 13, 2001, with the vast majority of the interviews completed by October 8.[4] The interviews averaged thirty minutes in length, and they covered a number of topics, including economic attitudes and behavior, personal health, evaluations of groups in American society and overseas, reactions to the attacks, and support for a number of likely and possible government policies and responses. A total of 752 interviews were completed with a response for the survey of 59 percent.

A second wave of the survey was conducted between March 11 and April 16, 2002, based on reinterviews of respondents from the first wave, supplemented by a small sample of new interviews. A total of 764 interviews were conducted, composed of 613 recontact (panel) interviews and 151 new interviews. This was again a thirty-minute interview, with about two-thirds of the content repeated from wave 1 and about ten minutes of new content added to the questionnaire.

In the first wave, respondents were asked how they had heard about the attacks, and then were asked the following open-ended question:

"People have different explanations for the terrorist attacks on New York and Washington, DC. What do you think are the reasons for it?"

Interviewing staff recorded up to eight answers mentioned by respondents. The team of investigators later coded these answers into a set of broad categories (see the appendix for a complete listing). The question and the coding procedure were repeated in wave 2 of the survey. A second key measure is the respondent's attention to news about the attacks. The following question was asked in wave 1:

"How closely have you been following the news about the recent terrorist attacks on New York and Washington, DC? Very closely, somewhat closely, a little, or not closely at all?"

A slightly different version of this question was asked in wave 2 of the study, approximately six months later:

"How closely have you been following the news about the "war on terrorism"? Very closely, somewhat closely, a little, or not closely at all?"

Other survey measures relevant to this analysis include an index of political knowledge, computed as the sum of correct answers to three questions about the positions held by relatively visible political figures,[5] as well as each respondent's age, level of education, race, and gender.

Patterns in the News Coverage and Citizen Responses

The results from the content analysis presented in Figure 10.1 show that there was immediate coverage of the attacks in *U.S. News & World Report*, and as expected, it consumed a significant portion of the magazine in the early weeks. Content related to September 11 found its way into several sections of the magazine, including "Nation and World," "Money and Business," "Culture and Ideas," "Health and Medicine," and "Science and Technology." In the first week after the event, roughly half of the coverage (47 percent) consisted of articles about the attacks. The proportion of the coverage devoted to the attacks grew to 85 percent by the fourth week, not counting complete coverage in special issues. Across the first five weeks, almost two out of three articles (65 percent) contained

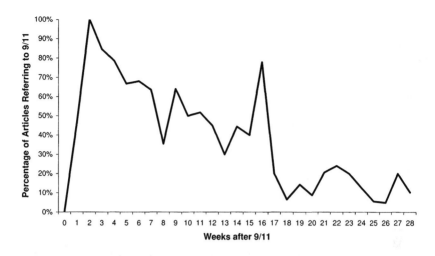

Fig. 10.1 The volume of coverage about 9/11 in *U.S. News & World Report.* Source: *How Americans Respond* content analysis.

a reference to the attacks. This initial surge in coverage of the attacks tapered off gradually through the end of the year and then oscillated between roughly 10 and 20 percent in the early months of 2002.

Despite all of this coverage, however, very few of the articles contained any information that provided explicit reasons or explanations for the attacks. In this early period, which corresponds to the fieldwork for wave 1 of the survey, approximately half of the articles (46 percent) about the attacks also contained a reason or explanation for them. The range of reasons and explanations was great, including inadequacies of US policies such as immigration or airport security; references to the motivations of groups like al Qaeda or individuals like Osama bin Laden; and cultural or religious explanations for opposition to US policies and hostility toward Americans. Many of the early articles contained multiple references to explanations for the attacks, but the overall number was not very large. Moreover, the number of reasons that were discussed dropped rapidly, as shown in Figure 10.2. By the middle of October, five weeks after the attacks, the number of explanations mentioned was five or fewer; by January, the number was essentially zero. For the remainder of the analysis in this chapter, we focus on the content of the coverage in the first five weeks after the attacks that corresponded to the field period for wave 1 of the surveys.

All told there were forty-seven articles in this period that contained ninety-four different explanations or reasons for the attacks.[6] Table 10.1 shows the distribution of explanations offered by the *U.S. News* coverage and by the public as captured by the first two waves of the surveys. The original explanations from

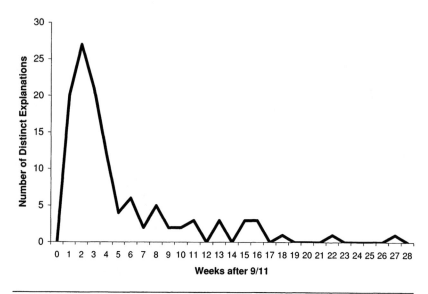

Fig. 10.2   The number of distinct explanations mentioned in coverage by *U.S. News & World Report.* Source: *How Americans Respond* content analysis.

both sources have been sorted into broader categories here (see the appendix for examples of more specific explanations that were classified into each category). The type of explanation most commonly cited in the news was that the US faces the threat of terrorist attacks because of inadequacies in airport security, immigration checks, and intelligence gathering (20.2 percent of all mentions appearing in 40.4 percent of all the articles). This set of reasons "explains" 9/11 in terms of those factors, particularly weaknesses in US defenses, that may have facilitated the success of the attacks. This was closely followed by explanations that focused on attributing responsibility to perpetrating individuals or groups, particularly Osama bin Laden (representing 19.1 percent of all reasons appearing in 38.4 percent of all articles). A third popular type of explanation centered on motives for the actions, including "hatred" or the desire to "start a war" or "destroy our way of life" (16.1 percent of all mentions appearing in 34 percent of the articles).

Table 10.1 shows similarities, but also some clear differences, between the reasons offered in the news and those offered by survey respondents. The most frequent type of explanation offered by the public fixed on motives such as the terrorists' hatred for the United States (slightly under half of respondents in wave 1, slightly over half in wave 2). Only one-in-five survey respondents cited "national security threats" posed by inadequate security or intelligence,

Table 10.1 Explanations for September 11

CATEGORY	U.S. NEWS COVERAGE COUNT N.	MENTIONS %	ARTICLES %	SURVEY WAVE 1 COUNT N.	MENTIONS %	RESPONDENTS %	SURVEY WAVE 2 COUNT N.	MENTIONS %	RESPONDENTS %
National security threats	19	20.2	40.4	29	2.5	4.8	43	3.2	7.0
Terrorist individuals or groups	17	19.1	38.4	58	4.9	9.5	70	5.3	11.4
Hatred, enmity	15	16.1	34.0	296	24.7	48.4	331	24.4	52.6
Aspects of terrorists	11	12.8	25.5	124	10.2	20.4	144	11.0	23.3
Religious Issues	11	11.8	23.4	136	12.2	22.1	140	10.7	22.8
Policies of other countries	8	8.6	17.0	17	1.4	2.9	26	2.0	4.2
Perceived problems with the U.S.	4	4.2	8.6	42	3.5	6.9	76	5.9	12.4
U.S. international policies	4	4.4	8.4	137	11.3	22.5	121	9.3	20.0
Differences between 'us' and 'them'	1	1.1	2.1	89	7.3	14.5	74	6.1	12.7
Aspects of human nature	1	1.1	2.1	43	3.7	7.2	31	2.4	5.0
Interest in control or power	–	–	–	65	5.4	10.6	88	6.7	14.5
Lack of understanding of others	–	–	–	42	3.5	6.9	64	4.8	10.4
Revenge	–	–	–	31	2.5	5.0	36	2.8	6.0
Other	1	1.1	2.1	18	1.5	2.9	16	1.2	2.6
Don't know	–	–	–	68	5.7	11.1	36	2.7	5.9
No Answer	–	–	–	8	0.6	0.3	21	1.6	3.4
Total responses	92	100	202	1,203	100	196	611	100	214.2

Note: Explanations given in the first month of *U.S. News and World Report* coverage and in both waves of the panel survey.
Source: *How Americans Respond* Panel Survey.

and only one-in-ten cited terrorist individuals or groups, including Osama bin Laden—both sets of reasons that were offered much more frequently in the news coverage. One other noteworthy difference in the distributions, produced by the distinct types of sources from which these explanations were culled, is that the survey respondents could admit that they "didn't know" what might explain the attacks, while journalists would not be expected to write this in news stories. One-in-nine respondents simply said they did not know the reason for the attacks in the first interview; this dropped to 5.9 percent by the second interview.

Comparison of these two sets of data in their present form is complicated by a number of factors. The conceptual link between the particular explanations offered in the news media and individuals' own explanations that may be derived from media exposure is ambiguous. It is also unclear how the two aggregate datasets should be methodologically related to one another, especially given the fact that multiple responses were possible. For example, there were not enough volunteered responses (about two on average) from each individual to be confident in using response order as an indicator of salience. Therefore, as far as explaining why individuals offered the particular explanations they did, we can use these data only to say that there is a significant overlap between certain popular explanations in news coverage and in public explanations, though there are notable exceptions to this overlap. However, taking note of changes in the volume of coverage that focused on explanations, we can potentially say something about why individuals offered more or fewer explanations and we turn now to multivariate analysis of the richness of respondent explanations.

We tested two principal hypotheses about the impact of media exposure on the number of explanations provided by respondents, one focusing on attentiveness to the news and the other focused on timing. For this portion of the analysis, we focus exclusively on the panel respondents in our surveys. In the panel portion of the study, there were 613 respondents interviewed right after the September attacks, during the period when both coverage and discussion of explanations were heaviest, and then reinterviewed six months later.

The first hypothesis is that greater attention to news about the attacks or the subsequent "war on terrorism" should provide individuals with a richer (i.e., more numerous) set of explanations for 9/11. Self-reported attention to news is a somewhat crude proxy for media exposure. Even so, our concern in this analysis is with the impact of overall levels of news exposure on the levels of information at individuals' fingertips. Thus, use of general attentiveness as a measure is appropriate in this case, because we are not trying to explain the impact of exposure to particular sources. Inclusion of the political knowledge measure also helps to control for some potentially confounding effects of interest in public affairs (as reflected in news attentiveness).

The second hypothesis is that the timing of the initial (wave 1) interview should affect the number of explanations respondents offer. As we saw in the content analysis of *U.S. News and World Report* above, the number of distinct explanations provided in the national new stream increased a great deal in the first couple weeks. Moreover, most of the explanations that would be discussed in news coverage were discussed over the course of the first month. We expect, therefore, that citizens on average were in a better position to make some sense of reasons for the attacks in mid-October than they had been immediately following 9/11. There is little doubt that such accumulated understanding probably owes something to the ordinary conversations citizens had with each other after watching the news, as well as from direct learning from exposure to the news itself. Since the amount of coverage tapered off significantly by the time of the second interview, attention to news reports on the attacks and timing of the first interview should lose much of their explanatory power.

In line with this hypothesis, initial coverage discussing explanations for the attacks was significant but hardly overwhelming. The distribution of articles that referred to the September 11 attacks and the subset of those that contained explanations for the attacks is shown in Figure 10.3. The distribution of articles spikes in the fifth week at forty-four articles, or 39 percent of the total number of articles in this period, due to the special focus of the one-month anniversary issue. The number of articles in a week that contained information about the reasons for the attacks ranged from four to fourteen, and the proportion of articles containing reasons ranged from 18 percent to 67 percent. These patterns underscore that citizens were likely to learn more as the first several weeks of coverage accumulated. However, given the fact that a significant share of articles

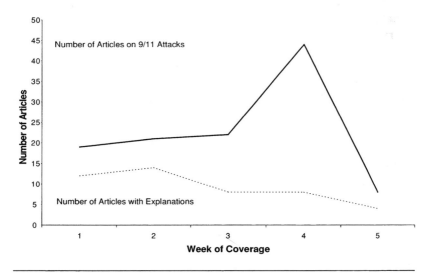

Fig. 10.3   Attention to explanations during the first five weeks of coverage in *U.S. News & World Report*. Source: *How Americans Respond* content analysis.

about September 11 never mentioned explanations, high levels of attention to the news would be required to learn of these explanations directly.

In testing the preceding hypotheses, we control for a number of individual attributes typically linked to individuals' beliefs or opinions about public affairs. As mentioned earlier, the ability of citizens to form or retain, as well as recall, explanations for the attacks should be a function of higher levels of education and political knowledge, respectively reflecting their general ability to process information and to relate it to what they have learned previously. We also controlled for standard demographic attributes of the respondents, including age, race, and sex. Although not our primary interest here, we might expect older citizens, drawing on a richer set of personal life experiences and perspectives, to offer more explanations. While it is possible that members of dominant social groups (e.g., men or whites) take a greater interest in foreign affairs and external threats to the nation, our initial expectations for race and sex were not strong.

We now take a closer look at the survey data. As expected, there is a substantial relationship between the number of explanations offered in the first interview and the second ($r = .37$), though it was not extremely strong. On average, respondents offered only slightly more reasons in their first interview (mean = 1.86, standard deviation = 1.17) than in their second (mean = 1.67, standard deviation = 1.49), but with considerable variance across individuals. Our central question is how the availability of explanations in the newstream influenced the number of explanations people could offer. Based on our assessment of patterns in the news coverage, our analysis of survey responses focuses on the timing of the interview (as a proxy for accumulated exposure) and attentiveness to the news. The results are shown in Table 10.2; the effects of the principal variables, along with controls, on the number of explanations were estimated using ordinary least squares (OLS) regression. We estimate the effects for both wave 1 and wave 2 of the panel. The first model contains independent variables measured only in the first wave, while the second model contains variables from both waves.

The model for wave 1 does not explain much of the total variance in responses ($R^2 = .074$), but our main interest is in the relative importance of the predictors. As expected, higher levels of education ($b = .066$, s.e. = .022) and political knowledge ($b = .138$, s.e. = .056) both significantly predict an increase in the number of explanations given. Individuals who are well educated and attuned to politics produce more explanations for the attacks. Taking that into account, those who were interviewed later in the initial period, and therefore were presumably exposed to more coverage about the attacks, also provide more explanations. The date of interview[7] is strongly significant ($b = .208$, s.e. = .050), and the impact is sizeable, if not great, with respondents interviewed during the fifth week likely to offer nearly one more explanation on average than those interviewed in the first week. Once we have controlled for the timing of the interview and levels of education, the impact of attention to the news is noteworthy but our confidence in the relationship is attenuated by

Table 10.2 Factors Affecting Explanations of 9/11

	WAVE 1 (SEPTEMBER–OCTOBER '01)			WAVE 2 (MARCH–APRIL '02)		
		ST.ERR	SIG.		ST.ERR.	SIG.
Constant	.285	(.421)		.065	(.404)	
Race (Nonwhite = 0, White = 1)	.122	(.126)		.495	(.123)	***
Sex (Male = 1, Female = 2)	.006	(.108)		.008	(.106)	
Age	.003	(.003)		.001	(.003)	
Education	.066	(.022)	***	.098	(.022)	***
Political Knowledge	.138	(.056)	**	.022	(.055)	
Follow news about attacks	.146	(.080)	*	.003	(.079)	
Date of interview	.208	(.050)	***	—		
Follow news about war on terrorism	—			.150	(.068)	**
Reasons given in wave 1	—			.325	(.040)	***
R	.271			.465		
Adjusted R^2	.074			.206		
Number of cases	611			611		

Notes: The unstandardized beta coefficients, standard errors and significance from regression analysis using OLS models with the number of explanations offered by respondents as the dependent variable.
*Significant at the .05 level.
**Significant at the .01 level.
***Significant at the .001 level.
Source: *How Americans Respond* Panel Survey.

borderline statistical significance (b = .146, s.e. = .080). Thus, the tendency of respondents in later weeks to offer more explanations may stem from general discussions with family, friends, and co-workers, once the news was "out there," rather than from their personal attentiveness to the news.

The rightmost column in Table 10.2 shows a model predicting the number of explanations offered by the same respondents when they were interviewed approximately six months later. While the overall predictive power of the model increased a good deal (R^2 = .206), our main interest is again in the relative explanatory power of the predictors. In the wave 2 model, we controlled for the number of explanations offered in the first interview. This was by far the most powerful predictor of explanations offered in the second interview (b = .325, s.e. = .040) and accounts for much of the increase in variance explained. The prior number of explanations no doubt serves as a baseline for individual differences stemming from personality factors such as talkativeness and the need for cognition not captured by measures in either survey. Education remains important (b = .098, s.e. = .022), as is being white (B = .495, s.e. = .123), but political knowledge is no longer significantly related to the number of explanations. Following news of "the war on terrorism" is a significant predictor of wave 2 explanations (b = .169, s.e. = 067), even though following news about the attacks in wave 1 was not.[8] The magnitude of the impact is nearly the same, but we now have much more confidence in its statistical significance. Six months after the attacks, many Americans had shifted their attention elsewhere or at least were not as attentive as in the immediate aftermath of September 11, and conversations also became less dominated by the topic. As a result, the impact of actual attention to the news is easier to observe in the data and, given the control for prior number of explanations, clearly shows a pay-off from persistent attention to the news through later months.

Conclusions

The analysis presented in this chapter took two forms. First, a review of patterns in US news magazine coverage of the September 11 attacks suggests that the patterns generally conformed to expectations about the volume and focus of news coverage established by earlier research. Patterns in the initial coverage somewhat resembled Picard's (1988) developmental sequence (i.e., from details of the incident, to government responses, to explanations for the incident). However, if this held true over the immediate period of five or six weeks, coverage that had anything to do with explanations or motivations for the attacks disappeared quickly thereafter. The emphasis on government perspectives conforms to observations others have previously made about the behavior of the press in covering overseas terrorist incidents (Paletz et al. 1985, Atwater 1987). In sum, the deviance model explains these patterns well.

Second, analysis of survey data sheds light on how news coverage affects the richness of American citizens' understanding of the events, as indicated by the number of answers they gave when prompted for the reasons for the attacks. The ability of Americans to explain what happened was influenced by accumulated exposure to news reports (or second-hand conversations about those reports) and by continued attention to the news once coverage thins. Familiar individual factors like education can also help to explain whether individuals form complex views of the world. In sum, these results suggest that beyond personal resources that citizens bring to learning about public affairs, such as education and political knowledge, persistent attentiveness to the news and the buildup of relevant exposure can increase people's ability to discuss and make sense of events like September 11.

In modern democracies, citizens typically depend on the mass media for information about events of public relevance and the actions of government officials. Even if most citizens learn about current affairs through conversations with others, mass mediated news is often the original source of information that makes those conversations possible. Thus, many people believe that one of the roles of the press in a democracy is to ensure an informed citizenry. Coverage in the aftermath of a major incident of domestic terrorism such as the September 11 terrorist attacks confirms this general pattern. Furthermore, our analysis highlights the potential of the press to increase citizens' understandings if news reports maintain a discussion of explanations over a period of weeks; moreover, these benefits do not require an exclusive focus on explanations, as these figured only modestly in the post-9/11 coverage. Yet even in these instances when general coverage reaches saturation levels, as we have seen, the content of the news does not linger long on efforts to explain the underlying causes and context of events. Thematic coverage of this sort quickly gives way to a continuing focus on episodic details of the "latest developments" and government responses (cf. Iyengar 1991). As a result, the press may fail to serve the needs of citizens as a whole, leaving only the most educated and attentive citizens capable of making full sense of these critical events.[9]

Appendix: Coding of Explanations Used in the Content Analysis and the HAR Survey

U.S. International Policies

101. U.S. support for Israel
102. United States does not support Palestinians
103. U.S. intervention in the Persian Gulf; Gulf War; Liberation of Kuwait; Desert Storm
104. Interference by United States; "stuck our nose in their business"
105. Iran; our support of the Shah; our actions in Iran
106. Libya; the bombing of Libya
107. Presence of United States in Middle East—n.e.c.
108. U.S. doesn't support them / opposes them / supports their enemies
109. U.S. foreign policy—(nothing further specified—n. f. s.)
110. U. S. involvement in Middle East conflicts—n. f. s.
111. We didn't do anything when terrorism happened in other countries
112. Afghanistan; what we did in Afghanistan; the plight of the Afghanis
113. Arab countries (in general); our trade restrictions / treatment of Arab countries
114. Iraq; starvation due to U.S. sanctions against Iraq
115. Israel (exc. 101); dislike or hatred of Israel or the Israelis; "Israeli conflict"
116. Palestine (exc. 102); the Palestinians / West Bank; "Palestinian conflict"
117. Saudi Arabia; our troops in Saudi Arabia; infidels in Mecca or other holy places
118. U.S. support of anti-Islamic causes—n.f.s.
119. President Bush's policies—n.f.s.
120. Camp David accords; Middle East peace efforts
121. Oil: big business; economic exploitation (overseas activities)

122. U.S. is too nice; sacrifice our self-interest for other countries
123. Indecision; inability of U.S. to carry policies to conclusion

Policies of other Countries

151. Terrorists are sheltered in some countries
152. They blame the U.S. for their problems / lack of power / bad governments; U.S. is a scapegoat for problems in terrorists' own countries
153. Oppression; oppressive states / governments / regimes

Religious Issues

201. Conflict between Islam or Muslims and Christianity
202. God's will; biblical prophecy; Bible fulfilling itself; sign or warning from God
203. Religious war—specific mention; Jihad
204. Religious zealotry; religious fanatics
205. They are against Christians / Christian nations
206. They are against the Jews; dislike / hatred of Jews; our helping the Jews
208. They don't know Jesus; have not been saved / are not Christians
209. Muslim beliefs; "Islam"—n.f.s.
210. They are spiritually blinded; misinterpret scripture / the Koran
211. They use religion as a mask; use Islam to achieve their goals
219. "Religion" or "religious" n.f.s; religious beliefs / religious reasons—n.f.s

Differences between United States and "THEM" (no mention of religion)

251. Beliefs; views; they don't believe in what we believe in
252. Cultural differences; "culture"—n.f.s.
253. Economic differences or "economics"—n.f.s.
254. Inequality; inequities; poverty; they don't have anything; "the haves and the have nots"
255. They are against freedom / our freedoms

Perceived Problems with the United States

301. Belief that the United States is bad; Americans are harmful
302. Capitalism; hostility toward (U.S.) capitalism; the World Trade Center as a symbol of capitalism; want to destroy banks / stocks / big business / economy; create economic instability in United States; want to destroy United States financial system
303. United States seen as decadent / immoral; want to protect themselves from our immorality

304. United States seen as arrogant, pushy; United States wants its own way
305. We gave them reasons to do things to us / incentives to attack us—n.f.s

Lack of Understanding

351. Cultural ignorance; ignorance of other cultures / ways of life
352. Our leaders are naïve / don't understand the world / don't know what to do
353. They have misguided views of our government, our country, or Americans; they are brainwashed, deluded; they need to grow up/act like civilized human beings
354. Need (to pray) for love / peace / understanding
355. Intolerance; intolerance of other cultures / ways of life; hatred of diversity
356. Culture of violence; been fighting for 2000 years; feuding for centuries

Control / Power

401. Our leaders can't do anything / have no control over it
402. They wanted to make a statement against America / the United States; they wanted to prove that they could do it; wanted to show they were equal to or stronger than America

Aspects of Human Nature

451. It's human nature
452. Greed—n.f.s
453. Nationalism—n.f.s
454. Prejudice—n.f.s
455. Racism—n.f.s
456. Politics, politicians; socio-political reasons, n.f.s.
457. Sin / evil in the world; homosexuality; atheism; abortion; "man is evil"

Aspects of Terrorists

501. It's a few crazy people; they're lunatics / mentally ill
502. Terrorists are evil or satanic
503. Fanaticism; a bunch of fanatics; they are radicals; place no value on human life; willing to die for their beliefs; will become martyrs for their cause
504. They are just murderers / killers
505. 〃 〃 bad; like to create trouble
506. 〃 〃 cowards
507. 〃 〃 ignorant, stupid, "bunch of dummies"
508. 〃 〃 unreasonable
509. They weren't raised right / bad upbringing / bad family background

510. They are unhappy / miserable people; can't stand anyone being happy
511. Self-righteous; feel favored by God; see themselves doing His will

Terrorist Individuals or Groups

551. Osama bin Laden
552. Taliban; the Taliban faction
553. Terrorist groups; terrorist organizations or networks; extremists, extremist groups, or hate groups
554. Saddam Hussein

Revenge

601. They want revenge
602. The trial / sentencing of the bomber

Hatred; Terrorism; Infliction of Damage; Enemies

651. Dislike / hatred / jealousy / anger toward the United States or Americans (non-economic reasons); jealous or envious of our power / way of life / freedoms; "they are our enemy"; dislike Western culture or civilization
652. Terrorism; general mention of terrorism or acts of terrorism; "to create terror"—n.f.s; they want to scare us, make us afraid, destroy our confidence
653. Want to create political instability in United States; cripple our government; "they want to damage our country"
655. They think we are their enemy
656. They want to get rid of us / destroy us / kill us
657. They think we want to get rid of them / destroy them / kill them
658. They want to destroy our way of life—n.f.s.
659. They think we want to destroy their way of life–n.f.s
660. They wanted to start a war; wanted to declare war on the United States
661. Want to destroy world trade / international economy
662. Want to take over the world / become the superpower
663. Want to end the world / destroy everything

National Security Threats

701. U.S. intelligence failure; ignored threats; didn't take warnings seriously; complacency; too comfortable; "asleep at the wheel"
702. United States has an open society; have open borders; "we're vulnerable"
703. Lack of security; have loose airport security; poor or no security
704. Immigration problems; don't investigate, regulate, or keep track of immigrants
705. Drug problems; heroin / opium issues; "the Golden Triangle"

706. Technology; technological threats from terrorism; nuclear proliferation; nuclear, chemical or biological weapons; Internet virus / attack

Other

996. None/ nothing/ not any/ no
997. Other
998. don't know; can't say; "no one knows"
999. refused
000. inappropriate, no further mention; no answer

Notes

1. The intended effects of such actions may vary for different audiences as well. Action against a regime or government may be designed to strike fear at the same time that widespread publicity elsewhere may build support for a terrorist group and its followers. The focus here is on the coverage of events in the United States and how they affected U.S. citizens; a study of the coverage in outlets like al Jazeera would have a very different focus.
2. This includes special issues on September 14 and October 12. The issue of October 15 was their long-planned "college guide" issue and contained almost no news content; as a result, it was dropped from the analysis since there was a special issue produced three days earlier on the one-month anniversary of the event.
3. Heather Schaar and Eric Groenendyk completed this coding. A comparison of their coding of a sample of twenty-five of the articles produced a 91% agreement in categories.
4. These data were collected with the support from internal funds at the Institute for Social Research. The study was designed by a group of 11 principal investigators from the Center for Political Studies, the Survey Research Center, and the Research Center for Group Dynamics. The Division of Surveys and Technology at the Survey Research Center supervised the data collection.
5. The exact question was:

    > "Now we have a set of questions concerning various public figures. We want to see how information about them gets out to the public from television, newspapers, and the like. The first name is Trent Lott. What job or political office does he hold?"

    The other individuals were William Rehnquist and Tony Blair. The number of correct answers was summed to form a four-point index with values ranging from 0 to 3.
6. The coding does not account for how lengthy an explanation was or how much prominence it received; it only recorded whether a particular explanation was offered. This is a gross measure of topical coverage (any mention at all) rather than a more proportionate measure (percent of the article in column-inches devoted to explanations).
7. This variable is coded as the week in which the interview took place after the starting date of the fieldwork. Its values range from 1 to 5.
8. The correlation between following the news about "the recent terrorist attacks" (wave 1) and following news about the "war on terrorism" wave (2) is .295.
9. Future analyses will take a deeper look at how citizens explain and interpret the attacks and track more closely citizen interpretations with those provided in the press. We have begun a massive project to code a number of aspects of the content of how the *New York Times* coverage explained and made sense of the attacks and their aftermath, for at least the entire six-month period covered by the How America Responds panel survey. Comparison of the evolution of daily coverage and corresponding evolution of citizen responses may shed even more light on this relationship.

References

Altheide, David L. 1985. 'Three-In-One News: Network Coverage of Iran.' *Journalism Quarterly* 59 (Autumn): 482–486.

Amanpour, Christiane. 2002. 'Excerpts from Christiane Amanpour's talk at the Goldsmith Awards—March 12, 2002.' *Press/Politics* (Summer): 10.

Atwater, Tony. 1987. 'Network Evening News Coverage of the TWA Hostage Crisis.' *Journalism Quarterly* 64 (Summer-Autumn): 520–525.

Bamford, James. 2002. 'Is the Press Up to the Task of Reporting These Stories?' *Nieman Reports* 55 (Winter): 19–22.

Converse, Philip E. 1964. 'The Nature of Belief in Mass Publics.' In *Ideology and Discontent,* edited by David Apter. London: Collier-Macmillan Ltd.

Crelisten, R. 1987. 'Power and Meaning: Terrorism as a Struggle over Access to the Communication Structure.' In *Contemporary Research on Terrorism,* edited by Paul Wilkinson and Alasdair Stewart. Aberdeen, Scotland: University of Aberdeen Press.

Crenshaw, Martha. 2000. 'Terrorism and International Violence.' In Manus I. Midlarsky (editor). *Handbook of War Studies II.* Ann Arbor: University of Michigan Press.

Enders, Walter, and Todd Sandler. 1999. 'Transnational Terrorism in the Post-Cold War Era.' *International Studies Quarterly* 43: 145–167.

Enders, Walter, and Todd Sandler. 2000. 'Is Transnational Terrorism Becoming More Threatening? A Time-Series Investigation.' *Journal of Conflict Resolution* 44: 307–332.

Enders, Walter, and Todd Sandler. 2002. 'Patterns of Transnational Terrorism, 1970–1999: Alternative Time-Series Estimates.' *International Studies Quarterly* 46: 145–165.

Epstein, E. C. 1977. 'The Uses of 'Terrorism': A Study in Media Bias.' *Stanford Journal of International Studies* 12:67–78.

Gans, Herbert J. 1979. *Deciding What's News.* New York: Pantheon Books.

Giles, Bob. 2002. 'Reporting Clashes with Government Policies.' *Nieman Reports* 55 (Winter): 3.

Gup, Ted. 2002. 'Secrecy and the Press in a Time of War.' *Nieman Reports* 55 (Winter): 11–13.

Huesmann, L. Rowell. 2002. 'How to Grow a Terrorist Without Really Trying.' Paper presented at the annual meeting of the American Psychological Association, Chicago, August 2.

Iyengar, Shanto. 1991. *Is Anyone Responsible?: How Television Frames Political Issues.* Chicago: University of Chicago Press.

Kelly, M. J. and T. H. Mitchell. 1981. 'Transnational Terrorism and the Western Elite Press.' *Political Communication and Persuasion* 1: 269–296.

Kirkpatrick, David D. 2001. 'Newsweeklies Run to Keep Up on Tricky Turf.' *New York Times* (October 22): C1.

Krimsky, George A. 2002. 'The View from Abroad.' *American Journalism Review* (January/ February): 54–57.

Lerner, Jennifer S., Roxana M. Gonzalez, Deborah A. Small, and Baruch Fischhoff. 2003. 'Effects of Fear and Anger on Perceived Risks of Terrorism: A National Field Experiment.' *Psychological Science* vol. 14, no. 2: 144–150.

Lipton, Joshua, and John Giuffo. 2002. 'Reverberations: Across the land, a new sense of vigor and purpose is spurring regional dailies since September 11.' *Columbia Journalism Review,* (July/August), retrieved at http://www.cjr.org/year/02/1/giuffoandlipton.asp.

Paletz, David, J. Z. Ayanian, and P. A. Fozzard. 1985. 'The I.R.A., the Red Brigades, and the F. A. L. N. in the *New York Times*,' *Journal of Communication* 32 (Spring): 162–172.

Picard, Robert G. 1993. *Media Portrayals of Terrorism.* Ames: Iowa State University Press.

Picard, Robert G. 1988. 'Stages in Coverage of Incidents of Political Violence.' *Terrorism and the News Media Research Project Monograph Series.* Boston: Emerson College.

Price, Vincent, and John Zaller. 1993. 'Who Gets the News? Alternative Measures of News Reception and Their Implications for Research.' *Public Opinion Quarterly* 57(2): 133–64.

Scherer, Michael. 2002. 'Framing the Flag.' *Columbia Journalism Review* (July/August), retrieved at http://www.cjr.org/year/02/2/Scherer.asp.

Shoemaker, Pamela J., T. Chang, and N. Brendlinger, 1987. 'Deviance as a Predictor of Newsworthiness; Coverage of International events in U.S. Media.' In *Communication Yearbook,* edited Margaret McLaughlin. Beverly Hills: Sage Publications. pp. 348–365.

Slone, Michelle. 2000. 'Responses to Media Coverage of Terrorism.' *Journal of Conflict Resolution*, 44 (August): 508–522.

Traugott, Michael, Ted Brader, Deborah Coral, Richard Curtin, David Featherman, Robert Groves, Martha Hill, James Jackson, Thomas Juster, Robert Kahn, Courtney Kennedy, Donald Kinder, Beth-Ellen Pennell, Matthew Shapiro, Mark Tessler, David Weir, and Robert Willis. 2002. 'How Americans Responded: A Study of Public Reactions to 9/11/01.' *PS: Political Science and Politics* 35 (3).

Weimann, Gabriel, and Hans-Bernd Brosius. 1991. 'The Newsworthiness of International Terrorism.' *Communication Research.* 18 (June): 333–354.

CHAPTER 11

Public Opinion Among Muslims and the West

PIPPA NORRIS
RONALD INGLEHART

In seeking to understand the causes of the events of September 11, 2001, many popular commentators have turned to Samuel P. Huntington's provocative and controversial thesis of a 'clash of civilizations'. This account emphasized that the end of the Cold War brought new dangers. "*In the new world,*" Huntington argued (1996:28),

> "*The most pervasive, important and dangerous conflicts will not be between social classes, rich and poor, or other economically defined groups, but between people belonging to different cultural entities. Tribal wars and ethnic conflicts will occur within civilizations . . . And the most dangerous cultural conflicts are those along the fault lines between civilizations . . . For forty-five years the Iron Curtain was the central dividing line in Europe. That line has moved several hundred miles east. It is now the line separating peoples of Western Christianity, on the one hand, from Muslim and Orthodox peoples on the other.*"

For Huntington, Marxist class warfare, and even the disparities between rich and poor nations, have been overshadowed in the twenty-first century by Weberian culture. This influential account appeared to offer insights into the causes of violent ethno-religious conflicts exemplified by Bosnia, the Caucuses, the Middle East, and Kashmir. It seemed to explain the failure of political reform to take root in many Islamic states, despite the worldwide resurgence of electoral democracies around the globe. The framework seemed to provide a powerful lens that the American media used to interpret the underlying reasons for the terrorist attack on the World Trade Center. Commentators often saw 9/11 as a full-scale assault on the global hegemony of America, in particular, and a reaction by Islamic fundamentalists against Western culture, in general. Nevertheless, the Huntington thesis has been highly controversial. The claim of rising ethnic conflict in the post-Cold War era has come under repeated and sustained attack (Gurr 2000; Russett, O'Neal, and Cox 2000; Fox 2001; Chirot 2001; Henderson and Tucker 2001). Many scholars have challenged the existence of a single Islamic culture stretching all the way from Jakarta to Lagos, let alone one that held values deeply incompatible with democracy (Kabuli 1994, Esposito and Voll 1996, Shadid 2001). What has been less widely examined, however, is systematic empirical evidence of whether the publics in Western and Islamic societies share similar or deeply divergent values, and, in particular, whether any important differences between these cultures rest on democratic values (as Huntington claims) or on social values (as modernization theories suggest).

This study seeks to throw new light on this issue by examining cultural values in seventy-five nations around the globe, including nine predominately Islamic societies, utilizing the World Values Survey 1995–2001. *Part I* briefly outlines the Huntington thesis and the response by critics. *Part II* lays out the study's research design, including the core hypothesis, comparative framework, and survey data. *Part III* analyzes the evidence. The conclusion summarizes the results and reflects on their implications. The evidence confirms the first claim in Huntington's thesis: culture *does* matter, and matters a lot: religious legacies leave a distinct and lasting imprint on contemporary values. But Huntington is mistaken in assuming that the core 'clash' between the West and Islamic societies concerns *political* values: instead the evidence indicates that surprisingly similar attitudes toward democracy are found in the West and the Islamic world. We do find significant cross-cultural differences concerning the role of religious leaders in politics and society, but these attitudes divide the West from many other countries around the globe, not just Islamic ones. The original thesis erroneously assumed that the primary cultural fault line between the West and Islam concerns government, overlooking a stronger cultural divide based on issues of gender equality and sexual liberalization. Cohort analysis suggests that as younger generations in the West have gradually become more liberal on these issues, this has generated a growing cultural gap, with Islamic nations remaining the most traditional societies in the world. The central values separating Islam and the West revolve far more centrally around Eros than Demos.

The 'Clash of Civilizations' Debate

The 'clash of civilizations' thesis advances three central claims. First, Huntington suggests that "culture matters"; in particular that contemporary values in different societies are path-dependent, reflecting long-standing legacies associated with core 'civilizations'. The concept of 'civilization' is understood by Huntington as a "culture writ large": *"It is defined both by common objective elements, such as language, history, religion, customs, institutions, and by the subjective self-identification of people."* (Huntington 1996: 41–43). Of these factors, Huntington sees religion as the central defining element (p.47), although he also distinguishes regional sub-divisions within the major world religions, such as the distinct role of Catholicism in Western Europe and Latin America, due to their different historical traditions and political legacies.

Second, the 'clash' thesis claims that there are sharp cultural differences between the core political values common in societies sharing a Western Christian heritage—particularly those concerning representative democracy—and the beliefs common in the rest of the world, especially Islamic societies. For Huntington, the defining features of Western civilization include the separation of religious and secular authority, the rule of law and social pluralism, the parliamentary institutions of representative government, and the protection of individual rights and civil liberties as the buffer between citizens and the power of the state: *"Individually almost none of these factors was unique to the West. The combination of them was, however, and this is what gave the West its distinctive quality"* (1996: 70–71). Other accounts have commonly stressed that the complex phenomenon of 'modernization' encompasses many additional social values that challenge traditional beliefs, notably faith in scientific and technological progress, belief in the role of economic competition in the marketplace, and the diffusion of modern social mores, exemplified by sexual liberalization and equality for women (Inglehart 1997, Inglehart and Baker 2000, Inglehart and Norris 2003). But Huntington's claim is that the strongest distinguishing characteristic of Western culture, the aspect which demarcates Western Christianity most clearly from the Muslim and Orthodox worlds, concerns the values associated with representative democracy. This claim is given plausibility by the failure of electoral democracy to take root in most states in the Middle East and North Africa (see Midlarsky 1998). According to the annual assessment made by the Freedom House (2002), of the 192 countries around the world, two-thirds (121) are electoral democracies. Of the 47 countries with an Islamic majority, one quarter (11) are electoral democracies. Furthermore, none of the core Arabic-speaking societies in the Middle East and North Africa falls into this category. Given this pattern, in the absence of survey evidence concerning the actual beliefs of Islamic publics, it is commonly assumed that they have little faith in the principles or performance of democracy, preferring strong leadership and rule by traditional religious authorities to the democratic values of pluralistic competition, political participation, and political rights and civil liberties.

Lastly, Huntington argues that important and long-standing differences in political values based on predominant religious cultures will lead to conflict between and within nation-states, with the most central problems of global politics arising from an ethno-religious "clash."[1] It remains unclear whether Huntington is claiming that the core cleavage concerns Western democratic values versus the developing world, or whether the main contrast lies as a fault line between the West and Islam, but the latter has been the primary popular interpretation of the thesis and the one which has aroused the most heated debate.

Middle Eastern area studies specialists, scholars of the Koran, and students of Islamic law have contested a series of issues about the 'clash' thesis. Critics have challenged the notion of a single Islamic culture, pointing to substantial contrasts found among one billion people living in diverse Islamic nations, such as Pakistan, Jordan, Azerbaijan, Indonesia, Bangladesh, and Turkey, and the differences between Muslims who are radical or moderate, traditional or modern, conservative or liberal, hard-line or revisionist (Hunter 1998; Esposito

1997; Fuller 2002). Observers stress the manifold differences within the Islamic world due to historical traditions and colonial legacies, ethnic cleavages, levels of economic development, and the role and power of religious fundamentalists in different states, claiming that it makes little sense to lump together people living in Jakarta, Riyadh, and Istanbul. Along similar lines, the idea that we can recognize a single culture of 'Western Christianity' is to over-simplify major cross-national differences, even among affluent postindustrial societies as superficially similar as the United States, Italy, and Sweden, for example the contrasts between Catholic Mediterranean Europe and Protestant Scandinavia, as well as among social sectors and religious denominations within each country.

Moreover, setting this issue aside for the moment, even if we accept the existence of a shared 'Islamic' culture, scholars have also argued that the core values and teaching of the Koran are not incompatible with those of democracy (Kabuli 1994; Esposito and Voll 1996; Shadid 2001). Edward Said (2001) decried Huntington's thesis as an attempt to revive the "black-white," "us-them," or "good-evil" world dichotomy that had been so prevalent during the height of the Cold War, substituting threats from "Islamic terrorists" for those from "Communist spies." Western leaders, seeking to build a global coalition against the followers of Osama bin Laden, took pains to distance themselves from the clash of civilizations thesis, stressing deep divisions within the Islamic world between the extreme fundamentalists and moderate Muslims. Leaders emphasized that the events of September 11 arose from the extreme ideological beliefs held by particular splinter groups of al Qaeda and Taliban fundamentalists, not from mainstream Muslim public opinion. Just as it would be a mistake to understand the 1995 bombing in Oklahoma City as a collective attack on the federal government by all Christian fundamentalists rather than the work of a few individuals, it may be inappropriate to view the attack by al Qaeda terrorists on symbols of American capitalism and financial power as a new 'clash of civilizations' between Islamic and Western cultures.

As well as challenging the basic premises of the clash of civilizations thesis, alternative explanations of radical Islamic fundamentalism suggest that the underlying root causes lie in deep disparities between rich and poor within societies, buttressed by the pervasive inequalities in political power in Middle Eastern regimes (Chirot 2001). Structural or neo-Marxist theories suggest that the best predictors of radical disaffection lie in uneven patterns of modernization around the world and the existence of pervasive inequalities *within* many Muslim societies. The most important cleavage may be between middle class, more-affluent, educated, and professional social sectors on the one hand—the teachers, doctors, and lawyers in Cairo, Beirut and Islamabad—and the substrata of poorer, uneducated, and unemployed younger men living in Saudi Arabia, Libya, and Syria who, if disaffected, may become willing recruits to Islamic fundamentalist causes. Huntington distinguishes certain demographic characteristics of Islamic societies, notably the phenomena of the 'youth bulge', but does not pursue the consequences of this generational pattern, in particular whether younger men from poorer sectors of society are particularly prone to political disaffection.

Yet there are plausible alternative theories about the major cultural contrasts we could expect to find between Islam and the West. In work presented elsewhere (Inglehart and Norris 2003) we document how the modernization process has transformed values by generating a rising tide of support for equality between women and men in post-industrial societies, and greater approval in these societies of a more permissive and liberal sexuality, including tolerance of divorce, abortion, and homosexuality. The version of modernization theory developed by Inglehart (1997) hypothesizes that human development generates changed cultural attitudes in virtually any society, although values also reflect the imprint of each society's religious legacies and historical experiences. Modernization brings systematic, *predictable* changes in gender roles. The impact of modernization operates in two key phases:

i.   Industrialization brings women into the paid work force and dramatically reduces fertility rates. Women attain literacy and educational opportunities. Women are enfranchised and begin to participate in representative government, but still have far less power than men.

ii.   The postindustrial phase brings a shift toward greater gender equality as women move into higher status economic roles in management and the professions and gain political influence within elected and appointed bodies. Over half of the world has not yet entered this phase; only the more advanced industrial societies are currently moving on this trajectory.

These two phases correspond to two major dimensions of cross-cultural variation: (i) a transition from traditional to secular-rational values; and (ii) a transition from survival to self-expression values. The decline of the traditional family is linked with the first dimension. The rise of gender equality is linked with the second. Cultural shifts in modern societies are not sufficient by themselves to guarantee women equality across all major dimensions of life; nevertheless through underpinning structural reforms and women's rights they greatly facilitate this process (Inglehart and Norris 2003). If this theory is applied to cultural contrasts between modern and traditional societies, it suggests that we would expect one of the key differences between the Western and Islamic worlds to focus around the issues of gender equality and sexual liberalization, rather than the democratic values that are central to Huntington's theory.

Hypotheses, Comparative Framework, and Data

To summarize, many issues arising from the 'clash' thesis could be considered, but here we focus upon testing two alternative propositions arising from the theoretical debate. Huntington emphasizes that the political values of democracy originated in the West with the separation of church and state, the growth of representative parliamentary institutions, and the expansion of the franchise. As such, he predicts that, despite the more recent emergence and consolidation of 'Third Wave' democracies in many parts of the world, democratic values will be most deeply and widely entrenched in Western societies. If true, we would expect to find *the strongest cultural clash in political values would be between the Western and Islamic worlds.* In contrast, Inglehart's modernization theory suggests that a rising tide of support for women's equality and sexual liberalization has left a particularly marked imprint on richer postindustrial nations, although traditional attitudes continue to prevail in poorer developing societies. Accordingly, given this interpretation, we also test the alternative proposition that *any deep-seated cultural divisions between Islam and the West will revolve far more strongly around social rather than political values, especially concerning the issues of sexual liberalization and gender equality.*

The issues of cultural conflict and value change have generated considerable controversy, but, as yet, almost no systematic survey data has been available to compare public opinion toward politics and society in many Middle Eastern and Western societies. Interpretations by area scholars and anthropologists have relied upon more qualitative sources, including personal interviews, observations and direct experience, and traditional textual exegesis of the literature, religious scriptures, and historical documents (see, for example, Lewis 2002). Recently commercial companies have started to conduct opinion polls that are representative of the public in a limited range of Muslim nations[2]; Gallup's survey examined attitudes toward other countries in nine Middle Eastern societies and the United States (Moore 2002), while Roper Reports Worldwide compared social values in the United States and Saudi Arabia (Miller and Feinberg 2002).

The latest waves of the World Values Survey (WVS), a global investigation of socio-cultural and political change, allow comparison of democratic values across a wide range of Western and Muslim nations, as well as in many other states.[3] The study has carried out representative national surveys of the basic values and beliefs of publics in more than seventy nations on all six inhabited continents, containing over 80% of the world's population. It builds on the European Values Surveys, first carried out in twenty-two countries in 1981. A second wave of surveys, in forty-three nations, was completed in 1990–1991, a third wave was carried out in fifty nations in 1995–1996, and a fourth wave with more than sixty nations took place in 1999–2001.[4] This total sample includes almost a quarter-million respondents, facilitating analysis of minority sub-groups, such as the Muslim populations living in Russia, India, Bulgaria, and Macedonia. This study focuses on analyzing attitudes and values in the last two waves of the survey, from 1995–2001. To test the evidence for the 'clash of civilizations' thesis, this study compares values at *societal*-level, based on the assumption that predominant cultures exert a broad and diffuse influence upon all people living under them.[5]

Classifying Cultural Regions

In Huntington's account nine major contemporary civilizations can be identified, based largely on the predominant religious legacy in each society:

- Western Christianity (a European culture that subsequently spread to North America, Australia, and New Zealand)
- Islamic (including the Middle East, Northern Africa, and parts of Southeast Asia)
- Orthodox (Russian and Greek)
- Latin American (predominately Catholic, yet with a distinct corporatist, authoritarian culture)
- Sinic/Confucian (China, South Korean, Vietnam, and Korea)
- Japanese
- Hindu
- Buddhist (Sri Lanka, Burma, Thailand, Laos, and Cambodia), and (possibly)
- Sub-Saharan Africa.[6]

Huntington treats states or societies as the core actors exemplifying these civilizations, although recognizing that populations with particular cultural and religious identities spread well beyond the border of the nation-state. Moreover some plural societies are deeply divided, so there is rarely a clean one-to-one mapping, apart from exceptional cases such as Japan and India.

To analyze the survey evidence for these propositions, societies were classified into these categories, (see Table 11.1) based on the predominant (plurality) religious identities within each nation. The survey includes nine societies with a Muslim majority (ranging from 71 to 96 percent), including Jordan, Pakistan, Turkey, Azerbaijan, Bangladesh, Albania, Morocco, Iran, and Egypt. This allows us to compare a range of states within the Islamic world, including semi-democracies with elections and some freedoms, exemplified by Albania, Turkey, and Bangladesh, as well as constitutional monarchies (Jordan), and suspended semi-democracies under military rule (Pakistan). Geographically these nations are located in Central Europe, the Middle East, and South Asia. In addition, the comparative framework includes twenty-two nations based on 'Western Christianity' (using Huntington's definition to include both predominately Catholic and Protestant postindustrial societies and countries like Australia and New Zealand which are not located regionally in the 'West' yet which inherited a democratic tradition from Protestant Britain). Other nations are classified into distinct civilizational traditions, including Latin America (eleven), Russian or Greek Orthodox (twelve), Central European (ten nations sharing a common Western Christian heritage with the West yet with the distinct experience of living under Communist rule), sub-Saharan Africa (five), South-East Asian (four

Table 11.1 Classification of Societies by the Historically Predominant Religion

PROTESTANT	CATHOLIC	MUSLIM	ORTHODOX	CENTRAL EUROPE	LATIN AMERICA	SINIC/ CONFUCIAN	SUB-SAHARAN AFRICA
Australia	Austria	Albania	Belarus	Croatia	Argentina	South Korea	Nigeria
Britain	Belgium	Azerbaijan	Bosnia	Czech Republic	Brazil	Taiwan	South Africa
Canada	France	Bangladesh	Bulgaria	East Germany	Chile	Vietnam	Tanzania
Denmark	Ireland	Egypt	Georgia	Estonia	Colombia	China	Uganda
Finland	Italy	Iran	Greece	Hungary	Dominican Rep.		Zimbabwe
Iceland	Malta	Jordan	Macedonia	Latvia	El Salvador		
New Zealand	Portugal	Morocco	Moldova	Lithuania	Mexico		
Netherlands	Spain	Pakistan	Montenegro	Poland	Peru		
Northern Ireland	Switzerland	Turkey	Romania	Slovakia	Uruguay		
Norway			Russia	Slovenia	Venezuela		
Sweden			Serbia				
United States			Ukraine				
West Germany							

Note: This study compares 72 nation-states and 75 societies, dividing states with distinctive historical traditions, cultural legacies and political institutions including the UK (Northern Ireland and Great Britain), Germany (East and West), and the Federal Republic of Yugoslavia (Serbia and Montenegro). The Catholic and Protestant societies are classified as 'Western Christianity'. In addition India and Japan are each treated as separate religious cultures.
Source: The World Values Survey/European Values Survey, 1995–2001.

societies reflecting Sinic/Confucian values), plus Japan and India. In addition, ten societies contain a significant *minority* Islamic population (ranging from 4 to 27 percent), including Bosnia, Macedonia, Nigeria, and India, although these nations have Orthodox, Protestant, or Hindu majority populations. In the multivariate regression models, each type of society was coded as a dummy variable and the 'Western' societies category was used as the (omitted) reference category. The models therefore measure the impact of living in each of these types of society, with controls, compared with living in the West.

To rule out intervening variables, multivariate regression models compare the influence of predominant religious cultures in each type of society controlling for levels of human and political development. Modernization theories suggest that this process brings certain predictable shifts in cultural values, including declining belief in traditional sources of religious authority and rising demands for more participatory forms of civic engagement (Inglehart 1997, Inglehart and Baker 2000, Norris 2002). The WVS survey contains some of the most affluent market economies in the world, such as the United States, Japan, and Switzerland, with per capita annual incomes as high as $40,000; middle-level industrializing countries such as Taiwan, Brazil, and Turkey; and poorer agrarian societies such as Uganda, Nigeria, and Viet Nam, with per capita annual incomes of $300 or less. It also includes many different types of states, including established and newer democracies, semi-democracies, and non-democracies. Accordingly structural differences among societies are measured by the United Nations Development Program (UNDP) Human Development Index (HDI) 2000—combining levels of per capita income, literacy and schooling, and longevity—and levels of democratization, which are classified based on the 1999–2000 Freedom House analysis of political rights and civil liberties.[7] The structural differences among groups within societies are measured by the standard social indicators, including income (as the most reliable cross-cultural measure of socioeconomic status in different societies), education, gender, age, and religiosity.

The latter was included to see whether the *strength* of religious beliefs influenced values more than the *type* of religious faith or identity (which, like being baptized as a Protestant or Catholic, can be purely nominal). To develop a religiosity scale, factor analysis was used with six indicators selected from the pooled World Values Survey, namely the proportion of the population in different societies: (i) who say that religion is 'very important' in their lives, (ii) who find comfort in religion, (iii) who believe in God, (iv) who identify themselves as religious, (v) who believe in life after death, and (vi) who attend a religious service regularly. All these items tap values and beliefs common throughout the world's religions and they were carried in all four waves of the WVS, to facilitate comparison over time. Factor analysis among the pooled sample (not reproduced here) showed that all the items fell into one dimension and formed a consistent and reliable "strength of religiosity" scale (Cronbach's Alpha = 0.48).

After recoding, the scale was standardized to 100-points, for ease of interpretation, where the higher score represents the strongest religiosity.

Measuring Political and Social Values

Attitudes were compared toward three dimensions of political and social values: (i) support for democratic ideals and performance, (ii) attitudes toward political leadership, and (iii) approval of gender equality and sexual liberalization. As argued elsewhere (Norris 1999), an important distinction needs to be drawn between support for the *ideals* of democracy and evaluations of the actual *performance* of democracy. Evidence from previous waves of the World Value Study (Klingemann 1999, Dalton 1999) suggests that citizens in many countries adhere strongly to the general principles of democracy, such as believing that it is the best form of government and disapproving of authoritarian alternatives, and yet at the same time many remain deeply dissatisfied with the way that democratic governments work in practice. The phenomenon of more "critical citizens" (Norris 1999) or "disenchanted democrats" (Putnam and Pharr 2001) has been widely observed. To examine these dimensions, attitudes toward the principles and performance of democracy are measured in this study using the items listed in Table 11.2, where respondents are invited to express agreement or disagreement with the statements. It should be noted that the performance items do not ask people about their experience of democracy in their own country, such as how well their government works, but rather taps their expectations of how well democratic governments generally function in taking decisions and maintaining order.

In addition, it is commonly assumed that one of the primary contrasts between Islamic and Western cultures relates to attitudes toward the role of religious leaders who exercise power by virtue of their spiritual authority or secular leaders who hold authority through elective office, reflecting deeper beliefs about the separation of church and state. We therefore also monitored support for the role of religious leaders in public life with the items listed in Table 11.2. Neither of these items cued respondents with any explicit reference to "democracy" and indeed, in principle, there is no inconsistency in believing both in the value of spiritual authorities and in the principles of democracy, if the religious leaders exercise power through elected office, exemplified by Christian Democrat parties or politicians from the Christian far right. We also sought to compare attitudes toward preferences for strong leadership, measured by questions tapping support for non-democratic forms of government by experts or by leaders unaccountable to parliament or elections. Factor analysis confirmed that these political items did indeed fall into four distinct dimensions. Accordingly summary scales were constructed, each standardized to 100 points for ease of interpretation and consistent comparison across measures.

Yet the alternative proposition is that the transformation of social values toward sexuality and women's equality, which has profoundly affected the younger generation in postindustrial societies, may lie at the heart of any

Table 11.2 Factor Analysis of Political Values

	DEMOCRATIC PERFORMANCE	DEMOCRATIC IDEALS	RELIGIOUS LEADERSHIP	STRONG LEADERSHIP
V170 *Democracies are indecisive and have too much squabbling*	.862			
V171 *Democracies aren't good at maintaining order*	.854			
V172 *Democracy may have its problems, but it's better than any other form of government*		.853		
V167 *Approve of having a democratic political system*		.780		
V200 *Politicians who do not believe in God are unfit for public office*			.881	
V202 *It would be better for [this country] if more people with strong religious beliefs held public office*			.879	
V165 *Approve having experts, not government, make decisions*				.838
V164 *Approve having strong leaders who do not have to bother with parliament and elections*				.721
% Of total variance	19.6	17.7	19.6	15.7

Note: Principal component factor analysis was used with varimax rotation and Kaiser normalization. The total model predicts 72.6% of cumulative variance. The democratic performance scale was reversed so that a positive response expressed greater satisfaction with democracy.
Source: The World Values Survey/European Values Survey, Waves III and IV (1995–2001).

Table 11.3 Mean Scores on the Political and Social Values Scales

TYPE OF SOCIETY	DEMOCRATIC POLITICAL VALUES				LIBERAL SOCIAL VALUES			
	APPROVE OF DEMOCRATIC PERFORMANCE	APPROVE OF DEMOCRATIC IDEALS	DISAPPROVAL OF RELIGIOUS LEADERS	DISAPPROVAL OF STRONG LEADERS	APPROVE OF GENDER EQUALITY	APPROVE OF HOMOSEXUALITY	APPROVE OF ABORTION	APPROVE OF DIVORCE
Western Christianity	**68**	**86**	**62**	**61**	**82**	**53**	**48**	**60**
Islamic	**68**	**87**	**39**	**61**	**55**	**12**	**25**	**35**
All Other	**63**	**80**	**53**	**55**	**67**	**28**	**36**	**47**
All Other								
Orthodox	61	78	54	55	64	22	46	51
Central Europe	63	81	62	56	67	36	48	56
Latin America	62	81	51	55	75	31	23	49
Sinic/Confucian	68	80	64	52	62	17	33	40
Sub-Saharan Africa	65	83	40	52	64	21	22	31
Hindu	60	84	N/a	53	61	17	25	31
Japanese	70	81	66	58	63	40	46	61
ALL	**65**	**83**	**53**	**57**	**67**	**33**	**38**	**50**
Difference between all group means	.18***	.20***	.49***	.19***	.46***	.45***	.38***	.33***
Difference between Western and Islamic group means	.02***	.03***	.30***	.01	.64***	.51***	.33***	.37***
N.	116629	117855	49903	83223	84932	135846	139841	139311

Note: For the classification of societies, see Table 1. All items have been scaled to 0–100. The significance of the difference between group means is measured by ANOVA (Eta) without any controls. *** Sig. P.000.
Source: The World Values Survey/European Values Survey, Waves III and IV (1995–2001).

cultural clash between modern and traditional societies in general and between the West and Islam in particular. In this regard, Huntington may have correctly identified the importance of civilizational values but may have misdiagnosed the root causes of any cultural differences. To explore this proposition we can compare support for gender equality, using a standardized scale developed elsewhere also based on factor analysis, monitoring attitudes toward the roles of women and men in the workforce, education, politics, and the family.[8] The Gender Equality items are similar to those commonly contained in the more comprehensive psychological scales of sex roles. The gender equality scale was summed across the component items and standardized to 100 points for ease of interpretation. We also compared attitudes using 10-point scales monitoring approval or disapproval of three related dimensions of changing sexual mores concerning homosexuality, abortion, and divorce.

Analysis of the Results

Table 11.3 compares the mean scores on these scales for each type of society without any prior social or demographic controls and the significance of the difference between societies. Figure 11.1 illustrates the contrasts between Western and Islamic societies. The results show that, contrary to the first hypothesis, Western and Islamic societies generally *agreed* on three of the four indicators of political values. Approval of how well democracy worked in practice was similar for those living in the West and in Islamic societies while, in contrast, far more critical evaluations were expressed in all other cultures around the globe, with the single exception of Japan. Similar patterns were evident when people were asked whether they supported democratic ideals, for example whether democracy was better than any other form of government. As others have reported (Klingemann 1999), in recent years high support for democratic ideals is almost universally found in most nations around the globe. Both Western and Islamic societies expressed similar levels of approval, while in contrast slightly less positive attitudes were evident elsewhere, with Sinic and Orthodox societies proving the least enthusiastic. Attitudes toward leadership by experts and by unaccountable government officials were also similar in Islamic and Western societies. Therefore the major political disagreement between Western and Islamic societies was found in attitudes toward the role of religious leaders, where Islamic nations proved far more favorable. Yet at the same time it would be an exaggeration to claim that this latter difference represents a simple dichotomous 'clash of values'. Although it is true that many more Muslims than Westerners supported the idea of religious authorities, there was widespread agreement with this idea in many other parts of the world, including sub-Saharan Africa and Catholic Latin America. The West proved more secular in orientation, as did Central Europe, the Sinic/Confucian nations, and Japan.

Yet comparing the simple means in each type of religious culture could be misleading if other endogenous factors are influencing the results, such as the level of democratization or economic affluence typically found in Western

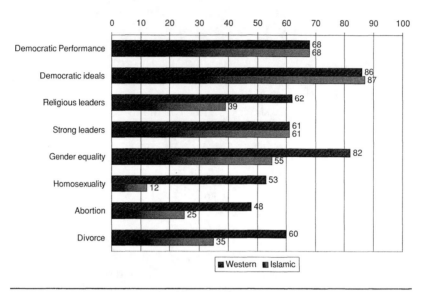

Fig. 11.1   Approval of political and social values in Western and Islamic Societies. Note: Mean approval. See Table 11.3 for details. Source: World Values Survey/European Values Survey (WVS), pooled sample 1995–2001.

and Islamic societies. The multivariate OLS regression models presented in Table 11.4 therefore compare the impact of living within each type of religious culture after including controls for the societal-level of human and political development and individual-level measures for age, gender, education, income, and strength of religiosity. In these models, each type of society was coded as a dummy (0/1) variable. The Western category was excluded from the analysis, so that the dummy coefficients can be interpreted as the effect of living in these societies, after applying prior controls, compared with the effect of living in the West. The data was entered in blocks, including development and social controls in the first block, then the additional effects of the full model in the second block, including the type of society as well.

The results show that after controlling for all these factors, contrary to Huntington's thesis, compared with Western societies, support for democracy was marginally slightly *stronger* (not weaker) among those living in Islamic societies. This pattern was evident on three indicators: approval of the way democracy works in practice, support for democratic ideals, as well as disapproval for the idea of strong government leaders. It should be stressed that the difference on these items between Islam and the West were extremely modest in size, as shown by the strength of the standardized beta coefficient, and the statistical significance is largely the product of the large number of respondents in the pooled sample, but nevertheless the difference was in the contrary direction

Table 11.4 Political Values by Type of Society, with Controls

SCALE	APPROVE OF DEMOCRATIC PERFORMANCE 0–100				APPROVE OF DEMOCRATIC IDEALS 0–100				FAVOR RELIGIOUS LEADERSHIP 0–100				FAVOR STRONG LEADERSHIP 0–100			
	B	ST. ERR.	BETA	SIG	B	ST. ERR.	BETA	SIG	B	ST. ERR.	BETA	SIG	B	ST. ERR.	BETA	SIG
Type of society																
Islamic	1.3	.34	.03	***	2.6	.27	.06	***	9.7	.41	.19	***	-2.8	.35	-.06	***
Orthodox	-8.9	.25	-.18	***	-7.9	.21	-.18	***	5.2	.33	.09	***	5.5	.27	.13	***
Central European	-5.4	.21	-.11	***	-5.3	.17	-.12	***	0.1	.27	.00	N/s	3.5	.24	.08	***
Latin American	-6.1	.24	-.11	***	-3.5	.19	-.08	***	3.8	.35	.05	***	3.3	.25	.07	***
Sinic/Confucian	1.4	.45	.01	**	-3.1	.37	-.03	***	-5.1	.79	-.03	***	16.6	.47	.16	***
Sub-Saharan African	-3.6	.43	-.05	***	-4.1	.34	-.07	***	7.6	.46	.13	***	4.3	.48	.07	***
Hindu	-8.9	.60	-.06	***	-2.5	.47	-.02	***	N/a			***	6.0	.62	.05	***
Japanese	3.3	.49	.02	***	-3.5	.39	-.03	***	-0.1	.59	.00	N/s	1.7	.54	.02	**
(Constant)	68.8				82.1				61.8				54.1			
Adjusted R² Block 1 (Control variables only)	.01				.01				.32				.01			
Adjusted R² Block 2 (Controls + type of society)	.05				.06				.33				.06			
N.	93965				95550				45209				64412			

Note: OLS regression models with blockwise entry with the political value scales as the dependent variables. The full model is illustrated in Table 11.6. Block 1 in all models control for the *level of human development* (Human Development Index 1998), *level of political development* (Freedom House 7-point index (reversed) of political rights and civil liberties 1999–2000), age (years), gender (male = 1), education (3 categories from low to high), income (10 categories), and religiosity. Block 2 then enters the type of society, based on the predominant religion, coded as dummy variables. Western societies represent the (omitted) reference category. The coefficients can be understood to represent the effect of living in each type of society compared with living in Western societies, net of all prior controls. *Political value scales*: For details see Table 2. *Type of society*: see Table 1. Sig. *** p.001 ** p.01 * p.05.

Source: All World Values Survey/European Values Survey (WVS), pooled sample 1995–2001.

to that predicted by the Huntington thesis. Moreover, as observed earlier, even after introducing controls, lower support for democratic values was found in many other types of non-Western society, especially countries in Eastern and Central Europe, and Latin America, while the Sinin/Confucian states showed the greater approval of strong government. At the same time, after introducing all the controls, Islamic societies did display greater support for a strong societal role by religious authorities than do Western societies. This pattern persists despite controlling for the strength of religiosity and other social factors, which suggests that it is not simply reducible to the characteristics of people living in Islamic societies. Yet this preference for religious authorities is less a cultural division between the West and Islam than it is a gap between the West and many other types of less secular societies around the globe, especially in Sub-Saharan Africa and, to a lesser extent, in Latin America.

To examine these results in more detail, Figures 11.2 and 11.3 compare the location of each nation on these scales. Of all countries under comparison, Russia proved a striking outlier in Figure 11.2, displaying widespread disillusionment with the way that democratic processes worked, as well as little enthusiasm for democratic ideas. Other Orthodox societies also showed minimal faith in democracy, including the Ukraine, Moldova, Belarus, Georgia, and Macedonia. A few other developing countries from different cultures proved extremely

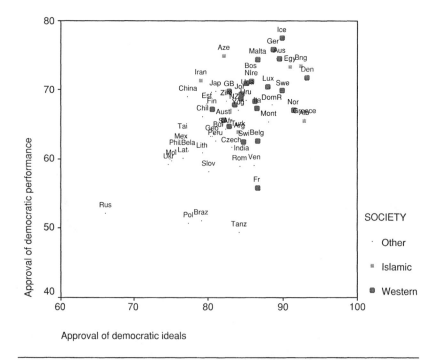

Fig. 11.2   Democratic values. Source: World Values Survey/European Values Survey (WVS), pooled sample 1995–2001.

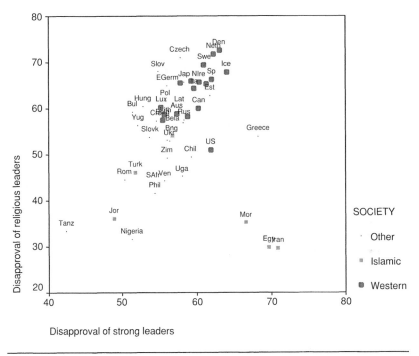

Fig. 11.3 Leadership attitudes. Source: World Values Survey/European Values Survey (WVS), pooled sample 1995–2001.

critical of the way that democracy worked in practice, although showing greater support for democratic ideals, including Tanzania, Brazil, and Poland. Many diverse cultures were located in the middle of the distribution, including Turkey and Jordan as Islamic societies, as well as the United States, Italy, and the Netherlands. Nations that gave the strongest endorsement for democratic ideals and practices included the Scandinavian societies of Denmark, Iceland, and Sweden, along with Germany and Austria, but high support was also registered in Muslim Bangladesh, Egypt, and Azerbaijan. Therefore in general slightly lower levels of support for democracy were evident in some Eastern European states, notably in Russia, lending some confirmation for claims of a division between the Orthodox and Western worlds. But attitudes toward democratic principles and performance generally showed a broad distribution across many diverse cultural groups, providing minimal support for the stronger claim that the West is particularly distinctive to Islam in its faith in democracy. Indeed the difference between public opinion in Eastern and Western Europe could be explained equally satisfactorily as reflecting a residual hangover from the Cold War era, and the poor performance of electoral democracies and states in these nations, rather than being interpreted as the result of cultural legacies or the emergence of any "new" ethno-religious cleavage.

Figure 11.3 compared leadership attitudes by nation. Support for religious leaders was lowest in many secular societies in Scandinavia and Western Europe, as well as in certain nations in Eastern Europe like the Czech Republic. The United States proved distinctive, showing higher than average support for religious leaders, compared with other Western nations, while Greece was another outlier. At the other extreme, support for religious leaders was relatively strong in African societies, including Nigeria, Tanzania, and South Africa, as well as the Philippines, all countries with strong religiosity. Compared with Western nations, many of the Islamic nations expressed greater support for the principle of religious authorities, but they were far from alone in this regard. There is also a fascinating split over the issue of strong leadership evident within the Islamic world; more democratic countries with greater political rights, civil liberties, and parliamentary traditions, exemplified by Bangladesh and Turkey, expressed greater reservations about strong leadership. To a lesser extent, Jordan also fell into this category. In contrast, the public living in Islamic countries characterized by more limited political freedoms, less democratic states, and by strong executives, expressed greater support for strong leadership, notably in Egypt, Iran, and Morocco.

Yet so far we have not compared the alternative modernization thesis that the social values of gender equality and sexual liberalization could plausibly lie at the heart of any "clash" between Islam and the West. The mean scores on these social attitudes in Table 11.3 reveal the extent of the gulf between Islam and the West, generating a far stronger cultural gap on these issues than across most of the political values. Regression models, including the same prior controls used earlier, show that many structural factors consistently help to predict attitudes, since egalitarian and liberal values are stronger among the young, women, the well-educated, and the less religious, as well as in modern societies with greater human and democratic development. After these controls are introduced, Table 11.5 shows that there remains a strong and significant difference across all the social indicators (including approval of gender equality, homosexuality, abortion, and divorce) among those living in Western v. Islamic societies. Figure 11.4 shows the distribution of nations on the scales for gender equality and homosexuality in more detail. The results confirm the consistency of the sharp differences between Islam and the West on these issues. All the Western nations, led by Sweden, Germany, and Norway, strongly favor equality for women and also prove tolerant of homosexuality. Many other societies show a mixed pattern, falling into the middle of the distribution. In contrast the Islamic nations, including Egypt, Bangladesh, Jordan, Iran, and Azerbaijan, all display the most traditional social attitudes, with only Albania proving slightly more liberal.

We lack time-series survey data that would allow us to trace trends in the postwar era, to see whether these cultural differences between societies have widened, as we suspect, due to the modernization process in post-industrial economies. Nevertheless, if we assume that people acquire their basic moral and social values

Table 11.5 Social Values by Type of Society, with Controls

SCALE	APPROVE OF GENDER EQUALITY 0–100				APPROVE OF HOMOSEXUALITY 0–10				APPROVE OF ABORTION 0–10				APPROVE OF DIVORCE 0–10			
	B	ST. ERR.	BETA	SIG	B	ST. ERR.	BETA	SIG	B	ST. ERR.	BETA	SIG	B	ST. ERR.	BETA	SIG
Type of society																
Islamic	−8.2	.35	−.18	***	−1.9	.05	−.18	***	−0.67	.05	−.07	***	−0.25	.05	−.03	***
Orthodox	−8.9	.30	−.17	***	−2.1	.04	−.26	***	0.24	.04	.03	***	−0.20	.04	−.03	***
Central European	−6.6	.30	−.09	***	−1.6	.03	−.18	***	0.24	.03	.03	***	0.01	.03	.01	N/s
Latin American	2.6	.25	.05	***	−1.0	.03	−.11	***	−1.20	.03	−.14	***	0.15	.04	.02	***
Sinic/Confucian	−0.3	.69	−.01	N/s	−2.9	.07	−.13	***	−2.10	.06	−.10	***	−2.30	.07	−.11	***
Sub-Saharan African	7.3	.42	13	***	−0.6	.06	−.05	***	−0.08	.06	−.01	N/s	0.29	.06	.03	***
Hindu	3.4	.53	.03	***	−1.2	.08	−.05	***	−0.05	.08	−.01	N/s	−0.10	.08	−.01	N/s
Japanese	−14.4	.52	−.09	***	−1.5	.06	−.06	***	−0.45	.06	−.02	***	−0.05	.07	−.01	N/s
(Constant)	32.7				1.6				3.1				2.16			
Adjusted R² Block 1 (Control variables only)	.26				.20				.23				.26			
Adjusted R² Block 2 (Controls + type of society)	.33				.21				.26				.31			
N.	63476				99980				103290				105432			

Note: OLS regression models with blockwise entry with the social value scales as the dependent variables. The full model is illustrated in Table 11.6. Block 1 in all models control for the *level of human development* (Human Development Index 1998), *level of political development* (Freedom House 7-point index (reversed) of political rights and civil liberties 1999–2000), age (years), gender (male = 1), education (10 categories), income (10 categories), and religiosity. Block 2 then enters the type of society, based on the predominant religion, coded as dummy variables. Western societies represent the (omitted) reference category. The coefficients can be understood to represent the effect of living in each type of society compared with living in Western societies, net of all prior controls. *Type of society:* see Table 1. *Gender equality scale:* For details see fn.7. *Sexual liberalization scales:* "Please tell me for each of the following statements whether you think it [Homosexuality/ abortion/ divorce] can always be justified, never be justified, or something in-between, using this card from 1 (never justifiable) to 10 (Always justifiable)." Sig. ***p.001 **p.01 *p.05. N/s Not significant.
Source: All World Values Survey/European Values Survey (WVS), pooled sample 1995–2001.

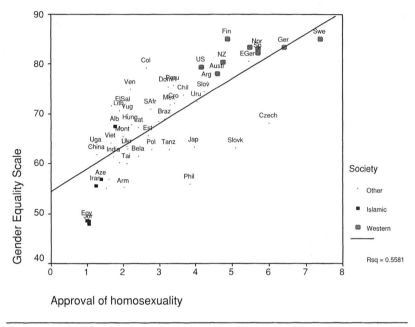

Fig. 11.4 Social values. Source: World Values Survey/European Values Survey (WVS), pooled sample 1995–2001.

as the result of the long-term socialization process in the family, school, and community leading to generational rather than life-cycle effects, we can analyze these attitudes for different ten-year cohorts of birth. The results in Figure 11.5 confirm two striking and important patterns: first, there is a persistent gap in support for gender equality and sexual liberalization between the West (which proves most liberal), Islamic societies (which prove most traditional), and all other societies (which are in the middle). Moreover, even more important, the figures reveal that the gap between the West and Islam is usually narrowest among the oldest generation, but that this gap has steadily widened across all the indicators as the younger generations in Western societies have become progressively more liberal and egalitarian, while the younger generations in Islamic societies remain as traditional as their parents and grandparents. The trends suggest that Islamic societies have not experienced a backlash against liberal Western sexual mores among the younger generations, but rather that young Muslims remain unchanged despite the transformation of lifestyles and beliefs experienced among their peers living in postindustrial societies.

Conclusion and Discussion

The thesis of a 'clash of civilizations' has triggered something of a "clash of scholarship" among those seeking to understand the causes and consequences of

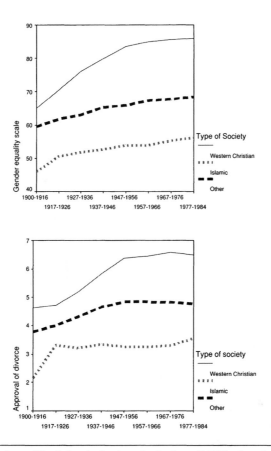

Fig. 11.5 Support for sexual liberalization values by cohort and society. Source: World Values Survey/European Values Survey (WVS), pooled sample 1995–2001.

ethnic-religious conflict. This task has long been of interest to academe but it has received fresh impetus by the dramatic events and aftermath of 9/11. Alternative interpretations of these issues are important for themselves but also because they carry important policy implications, not least for how far differences between the United States and Middle Eastern states primarily reflect the views of political elites and governing regimes or whether they tap into deeper currents of public opinion. To summarize the core components of the Huntington thesis, the claims are threefold: societal values in contemporary societies are rooted in religious cultures; the most important cultural division between the Western and Islamic world relates to differences over democratic values; and, in the post-Cold War era, this "culture clash" is at the source of much international and domestic ethnic conflict.

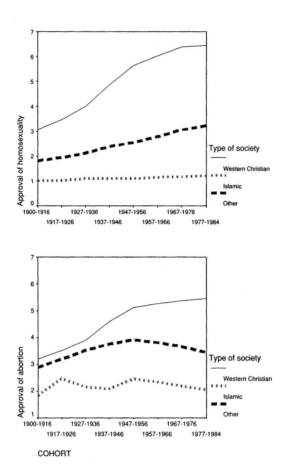

Fig. 11.5 *(Continued)*

The comparative evidence from this study, drawing upon public opinion toward democracy in more than seventy societies around the globe in 1995–2001, suggests four main findings:

i. First, when political attitudes are compared (including evaluations of how well democracy works in practice, support for democratic ideals, and disapproval of strong leaders), far from a "clash of values," there is minimal difference between the Islamic world and the West.

ii. Instead the democratic "clash" (if it can be called a clash) divides post-Communist states in Eastern European (exemplified by Russia, Ukraine, and Moldova), which display minimal support for democracy, from many other countries that display far more positive attitudes, including both

Western *and* Islamic nations. This pattern could be explained equally well as reflecting the residual legacy of the Cold War and a realistic evaluation of the actual performance of democracy in these states, rather than by the reemergence of ethnic conflict based on the values of the Orthodox church which are, after all, part of Christendom.

iii. Support for a strong societal role by religious authorities is stronger in Islamic societies than in the West, but here it is not a simple dichotomy, as many other types of society also support an active role for religious leaders in public life, including the sub-Saharan African countries under comparison as well as many Catholic nations in Latin America.

iv. Yet there *is* a substantial cultural cleavage, although one underestimated by Huntington, in social beliefs about gender equality and sexual liberalization. In this regard, the West is far more egalitarian and liberal than all other societies, particularly Islamic nations. Moreover cohort analysis suggests that this gap has steadily widened as the younger generation in the West has gradually become more liberal in their sexual mores while the younger generation in Islamic societies remains deeply traditional.

The results indicate that modern Western societies are indeed different, in particular concerning the transformation of attitudes and behavior associated with the 'sexual revolution' that has occurred since the 1960s, fundamental changes in the nature of modern families, and more expressive lifestyles. Equality for women has progressed much further, and transformed traditional cultural beliefs and values about the appropriate division of sex roles far more deeply, in affluent Western societies. But at the same time any claim of a 'clash of civilizations', especially of fundamentally different *political* values held by Western and Islamic societies, represents an over-simplification of the evidence. Across many political dimensions examined here, both Islamic and Western societies are similar in their positive orientation toward democratic ideals. Where Islamic societies do differ significantly from the West, in supporting religious authorities, they are far from exceptional around the world. Any black-and-white "Islam versus the West" interpretation of a 'culture clash' as conveyed by the popular media is far too simplistic. It would be desirable to be able to compare public opinion across more dimensions, and across a wider range of nations in the Middle East, Africa, and Asia. Moreover it remains unclear how far different understandings of democracy are culturally determined, giving rise to the familiar problems of equivalence in cross-national research. Nevertheless the results urge strong caution in generalizing from the type of regime to the state of public opinion in any particular country. Support for democracy is surprisingly widespread among Islamic publics, even among those who live in authoritarian societies. The most basic cultural fault line between the West and Islam does not concern democracy—it involves issues of gender equality and sexual liberalization.

Technical Appendix

Table 11.6 Illustration of the Full Regression Model Used in Tables 11.4 and 11.5

	APPROVE OF DEMOCRATIC PERFORMANCE			
	B	ST. ERR.	BETA	SIG
Developmental controls				
Level of human development (100-point scale)	−2.4	.1.0	−.02	**
Level of political development	0.16	.06	.01	**
Social controls				
Age (Years)	−0.05	.01	−.05	***
Gender (Male = 1)	0.41	.12	.01	***
Education (3 categories low to hi)	1.56	.07	.08	***
Income (10 categories low to hi)	0.01	.01	.02	***
Religiosity scale (100-pt low to hi)	−0.01	.01	−.02	***
Type of society				
Islamic	**1.3**	**.34**	**.03**	***
Orthodox	−8.9	.25	−.18	***
Central European	−5.4	.21	−.11	***
Latin American	−6.1	.24	−.11	***
Sinic	1.4	.45	.01	***
Sub-Saharan African	−3.6	.43	−.05	***
Hindu	−8.9	.61	−.06	***
Japanese	3.4	.50	.02	***
(Constant)	68.8	.94		
Adjusted R^2 Block 1 (Control variables only)	.01			
Adjusted R^2 Block 2 (Controls + type of society)	.05			

Note: This illustrates the full OLS regression model, with blockwise entry, in this case with the approval of democratic performance 100-point scale as the dependent variable. Block 1 of the model controls for the level of development of the society and the social background of respondents. Block 2 then enters the type of society, based on the predominant religion, coded as dummy variables. Western societies represent the (omitted) reference category. The coefficients represent the effects of living in each type of society compared with living in Western societies, net of all prior controls. *Democratic performance* scale: For details see Table 2. *Level of human development:* Human Development Index (HDI) 2000, including longevity, literacy and education, and per capita GDP in $US PPP (UNDP Development Report 2000). *Level of political development:* (Freedom House 7-point index (reversed) of political rights and civil liberties 1999–2000) (www.freedomhouse.org). *Type of society:* see Table 11.1. Sig. *** p.001 ** p.01 *p.05. N/s Not significant Source: World Values Survey/European Values Survey (WVS), pooled sample 1995–2001.

Notes

1. International relations scholars have strongly challenged the evidence for Huntington's claim that ethnic inter-state conflict has increased during the 1990s (Gurr 2000; Russett, O'Neal, and Cox 2000; Fox 2001; Chirot 2001; Henderson and Tucker 2001), although this body of work is not central to the argument presented here.

2. The main exceptions are the first-ever Gallup survey in nine predominately Islamic societies which was carried out to monitor reactions to the events of 9/11. Gallup surveyed 10,000 people in December 2001 and January 2002, with researchers conducting hour-long, in-person interviews in Saudi Arabia, Iran, Pakistan, Indonesia, Turkey, Lebanon, Kuwait, Jordan, and Morocco. For details see http://www.gallup.com/poll/releases/pr020305.asp. In addition Roper Reports Worldwide conducted an annual worldwide survey from October 2001-January 2002 in thirty nations, including an urban sample of 1000 residents in the metropolitan areas in Saudi Arabia. For details of the Roper results see Miller and Feinberg (2002).

3. The following analysis draws upon a unique database, the World Values Survey (WVS) and the European Values Surveys (EVS). These surveys provide data from more than seventy societies containing over 80 per cent of the world's population and covering the full range of variation, from societies with per capita incomes as low as $300 per year, to societies with per capita incomes one hundred times that high, and from long-established democracies with market economies, to authoritarian states and ex-socialist states. We owe a large debt of gratitude to the WVS and EVS participants for creating and sharing this invaluable dataset. Their names are listed in the WVS and WVS websites. For more information about the World Values Survey, see the WVS web sites http://wvs.isr.umich.edu/ and http://www.worldvaluessurvey.com. Most of the European surveys used here were gathered by the European Values Survey group (EVS). For detailed EVS findings, see Loek Halman, The European Values Study: A Sourcebook Based on the 1999/2000 European Values Study Surveys. Tilburg: EVS, Tilburg University Press, 2001. For more information, see the EVS website, http://evs.kub.nl.

4. Full methodological details about the World Values Survey/European Values Survey (WVS/EVS), including the questionnaires, sampling procedures, fieldwork procedures, principle investigators, and organization can be found at: http://wvs.isr.umich.edu/wvs-samp.html. The four waves of this survey took place from 1981 to 2001, although it should be noted that all countries were not included in each wave.

5. In addition a distinct 'Jewish' culture could be identified, but Israel was not included within the current release of the WVS.

6. Although it should be noted that despite the centrality of the concept, the definition, labeling and classification of 'civilizations' remains inconsistent in Huntington's work, for example it remains unclear whether Huntington believes that there is or is not a distinct African civilization, and the major discussion of types (pp.45–47) excludes the Orthodox category altogether.

7. These countries are ranked as equally 'free' according to the 2000–2001 Freedom House assessments of political rights and civil liberties Freedom House. 2000. *Freedom in the World 2000–2001*. www.freedomhouse.org.

8. The combined 100-pt gender equality scale is based on the following 5 items: MENPOL Q118: "On the whole, men make better political leaders than women do." (Agree coded low); MENJOBS Q78: "When jobs are scarce, men should have more right to a job than women." (Agree coded low); BOYEDUC Q.119: "A university education is more important for a boy than a girl." (Agree coded low); NEEDKID Q110 "Do you think that a woman has to have children in order to be fulfilled or is this not necessary?" (Agree coded low); SGLMUM Q112 "If a woman wants to have a child as a single parent but she doesn't want to have a stable relationship with a man, do you approve or disapprove?" (disapprove coded low). Three items used statements with Lickert-style 4-point agree-disagree responses, while two used dichotomies, and these items were all recoded so that higher values consistently represent greater support for gender equality. Principal component factor analysis revealed that all five items fell into a single consistent scale (not reproduced here), with a Cronbach's Alpha of 0.54. For details of the construction, reliability, validity, and distribution of this scale see Ronald Inglehart and Pippa Norris. 2003. *Rising Tide: Gender Equality and Cultural Change Around the World*. New York: Cambridge University Press.

References

Chirot, D. 2001. 'A clash of civilizations or of paradigms? Theorizing progress and social change.' *International Sociology*. 16(3): 341–360.

Dalton, Russell. 1999. 'Political Support in Advanced Industrialized Democracies.' In *Critical Citizens: Global Support for Democratic Governance*. Ed. Pippa Norris. Oxford: Oxford University Press.

Esposito, John L. and John O. Voll. 1996. *Democracy and Islam*. New York: Oxford University Press.

Esposito, John. Ed. 1997. *Political Islam: Revolution, Radicalism or Reform?* Boulder, CO: Lynne Reinner.

Fox, J. 2001. 'Two civilizations and ethnic conflict: Islam and the West.' *Journal of Peace Research*. 38(4): 459–472.

Freedom House. 2002. 'Freedom in the World 2002: The Democracy Gap.' New York: Freedom House. www.freedomhouse.org

Fuller, Graham E. 2002. 'The Future of Political Islam.' *Foreign Affairs* 81(2): 48–60.

Funkhouser, G.R. 2000. 'A world ethos and the clash of civilizations: A cross-cultural comparison of attitudes.' *International Journal of Public Opinion Research* 12(1): 73–79.

Gurr, Ted. 2000. *Peoples versus States*. Washington, DC: US Institute for Peace Press.

Henderson, R.A., and R. Tucker. 2001. 'Clear and Present strangers: The clash of civilizations and international politics.' *International Studies Quarterly*. 45(2): 317–338.

Hunter, Shireen T. 1998. *The Future of Islam and the West: Clash of Civilizations or Peaceful Coexistence?* Westport, CT: Praeger.

Huntington, Samuel P. 1993a. 'The Clash of Civilizations?' *Foreign Affairs*. 72(3): 22–49.

Huntington, Samuel P. 1993b. 'If Not Civilizations, what? Paradigms of the Post-Cold War World.' *Foreign Affairs*. 72(5): 186–194.

Huntington, Samuel P. 1996. *The Clash of Civilizations and the Remaking of World Order*. New York: Simon and Schuster.

Huntington, Samuel P. 1996. 'The West Unique, Not Universal.' *Foreign Affairs*. 75(6): 28–34.

Huntington, Samuel P. 1997. 'The Clash of Civilizations—Response.' *Millenium—Journal of International Studies*. 26(1): 141–142.

Inglehart, Ronald, and Pippa Norris. 2003. *Rising Tide: Gender Equality and Cultural Change Around the World*. New York: Cambridge University Press.

Inglehart, Ronald and Wayne E. Baker. 2000. 'Modernization, Globalization and the Persistence of Tradition: Empirical Evidence from 65 Societies.' *American Sociological Review*. 65: 19–55.

Inglehart, Ronald. 1997. *Modernization and Postmodernization: Cultural, Economic and Political Change in 43 Societies*. Princeton, NJ: Princeton University Press.

Kabuli, Niaz Faizi. 1994. *Democracy according to Islam*. Pittsburgh, PA: Dorrance Publications.

Klingemann, Hans Dieter. 1999. 'Mapping political support in the 1990s: A global analysis.' In *Critical Citizens: Global Support for Democratic Governance*. Ed. Pippa Norris. Oxford: Oxford University Press.

Lewis, Bernard. 2002. *What Went Wrong? Western impact and Middle Eastern response*. New York: Oxford University Press.

Midlarsky, M.I. 1998. 'Democracy and Islam: Implications for civilizational conflict and the democratic process.' *International Studies Quarterly*. 42(3): 485–511.

Miller, Thomas A.W. and Geoffrey Feinberg. 2002. 'Culture Clash.' *Public Perspective*. 13(2): 6–9.

Norris, Pippa. 2002. *Democratic Phoenix: Political Activism Worldwide*. NY/Cambridge: Cambridge University Press.

Norris, Pippa. Ed. 1999. *Critical Citizens: Global Support for Democratic Governance*. Oxford: Oxford University Press.

Putnam, Robert D. and Susan Pharr. Eds. 2001. *Disaffected Democracies: What's Troubling the Trilateral Countries?* Princeton, NJ: Princeton University Press.

Russett, B. M., J. R. O'Neal and M. Cox. 2000. 'Clash of Civilizations, or Realism and Liberalism Déjà Vu? Some Evidence.' *Journal of Peace Research*. 37(5): 583–608.

Said, Edward. 2001. 'A Clash of Ignorance'. *The Nation*.

Shadid, Anthony. 2001. *Legacy of the prophet: despots, democrats, and the new politics of Islam*. Boulder, CO: Westview Press.

CHAPTER 12

Rallies All Around: The Dynamics of System Support

PAUL BREWER
SEAN ADAY
KIMBERLY GROSS

Terrorist violence and media framing of it may well affect how citizens feel about their own government and political system. Attacks by terrorist groups may reinforce support for political leaders and trust in government institutions, in a 'rally' effect against an internal or external threat. Alternatively such attacks may undermine public support for leaders and confidence in institutions, if insurgent groups are regarded as challenging the ability of the authorities to defend the public effectively against dangerous security threats. In turn, mass support for the political system may have important and far-reaching political consequences.

In their seminal studies, Easton (1965, 1975) and Gamson (1968) argued that such support is crucial to the success and, ultimately, the survival of the political system. To be sure, political discontent rarely leads to fundamental state failure. Research has shown, however, that system support shapes mass political behavior and opinion even under less dramatic circumstances. For example, recent studies have found that support for the political system influences compliance with governmental authority (Scholz and Lubell 1998), voting behavior (Hetherington 1999), and policy preferences (Chanley et al. 2000, Hetherington and Globetti 2002).

Given these consequences, it is not surprising that scholars have devoted considerable attention to understanding trends in system support among various mass publics. Surveys conducted in the United States showed that many forms of system support declined substantially from the 1960s through the 1990s (Brody 1991, Craig 1993, Rosenstone and Hansen 1993, Hibbing and Theiss-Morse 1995, Hetherington 1998). For example, trust in government diminished from its peak in 1964, when 76% of Americans trusted the government in Washington to do what is right "just about always" or "most of the time," to levels that by the 1990s averaged about half of that (see Figure 12.1). American confidence in government institutions such as the presidency and Congress also suffered sizable declines (Lipset and Schneider 1983, Hibbing and Theiss-Morse 1995), and

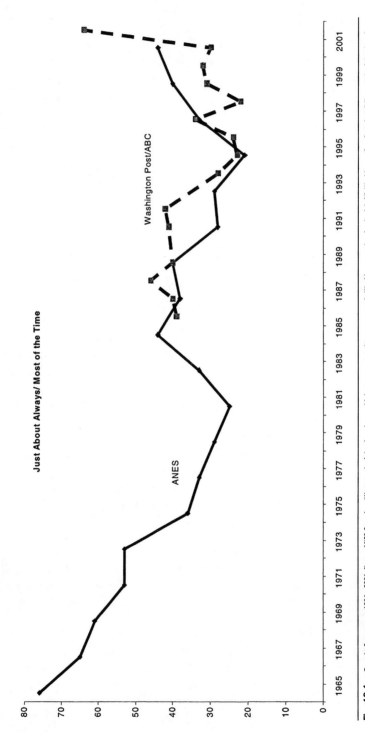

Fig. 12.1 Trust in Government 1964–2001. Notes: ANES Question: "How much of the time do you think you can trust the government in Washington to do what is right?" *Washington Post* Question: "How much of the time do you trust the government in Washington to do what they say?" Sources: American National Election Studies, 1958–2000, *Washington Post*/ABC News, 1985–2001.

presidential approval ratings reached lower peaks than they once had (Brody 1991). The decline in support for political institutions and actors was neither unique to the American public nor particularly severe when placed in an international context (Dalton 1999). Nor did it necessarily extend to the political community or the abstract principles of the system (Norris 1999). Nevertheless, the evidence for eroding system support among the American public was sufficient to provoke considerable alarm among many observers.

This evidence also inspired new research that went beyond documenting shifts in the aggregate levels of system support indicators to examine causal relationships among them at the individual level. Hetherington (1998), in particular, showed that mutually reinforcing relationships bind various forms of system support. His findings carried the troubling implication that "vicious cycles"—negative feedback loops among individual components of system support—might generate a downward spiral in system support across the board. Vicious cycles of this sort may be "problematic for governance," according Hetherington, because they "likely undermine the government's ability to solve problems," which in turn may further diminish support for the political system (1998: 791).

On a more optimistic note, the existence of "vicious cycles" may indicate that "virtuous cycles" are possible as well. Hetherington's (1998) research suggested that system support among the American public would remain low in the absence of an exogenous change triggering a positive, rather than negative, feedback loop among the components of system support. The events of September 11 may have provided just such a shock, at least in the short run. Surveys conducted in the months following the terrorist attacks recorded a dramatic surge in public support for the American political system. *Washington Post*/ABC News surveys found that the percentage of respondents who "trust[ed] the government in Washington to do what is right" just about always or most of the time more than doubled, rising from 30% to 64% (Milbank and Morin 2001). The Gallup Organization recorded the largest jump in presidential approval—thirty-five percentage points—that it had ever observed (Moore 2001). The National Opinion Research Center found that the proportion of Americans expressing a great deal of confidence in the military increased by twenty-seven percentage points; for Congress, by thirty-one points; and for the executive branch of the federal government, by thirty-four points (Smith et al. 2001). Other surveys showed that American confidence in the Federal Bureau of Investigation and the Central Intelligence Agency also increased in the immediate aftermath of the attacks (Brewer et al. 2002).

Why did this post-9/11 surge in system support take place in America? In particular, did "virtuous cycles"—that is, mutually reinforcing relationships among various forms of system support—contribute to the surge? To help answer these questions, we revisit the individual-level causal structure of trust in the aftermath of the terrorist attacks. Specifically, we examine panel survey data that allow us to analyze the relationships among the components of system support. To date, studies of the causal structure of system support have relied largely upon either aggregate time-series data or cross-sectional, individual-level data (often collected during election campaigns); thus, our panel design allows us new leverage in disentangling that structure. We collected two waves of panel data, one from October 2001 and one from March 2002.

In this chapter, we advance our understanding of the causal structure of American system support in three ways. First, we establish the dynamics of system support during a particularly interesting and important time period: The aftermath of a national crisis during which national security appeared to be threatened, the American public gave the political system an atypically enthusiastic vote of confidence, and political leaders drew upon that public support in undertaking dramatic initiatives, including launching military actions abroad and claiming broader domestic powers to fight terrorism. Second, we expand the scope of previous research into the causal structure of system support to address the simultaneous relationships among various forms of support for political institutions, the political community, and the social community. Finally, we look at whether findings from the "rally" phase—the period following 9/11 during which system support surged—parallel previous findings regarding the causal structure of system support (e.g., Brehm and Rahn 1997, Hetherington 1998).

The Concept of System Support

Before we examine how the various pieces of this puzzle may be related to one another, we should first say more about how they fit into our conceptual framework. Our understanding of system support is rooted in the frameworks developed by Easton (1965, 1975) and Norris (1999). Easton identified three levels of system support: support for the political community, support for the political regime, and support for political authorities. Norris (1999: 10-2) expanded this scheme into a five-level framework that distinguished between support for the political community ("basic attachment to the nation"), support for regime principles ("values of the political system"), support for regime performance ("function in practice"), support for regime institutions ("governments, parliaments, the executive, the legal system and police, the state bureaucracy, political parties, and the military"), and support for political actors ("politicians as a class and the performance of particular leaders"). Our account focuses on the first level, represented by patriotism, and the last two levels (which we combine for our purposes), represented by support for the president, Congress, the military, the intelligence community, and the government as a whole. However, we make two modifications to the Easton and Norris frameworks in our account of system support. First, within what Norris describes as support for political institutions and actors, we distinguish between political trust and trust in specific institutions. We argue that political trust, or generalized trust in government, exists at a more abstract level than trust in particular institutions or actors such as Congress or the presidency. Second, we link the various levels of system support to support for a construct outside of the political system, namely the social community.

Now let us consider each individual piece of our framework. A logical place to begin is with political trust, also known as trust in government. We define political trust as a general orientation toward the government as a whole (Stokes 1962, Hetherington 1998). Put another way, it is the broadest form of support for political institutions and the actors occupying them. Following previous studies of political trust in the American context, we focus on four indicators of political trust: Citizens' generalized beliefs about whether the government can be trusted to do what is right, wastes tax money, is run for the benefit of all the people, and is run by crooks (Stokes 1962, Miller 1974a, Hetherington 1998).[1]

Along with political trust, we are interested in support for specific government institutions and actors, particularly the president, Congress, the military, and the intelligence community. From the early years of survey research onward, scholars have measured—and attempted to explain—confidence in the presidency and approval ratings for specific presidents. One long-standing finding in this research is that the latter form of support typically increases during times of international crisis (e.g., Mueller 1970, 1973; Sigelman and Conover 1981). Hence it seems appropriate to consider presidential approval in our analysis of system support, particularly given that such approval is a crucial resource for exercising the powers of the presidency (Neustadt 1960). Because the distinction between the presidential approval and confidence in the presidency "is not often made by ordinary citizens" (Hibbing and Theiss-Morse 1995: 44), however, we fold these concepts into one, presidential support. As we will show, our results justify this decision.

We also investigate support for three institutions that played their own crucial roles during the aftermath of 9/11: Congress, which wielded the formal power to declare war; the military, which was swiftly called into action to respond to the attacks; and the intelligence community, which played a prominent role in the "war on terrorism" (and later received scrutiny for alleged failures prior to the attacks). Of the branches of government, Congress has borne the harshest public scorn in recent decades (Hibbing and Theiss Morse 1995); the military, meanwhile, has been an exception to the trend of eroding support. In examining support for the intelligence community we focus on confidence in the Central Intelligence Agency and the Federal Bureau of Investigation, its two most prominent components.

National pride or patriotism is another important component of system support, albeit one that occupies a higher level of abstraction than those previously discussed. Not surprisingly, research has shown that the American public consistently exhibits high levels of national pride (e.g., Dalton 1999). Indeed, previous surges in support for political leaders have often been described as "rally-round-the-flag" effects (e.g., Mueller 1970, 1973), although the causal role of patriotism in such rallies has received little direct scrutiny. Of the various dimensions of national pride we focus on "symbolic patriotism," which revolves around a strong emotional attachment to the nation and traditional patriotic symbols such as the flag (Sullivan, Fried, and Dietz 1992).

Finally, we include another level in our account of system support: support for the social community that surrounds the political system, represented by trust in one's fellow citizens. Such trust, variously referred to as social trust, interpersonal trust, or faith in human nature, has recently become the focus of scholarly research, particularly given evidence of its decline among the American public over the past four decades (Putnam 1995a, Rahn and Transue 1998). Taken by itself social trust has important political consequences: It affects civic engagement (Brehm and Rahn 1997, Putnam 2000), compliance with government (Scholz and Lubell 1998), tolerance (Uslaner 2002) and policy attitudes (Brewer and Steenbergen 2002, Uslaner 2002). More important for our purposes, there are theoretical grounds for expecting support for the social community to be intertwined with the various components of system support.

We discuss those grounds shortly. For now, let us simply note that there is also a strong empirical basis for expecting the various pieces in our framework to be bound by causal relationships: They all moved in tandem after 9/11. Not only did support for political institutions and actors increase; so did symbolic patriotism and even social trust. The National Opinion Research Center found that the percentage of Americans saying that they "would rather be citizen[s] of America than any other country in the world" rose from 90 percent to 97 percent (Smith et al. 2001). Similarly, trust in one's fellow citizens increased following 9/11, with some of NORC's measures of social trust reaching levels that broke or approached previously recorded highs (Smith et al. 2001).

Less clear are the directions of the relationships among these various constructs. Within the rising tide that lifted all boats, which forms of support did the pulling and which were pulled? For example, did generalized political trust spill over to support for specific government institutions and actors (namely, the president, Congress, the military, and the intelligence community), did it reflect faith in these components of government, or did it do both? Did patriotic fervor shape support for government institutions and actors, and did government institutions and actors inspire national pride? Did citizens who rallied around the president rally around the military, the Congress, and the intelligence community as well, and did confidence in these institutions buoy presidential support? What was the relationship between each of these forms of system support and generalized trust in one's fellow citizens? Last, was the structure of system support during this period characterized by mutually reinforcing relationships that could have produced an upward spiral across the board in system support?

Explaining the Causal Structure of System Support

Our theoretical account of system support dynamics is grounded in cognitive research on how people organize and use information. An individual's level of support for any aspect of the political system—be it a particular institution or actor, the government as a whole, or the political community—will be determined by the information linked to that object within the individual's memory (Erber and Lau 1990). People can draw connections among these representations; thus, various forms of system support may be related to one another (Hetherington 1998, Chanley et al. 2000). In addition, these forms of system support may be related to other constructs, such as support for the social community (Brehm and Rahn 1997).

Two perspectives on the nature of political belief systems may explain which sorts of connections are particularly powerful within the causal structure of system support. According to one perspective, people tend to form hierarchical belief systems in which generalized orientations shape more specific orientations (Hurwitz and Peffley 1987, Peffley and Hurwtiz 1993). Put another way, people engage in "theory-driven" processing: They use their abstract beliefs as heuristics, or information shortcuts, when forming evaluations of particular objects. According to the other perspective, general orientations tend to be reflections of specific orientations (Peffley and Hurwitz 1993). Applied to the case at hand, the first perspective suggests that people may reason from the most abstract construct in the model (support for the social community) to the broadest level of system support (support for political community) and then from both of these to more concrete forms of system support (political trust, presidential support, confidence in Congress, confidence in the military, and confidence in the intelligence community). The second perspective implies that people may reason along these same paths in the opposite directions. Figure 12.2 provides a schematic representation of our model, which incorporates both perspectives.

Among the constructs represented in Figure 12.2, social trust is the most general. According to Rahn and Transue (1998: 545) it serves a "standing decision"

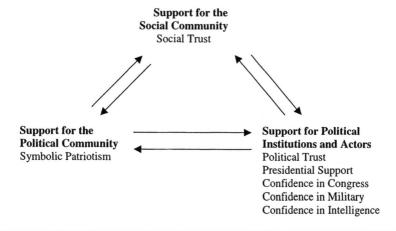

Fig. 12.2 A causal model of system support.

on whether to give others the benefit of the doubt in specific situations. In the case at hand, citizens may rely on this standing decision when deciding whether to trust political institutions and actors. Lane (1959: 164) has written that "if one cannot trust other people generally, then one can certainly not trust those . . . with the powers which come with public office." By the same logic, citizens who trust other people may infer that they can trust government institutions and actors. Indeed, Brehm and Rahn's analysis of individual-level data from 1972 to 1994 suggests that this is the case, although other scholars have disputed the existence of such a relationship (Newton 1999, Uslaner 2002). If Brehm and Rahn are correct, then one might expect social trust to influence each of our indicators of support for political institutions and actors: political trust, presidential support, confidence in Congress, confidence in the military, and confidence in government intelligence agencies. It may even be that social trust can produce positive feelings toward one's nation and its symbols if citizens base their evaluations of the political community on their evaluations of the social community.

In each case, however, the reverse may also be true. For example, citizens may infer that they can trust one another when they can count on political authorities to enforce the social contract and infer otherwise when they cannot. This logic, which lies at the heart of Hobbes's (1651 [1985]) argument for Leviathan (i.e., governmental authority), suggests that confidence in government institutions and actors should influence social trust—another proposition supported by individual-level data from 1972 to 1994 (Brehm and Rahn 1997, but see Uslaner 2002). Along the same lines, patriotic sentiment may produce a spirit of civic-mindedness and camaraderie, thereby shaping social trust not only in the aggregate (Putnam 2000) but also at the individual level.

The next broadest level of abstraction in our model is occupied by support for the political community in the form of patriotism. One might expect emotional attachments to the nation and its symbols to inspire greater political trust, presidential support, confidence in Congress, confidence in the military, and confidence in the intelligence community—particularly during times of crisis if the public truly rallies around the flag under such circumstances. At the same time, it is plausible that the various components of support for political institutions and actors might influence patriotism: a trustworthy government institution or actor could become a source of national pride, rather than merely a reflection of it. For example, faith in the president or the military might inspire patriotic sentiments.

In specifying the relationships among the various forms of support for political institutions and actors, we again allow for reciprocal relationships that flow from the general to the specific and from the specific to the general (see Figure 12.3). On the one hand, citizens may base their degree of faith in specific institutions and actors on their generalized evaluations of government, with political trust thereby serving as another standing decision for citizens. Indeed,

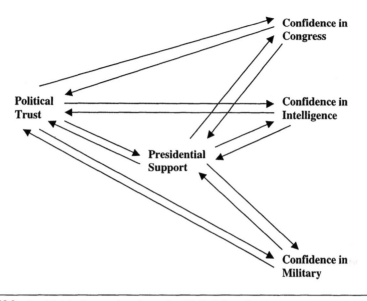

Fig. 12.3   Potential relationships among forms of support for political institutions and actors.

previous research has found that political trust influences evaluations of the president (Hetheringon 1998, Chanley et al. 2000) and Congress (Hetherington 1998, but see Chanley et al. 2000). By a similar logic, political trust may also affect confidence in the military and the intelligence community. Turning the causal arrows in the other direction, citizens may base their evaluations of the government as a whole on their evaluations of its components. For example, Hetherington (1998) found that in 1988 and 1996, feelings toward the president and Congress not only were influenced by but also influenced political trust (see also Citrin 1974, Feldman 1983, Citrin and Green 1986, but see Chanley et al. 2000). Previous research sheds no light on the effects of faith in the military or the intelligence community on political trust, but they may follow the same pattern. It may also be that evaluations of different components of government are differentially related to political trust. Several previous studies point to a particularly strong link between evaluations of Congress and political trust. Feldman (1983) and Hetherington (1998) concluded that evaluations of Congress play a central role in shaping political trust; looking at the reverse effect, Chanley et al. (2000) found that political trust has a greater impact on evaluations of Congress than on evaluations of the president.

Because the American political system has evolved into a president-dominated one (Fiorina 1992) and because the media typically provide the public with a president-centered view of American politics (Iyengar and Kinder

1987), one must also consider the potential relationships between presidential support and confidence in other government institutions. On the one hand, presidential support may spill over to other institutions. It seems plausible that citizens will evaluate the military and intelligence agencies in part on the basis of presidential support; after all, these institutions are under the president's authority. If citizens see the president as the center of American politics, then presidential support may even shape confidence in Congress. At the same time, president-centered politics could also lead citizens to give the president credit or blame for what goes on in government, regardless of whether the president is fully responsible (Ansolabehere et al. 1993). Thus, citizens may base their degree of presidential support on their degree of confidence in the military, the intelligence community, and Congress.

One final point suggested by our theoretical framework is that the causal structure of system support may change depending on the nature of information available to citizens. This raises questions about whether relationships observed by scholars in the pre-9/11 period carried over to the immediate aftermath of the terrorist attacks. For instance, did the reciprocal relationship between political trust and social trust observed by Brehm and Rahn (1997) persist in the aftermath of the attacks? Likewise, did the mutually reinforcing relationships between political trust and evaluations of both the president and Congress (see Hetherington 1998) continue after 9/11? Given that the post-9/11 period was a unique moment in modern American history, it is quite plausible that the relationships among the elements of our model would vary considerably in such a moment from what one might find in the midst of a partisan political campaign.

Data and Methods

Our data come from a two-wave national random digit dial telephone survey of Americans, eighteen years and older. The first wave of the survey, in which 1,235 respondents were interviewed, was conducted from 24 October to 5 November 2001. The second wave was in the field from 28 February to 26 March 2002, with the bulk of the interviews occurring in the first two weeks. Sixty-one percent (758) of the respondents from the first wave were re-interviewed.[2] In the account that follows, we restrict our attention to panel respondents (i.e., those who were interviewed in both waves). The appendix provides further details about the nature of the sample.

The first wave contained measures for gender, education, income, age, and party identification.[3] We include these variables in our model because past research suggests they may be related to system support. Our measures for education and income divided respondents into seven categories, whereas our measure for age placed them in one of six cohorts based on the decade in which they came of age (see Putnam 1995b). We used the traditional branching-format question series to produce a seven-point scale for party identification, coded so that high values indicated Republican partisanship and low values indicated Democratic partisanship.

Both waves included the following measures for the key variables in our model:

Social trust was measured through an index constructed from two traditional indicators (Wrightsman 1991, Rahn and Transue 1998): "Generally speaking, would you say that most people can be trusted, or that you can't be too careful in dealing with people?" and "Would you say that most of the time people try to be helpful, or that they are just looking out for themselves?" The reliability of this measure was .80 in the first wave and .76 in the second.

Symbolic patriotism was measured through an index constructed from two items: "How patriotic are you—would you say extremely patriotic, very patriotic, somewhat patriotic, or not especially patriotic?" and "When you see the American flag flying does it make you feel extremely good, very good, somewhat good, or not very good?" The reliability of this measure was .79 in the first wave and .83 in the second wave.

Political trust was measured through the traditional four-item index (Stokes 1962, Miller 1974a): "How much of the time can you trust the government in Washington to do what is right—just about always, most of the time or only some of the time?"; "Would you say the government is pretty much run by a few big interests looking out for themselves or that it is run for the benefit of all the people?"; "Do you think that quite a few of the people running the government are crooked, not very many are, or do you think hardly any of them are crooked?" and "Do you think that people in the government waste a lot of the money we pay in taxes, waste some of it, or don't waste very much of it?" Its reliability was .78 in the first wave and .81 in the second wave.

Presidential support was measured through an index that combined the traditional presidential approval measure ("Do you approve or disapprove of the way George W. Bush is handling his job as president") and a confidence measure ("How much confidence do you have in the presidency—a great deal, quite a lot, some, or very little?"). In each wave, the two items were highly correlated with one another, yielding reliability scores of .92 in the first wave and .83 in the second.

Confidence in Congress was measured through a single item that paralleled the confidence in the presidency measure.

Confidence in the military was measured through a similar item.

Confidence in intelligence was measured through an index that combined confidence in the "C.I.A., or Central Intelligence Agency," and the "F.B.I., or Federal Bureau of Investigation." We combined these indicators because they were strongly correlated in each wave. The reliability of the index was .88 in the first wave and .84 in the second.

Table 12.1 reports the means and standard deviations for these variables in each wave among the panel respondents for whom we have full data. Each

Table 12.1 Variables in the Model

	WAVE 1	WAVE 2
	Mean (standard deviation)	Mean (standard deviation)
Social Trust	.70 (.38)	.68 (.39)
Symbolic Patriotism	.74 (.22)	.71 (.23)
Political Trust	.41 (.27)	.38 (.27)
Presidential Support	.80 (.26)	.75 (.28)
Confidence in Congress	.48 (.28)	.46 (.25)
Confidence in Military	.80 (.24)	.76 (.25)
Confidence in Intelligence	.52 (.28)	.49 (.26)

Note: N = 490. Variables are coded 0–1 where 1 represents the confident or trusting position. Wave 1: 24 October to 5 November 2001. Wave II: 28 February to 26 March 2002.

variable was transformed to range from 0 to 1 where 1 represents maximum support. Note that although each form of support declined from the first wave to the second, these declines were modest; stability, rather than change, dominated during this period. Thus, it seems appropriate to consider both waves as falling within the initial rally phase following 9/11.

The next two tables present the correlations among the key variables in wave 1 (Table 2a) and wave 2 (Table 12.2b). Again, stability dominated. The correlations in wave 1 largely resembled those in wave 2, suggesting that the structure of system support was stable over this period.

Our analysis examined the causal structure of system support during the rally period. We constructed a cross-lagged effects model of system support, using the wave 1 measures as independent variables and the wave 2 measures as dependent variables (see Finkel 1995).[4] In our model, each form of support in wave 1 was allowed to influence itself in wave 2. We allowed gender, education, income, and age cohort to influence each form of support in wave 2, and we allowed party identification to influence all forms of support in wave 2 except social trust (for which there was no obvious reason to expect a partisanship effect).

We drew on our theoretical account to specify the paths representing the causal relationships among the various forms of support in the model. We allowed social trust, symbolic patriotism, and political trust in wave 1 to influence one another in wave 2; we also allowed them to influence presidential support, confidence in Congress, confidence in the military, and confidence in intelligence in wave 2. We allowed presidential support, confidence in Congress, confidence in the military, and confidence in intelligence in wave 1 to influence social trust, symbolic patriotism, and political trust in wave 2. We allowed presidential support in wave 1 to influence confidence in Congress, the military, and intelligence in wave 2; in addition, we allowed confidence in Congress, the military, and intelligence in wave 1 to influence presidential support in wave 2.

Table 12.2a Correlation among Wave 1 Variables

	INTERPERSONAL TRUST	SYMBOLIC PATRIOTISM	POLITICAL TRUST	PRESIDENTIAL SUPPORT	CONFIDENCE IN CONGRESS	CONFIDENCE IN MILITARY
Symbolic Patriotism	.05					
Political Trust	.24	.22				
Presidential Support	.15	.43	.45			
Confidence in Congress	.17	.22	.56	.38		
Confidence in Military	−.05	.47	.27	.47	.32	
Confidence in Intelligence	.07	.29	.41	.45	.37	.52

Note: Wave 1: 24 October to 5 November 2001. Number of observations = 490.

Table 12.2b Correlation among Wave 2 Variables

	INTERPERSONAL TRUST	SYMBOLIC PATRIOTISM	POLITICAL TRUST	PRESIDENTIAL SUPPORT	CONFIDENCE IN CONGRESS	CONFIDENCE IN MILITARY
Symbolic Patriotism	.04					
Political Trust	.25	.15				
Presidential Support	.08	.42	.45			
Confidence in Congress	.12	.13	.49	.35		
Confidence in Military	.07	.41	.31	.47	.30	
Confidence in Intelligence	.10	.30	.49	.50	.43	.44

Note: Wave II: 28 February to 26 March 2002. Number of observations = 490.

In keeping with the notion of vicious—or in this case, virtuous—cycles in system support, we expected positive coefficients for the causal paths among the various forms of support: In each instance, we hypothesized that higher levels of one would produce higher levels of the other.

Results

We used Weighted Least Squares in LISREL 8.52 to estimate the model (see Joreskog 1990). Table 12.3 reports the results.[5] The Adjusted Goodness of Fit index for the model was .97, indicating that it fit the data adequately.

To begin with, our findings suggest that social trust and political trust influenced one another. The effect of social trust in wave 1 on political trust in wave 2 was positive and significant; likewise, so was the effect of political trust in wave 1 on social trust in wave 2. These results suggest that the reciprocal relationship between social and political trust described by Brehm and Rahn (1997) persisted in the wake of 9/11.

Except for political trust and social trust itself, no other variable in the model exerted a significant effect on social trust in wave 2. Social trust in wave 1 did, however, influence several forms of system support in wave 2 besides political trust. One novel finding produced by our analysis was that greater trust in one's fellow citizens had a positive and significant effect on symbolic patriotism. We take this as evidence that social trust shaped emotional attachments to the nation and its symbols. We found no indication that social trust influenced presidential support, but it did exert positive and significant effects on confidence in Congress and confidence in intelligence. The effect of social trust on confidence in the military was similarly positive but fell short of statistical significance. Collectively, these results lend support to the argument that social trust influences evaluations of government institutions and actors (Lane 1959, Brehm and Rahn 1997, Putnam 2000).

Symbolic patriotism in wave 1 had no significant effect on either social or political trust in wave 2. On the other hand, it had a positive and significant effect on presidential support in wave 2: Citizens who rallied around the flag also rallied around the president. Thus, our results provide evidence for a causal mechanism underlying presidential approval during times of crisis that has long been hypothesized (e.g., Mueller 1970, 1973) but, until now, never examined directly. Symbolic patriotism in wave 1 had a similarly positive effect on confidence in the military in wave 2, indicating that citizens who rallied around the flag also rallied around the troops. Symbolic patriotism did not have a significant effect on either confidence in Congress or confidence in the intelligence community, which suggests that these institutions were not as closely tied as the White House or the armed forces to emotions regarding the nation and its symbols. Another intriguing and novel finding is that confidence in the military in wave 1 had a significant and positive effect on symbolic patriotism in wave 2. Citizens who rallied around the military also seem to have rallied around the

Table 12.3 Effect of Wave 1 Variables on Wave 2 Variables

WAVE 1 VARIABLES	WAVE 2 VARIABLES						
	SOCIAL TRUST	SYMBOLIC PATRIOTISM	POLITICAL TRUST	PRESIDENTIAL SUPPORT	CONFIDENCE IN CONGRESS	CONFIDENCE IN MILITARY	CONFIDENCE IN INTELLIGENCE
Social Trust	.69**	.11**	.14**	-.01	.12*	.09	.09*
	(.06)	(.04)	(.04)	(.05)	(.06)	(.06)	(.05)
Symbolic Patriotism	-.09	.69**	-.02	.10*	-.05	.12*	.06
	(.06)	(.06)	(.05)	(.05)	(.05)	(.06)	(.05)
Political Trust	.12*	-.02	.75**	.15**	.25**	.12*	.16**
	(.07)	(.05)	(.08)	(.07)	(.07)	(.06)	(.06)
Presidential Support	.06	.06	.03	.52**	.14*	.13*	.16**
	(.08)	(.08)	(.06)	(.08)	(.08)	(.07)	(.07)
Confidence in Congress	-.05	-.07	.04	.05	.40**	—	—
	(.07)	(.05)	(.05)	(.06)	(.07)		
Confidence in the Military	-.02	.13*	-.07	.00	—	.49**	—
	(.08)	(.06)	(.06)	(.06)		(.08)	

Confidence in Intelligence	−.01 (.06)	−.01 (.06)	.06 (.05)	.04 (.06)	—	—	.51** (.05)
Party Identification	—	−.04 (.04)	.08* (.04)	.21** (.05)	−.05 (.06)	.00 (.05)	.06 (.04)
Female	.03 (.06)	.02 (.04)	−.02 (.05)	−.02 (.05)	−.02 (.06)	.06 (.05)	−.12** (.05)
Education	.00 (.05)	−.07* (.04)	−.15** (.05)	−.06 (.05)	−.08 (.05)	−.05 (.06)	−.08 (.05)
Income	.06 (.05)	.03 (.04)	.06 (.04)	.00 (.04)	.03 (.05)	−.05 (.05)	−.05 (.05)
Age Cohort	.08 (.05)	.03 (.03)	.02 (.04)	.01 (.04)	−.01 (.05)	−.05 (.05)	.01 (.04)

Note: The figures are the unstandardized beta coefficients produced by Weighted Least Squares regression analysis with the standard errors in parentheses. Wave 1: 24 October to 5 November 2001. Wave II: 28 February to 26 March 2002. Number of observations = 490. Chi-Square = 71.81 (28 degrees of freedom). Adjusted Goodness of Fit index = .97. * $p < .05$; ** $p < .01$.

flag, not just the other way around. In contrast, support for the president, Congress, and the intelligence community had no such effects on patriotism.

Aside from political trust itself and social trust, no form of support influenced political trust in wave 2, whereas political trust in wave 1 influenced every wave 2 measure of support for specific institutions and actors. Specifically, political trust exerted positive and significant effects on presidential support, confidence in Congress, confidence in the military, and confidence in intelligence in wave 2. The findings regarding presidential support and confidence in Congress imply that the effects of political trust on evaluations of these institutions (Hetherington 1998; Chanley et. al. 2000) carried over from before 9/11 to its aftermath. The findings regarding the military and the intelligence community demonstrate that the impact of political trust on confidence extended to other institutions in this period. The finding that the effect of political trust on confidence in Congress was the strongest path in the model (excluding the effects of variables in wave 1 on themselves in wave 2) also reinforces Chanley et al.'s (2000) claim that the tie from political trust to evaluations of Congress is particularly strong. The absence of reciprocal effects for evaluations of the White House and Congress on political trust, however, is a departure from the pre-9/11 era (Hetherington 1998). Our evidence suggests that in this moment it was not simply evaluations of the current administration that drove system support, as Citrin (1974) contends is typically the case.

Presidential support in wave 1 exerted positive and significant effects on confidence in the military, intelligence, and Congress in wave 2. The reverse was not true, as the effects of confidence in the military, intelligence, and Congress in wave 1 on presidential support in wave 2 fell short of significance. Thus, the results suggest that presidential support spilled over to other parts of the government, which is consistent with a president-centered political mindset on the part of citizens. The results do not suggest, however, that presidential support was based on evaluations of other government institutions, even those under the authority of the White House.

From Vicious Cycles to a Virtuous Cycle and Back Again?

The results lead us to conclude that during the initial aftermath of 9/11, mass support typically flowed from the abstract to the specific (see Figure 12.4). Social trust shaped symbolic patriotism, political trust, confidence in Congress, and confidence in the intelligence community. Emotional attachments to nation and flag, in turn, shaped presidential support and confidence in the military (although our results imply that one cannot characterize the more general rally in system support as being driven solely by patriotic fervor). Moving down another step in abstraction, generalized political trust influenced presidential support, confidence in Congress, confidence in the military, and confidence in the intelligence. The two exceptions to the top-down structure of system support were the effect of political trust on social trust and the effect of confidence in the military on symbolic patriotism.

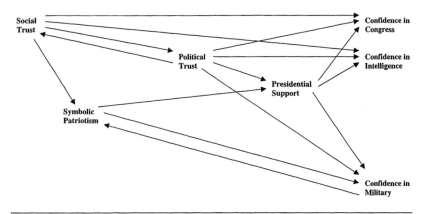

Fig. 12.4 Observed relationships among key variables in the model.

Our findings furthermore indicate that presidential support dominated confidence in other government institutions during the rally period following 9/11. Presidential support lifted confidence in institutions under presidential authority—namely, the military and intelligence agencies—and even another branch of government, Congress. This makes sense, particularly when one considers that the presidency-centered view of politics was probably even more evident than usual in the media coverage following the attacks. The spillover effects, however, only went in one direction. In short, citizens treated other parts of government as extensions of the presidency but not the other way around.

Some of our findings replicate those from the pre-9/11 period. For example, our findings regarding the reciprocal relationship between political trust and social trust reflect the pattern observed by Brehm and Rahn (1997) from 1972 to 1994. This result lends support to the claim that a reciprocal relationship does exist at the individual level.[6] Furthermore, our findings regarding the effects of political trust on presidential support and confidence in Congress parallel the results observed by Hetherington (1998) in 1988 and 1996. In contrast, our failure to find effects for presidential support and confidence in Congress on political trust breaks the pattern observed by Hetherington in 1988 and 1996. Why do we think this period is different? One possible reason is that the terrorist attacks were seen as an attack on the government as a whole, to which the government responded as a whole. Leaders on both sides of the aisle made great efforts to present a united front and the American public seems to have responded in kind. The nature of the terrorist attacks and the subsequent governmental response may have altered the normal structure of system support. Thus, it may be that the structure was unusually "top-down," or theory-driven, during the rally phase that followed the events of 9/11.

At the same time, the results suggest that the surge in system support was in part the product of a virtuous cycle linking system support and support for the social community: the mutually reinforcing relationship between political trust and social trust. Although our analysis did not directly compare system support before 9/11 to system support afterward, it demonstrated that these two beliefs were particularly important foundations of system support during the aftermath of the attacks. Thus, we may infer that the increases in these two forms of trust following 9/11 played an important role in lifting not only one another but other forms of system support upward as well—both directly and by shaping symbolic patriotism and presidential support, which in turn influenced confidence in other institutions. Put another way, political leaders in the White House, Congress, the military, and the intelligence community may have received greater opportunities to draw upon the resource of system support during this time of crisis because citizens decided that they could, at least for the time being, place generalized faith in both government and one another.

Of course, our results cannot fully explain how the exogenous shock of the terrorist attacks and subsequent events triggered increases in social trust, symbolic patriotism, and political trust, thereby feeding the upward spiral in system support. Our theoretical framework, however, suggests some plausible hypotheses revolving around the impact of changes in the flow of information that citizens could have connected to their beliefs about the political system, particularly government in general and their fellow citizens. One possibility, suggested by Brody's (1991) and Zaller's (1992) research, is that exposure to a pro-government consensus within public debate produced increased levels of political trust. Another potential explanation for the increase in political trust is that the media abandoned frames that previously dominated news coverage. Some accounts have blamed "game" or "horse race" coverage of politics for the decline in political trust among Americans, arguing that even if negative coverage does not cause cynicism it may activate and reinforce it (Patterson 1993, Cappella and Jamieson 1997). Thus, a decline in such coverage following 9/11 may have lifted political trust. Similarly, a boom in news stories about relief efforts and the heroism of ordinary citizens may have buoyed social trust in the wake of the terrorist attacks. The increase in civic engagement after 9/11 reported by observers (e.g., Smith et al. 2001) may also have contributed to—and been influenced by—increased social trust (see Brehm and Rahn 1997, Putnam 2000, but see Uslaner 2002). Finally, some accounts suggest that system support should rise during moments of international crisis. Using times series data from 1980–2001, Chanley (2001) has shown that concern over international crises is associated with greater political trust (though past research on this question has produced mixed results). When Americans turn their attention from domestic concerns to international crises they may lend support to the political system as the only way to address the concern; this seems especially likely when the international crisis is perceived as presenting a real threat to the nation, as in the case of 9/11. Our results do not speak directly to these explanations. We do believe, however, that the question of why Americans decided they could place their faith in the government and one another at this moment is worthy of further research.

Another topic that future research should address is the decline in system support that appeared to follow the post-9/11 surge. By the summer of 2002, the percentage of respondents saying that they could trust the government to do what is right just about always or most of the time decreased from its post-9/11 peak of around 60% to 40%, a figure nearly as low as the pre-9/11 level (Mackenzie and Labiner 2002, Stevenson and Elder 2002). Over the same span, President Bush's approval rating declined from its peak of around 90% to a more modest—though still high—70% (Stevenson and Elder 2002). Some observers concluded that political leaders had lost a rare opportunity to build a stronger foundation of system support. "Clearly, September 11 created a government moment, a time for citizens to recognize and appreciate the services that the government provides and the skill with which it performs," wrote Mackenzie and Labiner (2002: 3). "But just as clearly, the moment ha[d] passed," by the summer of 2002. Did the virtuous cycle of the immediate post-9/11 period give way to a return of the vicious cycles observed before 9/11? If so, why?

The answers to these questions may have profound implications for our understanding of system support and our evaluations of the prospect for a sustained increase in such support among the American public. Moreover, if the "rally" phase has given way to a return of the vicious cycles observed prior to 9/11, this may be more than simply a missed opportunity to build a stronger foundation of system support. Trust is related to policy preferences, with greater trust generating greater support for government spending (Chanley 2001, Hetherington and Globetti 2002). Specifically, trust may be necessary in order for political leaders to muster support for the kind of large scale programs that may be needed in what President Bush deems the ongoing war on terrorism. System support was available for political leaders to draw on in taking decisive action in Afghanistan and in undertaking sweeping domestic measures to ensure security. As system support declines, leaders may have trouble mustering similar support in the future.

Appendix: Sample Characteristics

The average length of the first interview was around fifteen minutes; the average length of the second was around ten. Of the 758 respondents interviewed in both waves, half were women and half were men. Twenty-nine percent had a high school education or less; another 29% had some education beyond high school but no college degree; 24% had earned a college degree, and 18% had postgraduate training. Family income broke down as follows: Less than $30,000, 26%; between $30,000 and $50,000, 23%; between $50,000 and $75,000, 25%, between $75,000 and $100,000, 14%; and over $100,000, 14%. Fifteen percent came of age (i.e., turned 18) in the 1990s or later, 18% came of age during the 1980s, 22% during the 1970s, 22% during the 1960s, 13% during the 1950s, and 9% during the 1940s or before. African Americans and Hispanics are underrepresented within the sample (under 5% for each). Moreover, the response rate for the first wave was low (16%). Thus, caution must be exercised in generalizing the results to the American public and to these groups in particular. A comparison on key indicators to other surveys conducted at about the same provides evidence, however, that our survey successfully captured what was happening to system support following September 11. For example, the percentage of Americans who "trust[ed] the federal government to do what is right" just about always or most of the time in the first wave of our panel sample (63%) fell within the range of percentages reported by the *Washington Post*/ABC News (64%; 25-7 September), Gallup (60%; 5-6 October), and the *New York Times*/CBS News (55%; 25-8 October). Similarly, the percentage approving of the president's performance in the first wave of our panel sample (89%) closely matched the percentages found by these organizations (90%, 25-7 September; 88%, 19-21 October; and 87%, 25-8 October, respectively).

Acknowledgements

This research was funded by the National Science Foundation under a grant to Paul R. Brewer, Sean Aday, Kimberly Gross, and Lars Willnat. The authors thank Richard Flickinger, Pippa Norris, Lee Sigelman, and Lars Willnat for their helpful comments.

Notes

1. Early research on political trust focused on whether measures of it reflect general orientations or specific evaluations. According to some scholars, political trust reflects diffuse support—that is, support for the political regime (Miller 1974a, 1974b); according to others, it reflects support for the particular government of the moment (Citrin 1974, Citrin and Green 1986). We do not dismiss the claim that the trust measures reflect views on the current government, but we think that evaluations of specific institutions (e.g., Congress, the Presidency) should be more dependent on the particular actors and actions undertaken by the current government. Thus, we include evaluations of specific institutions in our larger model of system support and examine the influence of these evaluations on the political trust measure, testing Citrin's claim in the post-9/11 period.

2. Although the cooperation rate for the second wave was quite high (78%), the response rate for the first wave was 16%. We computed response rate using AAPOR guidelines as follows: Response rate = completed interviews/completed interviews + partial interviews + refusals + language problems + unknown eligibility. We estimated the percentage of those numbers of unknown eligibility that would have been eligible by using the same proportion as we found to be eligible in those numbers we did reach.

3. Because the panel sample contains so few African Americans, we omitted race as a variable in the analysis (see the Appendix). The means and standard deviations for those demographic variables included in the analysis were: Party identification, mean .52, standard deviation .36; education, mean .66, standard deviation .25; income, mean .59, standard deviation .26; age cohort, mean .42, standard deviation .28.

4. We should note that caution is required in interpreting the results of the model, given that we were unable to model the potential effects of autocorrelation (Markus 1979a).

Finkel (1995), however, has argued that cross-lagged effects models typically provide strong indications of the causal ordering among variables. Moreover, by including key demographic variables in the model, we removed some of the most likely sources of spurious association between the dependent variables in the model.

5. Note that only three of the coefficients for the demographic controls attained statistical significance: Education exerted negative effects on political trust and symbolic patriotism, and men were more likely than women to express confidence in intelligence. As one might expect, Republicans expressed considerably higher levels of presidential support than Democrats; they also expressed higher levels of political trust.

6. This reciprocal relationship also emerged in a model that included two first wave measures of media consumption: A two-item index of national network news and cable news consumption and a single-item indicator of newspaper consumption.

References

Ansolabehere, Stephen, Roy Behr, and Shanto Iyengar. 1993. *The Media Game: American Politics in the Television Age.* New York: Macmillan.

Brehm, John, and Wendy Rahn. 1997. 'Individual-Level Evidence for the Causes and Consequences of Social Capital.' *American Journal of Political Science* 41(3): 999–1023.

Brewer, Paul R., Sean Aday, Kim Gross, and Lars Willnat. 2002. 'Crisis and Confidence: A Panel Study of Media Effects after September 11.' Paper presented at the annual meeting of the American Association for Public Opinion Research, May 2002, St. Petersburg, FL.

Brewer, Paul R., and Marco R. Steenbergen. 2002. 'All Against All: How Beliefs about Human Nature Shape Foreign Policy Opinions.' *Political Psychology* 23(1): 39–58.

Brody, Richard A. 1991. *Assessing the President: The Media, Elite Opinion, and Public Support.* Stanford, CA: Stanford University Press.

Cappella, Joseph N., and Kathleen Hall Jamieson. 1997. *Spiral of Cynicism: The Press and the Public Good.* New York: Oxford University Press.

Chanley, Virginia A. 2001. 'Trust in government in the Aftermath of 9/11: Determinants and Consequences.' *Political Psychology* 23(3): 469–81.

Chanley, Virginia A., Thomas J. Rudolph, and Wendy M. Rahn. 2000. 'The Origins and Consequences of Public Trust in Government.' *Public Opinion Quarterly* 64(3): 239–56.

Citrin, Jack. 1974. 'Comment: The Political Relevance of Trust in Government.' *American Political Science Review* 68(3): 973–88.

Citrin, Jack, and Donald Philip Green.1986. 'Presidential Leadership and the Resurgence of Trust in Government.' *British Journal of Political Science* 16(4): 431–53.

Craig, Stephen C. 1993. *The Malevolent Leaders: Popular Discontent in America.* Boulder, CO: Westview Press.

Dalton, Russell J. 1999. 'Political Support in Advanced Industrial Democracies.' In *Critical Citizens: Global Support for Democratic Governance,* ed. Pippa Norris. New York: Oxford University Press.

Easton, David. 1965. *A Systems Analysis of Political Life.* New York: Wiley.

Easton, David. 1975. 'A Re-Assessment of the Concept of Political Support.' *British Journal of Political Science* 5(4): 435–57.

Erber, Ralph and Richard R. Lau. 1990. 'Political Cynicism Revisited: An Information-Processing Reconciliation of Policy-Based and Incumbency-Based Interpretations of Changes in Trust in Government.' *American Journal of Political Science* 34(1): 236–53.

Feldman, Stanley. 1983. 'The Measurement and Meaning of Political Trust.' *Political Methodology* 9(3): 341–54.

Finkel, Steven E. 1995. *Causal Analysis with Panel Data.* Thousand Oaks, CA: Sage Publications.

Fiorina, Morris P. 1992. *Divided Government.* New York: Macmillan.

Gamson, William A. 1968. *Power and Disconnect.* Homewood, IL: Dorsey.

Hetherington, Marc J. 1998. 'The Political Relevance of Political Trust.' *American Political Science Review* 92(4): 791–808.

Hetherington, Marc J. 1999. 'The Effect of Political Trust on the Presidential Vote, 1968–96.' *American Political Science Review* 93(2): 311–26.

Hetherington, Marc J., and Suzanne Globetti. 2002. 'Political Trust and Racial Policy Preferences.' *American Journal of Political Science* 46(2): 253–75.

Hibbing, John R., and Elizabeth Theiss-Morse. 1995. *Congress As Public Enemy: Public Attitudes toward American Political Institutions*. New York: Cambridge University Press.

Hobbes, Thomas. [1651] 1985. *Leviathan*. New York: Penguin Books.

Hurwitz, Jon, and Mark Peffley. 1987. 'How Are Foreign Policy Attitudes Structured? A Hierarchical Model.' *American Political Science Review* 81(4): 1099–120.

Iyengar, Shanto, and Donald R. Kinder. 1987. *News That Matters: Television and American Opinion*. Chicago: University of Chicago Press.

Joreskog, Karl G. 1990. 'New Developments in LISREL: Analysis of Ordinal Variables Using Polychoric Correlations and Weighted Least Squares.' *Quality and Quantity* 24(4): 387–404.

Klingemann, Hans Dieter. 1999. 'Mapping Political Support in the 1990s: A Global Analysis.' In *Critical Citizens: Global Support for Democratic Governance*, ed. Pippa Norris. New York: Oxford University Press.

Lane, Robert E. 1959. *Political Life: Why and How People Get Involved in Politics*. New York: Free Press.

Lipset, Seymour Martin, and William Schneider. 1983. *The Confidence Gap: Business, Labor, and Government in the Public Mind*. New York: Free Press.

Mackenzie, G. Calvin, and Judith M. Labiner. 2002. 'Opportunity Lost: The Rise and Fall of Trust and Confidence in Government After September 11.' Washington, DC: Brookings Institution.

Markus, Gregory B. 1979a. *Analyzing Panel Data*. Beverly Hills, CA: Sage Publications.

Markus, Gregory B. 1979b. 'The Political Environment and the Dynamics of Public Attitudes: A Panel Study.' *American Journal of Political Science* 23(2): 338–59.

Milbank, Dana, and Richard Morin. 2001. 'Public Is Unyielding in War Against Terror: 9 in 10 Back Robust Military Response.' *Washington Post*, September 29.

Miller, Arthur H. 1974a. 'Political Issues and Trust in Government: 1964–1970.' *American Political Science Review* 68(3): 951–72.

Miller, Arthur H. 1974b. 'Rejoinder to 'Comment' by Jack Citrin: Political Discontent or Ritualism?' *American Political Science Review* 68(3): 989–1001.

Moore, David W. 2001. 'Confidence in Leaders: Record Rally Effect for President, Congress as Americans Support Government Leaders in Wake of Terrorist Attacks.' Princeton, NJ: Gallup Organization.

Mueller, John E. 1970. 'Presidential Popularity from Truman to Johnson.' *American Political Science Review* 64(1): 18–34.

Mueller, John E. 1973. *War, Presidents, and Public Opinion*. New York: John Wiley and Sons.

Neustadt, Richard E. 1960. *Presidential Power: The Politics of Leadership*. New York: Wiley.

Newton, Kenneth. 1999. 'Social and Political Trust in Established Democracies.' In *Critical Citizens: Global Support for Democratic Governance*, ed. Pippa Norris. New York: Oxford University Press.

Norris, Pippa. 1999. 'Introduction: The Growth of Critical Citizens?' In *Critical Citizens: Global Support for Democratic Governance*, ed. Pippa Norris. New York: Oxford University Press.

Patterson, Thomas E. 1994. *Out of Order*. New York: Vintage Books.

Peffley, Mark, and Jon Hurwtiz. 1993. 'Models of Attitude Constraint in Foreign Affairs.' *Political Behavior* 15(1): 61–90.

Putnam, Robert D. 1995a. 'Bowling Alone: America's Declining Social Capital.' *Journal of Democracy* 6(1): 65–78.

Putnam, Robert D. 1995b. 'Tuning In, Tuning Out: The Strange Disappearance of Social Capital in America.' *PS: Political Science and Politics* 8(4): 664–83.

Putnam, Robert D. 2000. *Bowling Alone: The Collapse and Revival of American Community*. New York: Simon & Schuster.

Rahn, Wendy and John Transue. 1998. 'Social Trust and Value Change: The Decline of Social Capital in American Youth, 1976–1995.' *Political Psychology* 19(3): 545–65.

Robinson, Michael J. 1976. 'Public Affairs Television and the Growth of Political Malaise: The Case of 'The Selling of the Pentagon.' *American Political Science Review* 70(2): 409–32.

Rosenstone, Steven J., and Mark Hansen. 1993. *Mobilization, Participation, and Democracy in America*. New York: Macmillan.

Scholz, John T., and Mark Lubell. 1998. 'Trust and Taxpaying: Testing the Heuristic Approach to Collective Action.' *American Journal of Political Science* 42(2): 398–417.

Sigelman, Lee, and Pamela Johnston Conover. 1981. 'The Dynamics of Presidential Support During International Conflict Situations: The Iranian Hostage Crisis.' *Political Behavior* 3(4): 303–18.

Smith, Tom W, Kenneth A. Rasinksi, and Marianna Toce. 2001. 'America Rebounds: A National Study of Public Response to the September 11th Terrorist Attacks, Preliminary Findings.' Chicago: National Opinion Research Center.

Stokes, Donald E. 1962. 'Popular Evaluations of Government: An Empirical Assessment.' In *Ethics and Bigness: Scientific, Academic, Religious, Political, and Military,* ed. Harlan Cleveland and Harold D. Lasswell. New York: Harper and Brothers.

Stevenson, Richard W., and Janet Elder. 2002. 'Poll Finds Concern that Bush is Overly Influenced by Business.' *New York Times,* July 18.

Sullivan, John L., Amy Fried, and Mary G. Dietz. 1992. 'Patriotism, Politics, and the Presidential Election of 1988.' *American Journal of Political Science* 36(1): 200–34.

Uslaner, Eric M. 2002. *The Moral Foundations of Trust.* New York: Cambridge University Press.

Wrightsman, Lawrence S. 1991. 'Interpersonal Trust and Attitudes Toward Human Nature.' In *Measures of Personality and Social Psychological Attitudes,* ed. John P. Robinson, Phillip R. Shaver, and Lawrence S. Wrightsman. New York: Academic Press.

Zaller, John R. 1992. *The Nature and Origins of Mass Opinion.* New York: Cambridge University Press.

CHAPTER 13

Fear and Terrorism: Psychological Reactions to 9/11

LEONIE HUDDY
STANLEY FELDMAN
GALLYA LAHAV
CHARLES TABER

The events of 9/11 had a powerful psychological impact for many Americans. Health researchers found elevated levels of depression, anxiety, and post-traumatic stress syndrome among American adults and children after the attacks (Galea et al. 2002; Schuster et al 2001; Silver et al. 2002). These reactions are in line with one of terrorism's central goals—to induce fear and anxiety in people through focused acts of brutality and violence that gain broad publicity (Crenshaw 1986; Jacobson and Bar-Tal 1995; Long 1990; Wardlaw 1982).

Researchers suggest that terrorists spread public fear in order to create a powerful bargaining tool. For example, Long (1990: 5) argues that terrorists often "use the unreasonable fear and the resulting political disaffection it has generated among the public to intimidate governments into making political concessions in line with its political goals." Indeed, Long claims that terrorism is essentially a psychological phenomenon, "with fear and publicity two of its most important elements" (1990: 6). His perspective is shared by Friedland and Merari (1985) who argue that widespread fear and anxiety engendered by terrorist violence is designed to force governments to make concessions that will further a political cause. From this perspective, fear induced by terrorism could undermine support for tough antiterrorist policies.

Terrorists may create public fear in order to influence their negotiations with targeted governments, but fear has secondary consequences that further undermine government authority. Researchers draw on classic case studies to suggest that fear fragments and isolates society into anxious groups of individuals concerned only with their personal survival (Allen 1984; Long 1990; Wardlaw 1982). As Hutchinson (1973) puts it: "Terrorism destroys the solidarity, cooperation, and interdependence on which social functioning is based, and substitutes insecurity and distrust." The breakdown of social trust and cooperation could have serious effects on how society functions. If trust is essential to the accumulation of social capital, mistrust is likely to undermine a society's social resources. An erosion of trust could diminish political involvement of all kinds, ranging from involvement in electoral politics to activity in local educational and community groups. In this sense, a decline in social capital furthers terrorist aims because it distances citizens from their government and each other, emphasizing personal security over the collective good.

The motives of terrorists contrast starkly, however, with the need of governments in countries that have been targeted by terrorists to take forceful action and reassert their control. As Berry (1987: 296) writes: "A target that is incapable of responding to terrorism will lose public support and lessen its capabilities and confidence to thwart terrorism in the future." As discussed in earlier chapters, democratic governments are faced with the difficult problem of reconciling actions necessary to counter terrorism with the protection of civil liberties and restrictions on the military in domestic politics. They walk a fine line between appearing powerless and impotent or overly repressive (Wardlaw 1982). It is therefore critical that governments obtain broad public support for counterterrorist policies. Terrorists' efforts to incite fear are thus directly at odds with the objectives of political leaders who hope to foster substantial citizen support for retaliation.

Public opinion then becomes the battleground on which terrorists combat governments. For terrorists to achieve their goals, the targeted public needs to experience fear. In the extreme, this should lead residents of a targeted community to clamor for negotiations with terrorists that will put an end to violence. In contrast, governments need their citizens to support counterterrorist policies, and must steel them for the potential hardship, restricted liberties, and possible loss of life that these policies entail. Governments should actively urge citizens toward stoicism in the face of adversity. This is consistent with U.S. politicians' actions after 9/11; many urged Americans to continue to follow their regular daily routine and not succumb to fear.

The media plays an especially critical role in framing and amplifying the effects of terrorism and we give special attention to its impact on psychological responses to terrorism. Hoffman (1998) goes so far as to equate the birth of international terrorism with the introduction of the first TV satellite in the late 1960s. Media reactions to the events of 9/11 demonstrate the pervasive broadcast and rebroadcast of visual images following a terrorist attack. Terrorists seek to use the media to convey their message, as exemplified by bin Laden's ability to transmit his message via al Jazeera in the months following 9/11. The obvious unanswered question is whether the replaying of images from a terrorist event serves to heighten public fear and anxiety, in line with terrorist objectives.

A deeper understanding of psychological reactions to 9/11 thus plays a central role in analyzing the effects of terrorism and the success of counter-terrorist actions. We address several critical questions in this chapter: Was fear a common reaction among Americans to the events of 9/11? Did it incline American citizens to oppose tough anti-terrorism policies? And did it increase a sense of social dislocation in the United States? A review of recent psychological literature provides some empirical support for the notion that fear and anxiety lead to risk-averse actions and other responses that could undercut American public support for counter-terrorism policy, especially when that policy might exacerbate further terrorist threats.

The Psychology of Fear and Anxiety

Psychological studies highlight three key consequences of fear and anxiety. First, fear tends to elevate risk perceptions (Lerner and Keltner 2000, 2001; Mathews and Macleod 1986). This is consistent with the more general finding that events which arouse negative feelings lead to an overestimation of risk (Johnson and Tversky 1983). Lerner, Gonzalez, Small, and Fischoff (2003) examined the effects of 9/11 in an experimental setting by showing research participants video clips that either heightened fear or anger in response to the attacks. They found that individuals with experimentally elevated fear levels judged the risk of future terrorism more highly than individuals in the anger condition. Moreover, individuals who felt fearful soon after the attacks appraised the risk of future terrorism more highly six to eight weeks later. In other words, anxiety and fear promote a heightened sensitivity to threat.

Second, fear leads to risk aversion. Research on threats that involve the potential for physical harm such as crime, natural disasters, and violent conflicts provide evidence that personal threat and fear leads to a change in personal behavior designed to minimize risk (and presumably fear). Consider crime research. A pervasive fear of crime (Warr 1990) motivates change in personal behavior, resulting in a link, for example, between the perceived risk of crime and gun ownership (Ferraro 1996; Smith and Uchida 1988). Residents of Queens and Long Island who felt they could personally be victimized by a terrorist act after 9/11 were more likely to have stopped using public transportation in Manhattan and had traveled less often by air (Huddy, Feldman, Capelos, Provost 2002).

Reactions to other terrorist events highlight "the transformation of reasonable fear into a kind of irrational hysteria" (Long 1990), as exemplified by American tourists' avoidance of Europe in response to a spate of terrorist incidents in 1985 and 1986, the deep reluctance of Americans to fly after 9/11, or the precipitous decline in tourism to Bali after the 2002 club bombing. Persuasion researchers provide related evidence that fearful and anxious individuals are more readily persuaded by information that reduces their level of fear, especially messages that convincingly reduce fear and threat (Hovland, Janis, and Kelly 1953; Janis and Feshbach 1953; Rogers 1983; Gleicher and Petty 1992; for an overview see Eagly and Chaiken 1993).[1]

Third, fear can have a deleterious effect on the rational processing of information because it leads to worsened cognitive functioning (Lerner and Keltner 2000, 2001; Mathews and Macleod 1986). This fits with research findings on the quality of elite and group decision-making under conditions of threat. Leader rhetoric is less integratively complex under conditions of threat (Suedfeld and

Tetlock 1977), and a heightened sense of crisis reduce the quality of elite decisions (Brecher, Wilkenfeld, and Moser 1988; Holsti 1965, 1972; Holsti, North,
and Brody 1968; Paige 1958; Lebow 1981; McCalla 1992; Jervis, Lebow, and Stein
1985).[2] Other evidence indicates that group decision-making processes deterio-
rate (resulting in poorer decision quality) under conditions of threat perception
and stress (Janis 1982; t'Hart 1990; Pruitt 1965). Most of these findings suggest
some degree of cognitive "shutdown" under threatening conditions, which has
also been a central theme in work on fear emotions (Cacioppo and Gardner
1999).[3]

Overall, fear and anxiety lead to less clear information processing, the overestimation of risk, and greater risk aversion. These reactions hold important
implications for support of anti-terrorism policies. National security policies
that have potentially violent consequences should be less popular among fearful
individuals than policies that address the threat of terrorism without increasing
the prospect of further retaliatory action. In other words, fear should decrease
support for risky overseas military action, but should not diminish support
for homeland security policies, such as domestic surveillance, identity checks,
and other forms of internal security that do not exacerbate threat. In addition,
fear may have even broader political and social ramifications through its other
psychological effects. It could lead to an overestimation of the negative consequences of both terrorist actions and government retaliation and reduce the
absorption of important information about national security because it diminishes cognitive processing capabilities. We explore one additional consequence
of fear suggested by the terrorism literature: social dislocation. As noted earlier,
terrorism researchers believe that fear leads to a greater mistrust of one's fellow
citizens and, thus, weakens social bonds.

Cognitive Reactions to Terrorism

We focus primarily here on the consequences of fear and anxiety as critical
reactions to terrorism because this is the primary psychological reaction desired
by terrorists. But heightened levels of fear and anxiety are not necessarily the only,
or even the primary response, of most Americans to 9/11. Indeed, as in chapter
10, researchers investigating the politics of 9/11 have focused more squarely
on the political consequences of cognitive reactions to terrorism, especially
perceptions of future terrorist risk. We compare the political impact of anxiety
and fear with these cognitive reactions, in line with evidence that cognitive
reactions to a terrorist threat and their political consequences are quite different
from the effects of fear and anxiety.

A number of researchers examined the perceived risk of terrorism after 9/11,
distinguishing between the political effects of perceived terrorist risks to the
nation and perceived risks to oneself and one's family (Davis and Silver 2002;
Huddy, Feldman, Capelos, and Provost 2002). This work draws on an extensive
body of past research that documents the more powerful effects of national or

sociotropic than personal self-interest on policy support across a broad range of policy areas (Sears and Funk 1991). Research conducted after 9/11 demonstrated that sociotropic threat does enhance support for homeland security policies that potentially dampen civil liberties, especially among individuals who trust the government (Davis and Silver 2002), and exacerbates negative views of the economy and the stock market (Huddy, Feldman, Capelos, and Provost 2002). The political effects of personal threat are much weaker or nonexistent, although personal threat curtails personally risky behaviors such as air travel and increases caution in handling the mail (around the time of the Anthrax scare). This research would seem to suggest that Americans put aside their personal fears after 9/11, and supported anti-terrorism measures to counteract the perceived threat of terrorism to the nation as a whole.

We find in our own research, however, that it is important to distinguish between fear and the cognitive perception of personal and national risk because they have differing effects, even though they are related (Huddy, Feldman, Taber, and Lahav 2002). In general, we find that fear and risk appraisal have clear and opposing effects on support for military intervention and U.S. isolationism. Fear reduces support for U.S. military intervention overseas in line with the general expectation that fear leads to the avoidance of potentially risky or dangerous action, whereas perceptions of risk increase it. These findings are mirrored to some degree in Traugott and Brader's analyses, in which fear heightens isolationism whereas perceived risk increases support for military action (see chapter 10). It is therefore important to contrast the political effects of fear and anxiety with those of future risk appraisal.

Research Design

The study is based on a national survey conducted via telephone with 1,549 adults over age eighteen between early October 2001 and early March 2002. The sample was drawn as a weekly rolling cross-section with roughly 100 individuals interviewed each week throughout this period. Numbers from each randomly selected sample were in use for a two-week period. The first month of data was collected by Schulman, Ronca, and Bukuvalis; the remaining bulk of the data was collected by the Stony Brook University Center for Survey Research. Up to fifteen callbacks were made at each number and an attempt made to convert individuals who initially refused.[4]

The survey was roughly twenty minutes in length and included questions on emotional reactions to 9/11, possible somatic symptoms, perceptions of perceived future threat, support for the Bush administration, military intervention in Afghanistan, policies aimed at tightening internal security, perceptions of Arab and Arab-Americans, and patriotism, in addition to standard political and demographic items. The wording of items that tap psychological reactions to 9/11 are included in the results section; the wording of all other items used in the analyses is presented in the Appendix.

Results

To what extent were Americans psychologically affected by the attacks of 9/11? Our survey included four items on fear and anxiety, and three on depression and related somatic symptoms. As seen in Table 13.1, the majority of Americans were not psychologically disturbed by the attacks, although a minority expressed considerable levels of fear and depression. We asked respondents how often they had felt four negative emotions: anxious, scared, worried, and frightened. Almost a half reported feeling anxious or worried at least sometimes; a small minority reported feeling these emotions very often. Just under a third reported feeling scared or frightened sometimes or very often. But that left a majority who did not feel frightened or scared, or felt that way only occasionally (over two-thirds said they never felt frightened or did not feel that way very often).

A minority of respondents also reported symptoms linked to depression, a second distinct but related psychological response to the events of 9/11. Our survey included three indicators of depression: feeling depressed, having trouble concentrating, and having trouble sleeping. Over a third of respondents reported feeling very or somewhat depressed in the week prior to the interview. A smaller number (21%) reported that it had been somewhat or very difficult to concentrate on their job and other normal activities in the past week, and an even smaller number (13%) reported having had difficulty sleeping in the previous week because of the terrorist attacks. These reactions are strongly tied to the experience of fear and anxiety (r = .63). This suggests that reported feelings of fear and anxiety may have real behavioral manifestations. In subsequent analyses, we treat depression as an outcome of fear and anxiety and do not consider its separate political effects. Our decision rests on both theory and empirical fact. Fear is thought to be a more potent influence on support for government anti-terrorist policy than depression. Moreover, depression had no additional political impact in subsequent analyses over and above the effects of fear. The determinants of depression and fear are analyzed in tandem to reinforce their affinity.

We contrast these psychological reactions with the perceived risk of future terrorist attacks. This comparison reveals that concern about possible future attacks was more pervasive than feelings of fear and anxiety. Risk appraisal was assessed by two questions on the risk of future terrorist attacks on the United States: "How concerned are you that there will be another terrorist attack on the U.S. in the near future?" and "How concerned are you that terrorists will attack the U.S. with biological or chemical weapons?" Levels of concern were quite high: 86% reported that they were very or somewhat concerned about another attack and 84% were very or somewhat concerned about the threat of biological or chemical attacks. Americans thus appraised the risk of future terrorism as high, but varied in the degree to which this perceived risk leads to strong negative emotional reactions to the attacks. Not surprisingly, risk appraisal was linked to fear and anxiety (r = .42) but was more weakly associated with depression (r = .33).

Table 13.1 Key Psychological Reactions to 9/11

Fear and Anxiety

As you think about the terrorist attacks and the U.S. response, how often have you felt....

	Very Often	Sometimes	Not Very Often	Never	DK/NA
Anxious?	11.4	35.7	27.9	23.6	1.4
Scared?	7.9	23.3	28.7	38.3	0.8
Worried?	13.0	36.9	25.9	22.9	1.2
Frightened?	5.6	24.5	27.4	41.3	1.2

Depression

	Very Difficult	Somewhat Difficult	Not Very Difficult	Not At All Difficult	DK/NA
In the past week, how difficult has it been, if at all, for you to concentrate on your job or your normal activities because of the way you feel about the terrorist attacks and the events since then?	4.6	17.7	22.1	54.6	1.1

	A Great Deal	Some	A Little	None	DK/NA
In the past week, how much trouble, if any, have you had sleeping because of the way you feel about the terrorist attacks and the events since then?	3.1	9.4	12.1	74.4	1.0

	Very Depressed	Somewhat Depressed	Not Very Depressed	Not At All Depressed	DK/NA
In the past week, how depressed have you felt, if at all, about the terrorist attacks and the events since then?	7.8	30.7	20.1	39.9	1.4

Risk Appraisal

	Very Concerned	Somewhat Concerned	Not Very Concerned	Not At All Concerned	DK/NA
How concerned are you that there will be another terrorist attack on U.S. soil in the near future?	49.8	36.5	9.7	3.5	0.4
How concerned are you that terrorists will attack the U.S. with biological or chemical weapons?	47.3	37.4	10.2	3.8	1.3

Note: Entries are percentages.

262 • Leonie Huddy, Stanley Feldman, Gallya Lahav, and Charles Taber

It is clear from these responses that Americans were extremely concerned about the risk of another terrorist attack in the months after 9/11. Fear and other negative emotional reactions were less prevalent, although evident nonetheless. These results suggest that terrorists achieved their psychological goal to a modest degree. A minority of Americans were quite shaken by the attacks and experienced additional symptoms associated with depression.

Correlates of Fear, Depression, and Risk

Evidence that a minority of Americans were made frightened and anxious by the events of 9/11 raises the obvious question of why some individuals were made more fearful than others by the attacks. We consider several likely factors that were distinctly related to heightened levels of fear and anxiety but not elevated perceptions of risk. In order to examine the determinants and consequences of perceived threat we created scales for risk appraisal, fear/anxiety, and depression by summing the questions that assess each concept. These items are displayed in Table 13.1. The three scales were re-coded to range from 0 to 1, with high scores indicating a high-perceived risk of another terrorist attack, strong feelings of fear and anxiety, and symptoms of depression.[5] We analyze the origins of fear, depression, and risk appraisal using regression analyses; these estimated equations are presented in Table 13.2.

Physical proximity to the attacks is an important source of fear and anxiety. We expected individuals physically closest to the event to be most emotionally aroused and fearful. This is consistent with Arian and Gordon's (1993) evidence that during the Gulf War residents of the Tel Aviv area—where scud missiles were aimed—were more likely to feel fearful than other Israelis. It also fits with evidence that physical proximity to the attacks lead to a greater sense of personal than national threat after 9/11 and heightened levels of post-traumatic stress syndrome (Galea et al 2002; Huddy, Feldman, Capelos, and Provost 2002). We also expected someone who knew a victim of the attacks (and who was thus emotionally closer to the event) to experience higher levels of fear. And, indeed, there is support for these predictions. Individuals who lived in the Northeast were more likely than other Americans to feel fear and report symptoms of depression, but did not perceive any higher level of risk to the nation as a whole. Having known someone who was missing or killed in the attacks led to higher levels of fear, depression, and risk, although it had greatest impact on levels of fear and depression (see Table 13.2).

Several other factors also selectively increased levels of fear and anxiety and depression, but not perceived risk. Interestingly, younger people felt more frightened and anxious than older people. Hispanics felt more depressed than non-Hispanics. And, Republicans experienced somewhat less fear, anxiety, and depression than Democrats. It thus appears that Republicans were reassured by the presence of George W. Bush as president.

Women were also more likely to report elevated levels of fear and depression. One of the most consistent findings to emerge from research on physical threat

Table 13.2 The Determinants of Threat Reactions

	FEAR/ANXIETY		DEPRESSION		RISK APPRAISAL	
Age (10 years)	−.013	−.018	.006	−.001	.007	.001
	(.004)	(.004)	(.004)	(.004)	(.004)	(.004)
Education	−.014	−.016	−.018	−.020	−.008	−.009
	(.003)	(.003)	(.003)	(.003)	(.003)	(.003)
Female	**.18**	**.18**	**.06**	**.07**	**.06**	**.07**
	(.01)	(.01)	(.01)	(.01)	(.01)	(.01)
Race/Ethnicity						
Black	.01	.01	**.09**	**.10**	**.07**	**.06**
	(.02)	(.03)	(.02)	(.02)	(.02)	(.02)
Hispanic	.05	.04	**.11**	**.11**	.04	.03
	(.03)	(.03)	(.03)	(.03)	(.03)	(.03)
Other	.00	.00	.05	.05	.04	.04
	(.03)	(.03)	(.03)	(.03)	(.03)	(.03)
Party ID (Republican)	−.05	−.05	−.06	−.05	.00	.01
	(.02)	(.02)	(.02)	(.02)	(.02)	(.02)
Ideology (Conservative)	**.05**	**.04**	**.06**	**.05**	**.05**	**.05**
	(.02)	(.02)	(.02)	(.02)	(.02)	(.02)
Know missing	**.08**	**.08**	**.06**	**.06**	**.02**	**.02**
	(.02)	(.02)	(.01)	(.01)	(.01)	(.01)
Northeast	**.05**	**.04**	**.05**	**.05**	.02	.01
	(.02)	(.02)	(.02)	(.02)	(.02)	(.02)
Television (days)		.014		.012		.011
		(.003)		(.003)		(.003)
Newspaper (days)		−.001		.003		.003
		(.002)		(.002)		(.002)
Constant	.52	.50	.37	.35	.76	.74
	(.05)	(.05)	(.05)	(.05)	(.04)	(.04)
R^2	.16	.18	.10	.12	.04	.06

Note: Entries are regression coefficient; standard errors are in parentheses. Coefficients in bold have t-values greater than 2.

is that women are more personally afraid of victimization than are men, despite the fact that men are more likely to be the victims of violent crime (Ferraro 1996; Stafford and Galle 1984; Warr 1984). Women are also more fearful of war and terrorism (Poikolainen, Kanerva, and Loennqvist 1998; Arian and Gordon 1993; Jacobson and Bar-Tal 1995; Raviv et al. 2000).[6] Consistent with our expectations, women reported higher levels of fear and anxiety, depression, and risk appraisal than men, although gender differences were most pronounced on fear and anxiety.

Several additional factors heightened both emotional reactions and perceived risk. Better educated individuals were expected to report lower levels of fear and perceived risk because they can use base rates to assess more accurately the cognitive likelihood of future attacks than less well educated individuals (Friedland and Merari 1985). This prediction is also supported by the data. Education had a pronounced effect on all three reactions, with better-educated individuals estimating lower levels of risk and feeling less fearful or depressed. In addition, blacks were somewhat more likely than whites to experience depression and assess a higher risk of terrorism, although they did not experience higher levels of fear and anxiety. Conservatives felt less fear and depression, and perceived less national risk.

The media are critical to terrorist aims because they publicize a terrorist event and may serve to amplify fearful reactions. Indeed, some view terrorists and the media as enjoying a symbiotic relationship (Wardlaw 1982; Wilkinson 1987). Watching TV news heightened emotional reactions to 9/11 and increased perceptions of future risk in our data. Individuals who reported watching a great deal of TV news were more likely to report feeling afraid, depressed, and viewed the future risk of terrorism as high (see Table 13.2). Before concluding that the media is responsible for elevating levels of fear and risk, we need to consider the alternative hypothesis that fear increases TV viewing. Our data are cross-sectional, making it difficult to disentangle the two. Nonetheless, in a series of two-stage-least-squares analysis (not reported here), TV viewing had considerable impact on fear, but fear had no significant impact on TV viewing. Our cautious conclusion based on these analyses is that TV viewing elevates perceptions of risk and fear and anxiety. As seen in Table 13.2, these effects are confined to visual media. Reading newspapers had no appreciable effect on fear and anxiety, depression, or risk appraisal.

Our data were collected over a five-month period, allowing us to observe changes in fear and depression over time. We began our data collection some five weeks after 9/11 and therefore did not capture the fairly steep decline in perceived national or personal risk observed in cross-sectional poll data in the first few weeks after 9/11 (Huddy, Khatib and Capelos 2002). In order to examine the effects of time we added a weekly time counter to the three regressions reported in Table 13.1. We then estimated the model allowing for non-linear effects of time through a flexible polynomial specification. The results are shown in Figure 13.1. Recall that risk appraisal, fear and anxiety, and depression are all coded to range from a minimum of 0 to a maximum of 1. We observe a slight decline in fear and risk appraisal from five weeks after 9/11 up until the end of November (some ten weeks after 9/11). After that there was no substantial decrease in the appraised risk of terrorism; if anything Figure 13.1 depicts a slight increase in fear and perceived risk at around twenty weeks after 9/11 (about the middle of February 2002). Symptoms of depression appear to diminish somewhat more consistently over this period. We can tentatively conclude from these data that psychological reactions to the attacks declined somewhat after 9/11 but were remarkably persistent over the five months of this study.

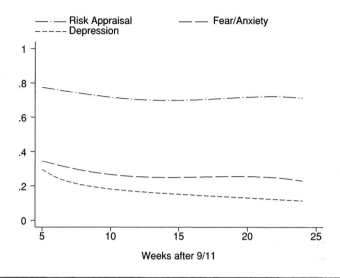

Fig. 13.1 Changes over time in reactions to 9/11.

All told, it appears that a combination of experiential, political, and cultural factors elevated levels of fear and depression without increasing the perceived risk of future terrorism. Younger people, Republicans, Hispanics, women, those who live in the Northeast, and people who knew someone who was killed or missing in the attacks experienced heightened psychological reactions to the attacks of 9/11. Moreover, there was a slight decline over time in such reactions. Education and regular viewing of TV news increased both the perceived risk of terrorism and emotional reactions to 9/11. The link between personal experience and physical proximity to the attacks suggests the additional power of terrorist events to frighten individuals most immediately affected by them.

Fear and Impaired Information Processing

Psychological research suggests that fear worsens cognitive functioning and we find supportive evidence of this in our data. Fearful individuals actually learned less from the news than others, as seen in ordered probit analyses presented in Table 13.3. We assessed knowledge by asking four factual questions about Afghanistan, Islam, and Osama bin Laden and constructed a measure by counting the number of correct answers. Since probit coefficients have no straightforward interpretation, we also present the expected change in the probability of correctly answering at least three of the four knowledge questions as each predictor varies across its range.[7] The impact of fear on knowledge levels is sizeable. Non-fearful individuals are 20% more likely than fearful respondents to get three out of four of the knowledge quiz questions correct. Lower knowledge

Table 13.3 Determinants of Knowledge about Afghanistan and bin Laden

	COEFFICIENT	CHANGE IN PROBABILITY	COEFFICIENT	CHANGE IN PROBABILITY
Fear/Anxiety	−.52	−.21	−.58	−.23
	(.12)		(.12)	
Risk Appraisal	.00	.01	−.05	−.02
	(.13)		(.13)	
Age (10 years)	.077	.18	.040	.10
	(.018)		(.019)	
Education	.161	.50	.153	.48
	(.013)		(.013)	
Female	−.52	−.20	−.46	−.18
	(.06)		(.06)	
Race/Ethnicity				
Black	−.21	−.09	−.23	−.09
	(.11)		(.11)	
Hispanic	−.17	−.07	−.18	−.07
	(.12)		(.12)	
Other	−.13	−.06	−.13	−.05
	(.13)		(.13)	
Party ID	.30	.11	.31	.12
(Republican)	(.09)		(.09)	
Ideology	−.15	−.06	−.17	−.06
(Conservative)	(.10)		(.10)	
Authoritarianism	−.76	−.30	−.75	−.29
	(.09)		(.09)	
Television (days)			.039	.11
			(.012)	
Newspapers			.038	.11
(days)			(.010)	

Note: Entries are regression coefficient; standard errors are in parentheses. Coefficients in bold have z-scores greater than 2. The change in probability indicates the likelihood that someone would get 3 out of 4 questions correct going from the lowest to highest value of the predictor variable.

levels among fearful individuals cannot simply be explained away by lower levels of attention to the news, however, because in the two-stage least squares analysis described earlier, fearful people were no more or less likely to watch the news than others. High levels of TV viewing increased levels of fear and this, in turn, lead to learning less about the situation overseas. It is important to note that simply watching more TV does not decrease knowledge. In fact, as seen in Table 13.2, once levels of fear and anxiety are controlled for, greater attentiveness to TV news and newspapers increased knowledge. Thus, there is tendency for TV viewing to increase fear, and those made fearful by the news learn less from it. But clearly, there are some individuals who are not made fearful by watching TV news, and they actually learn factual information from TV coverage. It is also clear in these analyses that newspapers convey information about terrorism even if they do not elevate levels of fear, anxiety and risk appraisal. Reading newspapers regularly had approximately the same effect on knowledge as regular TV viewing. It was, however, only TV viewing that increased fear and anxiety and perceptions of risk.

The coefficient estimates in Table 13.3 show that lower knowledge levels are a product of fear and not simply concern about a future attack. The latter had no additional impact on knowledge levels. The remaining predictors of knowledge are largely in line with previous findings on the determinants of political knowledge, particularly foreign policy knowledge. Increasing education, age, and lower levels of authoritarianism lead to substantially higher knowledge levels; men were more knowledgeable than women. Overall, the link between fear and knowledge hold intriguing implications for understanding the impact of terrorist action, especially among those made fearful by an attack. If fear diminishes information it may also lead to an erroneous estimation of the future risks posed by terrorists and impede understanding of the causes of terrorism.

Fear and Pessimism

One of the key psychological effects of fear is to elevate risk perceptions (Lerner and Keltner 2000, 2001; Mathews and Macleod 1986). Fear and risk perception are related in our data ($r = .42$). But it is difficult to know whether this is because perceived risk leads to fear, or vice versa. To get out of this quandary, we examine the link between fear and perceptions of the economy to better understand whether fear leads to heightened risk perceptions in an area less directly tied to the likelihood of future terrorist events. Three variables tap economic perceptions: holding a pessimistic view of the U.S. economy over the next twelve months, and being concerned that the attacks would seriously affect one's own finances, and the nation's economy. Once again, we run ordered probit analyses to examine the impact of fear and other control variables on economic estimates. These analyses are presented in Table 13.4. Fear has the expected effect and leads to more pessimistic views of the economy across all three questions. These effects are sizeable. Fear increases the probability of holding a negative view of the U.S. economy by 28% and of one's own personal finances by 38%. Caution needs to be used in interpreting these results because the word "worried" is used in asking about national and personal finances. Nonetheless, fear increases pessimism about the immediate trajectory of the national economy even when the word worried is not used.

Other factors also influence economic pessimism. The perceived risk of a future attack increases the perceived impact of the attack on the national economy and one's personal finances. Younger people, women, and Hispanics are also more pessimistic about the immediate future trajectory of the economy.

Table 13.4 Determinants of Economic Pessimism

	HURT US ECONOMY		HURT OWN FINANCES		ECONOMY BETTER/WORSE	
	Coefficient	*Change in Probability*	*Coefficient*	*Change in Probability*	*Coefficient*	*Change in Probability*
Risk Appraisal	**1.21**	.44	**1.05**	.40	.12	.03
	(.13)		(.13)		(.13)	
Fear/Anxiety	**.96**	.28	**1.04**	.38	**.55**	.15
	(.13)		(.13)		(.13)	
Age (10 years)	.025	.05	.007	.02	**−.067**	−.10
	(.019)		(.018)		(.018)	
Education	−.010	−.03	−.023	−.08	.014	.02
	(.012)		(.012)		(.012)	
Female	.09	.03	.03	.01	**.29**	.08
	(.06)		(.06)		(.06)	
Race/Ethnicity						
Black	.11	.03	.19	.07	.11	.03
	(.12)		(.11)		(.11)	
Hispanic	.08	.02	.14	.05	**−.42**	−.08
	(.12)		(.12)		(.12)	
Other	.08	.02	.08	.03	−.02	.00
	(.14)		(.13)		(.13)	
Party ID (Republican)	**−.42**	−.14	**−.26**	−.10	**−.37**	−.09
	(.10)		(.09)		(.09)	
Ideology (Conservative)	.01	.00	−.02	−.01	.00	.00
	(.10)		(.10)		(.10)	
Authoritarianism	**.23**	.07	**.21**	.08	.08	.02
	(.09)		(.09)		(.09)	

Note: Entries are regression coefficient; standard errors are in parentheses. Coefficients in bold have z-scores greater than 2. The change in probability indicates the likelihood that economic estimates worsen (somewhat and much worse combined) going from the lowest to highest value of the predictor variable.

Republicans are more buoyant about economic conditions in general; authoritarians are more pessimistic. Taken together, fear had large and consistent effects on economic pessimism. It was the largest source of pessimism concerning the course of the U.S. economy over the next twelve months; it was the second largest predictor of pessimism (following risk) concerning the impact of the 9/11 attacks on the national economy and one's personal finances. This suggests that fear and anxiety produced by terrorism can lead, quite generally, to substantially increased levels of risk perceptions.

Social Dislocation

Terrorism researchers have suggested that the fear elicited by a terrorist incident may also lead to social dislocation and disaffection (Long 1995; Hutchinson 1973). We find supportive evidence for this hypothesis in our data. The survey included two relevant questions. The first asked about the extent to which other Americans could be trusted; the second assessed the degree to which respondents thought that Arab-Americans supported the terrorist acts and thus were disloyal. Ordered probit analyses presented in Table 13.5 indicate that fear and anxiety increased Americans' level of distrustfulness on both measures, although they were unaffected by risk appraisal assessments. These findings reinforce speculation that the fear incited by terrorist acts increases suspicion of others, and may lead to greater social disaffection.

The notion that some Americans became distrustful and wary of other individuals is at odds with the popular conception that Americans pulled together cohesively after 9/11. Our results do not necessarily contradict this finding. Fearful individuals make up only a minority of the U.S. population, confining these results to a subset of Americans. Moreover, the results indicate that fearful individuals demonstrate less trust in others than non-fearful Americans but do not address any possible increase in trust before and after the attacks. Our findings remain consistent with the possibility that fearful Americans increased their trust in others after 9/11, but did so to a lesser degree than less frightened individuals. Either way, the results are intriguing. Additional analyses not shown here demonstrate that fear only produces disaffection from other individuals, not the nation as a whole. Fear actually increased positive feelings about the United States in a regression analysis of the determinants of patriotism.[8] Moreover the link between fear and greater distrust of Arab-Americans did not extend to Arabs in general. This became clear in a regression analysis of Arab stereotypes. Both fearful and non-fearful respondents held equally negative stereotypes of Arabs.[9] Taken together, these results suggest that fear and heightened distrust of other individuals inside the United States may have made people more wary in their daily interactions with other Americans.

National Security Policy

We expected fear to heighten one's sensitivity to risk and, therefore, diminish support for overseas military action and the Bush administration, because of its

Table 13.5 Determinants of Social Trust

	TRUST AMERICANS		ARAB-AMERICANS SUPPORT TERRORISM	
	Coefficient	*Change in Probability*	*Coefficient*	*Change in Probability*
Risk Appraisal	−.27	−.09	.15	.06
	(.16)		(.14)	
Fear/Anxiety	**−.42**	−.15	**.30**	.11
	(.15)		(.13)	
Age (10 years)	**.099**	.21	−.009	−.02
	(.022)		(.019)	
Education	**.053**	.16	−.023	−.07
	(.016)		(.013)	
Female	**−.16**	−.06	.02	.01
	(.08)		(.06)	
Race/Ethnicity				
Black	**−.64**	−.24	.16	.07
	(.14)		(.12)	
Hispanic	**−.30**	−.11	.05	.02
	(.14)		(.13)	
Other	−.03	−.01	.21	.08
	(.17)		(.14)	
Party ID (Republican)	.17	.06	−.04	−.02
	(.12)		(.10)	
Ideology (Conservative)	−.12	−.04	**.22**	.09
	(.12)		(.10)	
Authoritarianism	**−.61**	−.21	**.29**	.11
	(.12)		(.10)	

Note: Entries are regression coefficient; standard errors are in parentheses. Coefficients in bold have z-scores greater than 2. The change in probability indicates the likelihood of social mistrust or mistrust of Arab-Americans going from the lowest to highest value of the predictor variable.

support for such action. In contrast, the appraisal of risk should increase support for the administration and its military policies because it triggers a retaliatory response associated with the cognitive perception of risk (see Huddy, Feldman, Taber, and Lahav 2002 for a longer discussion of the rationale underlying this hypothesis). Consistent with other national polls (Huddy, Khatib, and Capelos 2002), 90% of respondents in our sample approved of the way Bush was handling his job, 88% approved of his handling of the terrorist situation, 72% supported increasing military action even if it meant significant U.S. casualties, and 84% believed it would be best if the United States took an active part in world affairs (see the Appendix for question wording).

Table 13.6 shows the results of ordered probit estimates of responses to each of these questions. Fear and anxiety promotes disapproval of President Bush and his handling of the situation, and leads to greater opposition to increased military action and overseas involvement, consistent with psychological evidence that fear promotes risk aversion. This fits with Wardlaw's (1982) view that one of the primary functions of terrorism is to sow disaffection with authorities by showing that the government is unable to fulfill primary security functions. In contrast, increasing risk appraisal has the opposite effect. It is associated with greater support for U.S. military intervention, U.S. overseas involvement, and approval of Bush. The fraction of the public who experience a highly fearful response to terrorism thus holds the key to understanding public support for national security policies that involve potentially dangerous policy options. When that number is small, there is minor opposition to overseas military engagement. If a majority of Americans feel fearful, however, the balance might tip toward opposition to military action.

The effects of fear and anxiety are substantial, as can be seen from the estimated changes in probability in Table 13.6; they are especially striking given the relatively high overall levels of support for Bush and overseas military action. The effects of fear are also large when compared to other predictors. Consider Bush approval. The impact of fear and ideology are comparable, and the effect of fear is only slightly less than that of partisanship. It is important to note that marginal changes in probability will always be small when predicted probabilities approach 1 (or 0) as a consequence of the functional form of the probit model. This can be seen in the limited effects of all predictors on Bush approval, including partisanship, risk appraisal, and negative emotions—all predictors including fear.

In addition to the effects of threat, there are several other factors that influence Bush approval and increase support for overseas military involvement. Black respondents were consistently more opposed to U.S. military and overseas involvement than were whites. Authoritarianism was associated with greater approval of Bush and increased support for military action, but greater reluctance toward increased U.S. involvement in world affairs. Not surprisingly, Republicans were significantly more likely than Democrats to support military action; conservatives were stronger supporters than liberals of military action and were more supportive of the United States taking a leading role in world affairs.

In the realm of foreign policy, fear and anxiety led to isolationism and less support for U.S. military activity. Potentially dangerous overseas military action is not appealing to fearful and anxious individuals. Bush's actions and rhetoric were also less reassuring to those who experienced fear and anxiety after 9/11 than to those who assessed a high risk of further terrorism but were not as deeply frightened by the attacks.

Conclusion and Future Implications

Experts suggest that terrorism has several central aims, but in all scenarios the public is used as a pawn in a game played with governments. Terrorist groups aim their actions at ordinary people, although their ultimate target

Table 13.6 Determinants of Bush Approval and Interventionist Policies

	BUSH APPROVAL		BUSH: TERRORISM		MILITARY ACTION		ACTIVE IN WORLD AFFAIRS	
	Coefficient	Change in Probability	Coefficient	Change in Probability	Coefficient	Change in Probability	Coefficient	Change in Probability
Risk Appraisal	**.66**	.11	.35	.05	**.65**	.20	**.58**	.15
	(.22)		(.23)		(.15)		(.19)	
Fear/Anxiety	**−.45**	−.07	**−.58**	−.08	**−.33**	−.09	**−.38**	−.09
	(.21)		(.21)		(.14)		(.18)	
Age (10 years)	.028	.04	.040	.03	.018	.02	**.066**	.09
	(.032)		(.033)		(.020)		(.027)	
Education	.025	.03	.009	.01	−.009	−.03	**.050**	.09
	(.021)		(.106)		(.013)		(.019)	
Female	.01	.00	.09	.01	**−.35**	−.12	.05	.01
	(.11)		(.11)		(.07)		(.09)	
Race/Ethnicity								
Black	**−.56**	−.11	**−.59**	−.12	**−.48**	−.15	**−.42**	−.11
	(.16)		(.15)		(.12)		(.15)	
Hispanic	−.17	−.03	−.24	−.04	**−.41**	−.13	−.09	−.02
	(.19)		(.19)		(.13)		(.16)	
Other	−.25	−.04	−.35	−.04	−.27	−.07	−.12	−.03
	(.20)		(.20)		(.14)		(.19)	
Party ID (Republican)	**.84**	.12	**.86**	.12	**.60**	.16	**.34**	.08
	(.17)		(.18)		(.10)		(.14)	
Ideology (Conservative)	**.51**	.07	.18	.02	**.29**	.09	.17	.04
	(.17)		(.17)		(.11)		(.14)	
Authoritarianism	**.36**	.05	.14	.02	**.25**	.07	**−.54**	−.12
	(.16)		(.17)		(.10)		(.14)	

Note: Entries are regression coefficient; standard errors are in parentheses. Coefficients in bold have z-scores greater than 2. The change in probability indicates the likelihood of disapproval of Bush, support for military intervention, or U.S. engagement in world affairs going from the lowest to highest value of the predictor variable.

remains the political authorities, whom terrorists hope to force into meeting their demands (Long 1990; Wardlaw 1982). Fear plays an important role in this process. Terrorists hope to sow public disaffection with government, weaken public support for tough antiterrorism policies, and disrupt social ties through the creation of fear and anxiety (Wardlaw 1982). As Wardlaw (1982) notes, "While the primary effect [of terrorism] is to create fear and alarm, the objectives may be to gain concessions, obtain maximum publicity, provoke repression, break down social order, build morale in the movement" (1982: 42).

To what extent did terrorists succeed in spreading fear and anxiety among Americans through the 9/11 attacks? Only to a very limited degree based on the small number of Americans who reported feeling fearful and anxious in the current survey. But those minority responses held clear social and political consequences. Fear hindered information processing, heightened pessimism about the economy, increased social distrust of other Americans, weakened support for aggressive anti-terrorism military action, increased isolationism, and aroused disapproval of President Bush's performance.

The findings reported here confirm the role of television in shaping psychological reactions to a terrorist event. Americans who watched television news more frequently reported higher levels of fear and anxiety after 9/11. These findings raise questions, for example, about the wisdom of replaying coverage of the demise of the World Trade Center towers. Such images are impossible to forget and replaying them may serve to maintain or further amplify fear and anxiety, long after a terrorist incident. The visual imagery of TV seems to be the key to the heightened levels of fear and anxiety among avid media consumers. Reading newspapers increases knowledge levels just as much as television viewing, but has no effect at all on fear and perceptions of risk.

The impact of fear on support for national security policy holds important implications for the Bush administration's war on terrorism. Will Americans continue to rally behind the president, as has happened so often in past conflicts? Or has the landscape been altered by the events of 9/11, so that more caution about overseas action has now crept into public deliberation? Are Americans whose sense of security was shattered by 9/11 reassured by talk of "preemptive strikes" against countries that harbor terrorists, or will they feel even less secure? Our findings provide an interesting twist to the usual explanation of rally effects which rely on the existence of elite consensus concerning overseas military action (Zaller 1994). At odds with past studies that report a uniform and strong rally effect when the president initiates overseas military action, was found a smaller rally effect among fearful and anxious Americans who were less supportive than other Americans of the President and his foreign policy agenda.

Our findings also lend insight into the future trajectory of support for anti-terrorism measures in the United States. In general, acts of terrorism tend to harden opposition to an enemy and promote support for a belligerent response, especially when the attacks elicit low-to-moderate levels of fear. But when levels of fear increase, support for belligerent action against terrorists decreases, presumably because it raises the likelihood of further terrorist retaliation. In the aftermath of 9/11, several factors were associated with heightened levels of fear in America, including living in the Northeast and knowing someone who was hurt or killed in the attacks. We have emphasized the effects of fear throughout this analysis. But it is important to remember that Americans' dominant reaction to 9/11 was not one of fear. Most Americans felt a heightened concern about future terrorist attacks in the United States and in the absence of fear this heightened sense of risk galvanized support for government anti-terrorist policy. In this sense, the 9/11 terrorists failed to arouse sufficient levels of fear and anxiety to counteract American's basic desire to strike back in order to increase future national security. Possible future acts of terrorism or a newly emergent enemy, however, could change the fine balance between a public attuned to future risks and one dominated by fear. If that were to occur, the reactions discussed here could escalate creating a more isolationist and pessimistic country in which distrust characterizes Americans' social relations.

Appendix
TV
- How many days in the past week did you watch the national TV news on ABC, CBS, CNN, FOX, or NBC?

Newspaper
- How many days in the past week did you read about national events in a daily newspaper?

Knowledge
- We are interested in what people have learned about the individuals and countries implicated in the attacks. Can you tell me the name of ONE country that shares a border with Afghanistan?
- Is Afghanistan an Arab country?
- Can you name the country that Osama bin Laden is originally from?
- Can you tell me the name of the Muslim holy book?

Authoritarianism
- Although there are a number of qualities that people feel children should have, every person thinks that some are more important than others. Would you say that it is more important for a child to be independent or respectful of their elders?
- Would you say that it is more important for a child to be curious or good mannered?
- Would you say that it is more important for a child to be obedient or self-reliant?

Economic Pessimism

- How worried are you that the financial effects of the attacks will seriously hurt the U.S. economy over the next few years?
- How worried are you that the financial effects of the attacks will seriously hurt your personal financial situation over the next few years?
- In the next twelve months, do you expect the economy, in the country as a whole, to get: much better, somewhat better, somewhat worse, much worse, or stay about the same?

Social Dislocation

- Generally speaking, would you say that most Americans can be trusted, **OR** do you believe that you can't be too careful in dealing with other people?
- Roughly how many Arab-Americans, do you think, support the actions of the terrorists?

Bush Approval

- Do you approve or disapprove of the way George Bush is dealing with the terrorist attacks on the World Trade Center in New York City and the Pentagon in Washington?

Bush Approval: Terrorism

- Do you approve or disapprove of the way George W. Bush is dealing with the terrorist attacks on the World Trade Center in New York City and the Pentagon in Washington?

Military Action

- How strongly do you favor or oppose increasing the level of military action, even if it means that U.S. armed forces might suffer a substantial number of casualties: strongly favor, somewhat favor, somewhat oppose, strongly oppose, or don't believe there will be casualties?

Active in World Affairs

- Do you think it will be best for the future of the United States if the country takes an active part in world affairs, or if the country stays out of world affairs.

Notes

1. Eagly and Chaiken (1993) refute Janis and Feshbach's notion that high levels of fear are unpersuasive. In their words, 'higher levels of threat lead to greater persuasion than lower levels' (p. 443).
2. Maoz (1990, 1997) has modified this conclusion to suggest that moderate levels of threat perception improve decision-making quality, while low and high levels of threat reduce decision quality.

3. This prediction is somewhat at odds with the finding that anxiety can improve the quality of decision-making by resulting in a more complete search for information (Vertzberger 1998; Marcus and MacKuen, 1993; Marcus, Neuman and MacKuen 2000). The difference may lie in the amount of fear or anxiety elicited by an event. Higher levels of fear can impair cognitive reasoning.

4. The cooperation rate for the survey was 52% and there was no difference in response rate between the two survey organizations.

5. All three scales are quite reliable. Coefficient alphas are .77 for risk appraisal, .85 for fear and anxiety, and .80 for depression.

6. Women's greater fear of personal crime such as murder, burglary, or assault arises almost completely out of their greater fear of rape (Ferraro 1996). This does not explain, however, women's greater fear of nuclear weapons or the risks posed by violent conflicts, such as terrorism.

7. The specific range for each variable is: age, 20 years to 80 years old; education, 11 years to 20 (postgraduate degree) years; gender, male to female; race/ethnicity, white to black/Hispanic/other; authoritarianism, lowest to highest score; party identification, strong Democrat to strong Republican; ideological identification, very liberal to very conservative; attendance at religious services, 0 to 8 times per month. Since risk appraisal and negative emotional arousal are continuous latent variables, we varied them over a range from the 5th to 95th percentile. The changes in probability were computed holding all other variables constant at the means of risk appraisal, negative emotions, age, education, authoritarianism, and religious attendance, for an independent and ideologically moderate white male.

8. Patriotism was measured with four items: *"Have you displayed an American flag outside your home, in your car, or at work at any time since the September 11 attacks?", "How angry does it make you feel, if at all, when you hear someone criticizing the United States?"; "How proud are you to be an American?"; "How good does it make you feel when you see the American flag flying?"*

    Negative stereotypes were assessed by four trait terms: trustworthy, violent, honest, and extremist.

References

Note: This research was supported by Grant SES-0201650 from the National Science Foundation.

Allen, William S. (1984). *The Nazi Seizure of Power: The Experience of a Single German Town, 1922–1945.* New York: Franklin Watts, revised (1965 original).

Arian, Asher and Carol, Gordon. 1993. 'The Political and Psychological Impact of the Gulf War on the Israeli Public.' In *The Political Psychology of the Gulf War: Leaders, Publics and the Process of Conflict,* ed. S. A. Renshon. Pittsburgh: University of Pittsburgh Press.

Brader, Ted. 2002. 'Citizen Responses to Threat and Fear: New Developments and Future Directions.' Paper presented at the annual meeting of the American Political Science Association, Boston, September, 2002.

Brecher, Michael, Jonathan Wilkenfeld, and Sheila Moser. 1988. *Crises in the Twentieth Century: Handbook of International Crises.* Oxford: Pergamon Press.

Cacioppo, J. T., and W. L. Gardner. 1999. Emotion. *Annual Review of Psychology, 50,* 191–214.

Crenshaw, Martha. 1986. 'The Psychology of Political Terrorism.' In *Political Psychology,* ed. Margaret G. Hermann. New York: Jossey-Bass.

Doty, R. M., B. E. Peterson and D. G. Winter. 1991. 'Threat and Authoritarianism in the United States, 1978–1987.' *Journal of Personality and Social Psychology, 61,* 629–640.

Davis, Darren W., and Brian D. Silver. 2002. 'Civil Liberties vs. Security in the Context of the Terrorist Attacks on America.' Paper presented at the annual meeting of the American Political Science Association, Boston, September, 2002.

Eagly, A. H., and S. Chaiken. 1993. *The Psychology of Attitudes.* Ft. Worth, TX: Harcourt Brace Jovanovich College Publishers.

Ferraro, K. A. 1996. 'Women's fear of victimization: Shadow of Sexual Assault?' *Social Forces, 75,* 667–690.

Friedland, Nehemia, and Ariel Merari. 1985. 'The Psychological Impact of Terrorism: A Double-Edged Sword.' *Political Psychology, 6:* 591–604.

Galea, Sandro, Jennifer Ahern, Heidi Resnick, Dean Kilpatrick, Michael Bucuvalas, Joel Gold, and David Vlahov. 2002. 'Psychological Sequelae of the September 11 Terrorist Attacks on New York City.' *New England Journal of Medicine* 346(13): 982–987.

Gleicher, Faith, and Richard E. Petty. 1992. 'Expectations of Reassurance Influence the Nature of Fear-Stimulated Attitude Change.' *Journal of Experimental Social Psychology*, 28: 86–100.

Hoffman, Bruce. 1998. *Inside Terrorism*. New York: Columbia University Press.

Hovland, Carol, I Janis, L. Irving, and Harold H. Kelley. 1953. *Communication and Persuasion*. Westport, Conn.: Greenwood Press.

Holsti, Ole R. 1965. 'The 1914 Case.' *American Political Science Review* 59: 365–378.

Holsti, Ole R. 1972. *Crisis, Escalation, and War*. Montreal: McGill-Queens University Press.

Holsti, Ole R., Robert C. North, and Richard A. Brody. 1968. 'Perception and Action in the 1914 Crisis.' In J. David Singer, ed., *Quantitative International Politics*. New York: Free Press.

Huddy, Leonie, Nadia Khatib, and Theresa Capelos. 2002. 'The Polls-Trends: Reactions to the Terrorist Attacks of September 11, 2001.' *Public Opinion Quarterly*.

Huddy, Leonie, Stanley Feldman, Theresa Capelos, and Colin Provost. 2002. 'The Consequences of Terrorism: Disentangling the Effects of Personal and National Threat.' *Political Psychology*, 23: 485–509.

Huddy, Leonie, Stanley Feldman, Charles Taber, and Gallya Lahav. 2002. 'The Politics of Threat: Cognitive and Affective Reactions to 9/11.' Paper presented at the annual meeting of the American Political Science Association, Boston, September.

Hutchinson, Martha C. 1973. 'The Concept of Revolutionary Terrorism.' *Journal of Conflict Resolution*, 6, 388.

Jacobson, D., and Daniel Bar-Tal. 1995. 'Structure of Security Beliefs among Israeli Students.' *Political Psychology*, 16, 567–590.

Janis, Irving L. 1982. *Groupthink*. Boston: Houghton-Mifflin.

Janis, Irving L., and Seymour Feshbach. 1953. 'Effects of Fear-Arousing Communications.' *Journal of Abnormal and Social Psychology*, 48, 78–92.

Jervis, Robert, Richard Ned Lebow, and Janice Gross Stein. 1985. *Psychology and Deterrence*. Baltimore: Johns Hopkins University.

Johnson, E. J., and Amos Tversky. 1983. 'Affect, Generalization, and the Perception of Risk.' *Journal of Personality and Social Psychology* 45: 20–31.

Lebow, Richard Ned. 1981. *Between Peace and War: The Nature of International Crisis*. Baltimore: Johns Hopkins University Press.

Lerner, Jennifer S., Roxana M. Gonzalez, Deborah A. Small, and Baruch Fischhoff. 2003. 'Effects of Fear and Anger on Perceived Risks of Terrorism: A National Field Experiment.' *Psychological Science* 14, 144–150.

Lerner, Jennifer S., and Dacher Keltner, 2000. 'Beyond Valence: Toward a model of emotion-specific influences on judgment and choice.' *Cognition and Emotion* 14(4): 473–493.

Lerner, Jennifer S., and Dacher Keltner. 2001. 'Fear, Anger, and Risk.' *Journal of Personality and Social Psychology* 81(1): 146–159.

Long, David E. 1990. *The Anatomy of Terrorism*. New York: Free Press.

Maoz, Zeev. 1990. *National Choices and International Processes*. Cambridge, UK: Cambridge University Press.

Maoz, Zeev. 1997. 'Decision Stress, Individual Choice, and Policy Outcomes: The Arab-Israeli conflict.' In Nehemia Geva and Alex Mintz, eds., *Decision-making on War and Peace: The Cognitive-Rational Debate*. Boulder, CO: Lynne Rienner.

Marcus, G. E. and M. B. MacKuen. 1993. 'Anxiety, Enthusiasm, and the Vote: The emotional underpinnings of learning and involvement during presidential campaigns.' *The American Political Science Review*, 87, 672–685.

Marcus, G. E., W. R. Neuman, and M. B. MacKuen. 2000. *Affective Intelligence and Political Judgment*. Chicago: University of Chicago Press.

Mathews, A., and C. MacLeod 1986. 'Discrimination of Threat Cues without Awareness in Anxiety States.' *Journal of Abnormal Psychology* 95: 131–138.

McCalla, Robert. 1992. *Uncertain Perceptions*. Ann Arbor, MI: University of Michigan Press.

Poikolainen, K., R. Kanerva and J. Loennqvist. 1998. 'Increasing Fear of Nuclear War among Adolescents before the Outbreak of the Persian Gulf War.' *Nordic Journal of Psychiatry*, 52, 197–202.

Pruitt, Dean G. 1965. 'Definition of the Situation as a Determinant of International Action.' In Herbert C. Kelman, ed., *International Behavior: A Social-Psychological Analysis*. New York: Holt, Rinehart and Winston.

Raviv, A., A. Sadeh, A. Raviv, O. Silberstein, and O. Diver. 2000. 'Young Israelis' Reactions to National Trauma: The Rabin assassination and terror attacks.' *Political Psychology, 21,* 299–322.

Rogers, R. W. 1983. 'Cognitive and Physiological Processes in Fear Appeals and Attitude Change.' In J. T. Cacioppo and R. E. Petty, eds., *Social Psychophysiology: A Sourcebook.* New York: Guilford, pp. 153–176.

Schuster, Mark A., Bradley D. Stein, Lisa H. Jaycox, Rebecca L. Collins, Grant N. Marshall, Marc N. Elliott, Annie J. Zhou, David E. Kanouse, Janina L. Morrison, and Sandra H. Berry. A National Survey of Stress Reactions after the September 11, 2001 Terrorist Attacks. *New England Journal of Medicine,* 345(20), 1507–1512.

Sears, Donald O., and C. Funk. 1991. 'The role of Self-interest in Social and Political Attitudes.' *Advances in Experimental Psychology, 24,* 1–91.

Silver, Roxanne, C. Alison E., Holman, Daniel, McIntosh, Poulin, N., Michael, Gil-Rivas, Virginia. 2002. 'Nationwide Longitudinal Study of Psychological Responses to September 11'. *Journal of the American Medical Association,* 288, 1235–1244.

Smith, D. A. and C. D. Uchida. (1988). 'The Social Organization of Self-help: A study of defensive weapon ownership.' *American Sociological Review, 53,* 94–102.

Stafford, M. C., and O. R. Galle. 1984. 'Victimization rates, exposure to risk, and fear of crime.' *Criminology, 22,* 173–85.

Suedfeld, Peter, and Philip Tetlock. 1977. Integrative Complexity of Communications in International Crises. *Journal of Conflict Resolution* 21: 169–184.

t'Hart, Paul. 1990. *Groupthink in Government.* Baltimore: Johns Hopkins.

Traugott, Michael, Ted Brader, Deborah Coral, Richard Curtin, David Featherman, Robert Groves, Martha Hill, James Jackson, Thomas Juster, Robert Kahn, Courtney Kennedy, Donald Kinder, Beth-Ellen Pennell, Matthew Shapiro, Mark Tessler, David Weir, and Robert Willis. 2002. 'How Americans Responded: A Study of Public Reactions to 9/11.' *PS,* XXXV (3).

Vertzberger, Y. Y. I. 1998. *Risk Taking and Decision-Making.* Stanford, CA: Stanford University Press.

Wardlaw, Grant. 1982. *Political Terrorism.* Cambridge, UK: Cambridge University Press.

Warr, M. 1984. 'Fear of Victimization: Why are women and the elderly more afraid?' *Social Science Quarterly,* 65, 681–702.

Warr, M. 1990. 'Dangerous Situations: Social context and fear of Victimization.' *Social Forces,* 68, 891–907.

Zaller, John. 1994. 'Elite Leadership of Mass Opinion: New Evidence from the Gulf War.' In W. Lance Bennett and David L. Paletz (Eds), *Taken by Storm: The Media, Public Opinion, and U.S. Foreign Policy in the Gulf War.* Chicago: University of Chicago Press.

Conclusion

CHAPTER **14**
The Lessons of Framing Terrorism

MONTAGUE KERN
MARION JUST
PIPPA NORRIS

It is often difficult to disentangle how news frames shape the social construction of reality from the "actual" reality of events. It is like being surrounded by an endless hall of mirrors. This is especially true if a consensual interpretation predominates in any society so that one-sided frames become taken for granted uncritically by politicians, reporters, and the public. To understand this process further, news coverage of an event needs to be compared against an independent benchmark. In particular, evidence of trends in terrorist incidents is needed for comparison with how the news media reported the threat of terrorism, and how this coverage in turn led toward the widespread American perception that international threats to U.S. domestic security suddenly surged to unprecedented levels post-9/11. A similar approach would compare official police crime statistics against reporting of these incidents, or government measures of the proportion of population below the poverty level compared with news stories about poverty. Admittedly official statistics also provide a social construction of reality, and these can also be affected by the news media, for example if the publicity surrounding cases of violent rape deters or encourages other victims to come forward to report cases to the police. Yet official statistics provide an alternative way to calculate the statistical risk of terrorism, especially if their construction is relatively independent of the media.

Attempts to monitor trends in the incidents of terrorism are often flawed and inconsistent, remaining heavily dependent on the particular definition and classifications used by official agencies, and affected by the reliability of the record provided by the media's reporting of these events. Estimates vary depending on whether they count the frequency of terrorist events, or their effects in terms of the number of fatalities or wounded, or the costs of damage to property. It is difficult to compare cases since some types of terrorism are relatively common, although they may involve only one or two victims in each event, exemplified by kidnappings in Colombia, while others may be rare but may involve many more victims when they occur, such as the airline bombing over Lockerbie. Different weightings of these factors can obviously generate alternative assessments of the statistical risks. It is also most difficult to compare domestic terrorist incidents, since national crime statistics collected by Interpol's database covering 180 nations depend on the statutory definition of terrorism used in each country and the reliability of official records by member states, and the major crime statistics collected by Interpol since 1950 are not disaggregated in a way that could identify terrorist incidents.[1] The U.S. State Department report *Patterns of Terrorism, 2001* provides the most consistent annual estimates of the number of international terrorist incidents around the world since 1969.[2] This data has been used by many scholars for secondary time-series analysis of the risks of international terrorism.[3] The definition of international terrorism used by the State Department has been slightly broadened over the years, introducing some inconsistencies, but the data presented in *Patterns of Terrorism 2001* has been adjusted to form a reliable time-series based on current definitions. For comparison, we can turn to the frequency of international terrorist incidents monitored from 1968 to 1997 by an independent source, the RAND-Memorial Institute for the Prevention of Terrorism (RAND-MIPT). The major trends documented by the RAND-MIPT series closely parallel the U.S. State Department evidence, which lends greater confidence in the reliability of the official estimates.[4] The FBI and U.S. Department of Justice collected comparable official statistics on incidents of domestic terrorism occurring within the United States borders from 1987 to 1999.[5]

The evidence about trends in terrorism in Figure 14.1, collected by the U.S. State Department and corroborated by the RAND-MIPT indicators, indicates that the frequency of international terrorist incidents fell significantly during the 1990s, rather than rising. Far from high risks, United States citizens have lived in the safest region in the world, whether measured by the number of attacks or the number of casualties on domestic soil, not the most vulnerable. These statistical indicators, extrapolating from past events, suggest that the Bush administration's claims that threats from world terrorism have sharply worsened with 9/11, so that Americans live in an especially dangerous place, are exaggerated. The evidence suggests that the public misperceived the statistical risk of terrorist acts, which is not surprising given the general difficulty the public has in calculating risk and particular types of risks. In this regard, the threat of terrorist events is similar to the exaggeration or underestimation of many other social and physical risks, whether from car accidents, violent crime, or cancer.[6]

Clearly 9/11 had a devastating impact on American perceptions of vulnerability and security, especially coming after a period of declining terrorism risk. The experience of 9/11 may be an aberration or a harbinger of heightened risk in the new decade of the 21st century. But even the scale of the tragedy of 9/11 incidents did not put the United States in a category of high terrorist vulnerability comparable to that of many other states in the world. In Peru alone, for example, it is widely estimated that long-standing conflict between the state and the Shining Path rebel movement, involving terrorism on both sides, caused

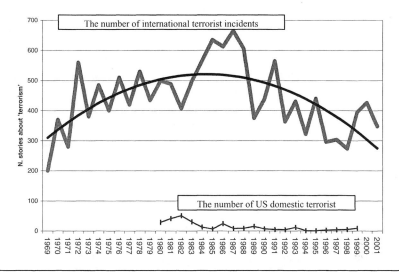

Fig. 14.1 Annual trends in terrorist incidents, 1969–2001. Sources: US Department of Justice. 1999. *Terrorism in the United States, 1999: 30 Years of Terrorism.* Washington, DC: FBI. US State Department. *Patterns of Terrorism, 2001.* Washington, DC.

30,000 deaths from the late-1960s until 1992, when the movement was severely weakened by the arrest of several rebel commanders. In the Philippines, three decades of fighting between the New People's Army (NPA) and the government killed an estimated 40,000 people. In Sri Lanka, from 1983 when war began to the 2002 Oslo peace settlement, about 60,000 people were killed in conflict between the Tamil Tigers and the government.

Of course many factors contributed toward American feelings of vulnerability after 9/11. For example, there were dramatic changes in homeland security and transportation policy that directly affected hundreds of thousands of Americans. Official government policy and leadership speeches by the Bush administration heightened public fears by recommending that Americans build safe rooms with plastic sheeting and duct tape and by issuing a series of "yellow" and "orange" warnings of terrorist dangers—which have not yet materialized. The Bush administration also claimed that there were direct links between the al Qaeda organization and Iraqi President Saddam Hussein, links that other governments in France, Germany and Russia, as well as elsewhere, argued were never convincingly substantiated.

The power of consensual news frames, exemplified by the "war on terrorism" frame in America cannot be underestimated. A one-sided news frame can block the reception of contrary independent evidence. Feelings of threat are magnified by the constant use of the frame, although in the American case, it appears to have hardened the will to resist (see Leona Huddy et al., Chapter 13). The events, depicted so vividly live on American television screens, carried tremendous visual immediacy and symbolic weight, from threats to Wall Street to the attack on the Pentagon, and rumors about potential threats to the White House. The events were shocking because prior to 9/11, foreign attacks on American soil had been unknown since the Second World War. The closest parallel in recent years was the Oklahoma City bombing, a product of domestic terrorism. As Todd Schaefer has shown (Chapter 6), the local angle of terrorism is often the most powerful frame in reporting. When terrorists strike, concern rises most within the society being attacked. Even among the U.S. population, New Yorkers felt more vulnerable to terrorist attacks than Americans living in other parts of the country.

The 9/11 attacks also exerted powerful effects because they involved suicidal perpetrators, religious extremists, and thousands of deaths. Novel terrorist tactics involving mass casualties or deaths, such as airplane hijacking in the 1970s or suicide bombers in the early 21st century, may elicit greater news coverage and fear reactions than continuing "routine" threats affecting individual casualties, such as kidnappings in Colombia. When the government takes effective steps to counter terrorist threats, then news coverage, and perceived vulnerability, decline. There are therefore multiple reasons why the government authorities warned, the news media reported, and why many Americans felt, that there was indeed a new security threat to their everyday lives after 9/11, whether from airports, anthrax spores in the mail, or possibly some new deadly biological hazard, loose nukes, dirty bombs, or mass poisonings. But these fears should be put in historical and geopolitical context, and understood in terms of the statistical probability and trends of terrorist events.

Long-term Trends in Terrorism

To understand the framing of terrorism, we need to consider long-term trends and the origins of this phenomenon, which lie in acts of assassinations, repression, and massacres common down the ages, whether perpetuated by states or by dissident groups.[7] Although practices can be identified since the earliest history of the Greek city-states, the concept was first used in 1795, to describe government by intimidation, arising from Robespierre's reign of terror during the French Revolution.[8] In this regard, the systematic use of terror was first understood as a coercive technique or method of subjection used by rulers to control the people. The term "terrorists" was rapidly extended to those groups or individuals who employed violent intimidation to further their views, especially members of extreme revolutionary societies in Russia. The nineteenth and early twentieth century saw sporadic outbursts from diverse insurgent groups using assassinations and bombs to attack monarchs, aristocrats and government officials, as exemplified by the Fenians (the Irish Republican Brotherhood), militant anarchists in Europe, and disaffected Russian revolutionaries.

Terrorism came somewhat later to the United States, although political violence was far from unknown, as illustrated by the assassination of President

Lincoln. After the American Civil War (1861–65) defiant Southerners formed the Ku Klux Klan to intimidate supporters of Reconstruction and to coerce the African American population. The 1890s experienced multiple regicides in Europe, and estimates suggest that chiefs of state were murdered at the rate of nearly one per year.[9] From the 1920s onward, the resurgence of terrorism was closely associated with nationalist independence movements struggling against colonial powers, exemplified by the Mau Mau rebellion in Kenya, the National Liberation Front of Algeria, and the Viet Minh fighting against French rule in Vietnam, with terrorism focused largely against governments within national borders. State terrorism during this era was exemplified by Stalin's use of the Great Terror as a mechanism of Soviet control, as well as repression and death squads employed routinely by military juntas and authoritarian regimes in many Latin America countries.

Terrorism During the 1970s and 1980s

The modern era of terrorism is conventionally demarcated from the early-1970s onward, a period that saw the growing spread of terrorism across national borders, in line with other trends in globalization. The trends in international terrorism around the world as monitored by the US State Department, illustrated in Figure 14.1, suggest that the number of incidents grew erratically from the early 1970s, after the Munich Olympic crisis, rising until they peaked around the mid-to-late 1980s. The most well-known incidents of *spectacular* terrorism in this era, widely reported in the international press, were exemplified by the Black September (pro-Palestinian) capture and killing of Israeli hostages at the Munich Olympics in 1972, plane hijackings in 1975 by the Baader Meinhof organization in Germany, assassinations and kidnapping by the extreme left-wing anti-capitalist Red Brigade in Italy in 1977, the Iranian U.S. Embassy hostage-taking in 1979, the hijacking of TWA-847 by Islamic Jihad in Athens in 1985, and the Libyan downing of PanAm-103 over Lockerbie in Scotland in 1988. Although receiving far less international media attention,[10] more routine and deadly incidents of terrorism continued in many world regions, especially throughout much of Africa and Latin America. Sporadic terrorist violence, including occasional bombings, hostage-takings, hijackings, assassinations, arson, and armed assaults, was evident in many areas with multiple incidents in deeply divided plural societies, exemplified by Israel and the West Bank, Spain, and Northern Ireland.[11]

For the last three decades, planes have been downed, bombs exploded, and victims hurt. In Europe, Baader Meinhof, Carlos the Jackal, the Red Brigades, the IRA, and ETA killed and maimed their way across the 1970s and 1980s. During these years, groups using terrorist tactics around the world were as diverse as Shining Path in Peru, the PLO in Israel and the West Bank, Marxist guerillas in Colombia, and the Afghan mujahadeen fighting the Soviet invaders. Latin America, Asia, and Africa learnt to live with varying degrees of civil violence and political terror. Given the importance of the local angle in news reporting, during the 1970s and 1980s the U.S. news media, especially network TV news, paid little attention to terrorism in many parts of the world except in cases where American citizens, interests, or cultural affinities were directly involved.[12] The most comprehensive study by Gabrielle Weimann and Conran Winn, comparing the number of terrorist incidents from 1968 to 1980 recorded in the RAND database against news coverage of these events by the three main American television networks in the Vanderbilt archive, estimated that only between 15–18 percent of terrorist acts were ever reported.[13] The study also found that the *New York Times,* while more comprehensive, still covered only a third of all such incidents. Following the general pattern of international news coverage, U.S. networks covered terrorist events in Africa and Latin America the least, and on North America and the Middle East the most.[14] The relative neglect of U.S. media coverage of terrorism in countries such as Colombia, Peru, Sri Lanka and the Philippines persisted despite the existence of widespread armed conflict, major violations of human rights, and substantial civil unrest.[15]

Terrorism During the 1990s

The end of the Cold War in the late-1980s and early-1990s generated a significant peace-dividend. Far from a growing threat, the 1990s witnessed a substantial *fall* in the frequency of international terrorist events. The mean number of international terrorist incidents per annum was estimated in *Patterns of Terrorism 2001* by the U.S. State Department. There were 437 incidents per year during the 1970s, rising to 535 per year during the 1980s, before falling to 383 per year during the 1990s. In total, 348 incidents occurred during 2001, the lowest level since the series started.[16] Nor was this just a statistical aberration or change of classification: similar trends were confirmed in the RAND-MIPT series.[17] Larry C. Johnson concluded that during the last decade of the 20th century, fewer countries confronted significant terrorist threats, the number of terrorist groups fell, and fatalities from international terrorism also declined.[18] The main factors driving this development can be found in the dramatic spread of democratization that occurred worldwide since the late 1980s, which facilitated greater autonomy or self-determination for many ethno-political groups, and the end of some of the most repressive state regimes.[19] The most reliable independent estimates of long-term trends in armed conflict and ethnic conflict, provided by the Minorities at Risk (MAR) project based at the University of Maryland, confirms that the 1990s saw a sizeable and consistent fall in the number of incidents of ethnic conflict and of armed conflict around the globe: "The number and magnitude of armed conflict within and among states have lessened since the early 1990s by nearly half."[20]

Of course global incidents of international terrorism could fall while cases of local terrorism grew on American soil, but in fact the FBI also documented fewer cases of domestic terrorism.[21] Incidents monitored by the FBI dropped from 23 cases per annum during the 1970s down to only 5 cases per annum during the 1990s. During the 1970s many domestic incidents were attributed to radical left-wing groups, anti-war extremists, and Puerto Rican separatists, including the Weather Underground, Armed Forces of Puerto Rican Liberation (FALN), the Black Liberation Army and the Symbionese Liberation Army. The fortunes of these groups declined in the mid-1980s, due to law enforcement initiatives and changes in the political culture. During the last decade the overall number of domestic incidents remained low, although some right-wing anti-government and racist fringe radicals, militia and 'patriot' groups became more active in the US, such as Aryan Nation, along with some radical environmental and animal rights activists.

During the 1990s, however, terrorist events, which had been common in many countries, sometimes came closer to home for Americans. The most spectacular acts that affected Americans during the last decade included the bombing of the New York World Trade Center underground car park in 1993, the 1995 demolition of the Alfred P. Murrah Federal Building in Oklahoma City, the Unabomber's 18-year campaign that ended in 1996, the 1998 destruction of the U.S. Embassies in Kenya and Tanzania, as well as the dramatic events of 9/11. What is remarkable with hindsight, however, is how few terrorist events had occurred within the borders of the United States prior to 9/11 compared with regional patterns elsewhere. The U.S. State Department noted only 15 international terrorist attacks took place from 1996 to 2000 within North America (see Figure 14.2), compared with 151 incidents in Africa, 159 in the Middle East, 251 in Asia, 309 in Western Europe, and 637 in Latin America.[22] A comparison of the total casualties produced by international terrorist incidents shows only 7 casualties within North America from 1996 to 2000, compared with 253 hurt in Latin America, 404 in Asia, 945 in Western Europe, 1754 in the Middle East, and a remarkable 6411 casualties in Africa. Against this background, threats from international terrorism that had become widely familiar to citizens in many nations around the world, as well as to U.S. citizens when traveling abroad, were largely unknown within U.S. borders. Figure 14.3 shows the number of American citizens hurt or killed by incidents of terrorism from 1991 to 2001, with relatively low numbers throughout the decade, with the clear exceptions of the Oklahoma bombing and 9/11.

Trends in Terrorism Coverage

So how did the U.S. news media cover these developments? The levels of coverage of terrorism in the U.S. national news can be compared from 1969 to 2002 using simple keyword searches for stories featuring the term 'terrorism'. We can compare coverage on the major network TV evening news programs ABC, CBS, NBC, PBS and CNN, using the Vanderbilt archive, and we can use a similar process to analyze coverage in the *New York Times,* using the

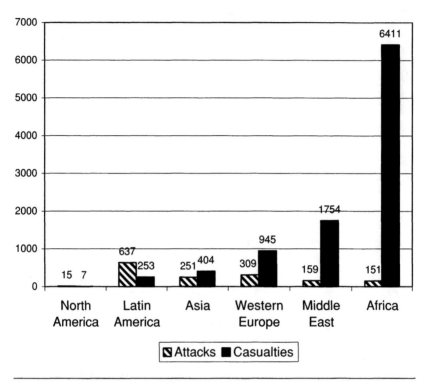

Fig. 14.2 Location of casualties and attacks from international terrorism, 1996–2000. Source: US State Department. *Patterns of Terrorism, 2001.* Washington, D.C. "It should be noted that the US State Department report *Patterns of Terrorism 2002* published in April 2003 saw a further drop in the total number of international terrorist attacks to 199 incidents in 2002."

Lexis-Nexis database.[23] Clearly the keyword search procedure is only an approximate indicator, and more refined analysis could examine coverage using alternative keyword terms such as 'political violence', or specific types of terrorism employed in different regions. Nevertheless the broad search for story summaries including the term 'terrorism' provides at least a rough gauge of the extent of coverage.

The results (see Figure 14.4) confirm what many previous studies have documented, namely that international terrorism attracted the greatest attention in the American press in the most dramatic cases, particularly those involving American victims. Weimann and Winn found that certain factors helped to predict which terrorist incidents attracted the most coverage in U.S. network news during this period, including the level of violence (the number of injuries or deaths involved), the location (in the Middle East or North America), the type of event (with most coverage for airline hijackings), and if responsibility for the incident was known.[24] These traits were exemplified by the Iranian U.S. Embassy hostage-taking in 1979, the Hezbollah truck bombings of the U.S.

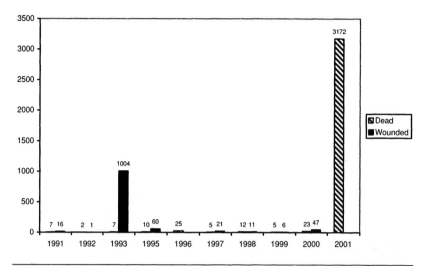

Fig. 14.3 U.S. Citizens wounded or killed by international terrorism, 1991–2001. Source: US State Department. *Patterns of Terrorism, 2001.* Washington, DC. Appendix C. Note that this does not include the case of the Oklahoma City bombing in 1995, where 842 people were wounded and 168 were killed, as this was classified as an act of domestic terrorism.

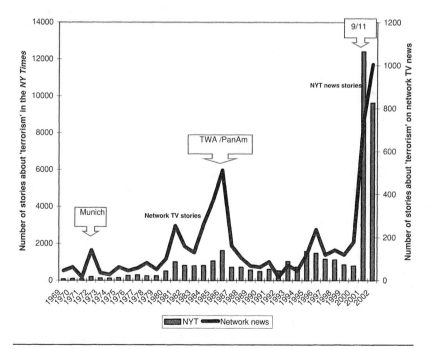

Fig. 14.4 Annual trends in coverage of terrorism in the *New York Times* and US TV network news, 1969–2002. Sources: Number of network TV evening news stories about 'terrorism' estimated from a keyword search of the Vanderbilt News Archive. The number of *New York Times* stories about terrorism estimated from a keyword search in Lexis-Nexis. See footnote 46.

Embassy and U.S. Marine barracks in Beirut in 1984, the hijacking of TWA-847 by Islamic Jihad in Athens in 1985, the Libyan state sponsorship of the bombing of La Belle disco in Berlin in 1986, and the downing of PanAm-103 over Lockerbie in Scotland in 1988. These 'spectacular' events generated distinctive peaks of coverage in American news media. During the 1970s, the *New York Times* contained on average one story about terrorism every other day. Coverage doubled to just over two stories per day on average during the 1980s. U.S. network TV evening news covered on average about one story about terrorism every week during the 1970s, and rose to 4 stories per week during the 1980s. In addition the American news media also provided coverage of routine domestic terrorist conflict in countries and regions with long-established cultural ties to the United States, particularly events in Israel and in Northern Ireland.[25]

During the 1990s the trends in U.S. TV news followed the real-world decline. The average number of stories about terrorism on the U.S. network news was four stories per week during the 1980s but this dropped to two stories per week during the 1990s (when international coverage in general was sharply reduced on U.S. TV news).[26] The events of 9/11 were therefore all the more shocking to Americans, in part because of the sheer extent of the death and destruction in New York and Washington DC, but also because the United States had seemed so immune from these risks at home for so long. As expected, news coverage of terrorism following 9/11 reached record levels; one simple indicator is that the number of news stories about terrorism on the three major networks jumped from around 178 in the 12-months prior to September 2001 to 1345 stories in the twelve months afterwards, not counting, of course, the extensive number of 24/7 extended news bulletins, round-the-clock cable news, local news programs, news magazine special reports, and documentaries.[27]

Not surprisingly, public concern mirrored the network news coverage. Chapters in this book have explored the direction of causality in this relationship, but simple correlations here can be examined by comparing the public's concern about terrorism with levels of TV network news of this subject. When Americans were asked by the Gallup Report about "the most important problem facing the country" the proportion nominating "terrorism" shot up from zero in the three months prior to September 2001 to almost half the population (46%) immediately after 9/11. Levels of anxiety subsided again in subsequent months, although remaining at relatively high levels. As illustrated in Figure 14.5, without assuming the direction of causality in this relationship, levels of public concern roughly reflected patterns of coverage of terrorism shown on national TV network evening news. Twelve months after September 11, despite continuing economic problems, and the persistence of major domestic issues such as health care and social security, one fifth of the public continued to regard terrorism as the "most important problem" facing America. By spring 2003, the levels of public concern about terrorism were about half what they were just after 9/11, but five times what they were before 9/11. Clearly the decline over time represents a "distance from the event" phenomenon, which is also

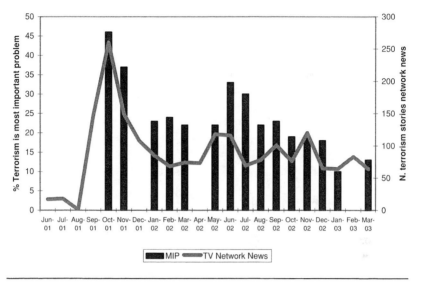

Fig. 14.5   Monthly trends in network TV news coverage of terrorism and public concern around 9/11. Sources: *TV network evening news:* The number of stories about 'terrorism' estimated from a keyword search of the Vanderbilt University Television News Archive. *MIP:* The percentage of the American public nominating 'terrorism' as '*The most important problem facing the country*'. The Gallup Report.

common to other kinds of misperceptions of risk (such as of earthquake fault lines), while the increase over the pre-9/11 period may represent an exaggerated sense of risk. The question remains whether we can expect a further continued decline in the perceived risk of terrorism, as memories fade, as with previous incidents such as Lockerbie or Oklahoma, or whether the government, the news media, and possibly events themselves, continue to fuel this sense of threat, so that concern about terrorism remains relatively high on the American public's agenda.

Public concern in America needs to be set in context: what changed with 9/11 were not the overall levels of international terrorist incidents in the world. Obviously American citizens had long been directly affected by terrorism prior to 9/11, with lives lost and people hurt both abroad (as exemplified by the Iranian hostage crisis in 1979, the Athens hijacking of TWA-847 in 1985, or the downing of PanAm-103 over Lockerbie in 1988) and also at home (as shown most dramatically by the Oklahoma City bombing in 1995). Certainly risks remain difficult to assess and some new threats against American interests may have been either deterred or prevented by strengthened security measures at airports, border crossings, or official buildings. Given the vulnerability of modern societies, terrorist threats directed against American citizens will continue, even with increased security. There could always be a 'contagion' effect from 9/11, if other groups seek to replicate the suicide attack to gain global publicity. The events of 9/11 were also different from many previous terrorist incidents since no political demands were made prior to the attacks, and religious fanatics willing to commit suicide committed the acts. The multiple coordinated simultaneous attacks upon different symbolic American targets, as well as their visual immediacy and live coverage, also immeasurably strengthened their impact. The events of 9/11 understandably brought a new feeling of vulnerability to many Americans, as security threats that were long familiar elsewhere around the globe directly affected U.S. citizens in New York and Washington DC, creating the broader climate of support for the 'war on terrorism'. For many Americans, and for the Bush administration, the events of 9/11 justified the subsequent attacks on Afghanistan and on Iraq, even if many critics deeply questioned the claimed linkage of al Qaeda with President Saddam Hussein.

Terrorism and the "Framing" Model

What then does this book tell us about the role of the press, government, and public opinion in the framing process, especially when the War on Terrorism frame emerged in the period immediately after 9/11? Here we evaluate this question in the light of the framing model (Chapter 1) that underpins the analysis in this book. The schematic model presented earlier in figure 1.1 distinguishes between the factors leading to the news frame—including the societal culture, the competing government and terrorist frames, and the events themselves—and the consequences of the news frame for public opinion and the policy process.

Influences on News Frames

Culture   The comparative focus of this book offers important insights into how societal cultures affected the framing of terrorism. As Tamar Liebes and Anat First point out (Chapter 4), the comparison of Israel and the West Bank shows how events may be manipulated to limit, or attract press attention, in order to achieve a narrative or iconic victory. Although accurate portrayal of factual events is the goal of journalism, reporters necessarily engage in processes of selection and emphasis as they construct the news. Problems of reportorial omission and commission are contentious, especially when there is no consensus on the frames or where different communities within the same nation adopt conflicting frames for events. Conflicting news frames of terrorism embody the difficulty journalists face in representing "reality." Given the potential for manipulation by state and non-state combatants, such as the Israel Defense Forces or the Palestine Liberation Organization, what does it mean for journalists to produce accurate news coverage? The difficulties are enormous. Simply staying alive in the face of opposing forces is a problem for journalists around the world. According to the Committee to Protect Journalists, 389 journalists were killed around the world for practicing their profession from 1992 to 2001.[28] Covering conflict, including terrorism, represents an ongoing and dangerous challenge for the press.

The case of Northern Ireland points to a different way that society influences the terrorism frame. As the British government welcomed the IRA pledge to renounce violence, Tim Cooke (Chapter 5) documents how journalists struggle to define new ways to characterize the struggle between the IRA and the Unionists. Former 'terrorists', whose views have previously been delegitamized due to use of violence, have become elected politicians. They may even become a central figure on the global political scene, as in the case of Nelson Mandela. Mandela was the former leader of the African National Congress, a movement long delegitimized by the U.S. government, and by global news coverage because of its embrace of terrorism against the minority Apartheid regime. The question for journalists and media scholars is: Whose cues should journalists follow in characterizing non-governmental organizations? How should they understand conflict in events that may involve insurgent action, especially when those rebel groups might transition to partners in waging peace?

As many previous studies have found, contributors stress that geopolitical position, and domestic political perspectives strongly shape news coverage of political violence. It is hardly surprising that terrorism is framed from a geopolitical perspective since news has, as Robin Brown (Chapter 3) points out, emerged as diplomacy by other means. Journalists around the world cover terrorism from a local angle, in terms of either the location of events or the nationality of victims and perpetrators. The result is a record of frustration. As Schaeffer points out in Chapter 6 the focus of the U.S. media was on the meaning of the Kenyan embassy terrorist attacks for the U.S. and what America should do in response. U.S. news stories ignored African perceptions, and concerns, for example, for aid for African victims. Similarly, in conveying the meaning of the September 11 attacks, African media depicted American viewpoints through news coverage of government officials and to some extent, those of average American victims (using global news which included this focus), and their editorial interpretations were almost entirely in line with African governmental points of view. Both media de-emphasized the global concerns of the other and searched for local angles.

While news of 9/11 portrayed American politics as defined by a renewed sense of national community and purpose, Brigitte Nacos and Torres Reyna (Chapter 8) describe the influence of culture in the use of stereotypes in news coverage. Stereotypes have had a significant impact on all media in all cultures, and over the course of American history. Prior to 9/11, news coverage particularly in New York, but also national newspapers, characteristically employed negative frames for Arabs and Muslims. Despite improving images of Arab Americans and Muslim Americans during the post-9/11 period, Huddy et al. found that negative stereotypes had a persistent impact on public opinion of Arab Americans after 9/11 (Chapter 13).

Government   Another force shaping frames on terrorism is censorship and self-censorship of journalists. Governments have what is widely perceived to be legitimate power to constrain press coverage in wartime. As Doris A. Graber (Chapter 2) points out, however, balancing the security interests and freedom of the press is a critical goal in democratic societies. The preservation of civilian oversight of the military, and popular oversight of government, depend on an informed public. It is extremely difficult for journalists to exercise their watchdog roles when they share official frames of events in the news. Given the inter-penetration of news and governance even in time of war, as explained by Brown (Chapter 3), it is in the interest of the military and the government to provide journalists with access to the news. The government and the military, on the one hand, and journalists, on the other, exist in a symbiotic relationship and struggle for control. The way that journalists were 'embedded' with the military during the Iraq war, and able to provide live coverage from the front-line, provides the latest important twist on this story. Recognizing the needs of other players and establishing trade-offs can help officials and the press to meet the needs of democratic citizens. Graber's review of the history of free press in wartime suggests, however, that journalists need to err on the side of getting the story if they are going to give the public information vital for democratic governance.

Content analyses conducted for this book show that U.S. news had a common theme in the post-9/11 period—that America had been attacked, the world had changed, and the U.S. must respond when threatened. Narratives portrayed the United States and its allies as besieged, and placed the blame for the attack squarely on Osama bin Laden and his supporters. As is common in crisis coverage, American news closely tracked official views both in national newspapers (Schaefer Chapter 6) and on CNN television (Jasperson and El-Kikhia, Chapter 8). President George W. Bush went on television, echoing the rhetoric of World War II to rally and comfort the nation ("We are beginning another front in our war against terrorism, so freedom can prevail over fear.")[29] His ratings soared. Immediately after 9/11, political leaders from around the world, including European allies, repeated Bush's message. Elite messages blended with "ordinary, heroic American" interviews that focused on the bravery of Americans and their renewed sense of national pride and purpose. At the same time, U.S. television also visually emphasized the savagery of the terrorist acts, and their impact on innocent victims, families, and communities.

Real World Events   As we have seen, government and other political actors can shape news coverage. Journalists' use of alternative frames has been rare in the post-Vietnam era of American war journalism, due to censorship and self-censorship. In early October 2001, however, CNN, which was generally deferential in regard to the framing efforts of the U.S. president and generals (Jasperson and El-Khikia Chapter 7), also aired some news stories based on information obtained from an Arabic-language news service, al Jazeera.[30] These stories included frames that referenced the human cost of the U.S. attack on al Qaeda, the Taliban, and the population in Afghanistan. Since CNN is itself a global network, its use of an Arabic-language TV news source no doubt enhanced its credibility in other parts of the world—although it may have offended the U.S. government. At the same time, the use of alternative frames by a widely watched news network expanded American media and public resources for deliberation.

Public Opinion   How did the American public react to the news coverage of 9/11 and its aftermath? Did the public find information that facilitated the cognitive construction of judgments necessary to understand events? In general, media coverage is an important resource for public opinion.[31] In this case, did news frames build, or disrupt bonds of national, social, and political trust? And did they contribute to emotional reactions that could immobilize citizens, making them fearful and unable to respond rationally to future terrorism risks? If this latter goal in particular was achieved, it could be argued that news coverage of 9/11 served the terrorists rather than American public interest.

At one level, news coverage clearly served U.S. interest. As Michael Traugott and Ted Brader (Chapter 10) point out, newsmagazine frames held terrorists responsible for their own actions, and public attention to such news far exceeded normal information-seeking demographics. It can be concluded that although newsmagazines helped put terrorism on the public agenda, it did not prime public opinion in a fashion sympathetic to terrorists, indeed the reverse.

Nor does it appear that a terrorist attack, amplified in press coverage, is likely to lead to major problems of social disaffection on the national level, another terrorist goal. Instead, during the months following 9/11, it became clear (Brewer et al. Chapter 12) that a worrisome trend toward increasing distrust of political institutions was reversed by 9/11. In the wake of the news event, greater trust in one's fellow citizens had a positive effect on symbolic patriotism, or attachment to the nation and its symbols. Increasing levels of social trust led to positive, mutually reinforcing evaluations of government institutions. The president was a particular beneficiary of this process—as citizens who rallied around the flag also rallied around George W. Bush. Interestingly, system support fueled the dramatic rise in Bush's approval ratings. In this case, popular support for an administration did not drive system support, but rather the other way round.

Beyond that, on the psychological level, did the United States experience an increase in fear and anxiety sufficient to preclude rational response to terrorist actions? Huddy and colleagues make it clear that Americans were extremely concerned about the risk of a future attack in the months following 9/11 (Chapter 13). Debilitating fear and other negative emotional reactions were less prevalent, although evident in a small minority of cases. A small number of Americans were emotionally shaken by the attacks, including younger people, Hispanics, Republicans, women, northeasterners, and those who knew a victim. Education and regular viewing of TV news increased both the perceived risk of terrorism, as well as fear and anxiety. The link between personal experience and physical proximity to the attacks clarified the additional power of terrorist events to frighten individuals most immediately affected by them.

Huddy et al. caution that the great majority of Americans were not affected emotionally by the terrorist attacks. Still, in a finding with important implications for the field of political communication, television viewing of repetitive, and rebroadcast visual images of homeland terrorist attacks increased fear, and those made fearful were less able to learn cognitively from news. Fear elicited by the 9/11 terrorist incidents had two further implications in regard to social dislocation and disaffection: 1) the extent to which other Americans can be trusted, on the individual level and 2) the extent to which respondents thought that Arab-Americans supported the 9/11 terrorist acts, and thus were disloyal. Interestingly, these findings square with high levels of anti-Arab American sentiment reported in public opinion polls, and significant stereotyping of Arab Americans, Arabs, and Muslims, as terrorist sympathizers, both before and after 9/11 (Nacos and Torres-Reyna Chapter 8). Finally, according to Huddy, et al. in the United States fear and anxiety increased patriotism and positive feelings about America, while making people more wary in their daily interactions with others, particularly Arab-Americans. These are significant findings, which indicate that, although the vast majority of Americans did not experience debilitating emotional responses to 9/11, some did, with consequences both for the emergence of patriotism and social wariness, particularly in regard to an enemy "within." This psychological effects research lends support to Nacos and Torres-Reyna's conclusion, based on content analysis, that news frames gave legitimacy to anti-Arab and anti-Muslim policies. Huddy et al.'s public opinion findings demonstrate that news can have a positive impact on the audience's political knowledge and ability to assess risks. Television frames also increase the levels of the audience's emotional responses, which were significantly greater among individuals who watched television and who lived in proximity to terrorism incidents or experienced loss as a result of terrorism. People who had strong emotional experiences in regard to 9/11, were more likely to stereotype Arabs and Muslims, and were more wary of their fellow citizens, but also felt increased patriotism.

The chapters in this book have shown how interdependent the press, the military, and the government are in wartime, even in a conflict as diffuse as that caused by terrorism. In democratic societies, public opinion is an important player in this game. Politicians and generals require public support for their military efforts and seek to stimulate that support by promoting and discouraging dissent. To promote their messages, however, public officials must have the cooperation of journalists. In times of shared crisis, a sense of threat often means that journalists freely offer their collaboration. Even if journalists seek opposing views on government war policies, they are constrained by their dependence on government access in order to write the news. Balanced presentation is difficult in wartime if official opposition leaders are unwilling to counter government views—either because they concede leadership to the party in government or out of fear of being accused of lack of patriotism. Mass media scholars have observed a phenomenon in which news is "indexed" to the policy debates of official or what journalists perceive to be "legitimate" sources.[32] In the case of U.S. foreign policy, this index is based heavily on views expressed by the Administration and the opposition party in Congress. That debate in the U.S. was absent or muted from 9/11, through the war in Afghanistan, and for many months of the troop build-up for the war in Iraq. It was not until the diplomatic failures of the Administration to secure broad allied support and the imprimatur of the U.N. Security Council for war with Iraq that members of Congress and aspiring presidential candidates raised questions.[33] The press carried these criticisms of the President's policies both at home and abroad, covered domestic and foreign peace demonstrations against the war, and reported ambivalence in public support for the war based on opinion polls. Several surveys that probed opinion about going to war against Iraq found significant public concern that the Administration had not sufficiently made its case for war against Iraq and worried about a preemptive war without broader allied and U.N. support. The divide between the President's supporters and those who hung back was marked by partisanship, gender, and race—factors, which tended to coincide.[34]

The core of President George W. Bush's support for War on Iraq, before March 19, 2003, was made up of Republicans and conservatives who voted for him in 2000. Thus, just as Democrats and liberals were more hawkish in support of President Bill Clinton's attack on Serbian-led Yugoslavia in 1999, sectors of the public that had supported Bush in 2000, notably white evangelical Protestants and rural citizens, were his greatest supporters on the war front. Men were also more hawkish than women were, although the gender gap was not terribly large, except in California. Polls taken after the invasion found that support for the war (and for President Bush) was weakest among African Americans. In fact African Americans were the only group to register a majority opposition to the war and to the President.[35]

One aspect of the opinion divide is particularly relevant for media framing of terrorism. Survey respondents who believed that Saddam Hussein was directly involved in the September 11 attack were disproportionately strong supporters of the war.[36] One journalist, who analyzed eight press and Pew Research Center polls dealing with the issue from September 13, 2001–February 10–12, 2003, in comparison with carefully worded explicit and implicit claims by the President, members of his administration, intelligence agencies, Congress, the President of the Czech Republic, and Osama bin Laden, concluded that the theory of a link between al Qaeda and Iraq was "explored, dispelled, suggested, dismissed and approximated over a year and a half."[37] The finding that misinformation and impressionistic clues were closely tied to American support for the war in Iraq suggests broad governmental power to shape public opinion, given news routines, and the expressed desirability of self-censorship among a significant segment of the press.[38]

The chapters in this book demonstrate that news coverage that unquestioningly adopts government frames—such as the war on terrorism—does not serve the public well. Official frames may not only exaggerate levels of terrorist activity, as in the U.S. case, but also fail to explain the complex range of economic and national issues that confront the world today. If news organizations take advantage of global resources they will be able to counter the gun-barrel vision produced by political, military, and cultural frames at home. The way news about terrorism is framed is both contentious and consequential. In a society that is consensual around acts of terrorism, the domestic news frames of terrorism can go unchallenged. Government elites and journalists will usually largely concur in their perceptions about the conflict and the most appropriate steps necessary to contain the threat. Even if politicians and journalists have doubts or disagreements, they will probably suppress explicit criticism out of concern for damaging public morale or fear of public backlash.

The U.S. in the immediate aftermath of 9/11 is a case in point. The consensual or one-sided news frame leaves little room for democratic debate. In divided societies, opposing sides can frame news about conflict differently, such as by Catholics and Protestants in Northern Ireland. These competing frames provide the possibility of debate, to the extent that they penetrate the warring communities, although this process will probably not lead to the kind of deliberation bridging social divides that helps to resolve conflict. In the age of global media, the reach of competing frames may be enhanced. Information about 9/11 that had been withheld from the U.S. public, penetrated the media via reports of debates in the British House of Commons. CNN reported information about U.S. operations in Afghanistan that had been similarly withheld from U.S. audiences, by utilizing news coverage from al Jazeera. Official hostility to media inclusion of competing global frames was exemplified when U.S. National Security Advisor Condoleeza Rice, called on American network television executives to refrain from broadcasting statements by Osama bin Laden (Graber, Chapter 2). This incident illustrates the extent to which global media is a recognized threat to official frames, even in an open and democratic society. This volume shows that people do learn from news and improving the quality of news can produce a more informed, trusting public, *even in crises characterized by terrorism frames.*

It is important to understand the framing process, not just for its own sake, but also because of the influence that frames can have on the political process, public policy, and international affairs. We argued in the introduction to the book that the War on Terrorism frame had replaced the older Cold War frame in American foreign policy. This process was dramatically illustrated by subsequent events in Afghanistan and then in Iraq. The hunt for the perpetrators of 9/11 was expanded to the war in Afghanistan, where members of al Qaeda and Osama bin Laden were thought to be hiding. Then by extension, President Bush, in alliance with Prime Minister Tony Blair, launched war against President Saddam Hussein in Iraq, on the grounds that President Hussein constituted a potential risk if he possessed "weapons of mass destruction" which could make their way into the hands of terrorists. As President Bush declared in his speech justifying the declaration of war on Iraq:

> "It (Iraq) has a deep hatred of America and our friends and it has aided, trained and harbored terrorists, including operatives of al Qaeda. The danger is clear: using chemical, biological or, one day, nuclear weapons obtained with the help of Iraq, the terrorists could fulfil their stated ambitions and kill thousands or hundreds of thousands of innocent people in our country or any other.

> The United States and other nations did nothing to deserve or invite this threat, but we will do everything to defeat it. Instead of drifting along toward tragedy, we will set a course toward safety. Before the day of horror can come, before it is too late to act, this danger will be removed. The United States of America has the sovereign authority to use force in assuring its own national security.

> That duty falls to me as commander-in-chief by the oath I have sworn, by the oath I will keep. Recognizing the threat to our country, the United States Congress voted overwhelmingly last year to support the use of force against Iraq. . . . The terrorist threat to America and the world will be diminished the moment that Saddam Hussein is disarmed."

For the first time, the complex balance of power of multilateral organizations was left divided and in disarray and the United States, the only global superpower, launched a preemptive war, not because a specific terrorist act by President Hussein *had* actually occurred against America's interests, but because such an act *could* have occurred at some undefined time in the future. The power of the War on Terrorism frame in America was such that, although there was no published intelligence of a proven link connecting President Hussein directly to the events of 9/11, in early-March 2003, prior to military intervention, when a representative sample of the American public was asked by Gallup polls whether they thought that Saddam Hussein was involved in supporting terrorist groups that had plans to attack the United States, most people agreed. When asked whether they thought that Saddam Hussein 'was *personally* involved in the September 11th attacks, or not', the majority agreed.[39] The fact that many other countries may not have shared these perceptions could be one reason why the world became so divided over the rationale for the Iraq war. Whether the War on Terrorism frame eventually diminishes as memories of 9/11 gradually fade in the public mind, or whether it continues to influence the future direction of American foreign policy and conflict in international affairs, becoming a self-reinforcing prophecy, remains to be seen.

Notes

1. http://www.interpol.int/Public/Statistics/ICS/Default.asp
2. U.S. State Department. *Patterns of Terrorism* 2001. Washington DC: U.S.Department of State (and previous annual reports in this series). "The US Department of State. 2003. *Patterns of Terrorism 2002*. Washington DC: US Department of State was published when our book was in press. The report notes a dramatic fall in the number of incidents of international terrorism, down from 355 attacks recorded during 2001 to 199 attacks

in 2002. The number of anti–US attacks was 77, down 65% from the previous year's total of 219. The number of those killed or wounded in 2002 was also less than in the previous year."

3.   See also the analysis of this data by Larry C. Johnson. 2001. 'The future of terrorism.' *American Behavioral Scientist.* 44(6): 894–913; Walter Enders and Todd Sandler. 1999. 'Transnational Terrorism in the Post-Cold War Era.' *International Studies Quarterly* 43: 145–167; Walter Enders and Todd Sandler. 2000. 'Is Transnational Terrorism Becoming More Threatening? A Time-Series Investigation.' *Journal of Conflict Resolution* 44: 307–332; Walter Enders and Todd Sandler. 2002. 'Patterns of Transnational Terrorism, 1970–1999: Alternative Time-Series Estimates.' *International Studies Quarterly* 46: 145–165.

4.   Data from the RAND-MIPT series is available from the website of the Oklahoma City National Memorial Institute for the Prevention of Terrorism (MIPT). http://db.mipt.org/6898_rep_in_out.cfm. As the series collection changed after 1997 and currently remains incomplete for 1999, the continuous U.S. State Department data was selected instead for analysis in this chapter.

5.   U.S. Department of Justice. 1999. *Terrorism in the United States, 1999: 30 Years of Terrorism.* Washington, DC: FBI.

6.   David L. Altheide. 2002. *Creating Fear: News and the Construction of Crisis.* New York: Aldine de Gruyter.

7.   D. Rapoport. Ed.1988.*Inside the Terrorist Organization.* New York: Columbia University Press.

8.   Oxford English Dictionary.

9.   Jessica Stern. 2001. *The Ultimate Terrorists.* Cambridge, MA: Harvard University Press. P. 16.

10.   Michael Delli Carpini and Bruce A. Williams. 1987. 'Television and terrorism: Patterns of presentation and occurrence 1969 to 1980.' *Western Political Quarterly.* 40(1): 45–64; Gabrielle Weimann and Conrad Winn, 1994. *The Theater of Terror: The Mass Media and International Terrorism.* New York: Longman Publishing/Addison-Wesley.

11.   For a comprehensive overview and chronology of these and other terrorist events see Cindy C. Combs and Martin Slann. 2002. *Encyclopedia of Terrorism.* New York: Facts on File.

12.   Michael Delli Carpini and Bruce A. Williams. 1987. 'Television and terrorism: Patterns of presentation and occurrence 1969 to 1980.' *Western Political Quarterly.* 40(1): 45–64.

13.   Gabrielle Weimann and Conrad Winn, 1994. *The Theater of Terror: The Mass Media and International Terrorism.* New York: Longman Publishing/Addison-Wesley. P. 68.

14.   "Fewer than one in 10 terrorist incidents in Latin America or Africa are reported on American television compared with almost one-quarter of such events taking place in North America and the Middle East." Gabrielle Weimann and Conrad Winn, 1994. *The Theater of Terror: The Mass Media and International Terrorism.* New York: Longman Publishing/Addison-Wesley. P. 76.

15.   In Colombia, there were usually about 3000 kidnappings a year, including prominent religious leaders, politicians, businessmen, and journalists.

16.   The U.S. State Department. *Patterns of Terrorism* 2001. Washington DC: U.S. Department of State.

17.   http://db.mipt.org/6898_rep_in_out.cfm

18.   Larry C. Johnson. 2001. 'The future of terrorism.' *American Behavioral Scientist.* 44(6): 894–913. There is some dispute about levels of fatality from each incident, and whether each event may have become more lethal, but the time-series evidence currently remains inconclusive on this point.

19.   For the trends in democratization see Freedom House. www.freedomhouse.org

20.   Ted Robert Gurr, Monty Marshall and Deepa Khosla. 2000. 'Global Conflict Trends.' University of Maryland, Center for Systemic Peace/Minorities At Risk. http://members.aol.com/CSPmgm/cspframe.htm

21.   U.S. Department of Justice. 1999. *Terrorism in the United States, 1999: 30 Years of Terrorism.* Washington, DC: FBI. Domestic terrorism is defined in this report as 'the unlawful use, or threatened use, of force or violence by a group or individual based and operating entirely within the United States or its territories without foreign direction committed against persons or property to intimidate or coerce a government, the civilian population, or any segment thereof, in furtherance of political or social objectives.'

22. Note that the U.S. State Department defines 'international terrorist attacks' as terrorism involving the citizens or territory or more than one country.' The U.S. State Department. *Patterns of Terrorism* 2001. Washington DC: U.S. Department of State. The report does not monitor purely domestic terrorist incidents such as the Oklahoma bombing. A comparison of the total number of U.S. citizens killed or wounded by international terrorist attacks in the four years prior to 9/11 was 636 in 1996, 27 in 1997, 23 in 1998, 11 in 1999, and 70 in 2000.

23. The number of stories about 'terrorism' in the network evening news broadcasts from the major U.S. national broadcast networks, ABC, CBS, NBC, PBS and CNN, was estimated from a keyword search of the summary records provided since 1968 by the Vanderbilt News Archive, excluding special news programs such as current affairs documentaries as well as commercials. http://tvnews.vanderbilt.edu/

24. Gabrielle Weimann and Conrad Winn, 1994. *The Theater of Terror: The Mass Media and International Terrorism.* New York: Longman Publishing/Addison-Wesley. P. 131.

25. Gabrielle Weimann and Conrad Winn, 1994. *The Theater of Terror: The Mass Media and International Terrorism.* New York: Longman Publishing/Addison-Wesley.

26. Pippa Norris. 1996 'The Restless Searchlight: Network News Framing of the Post Cold-War World.' *Political Communication* 12(4): 357–370. Although it is worth noting that during the 1990s coverage of terrorism in the *New York Times* followed a slightly contrary trend, increasing from just over two stories about terrorism per day to about two-and-a-half stories per day during the 1990s.

27. For more details, see Brigitte L. Nacos. 2002. *Mass-Mediated Terrorism.* Lanham: Rowman & Littlefield; Bradley S. Greenberg and Marcia Thomson. 2002. *Communication and Terrorism: Public and Media Responses to 9/11.* Hampton Press.

28. See the Committee to Protect Journalists. http://www.cpj.org/killed/Ten_Year_Killed/stats.html

29. President George Bush, CNN 7 October, 2001.

30. This represented about 17 percent of a selective thematic sample, which does not represent all CNN stories.

31. Benjamin I. Page and Robert Y. Shapiro. 1992. *The Rational Public: Fifty Years of Trends in Americans' Policy Preferences.* Chicago: University of Chicago Press; Russell W. Neuman, Marion R. Just and Ann N. Crigler. 1996. *Common Knowledge: News and the Construction of Political Meaning.* Chicago: University of Chicago Press.

32. Jonathan Mermin, 1999. *Debating War & Peace: Media Coverage of U.S. Intervention in the Post-Vietnam Era.* Princeton, N.J.: Princeton University Press; Richard Brody, 1991. *Assessing the President.* Stanford, California: Stanford University Press. Montague Kern, Patricia W. Webb and Ralph B. Levering, 1983. *The Kennedy Crises: The Press, the Presidency and Foreign Policy.* Chapel Hill, North Carolina. Leon V. Sigal. 1973. Reporters and Officials: The Organization and Politics of Newsmaking. Lexington, Massachusetts: D. C. Heath.

33. Tom Daschle, the Senate Minority Leader, questioned the quality of the diplomatic effort, the strength of the administration's case against Iraq, and its application of preemptive war doctrine in this case. The leading Democratic contender, Senator John Kerry, raised questions about the relative threat of Iraq vs. North Korea in the context of the War on Terrorism (although he maintained support for the President's war policies). Other Democratic candidates such as Governor Howard Dean of Vermont, former Senator Carol Mosely Brown and the Reverend Al Sharpton were overtly critical of the Iraq war policy, but were marginalized in the media based on their modest levels of public support.

34. Steve Sailer, "Analysis: Which American Groups Back War?" *UPI*, Los Angeles, March 20, 2003. Also see Adam Nagourney and Janet Elder, "Support for Bush Surges at Home, But Split Remains" The *New York Times* March 22, 2003, A1.

35. Richard Morin and Claudia Deane "Public Support Remains Strong for War Effort" www.washingtonpost.com/ac2/wp-dyn/A18075-2003Mar24. *Washington Post* Monday, March 24, 2003. The Washington Post poll was based on an RDD sample of 580 Americans interviewed on March 23rd. A separate sub-sample of 69 African Americans was also interviewed, for a total of 103. Margin of sampling error for the overall results is plus or minus 4 percentage points.

36. Overall 84% of those who believed Saddam Hussein was involved in 9/11 supported the war, compared with 49% who did not believe it, according to cross-tabulations of *New York Times*/CBS News poll of March 10 provided to Hank Zuker, Creative Research Systems www.surveysystem.com and reported on AAPOR-Net March 21, 20003. The level of misinformation was highlighted in a summary article about support for the war. "A recent *New York Times*/CBS News Poll showed that nearly half of Americans said they believed that Saddam Hussein was personally involved in the Sept. 11 attacks. A Knight Ridder poll taken in early January showed that half said they believed that at least some of the 19 hijackers on Sept. 11 were Iraqis. None were." Jim Rutenberg and Robin Toner, "Critics Say Coverage Helped Lead to War," *New York Times* March 22, 2003.
http://www.nytimes.com/2003/03/22/international/worldspecial/22MEDI.html?ex=1049364018&ei=1&en=333a1e7f5f811d9d.
37. Tom Zeller, "How Americans Link Iraq and September 11th" The *New York Times*. March 2, 2003.
38. "Some reporters investigating claims against Iraq said they felt no compunction to poke holes in the administration's case because they did not find it to be so off base. Many reported being in the same position as the administration: confident that Mr. Hussein is hiding weapons of mass destruction but unable to definitively prove it." Jim Rutenberg and Robin Toner, "Critics Say Coverage Helped Lead to War," *New York Times*, March 22, 2003.
http://www.nytimes.com/2003/03/22/international/worldspecial/22MEDI.html?ex=1049364018&ei=1&en=333a1e7f5f811d9d.
39. CNN/USA Today/Gallup Poll. March 3, 2003. N = 1,007 American adults nationwide. "Do you think Saddam Hussein is involved in supporting terrorist groups that have plans to attack the United States, or not?" Form A (N = 488, MoE ± 5). Yes 88%, No 9%, no Opinion 3%. "Do you think Saddam Hussein was personally involved in the September 11th terrorist attacks, or not?" Form B (N = 519, MoE ± 5) Yes 51%, No 41%, No opinion 8%.

Select Bibliography

Abramson, Paul. 1983. *Political Attitudes in America.* San Francisco: Freeman and Co.

Adams, William C. Ed. 1981. *Television Coverage of the Middle East.* Norwood, NJ: Ablex Press.

Addison, Michael. 2002. *Violent Politics: Strategies of Internal Conflict.* New York: Palgrave.

Alali, Odasuo A. and Gary W. Byrd. Eds. 1994. *Terrorism and the News Media: A Selected, Annotated Bibliography.* New York: McFarland & Company.

Alali, Odasuo A. and Kenoye Kelvin Eke. Eds. 1991. *Media Coverage of Terrorism: Methods of Diffusion.* Thousand Oaks, CA: Sage Publications.

Alexander, Yonah and Robert Picard. 1991. *In the Camera's Eye: News Coverage of Terrorist Events.* Washington, DC: Brasseys.

Almond, Gabriel A., and Sidney Verba. 1963. *The Civic Culture: Political Attitudes and Democracy in Five Nations.* Princeton: Princeton University Press.

Alper, S. William and Thomas Liedy. 1969–1970. 'The Impact of Information Transmission Through Television.' *Public Opinion Quarterly* 33: 556–562.

Altheide, David L. 1987. 'Format and Symbols in TV Coverage of Terrorism in the United States and Great Britain.' *International Studies Quarterly 31:* 161–76.

Ansolabehere, Stephen, Roy Behr, and Shanto Iyengar. 1993. *The Media Game: American Politics in the Television Age.* New York: Macmillan.

Ansolbehere, Stephen, Shanto Iyengar, and Nicholas Valentino. 1994. 'Does Attack Advertising Demobilize the Electorate?' *American Political Science Review* 88: 829–838.

Aufderheide, Pat. 2002. 'All-too-reality TV: Challenges for Television Journalists after September 11.' *Journalism: Theory, practice and criticism* 3(1).

Ayish, M. I. 2002. 'Political Communication on Arab World Television: Evolving Patterns.' *Political communication.* 19(2): 137–154.

Bahry, Donna L, and Brian D. Silver. 1990. 'Soviet Citizen Participation on the Eve of Democratization.' *American Political Science Review* 84 (September): 821–848.

Bahry, Donna L., and Brian D. Silver. 1987. 'Intimidation and the Symbolic Uses of Terror in the USSR.' *American Political Science Review* 81 (December): 1065–1098.

Barnhurst, Kevin. 1991. 'Contemporary Terrorism in Peru: Sendero-Luminoso and the Media.' *Journal of Communication.* 41(4): 75–89.

Barnhurst, Stephen R. 2002. *International Terrorism and Political Violence.* Victoria, BC: Trafford.

Bartels, Larry M. 1993. 'Messages Received: The Political Impact of Media Exposure.' *American Political Science Review,* 87(2): 267–285.

Bennett, W. Lance and David L. Paletz (Eds.) 1994. *Taken by Storm: The Media, Public Opinion, and U.S. Foreign Policy in the Gulf War.* Chicago: University of Chicago Press.

Bennett, W. Lance. 2000. *News: The Politics of Illusion.* 4th Ed. New York: Longman.

Birkland, Thomas A. 1997. *After Disaster: Agenda setting, Public Policy, and Focusing Events.* Washington, D.C.: Georgetown University Press.

Birkland, Thomas A., and Regina G. Lawrence. 2001. 'The *Exxon Valdez* and Alaska in the American Imagination.' In *American Disasters,* edited by S. Biel. New York: New York University Press.

Brehm, John, and Wendy Rahn. 1997. 'Individual-Level Evidence for the Causes and Consequences of Social Capital.' *American Journal of Political Science* 41(3): 999–1023.

Brewer, Paul R., and Marco R. Steenbergen. 2002. 'All Against All: How Beliefs about Human Nature Shape Foreign Policy Opinions.' *Political Psychology* 23(1): 39–58.

Brody, Richard A. 1991. *Assessing the President: The Media, Elite Opinion, and Public Support.* Stanford, CA: Stanford University Press.

Campbell, Christopher P. 1995. *Race, Myth, and the News.* Thousand Oaks, CA: Sage.

Cappella, Joseph N., and Kathleen Hall Jamieson. 1997. *Spiral of Cynicism: The Press and the Public Good.* New York: Oxford University Press.

Carruthers, Susan L. 2000. *The Media at War.* New York: St. Martin's Press.

Chanley, Virginia A., Thomas J. Rudolph, and Wendy M. Rahn. 2000. 'The Origins and Consequences of Public Trust in Government.' *Public Opinion Quarterly* 64(3): 239–56.

Chomsky, Noam. 2002. *9/11*. New York: Seven Stories Press.

Citrin, Jack, and Donald Philip Green.1986. 'Presidential Leadership and the Resurgence of Trust in Government.' *British Journal of Political Science* 16(4): 431–53.

Citrin, Jack, Beth Reingold, and Donald P. Green. 1990. 'American Identity and the Politics of Ethnic Change,' *Journal of Politics* 52 (November): 1124–1154.

Citrin, Jack. 1974. 'Comment: The Political Relevance of Trust in Government.' *American Political Science Review* 68(3): 973–88.

Cole, Thomas B. 2000. 'When a Bio-weapon Strikes, Who Will be in Charge?' *Journal of the American Medical Association,* 284(8): 944–948.

Cooper, H. H. A. 1977. 'Terrorism and the Media.' In *Terrorism: the Interdisciplinary Perspectives.* Eds. Y. Alexander and S. M. Finger. New York: John Jay Press.

Craig, Stephen C. 1993. *The Malevolent Leaders: Popular Discontent in America.* Boulder, CO: Westview Press.

Crelinsten R. D. 1989. 'Images of Terrorism in the Media: 1966–1985.' *Terrorism.* 12(3): 167–198.

Crelinsten, R. D. 1998. 'The Discourse and Practice of Counter Terrorism in Liberal Democracies.' *Australian Journal of Politics and History.* 44(3): 389–413.

Crelinsten, R. D. 1986. 'Power and Meaning: Terrorism as a Struggle over Access to the Communication Structure.' In *Contemporary Research on Terrorism.* Paul Wilkinson and A. M. Stewart. Eds. Aberdeen: Aberdeen University Press.

Crenshaw, Martha. 1989. *Terrorism and International Cooperation.* Boulder, CO: Westview Press.

Crenshaw, Martha. 1990. 'The Logic of Terrorism: Terrorist Behavior as a Product of Strategic Choice.' In *Origins of Terrorism.* Ed. W. Reich. Cambridge: Cambridge University Press.

Crenshaw, Martha. 1995. Ed. *Terrorism in Context.* Pennsylvania: Pennsylvania State University.

Crenshaw, Martha. 1997. *Encyclopedia of World Terrorism.* Armonk, N.Y: Sharpe Reference.

Crenshaw, Martha. 2000. 'Terrorism and International Violence.' In Manus I. Midlarsky (editor). *Handbook of War Studies II.* Ann Arbor: University of Michigan Press.

Davis, Darren W. 1995. 'Exploring Black Political Intolerance.' *Political Behavior* 17: 1–22.

Davis, James A. 'Communism, Conformity, Cohorts, and Categories: American Tolerance in 1954 and 1972–73.' *American Journal of Sociology* 81 (November): 491–513.

Dearing, James W. and Everett M. Rogers. 1996. *Agenda-setting.* Thousand Oaks: Sage.

Delli Carpini, Michael and Bruce A. Williams. 1987. 'Television and Terrorism: Patterns of Presentation and Occurrence 1969 to 1980.' *Western Political Quarterly.* 40(1): 45–64.

Dobkin, Bethami A. 1992. *Tales of Terror: Television News and the Construction of the Terrorist Threat.* New York: Praeger.

Dowley, Kathleen M., and Brian D. Silver. 2000. 'Sub-national and National Loyalty: Cross-National Comparisons,' *International Journal of Public Opinion Research* 12 (November): 357–371.

Dowley, Kathleen M., and Brian D. Silver. 2002. 'Social Capital, Ethnicity, and Support for Democracy in the Post-Communist States.' *Europe-Asia Studies* 44 (June): 505–527.

Dowling, R. E. 1986. 'Terrorism and the Media: A Rhetorical Genre.' *Journal of Communication.* 36(1): 12–24.

Easton, David. 1965. *A Systems Analysis of Political Life.* New York: Wiley.

Easton, David. 1975. 'A Re-Assessment of the Concept of Political Support.' *British Journal of Political Science* 5(4): 435–57.

Edelman, Murray. 1985. *The Symbolic Uses of Politics.* Urbana and Chicago: The University of Chicago Press (1967).

Edelman, Murray. 1988. *Constructing the Political Spectacle.* Chicago: University of Chicago Press.

El-Nawawy, Mohammed and Adel Iskandar. 2002. *Al Jazeera: How the Free Arab News Network Scooped the World and Changed the Middle East.* Boulder, CO: Westview Press.

Enders, Walter, and Todd Sandler. 1999. 'Transnational Terrorism in the Post-Cold War Era.' *International Studies Quarterly* 43: 145–167.

Enders, Walter, and Todd Sandler. 2000. 'Is Transnational Terrorism Becoming More Threatening? A Time-Series Investigation.' *Journal of Conflict Resolution* 44: 307–332.

Enders, Walter, and Todd Sandler. 2002. 'Patterns of Transnational Terrorism, 1970–1999: Alternative Time-Series Estimates.' *International Studies Quarterly* 46: 145–165.

Entman, Robert M. and Andrew Rojecki. 2000. *The Black Image in the White Mind.* Chicago, IL: University of Chicago Press.

Erber, Ralph and Richard R. Lau. 1990. 'Political Cynicism Revisited: An Information-Processing Reconciliation of Policy-Based and Incumbency-Based Interpretations of Changes in Trust in Government.' *American Journal of Political Science* 34(1): 236–53.

Falkenrath, Richard A., Robert D. Newman, and Bradley A. Thayer. 1998. *America's Achilles' Heel: Nuclear, Biological, and Chemical Terrorism and Covert Attack.* Cambridge, MA: MIT Press.

Fallows, James. 1996. *Breaking the News.* New York: Vintage.

Feldman, Stanley and Lee Seligman. 1985. 'The Political Impact of Prime-Time Television: The Day After.' *Journal of Politics,* 47: 557–578.

Feldman, Stanley, and Karen Stenner. 1997. 'Perceived Threat and Authoritarianism.' *Political Psychology* 18 (December): 741–770.

Feldman, Stanley. 1983. 'The Measurement and Meaning of Political Trust.' *Political Methodology* 9 (3): 341–54.

Fischoff, Baruch. 1996. 'Reporting on Environmental and Health Risks.' *The Quill* 83(6) (July–August), 43–7.

Frey, R. G. and Christopher W. Morris. Eds. 1991. *Violence, Terrorism and Justice.* New York: Cambridge University Press.

Friedman, Sharon M. 1991. 'Two Decades of the Environmental Beat.' In *Media and the Environment.* Ed. Craig L. LaMay and Everette E. Dennis, 17–28. Washington: Island Press.

Gamson, William A. 1968. *Power and Disconnect.* Homewood, IL: Dorsey.

Gamson, William A. and A. Modigliani. 1989. 'Media Discourse and Public Opinion on Nuclear Power: A Constructionist Approach.' *American Journal of Sociology.* 95: 1–37.

Gamson, William A., D. Croteau, W. Hoynes, and T. Sasson. 1992. 'Media Images and the Social Construction of Reality.' *Annual Review of Sociology* 18: 373–93.

Gans, Herbert. 1980. *Deciding What's News.* New York: Vintage.

George, A. 1991. *Western State Terrorism.* New York: Routledge.

Gibson, James L. 1987. 'Homosexuals and the Ku Klux Klan: A Contextual Analysis of Political Intolerance.' *Western Political Quarterly* 40: 427–448.

Gibson, James L. 1989. 'The Policy Consequences of Political Intolerance: Political Repression During the Vietnam War Era.' *Journal of Politics* 51: 13–35.

Gibson, James L. 1993. 'Perceived Political Freedom in the Soviet Union.' *Journal of Politics* 55: 936–974.

Gibson, James L. 1995. 'The Political Freedom of African Americans: A Contextual Analysis of Racial Attitudes, Political Tolerance, and Individual Liberty.' *Political Geography* 14: 571–599.

Gibson, James L. 1996. 'A Mile Wide But an Inch Deep: The Structure of Democratic Commitments in the Former USSR,' *American Journal of Political Science* 40 (May): 396–420.

Gibson, James L. 1998. 'A Sober Second Thought: An Experiment in Persuading Russians to Tolerate.' *American Journal of Political Science* 42 (July): 819–850.

Gibson, James L., and Amanda Gouws. 2000. 'Social Identities and Political Intolerance: Linkages Within the South African Mass Public.' *American Journal of Political Science* 44: 278–292.

Gibson, James L., and Richard D. Bingham. 1985. *Civil Liberties and Nazis: The Skokie Free Speech Controversy.* New York: Praeger.

Gibson, James L., Raymond M. Duch, and Kent L. Tedin. 1992. 'Democratic Values and the Transformation of the Soviet Union,' *Journal of Politics* 54: 329–371.

Gilbert Allison, Robyn Walensky, Melinda Murphy, Phil Hirschkorn, Mitchell Stephens. Editors. 2002. *Covering Catastrophe: Broadcast Journalists Report September 11.* NY: Bonus Books.

Gomberg, Paul. 2002. 'Patriotism is Like Racism.' In Igor Primoratz Ed. *Patriotism*. Amherst, New York: Humanity Books.

Graber, Doris. 1980. *Mass Media and American Politics*. Washington, DC: Congressional Quarterly.

Greenberg, Bradley S. 1986. 'Minorities and the Mass Media.' In Jennings Bryant and Dolf Zillmann, Eds. *Perspectives on Media Effects*. Hillsdale, N.J.: Lawrence Erlbaum.

Greenberg, Bradley S. and Marcia Thomson. 2002. *Communication and Terrorism: Public and Media Responses to 9/11*. Hampton Press.

Hafez, Kai. 2000. *Mass Media, Politics and Society in the Middle East*. Hampton Press.

Hafez, Kai. Ed. 2000. *Islam and the West in the Mass Media: Fragmented Images in a Globalizing World*. Hampton Press.

Hafez, Kai. Ed. 2001. *Mass Media and Society in the Middle East*. Hampton Press.

Hahn, Robert W. Ed. 1996. *Risks, Costs and Lives Saved: Getting Better Results from Regulation*. Washington: AEI Press.

Hallin, Daniel C. 1986. *The 'Uncensored War': The Media and Vietnam*. Berkeley, CA: University of California Press.

Hembroff, Larry A. 2002. 'The Civil Liberties Survey, 2001: Methodological Report,' Institute for Public Policy and Social Research, Michigan State University.

Herman, Edward S. and Gerry O'Sullivan. 1989. *The Terrorism Industry: The Experts and Institutions that Shape our View of Terror*. New York: Pantheon.

Herman, Edward S. and Noam Chomsky. 1988. *Manufacturing Consent: The Political Economy of the Mass Media*. New York: Pantheon.

Hetherington, Marc J. 1998. 'The Political Relevance of Political Trust.' *American Political Science Review* 92(4): 791–808.

Hetherington, Marc J. 1999. 'The Effect of Political Trust on the Presidential Vote, 1968–96.' *American Political Science Review* 93(2): 311–26.

Hetherington, Marc J., and Suzanne Globetti. 2002. 'Political Trust and Racial Policy Preferences.' *American Journal of Political Science* 46(2): 253–75.

Hibbing, John R., and Elizabeth Theiss-Morse. 1995. *Congress As Public Enemy: Public Attitudes toward American Political Institutions*. New York: Cambridge University Press.

Hoffman, Bruce. 1998. *Inside Terrorism*. New York: Columbia University Press.

Hoffman, D. 2002. 'Beyond Public Diplomacy.' *Foreign Affairs*. 81(2): 83–90.

Hornig, Susanna. 1993. 'Framing risk: Audience and reader factors.' *Journalism Quarterly* 69(3): 679–690.

Howell, Susan F., and Deborah Fagan. 1988. 'Race and Trust in Government: Testing the Political Reality Model.' *Public Opinion Quarterly* 52(3): 343–350.

Huddy, Leonie, Nadia Khatib, and Theresa Capelos. 2002. 'The Polls—Trends: Reactions to the Terrorist Attacks of September 11, 2001.' *Public Opinion Quarterly* 56(3): XXX–XXX.

Hurwitz, Jon, and Mark Peffley. 1987. 'How Are Foreign Policy Attitudes Structured? A Hierarchical Model.' *American Political Science Review*, 81(4): 1099–1120.

Hurwitz, Jon, and Mark Peffley. 1990. 'Public Images of the Soviet Union: The Impact on Foreign Policy Attitudes.' *Journal of Politics* 52(1): 3–28.

Inglehart, Ronald. 1997. *Modernization and Postmodernization: Cultural, Economic and Political Change in 43 Societies*. Princeton: Princeton University Press.

Ito, Y. 1990. 'Mass Communication Theories from a Japanese Perspective.' *Media, Culture and Society* 12: 423–464.

Iyengar, Shanto and Donald Kinder. 1987. *News That Matters: Television and American Opinion*. Chicago: University of Chicago Press.

Iyengar, Shanto and Silvo Lenart. 1988. 'Beyond 'Minimal Consequences:' A Survey of Media Political Effects.' In Samuel Long, ed. *Political Behavior Annual*. Boulder, CO: Westview.

Iyengar, Shanto. 1991. *Is Anyone Responsible? How Television Frames Political Issues*. Chicago: University of Chicago Press.

Jackman, Robert W. 1972. 'Political Elites, Mass Publics, and Support for Democratic Principles.' *Journal of Politics* 34(3): 753–773.

Jackson, David J. 2001. 'Outside of a Small Circle of *Friends*: The Political Influence of Entertainment Television.' Paper presented at the 2001 annual meeting of the American Political Science Association, August 30–September 2, San Francisco, CA.

Johnson, Donald. 1963. *The Challenge to American Freedoms: World War I and the Rise of the American Civil Liberties Union*. Lexington, KY: University of Kentucky Press.

Johnson, Larry C. 2001. 'The Future of Terrorism.' *American Behavioral Scientist*. 44(6): 894–913.

Just, Marion, Ann Crigler, Dean Alger, Timothy Cook, Montague Kern and Darrell West, 1996. Crosstalk: Citizens, Candidates and the Media in a Presidential Campaign. University of Chicago Press.

Keene, Karlyn. 1980. 'Rally 'Round the President.' *Public Opinion* 3(2): 28–9.

Kellner, D. 2002. 'September 11, the Media, and War Fever.' *Television & New Media* 3(2): 143–151.

Kerbel, Matthew Robert. 1994. *Edited for Television*. Boulder, CO: Westview.

Kern, Montague and Marion Just. 1995. "The Focus Group Method, Political Advertising, Campaign News and the Construction of Candidate Images," *Political Communication*, April–June.

Kern, Montague, Patricia W. Levering, and Ralph B. Levering. 1984. *The Kennedy Crises: The Press, the Presidency and Foreign Policy*. University of North Carolina Press.

Knightley, Philip. 1975. *The First Casualty*. N.Y.: Harcourt Brace and Jovanovitch.

Kuklinski, James H., Ellen Riggle, Victor Ottai, Norbert Schwarz, and Robert S. Wyer, Jr. 1991. 'The Cognitive and Affective Bases of Political Tolerance Judgments.' *American Journal of Political Science* 35(1): 1–27.

Lakos, A. 1986. *International Terrorism: A Bibliography*. Boulder, CO: Westview Press.

Lane, Robert E. 1959. *Political Life: Why and How People Get Involved in Politics*. New York: Free Press.

Laqueur, Walter. 1977. *Terrorism*. Boston: Little Brown.

Lasswell, Harold. 1988. *Psychopathology and Politics*. Chicago: University of Chicago Press. (1930).

Lawrence, Regina G. 2000a. 'Game-framing the issues: Tracking the strategy frame in public policy news.' *Political Communication* 17(2): 93–114.

Lawrence, Regina. 2000b. *The Politics of Force*. Berkeley: University of California Press.

Lenart, Slivo and Kathleen M. McGraw. 1989. 'America Watches *America*: Television Docudrama and Political Attitudes.' *Journal of Politics* 51: 698–712.

Lesser, Ian O., Bruce Hoffman, John Arquilla, Michele Zanini, and David Ronfeldt. 1999. *Countering the New Terrorism*. Rand Corporation.

Levi, Margeret. 1996. 'Social and Unsocial Capital: A Review Essay of Robert Putnam's 'Making Democracy Work'.' *Politics and Society* 24(1):45–55.

Levy, Leonard W. 1963. *Jefferson and Civil Liberties: The Darker Side*. Cambridge, MA: Harvard University Press.

Lewis, C. W. 2000. 'The terror that failed: Public opinion in the aftermath of the bombing in Oklahoma City.' *Public Administration Review*. 60(3): 201–210.

Liebes, Tamar. 1997. *Reporting the Arab Israeli Conflict: How Hegemony Works*. London: Routledge.

Linfield, Michael. 1990. *Freedom Under Fire: U.S. Civil Liberties in Times of War*. Boston: South End Press.

Lippmann, Walter. 1946. *Public Opinion*. New York, N.Y.: Free Press.

Lipset, Seymour Martin, and William Schneider. 1983. *The Confidence Gap: Business, Labor, and Government in the Public Mind*. New York: Free Press.

Livingston, Steven. 1994. *The Terrorism Spectacle*. Boulder, CO: Westview Press.

Luce, Mary Frances, James R. Bettman, and John W. Payne. 1997. 'Choice Processing in Emotionally Difficult Decisions.' *Journal of Experimental Psychology*, 23(1): 384–405.

Mackenzie, G. Calvin, and Judith M. Labiner. 2002. *Opportunity Lost: The Rise and Fall of Trust and Confidence in Government After September 11*. Washington, DC: Brookings Institution.

Mamdani, M. 2002. 'Good Muslim, Bad Muslim: A Political Perspective on Culture and Terror.' *American Anthropologist*. 104(3): 766–775.

Markus, Gregory B. 1979a. *Analyzing Panel Data*. Beverly Hills, CA: Sage Publications.

Markus, Gregory B. 1979b. 'The Political Environment and the Dynamics of Public Attitudes: A Panel Study.' *American Journal of Political Science* 23(2): 338–59.

Martín Barbero, Jesús. 1998. 'De los medios a las mediaciones.' *Comunicación, Cultura y Hegemonía*. México. Ediciones G. Gili.

Maslow, Abraham. 1954. *Motivation and Personality*. New York: Harper and Row.

Mazur, Allan. 1981. 'Media Coverage and Public Opinion on Scientific Controversies.' *Journal of Communication* 31(2): 106–115.

McBride, Allan and Robert K. Toberen. 1996. 'Deep Structures: Pol-pop Culture on Primetime Television.' *Journal of Popular Culture.* 29:181–200.

McBride, Allan. 1998. 'Television, Individualism, and Social Capital.' *PS: Politics and Political Science,* 31: 542–553.

McChesney, Robert W. 2002. 'The Zillionth Time as Tragedy.' *Television & New Media.* 3(2): 133–137.

McChesney, Robert W. 2002. 'The US News Media and World War III.' *Journalism: Theory, Practice and Criticism* 3(1).

McClosky, Herbert and Alida Brill. 1983. *Dimensions of Tolerance: What Americans Believe About Civil Liberties.* New York: Russell Sage.

McClosky, Herbert. 1964. 'Consensus and Ideology in American Politics.' *American Political Science Review* 58(2): 361–382.

McCombs, Maxwell and Donald Shaw. 1972. 'The agenda-setting function of the mass media.' *Public Opinion Quarterly.* 36: 176–187.

McCombs, Maxwell, Donald Shaw and David Weaver. Eds. 1997. *Communication and Democracy: Exploring the Intellectual Frontiers in Agenda-Setting Theory.* New York: Lawrence Erlbaum Assoc.

McCombs, Maxwell. 2002. *Setting the Agenda: The News Media and Public Opinion.* Oxford, England and Malden, MA. Polity Press an imprint of Blackwell.

McCutcheon, Allan L. 1985. 'A Latent Class Analysis of Tolerance for Nonconformity in the American Public,' *Public Opinion Quarterly* 49(4): 474–488.

Midlarsky, Manus I., Martha Crenshaw and Fumihiko Yoshida. 1980. 'Why violence spreads: The contagion of international terrorism.' *International Studies Quarterly.* 24(2): 262–298.

Milbank, Dana, and Richard Morin. 2001. 'Public Is Unyielding in War Against Terror: 9 in 10 Back Robust Military Response.' *Washington Post,* September 29.

Miller, D. 2002. 'Opinion Polls and the Misrepresentation of Public Opinion on the War with Afghanistan.' *Television & New Media.* 3(2):153–161.

Miller, Arthur H. 1974a. 'Political Issues and Trust in Government: 1964–1970.' *American Political Science Review* 68(3): 951–72.

Miller, Arthur H. 1974b. 'Rejoinder to 'Comment' by Jack Citrin: Political Discontent or Ritualism?' *American Political Science Review* 68(3): 989–1001.

Mindich, David T. Z. 2002. 'September 11 and its challenge to journalism criticism.' *Journalism: Theory, practice and criticism* 3(1).

Moore, David W. 2001. *Confidence in Leaders: Record Rally Effect for President, Congress as Americans Support Government Leaders in Wake of Terrorist Attacks.* Princeton, NJ: Gallup Organization.

Mowlana, Hamid. 1985. *International Flow of Information: Global Report and Analysis.* Paris: UNESCO.

Mowlana, Hamid. 1993. 'Towards a NWICO for the Twenty-First Century.' *Journal of International Affairs* 47(1): 59–72.

Mueller, John E. 1970. 'Presidential Popularity from Truman to Johnson.' *American Political Science Review* 64(1): 18–34.

Mueller, John E. 1973. *War, Presidents, and Public Opinion.* New York: John Wiley and Sons.

Nacos, Brigitte L. 1990. *The Press, Presidents, and Crises.* New York, NY: Columbia University Press.

Nacos, Brigitte L. 1996. *Terrorism and the Media: From the Iran Hostage Crisis to the Oklahoma City Bombing.* New York, NY: Columbia University Press.

Nacos, Brigitte L. 2000. 'Accomplice or witness? The media's role in terrorism.' *Current History* 99(636): 174–178.

Nacos, Brigitte L. 2002. *Mass-Mediated Terrorism.* Lanham: Rowman & Littlefield.

Nacos, Brigitte L, Robert Y. Shapiro and Pierangelo Isernia. Eds. 2002. *Decision-making in a Glass House: Mass Media, Public Opinion, and American and European Foreign Policy in the 21st Century.*

Nacos, Brigitte L. and Natasha Hritzuk, 2000. 'The Portrayal of Black America in the Mass Media.' In *Black and Multicultural Politics in America.* Eds. Yvette M. Alex Assensoh and Lawrence Hanks. New York, NY: New York University Press.

Nacos, Brigitte L., David P. Fan, and J. T. Young. 1989. 'Terrorism and the print media: The 1985 TWA Hostage Crisis.' *Terrorism.* 12(2): 107–115.

National Research Council, Committee on Risk Characterization, 1996. *Understanding Risk: Informing Decisions in a Democratic Society.* Washington, D.C.: National Academy Press.

Neely, Mark E., Jr. 1991. *The Fate of Liberty: Abraham Lincoln and Civil Liberties.* New York: Oxford University Press.

Nelkin, D. 1989. 'Communicating Technological Risk: The Social Construction of Risk Perception.' *Annual Review of Public Health* 10: 95–113.

Nelson, Michael. Ed. 1989. *The Elections of 1988.* Washington: *Congressional Quarterly.*

Nelson, P. S. and J. L. Scott. 1992. 'Terrorism and the media: An empirical analysis.' *Defence Economics* 3(4): 329–339.

Neuman, Russell W., Marion R. Just and Ann N. Crigler. 1996. *Common Knowledge: News and the Construction of Political Meaning.* Chicago: University of Chicago Press.

Neustadt, Richard E. 1960. *Presidential Power: The Politics of Leadership.* New York: Wiley.

Newton, Kenneth, and Pippa Norris. 2000. 'Confidence in Public Institutions: Faith, Culture, or Performance?' in *Disaffected Democracies: What's Troubling the Trilateral Countries?,* Ed. Susan J. Pharr and Robert D. Putnam. Princeton: Princeton University Press.

Noakes, J. A., and K. G. Wilkins. 2002. 'Shifting Frames of the Palestinian Movement in US News.' *Media, Culture and Society.* 24(5): 649–655.

NORC. 2001. 'America Rebounds: A National Study of Public Response to the September Terrorist Attacks: Preliminary Findings.' NORC, University of Chicago (prepared by Tom W. Smith, Kenneth A. Rasinski, and Marianna Toce).

Norris, Pippa. 1999. *Critical Citizens: Global Support for Democratic Governance.* New York: Oxford University Press.

Nunn, Clyde A., Harry J. Crockett Jr., and Allen J. Williams, Jr. 1978. *Tolerance for Nonconformity: A National Survey of Changing Commitment to Civil Liberties.* San Francisco: Jossey-Bass.

O'Heffernan, Patrick. 1994. 'A Mutual Exploitation Model of Media Influence in U.S. Foreign Policy,' pp. 231–249 in *Taken By Storm: The Media, Public Opinion, and U.S. Foreign Policy in the Gulf War,* Eds. W. Lance Bennett and David L. Paletz. Chicago: University of Chicago Press.

Oliverio, Annemarie. 1998. *The State of Terror.* Albany, NY: State University of New York Press.

Page, Benjamin. 1996. *Who Deliberates? Mass Media in Modern Democracy.* Chicago: University of Chicago Press.

Paletz, David L. and Alex P. Schmid, Eds. 1992. *Terrorism and the Media.* Newbury Park, CA: Sage.

Palmer, Nancy. 2003. (editor) *Terrorism, War and the Press.* The Joan Shorenstein Center on the Press, Politics and Public Policy, John F. Kennedy School of Government, Harvard University.

Parker, Suzanne L. 1995. 'Toward an Understanding of 'Rally' Effects: Public Opinion in the Persian Gulf War.' *Public Opinion Quarterly* 59(4): 526–46.

Peffley, Mark, and Jon Hurwitz. 1992. 'International Events and Foreign Policy Beliefs: Public Response to Changing U.S.-Soviet Relations.' *American Journal of Political Science* 36(2): 431–61.

Peffley, Mark, and Jon Hurwitz. 1993. 'Models of Attitude Constraint in Foreign Affairs.' *Political Behavior* 15(1): 61–90.

Pharr, Susan J., and Robert D. Putnam, Eds. 2000. *Disaffected Democracies: What's Troubling the Trilateral Countries?* Princeton: Princeton University Press.

Picard, Robert G. 1993. *Media Portrayals of Terrorism: Functions and Meaning of News Coverage.* Iowa: Iowa State University Press.

Pillar, Paul R. and Michael H. Armacost. 2001. *Terrorism and U.S. Foreign Policy.* Washington, D.C.: The Brookings Institution.

Pomper, Gerald. Ed. 1989. *The Election of 1988.* Chatham, NJ: Chatham House.

Pomponio, Arthur T. 2002. *Psychological Consequences of Terrorism.* New York: Wiley.

Postman, Neil. 1985. *Amusing Ourselves to Death: Public Discourse in the Age of Show Business.* New York: Penguin.

Presidential/Congressional Commission on Risk Assessment and Risk Management, 1997. *Risk Assessment and Risk Management in Regulatory Decision-Making.* Washington, D.C.: Government Printing Office.

Prothro, James W., and Charles W. Grigg. 1960. 'Fundamental Principles of Democracy: Bases of Agreement and Disagreement,' *Journal of Politics* 22(2): 276–294.

Putnam, Robert D. 1995a. 'Bowling Alone: America's Declining Social Capital.' *Journal of Democracy* 6(1): 65–78.

Putnam, Robert D. 1995b. 'Tuning In, Tuning Out: The Strange Disappearance of Social Capital in America.' *PS: Political Science and Politics* 8(4): 664–683.

Putnam, Robert D. 2000. *Bowling Alone: The Collapse and Revival of American Community.* New York: Simon & Schuster.

Putnam, Robert. 'Bowling Together.' *The American Prospect.* February 11, 2002.

Rahn, Wendy and John Transue. 1998. 'Social Trust and Value Change: The Decline of Social Capital in American Youth, 1976–1995.' *Political Psychology* 19(3): 545–565.

Rapoport, D. Ed. 1988. *Inside the Terrorist Organization.* New York: Columbia University Press.

Reich, Walter. Ed. 1998. *Origins of Terrorism: Psychologies, Ideologies, Theologies, States of Mind.* Washington, D.C.: Woodrow Wilson Center Press.

Reid, E. O. F. 1997. 'Evolution of a Body of Knowledge: An Analysis of Terrorism Research.' *Information Processing and Management.* 33(1): 91–106.

Robinson, Michael J. 1976. 'Public Affairs Television and the Growth of Political Malaise: The Case of 'The Selling of the Pentagon.'' *American Political Science Review* 70(2): 409–32.

Rokeach, Milton.1960. *The Open and Closed Mind: Investigations into the Nature of Belief Systems and Personality Systems.* New York: Basic Books.

Rosen, Jay. 2002. 'When the Networks Ran in Reverse: Reflections on the Terror in New York.' *Journalism: Theory, Practice and Criticism* 3(1).

Rosenberg, Morris A. 1956. 'Misanthropy and Political Ideology,' *American Sociological Review* 21(4): 690–695.

Rosenstone, Steven J., and Mark Hansen. 1993. *Mobilization, Participation, and Democracy in America.* New York: Macmillan.

Rudenstine, David, 1996. *The Day the Presses Stopped: A History of the Pentagon Papers Case.* Berkeley: University of California Press.

Rusciano, Frank Louis. *World Opinion and the Emerging International Order.* Westport, CT: Praeger, 1998.

Sajó, András and Monroe Price. Eds. 1996. *Rights of Access to the Media.* The Hague: Kluwer Law International.

Schaffert, Richard W. 1992. *Media Coverage and Political Terrorists: A Quantitative Analysis.* New York: Praeger.

Schatz, Robert T., and Ervin Staub. 1996. 'Manifestations of Blind and Constructive Patriotism: Personality Correlates and Individual-Group Relations,' In Daniel Bar-Tal and Ervin Stab Eds. *Patriotism: In the Lives of Individuals and Nations.* Chicago: Nelson-Hall Publishers.

Schecter, Danny. 2002. *Media Wars: News at a Time of Terror, Dissecting News Since 9/11,* Innovation.

Schiff, Z. & Ya'ari E. 1990. *Intifada: The Palestinian Uprising—Israel's Third Front.* NY: Simon and Schuster.

Schlesinger, Philip, Graham Murdock and Philip Elliott. 1983. *Televising Terrorism: Political Violence in Popular Culture.* London: Commedia Publishers.

Schlesinger, Philip. 1991. *Media, State and Nation: Political Violence and Collective Identities.* London: Sage.

Scholz, John T., and Mark Lubell. 1998. 'Trust and Taxpaying: Testing the Heuristic Approach to Collective Action.' *American Journal of Political Science* 42(2): 398–417.

Schubert, J. N., P. A. Stewart and M. A. Curran. 2002. 'A Defining Presidential Moment: 9/11 and the Rally Effect.'*Political Psychology.* 23(3): 559–583.

Schuster, Mark A. *et al.* 2001. 'A National Survey of Stress Reactions After the September 11, 2001, Terrorist Attacks,' *The New England Journal of Medicine* 345: 1507–1512.

Schwartz, D. M. 1998. 'Environmental terrorism: Analyzing the concept.' *Journal of Peace Research.* 35(4): 483–496.

Scraton, Phil. Ed. 2002. *Beyond September 11: An Anthology of Dissent.* London: Pluto Press.

Shaheen, Jack. 1997. *Arab and Muslim Stereotypes in American Popular Culture.* Washington, D.C.: Center for Muslim-Christian Understanding.

Shaheen, Jack. 2001. *Reel Bad Arabs: How Hollywood Vilifies a People.* Northampton, MA: Interlink Publishing Group.

Shamir, J. and K. Shikaki. 2002. 'Self-serving perceptions of terrorism among Israelis and Palestinians.' *Political Psychology.* 23(3): 537–557.

Shin, Michael and Michael D. Ward, 1999. 'Lost on Space: Political Geography and the Defense-Growth Trade-Off,' *Journal of Conflict Resolution,* 43(6): 793–817.

Sigelman, Lee and Carol Sigelman. 1974. 'The Politics of Political Culture: Campaign Cynicism and *The Candidate.*' *Sociology and Social Research* 58: 272–277.

Sigelman, Lee, and Pamela Johnston Conover. 1981. 'The Dynamics of Presidential Support During International Conflict Situations: The Iranian Hostage Crisis.' *Political Behavior* 3(4): 303–18.

Silberstein, Sandra. 2002. *War of Words,* London: Routledge.

Silverberg, Marshall, 1991. 'Constitutional Concerns in Denying the Press Access to Military Operations,' pp. 165–175 in *Defense Beat: The Dilemmas of Defense Coverage,* Loren B. Thompson, Ed. New York: Lexington Books, 1991.

Simon, Reeva. 1989. *The Middle East in Crime Fiction.* New York, N.Y.: Lilian Barber Press.

Slone, M. 2000. 'Responses to Media Coverage of Terrorism.' *Journal of Conflict Resolution.* 44(4): 508–522.

Slovic, P. 1987. 'Perception of Risk.' *Science* 236 (17 April): 280–285.

Smith, Tom W., Kenneth A. Rasinksi, and Marianna Toce. 2001. *America Rebounds: A National Study of Public Response to the September 11th Terrorist Attacks, Preliminary Findings.* Chicago: National Opinion Research Center.

Sniderman, Paul M.; Joseph F. Fletcher, Peter H. Russell, and Philip E. Tetlock. 1996. *The Clash of Rights: Liberty, Equality, and Legitimacy in Pluralist Democracy.* New Haven: Yale University Press.

Stern, Jessica. 1999. *The Ultimate Terrorists.* Cambridge, MA: Harvard University Press.

Stokes, Donald E. 1962. 'Popular Evaluations of Government: An Empirical Assessment.' In *Ethics and Bigness: Scientific, Academic, Religious, Political, and Military,* Eds. Harlan Cleveland and Harold D. Lasswell. New York: Harper and Brothers.

Sullivan, John L., Amy Fried, and Mary G. Dietz. 1992. 'Patriotism, Politics, and the Presidential Election of 1988.' *American Journal of Political Science* 36 (February): 200–234.

Surlin, Stuart H. 1978. '*Roots* Research: A Summary of Findings.' *Journal of Broadcasting,* 22: 309–320.

Tetlock, Philip E. 1986. 'A Value Pluralism Model of Ideological Reasoning.' *Journal of Personality and Social Psychology* 50 (April): 819–827.

Thompson, Loren B. 1991. 'The Media Versus the Military: A Brief History of War Coverage in the United States.' pp. 3–56 in *Defense Beat: The Dilemmas of Defense Coverage,* Loren B. Thompson, Ed. New York: Lexington Books, 1991.

Thrall, A. Trevor. 2000. *War in the Media Age.* Cresskill, NJ: Hampton.

Tuchman, Gaye. 1978. *Making News.* New York: Free Press.

Tyler, T. R. and Fay Lomax Cook. 1984. 'The mass media and judgments of risk: Distinguishing impact on personal and societal level judgments.' *Journal of Personality and Social Psychology* 47(4): 693–708.

U.S. State Department. *Patterns of Terrorism* 2001. Washington, D.C.: U.S. Department of State.

Uslaner, Eric M. 2002. *The Moral Foundations of Trust.* New York: Cambridge University Press.

Wallack, Lawrence M, Lori Dorfman, David Jernigan, and Makani Themba. 1993. *Media Advocacy and Public Health: Power for Prevention.* Newbury Park, CA: Sage Publications.

Wanta, W. and Y. W. Hu. 1993. 'The Agenda-Setting Effects of International News Coverage: An Examination of Differing News Frames.' *International Journal of Public Opinion Research.* 5(3): 250–264.

Wardlaw, Grant. 1982. *Political Terrorism.* Cambridge, UK: Cambridge University Press.

Weatherford, M. Stephen. 1984. 'Economic 'Stagflation' and Public Support for the Political System.' *British Journal of Political Science* 14(2): 187–205.

Weimann, Gabriel and Conrad Winn, 1994. *The Theater of Terror: The Mass Media and International Terrorism.* New York: Longman Publishing/Addison-Wesley.

Weimann, Gabriel and H. B. Brosius. 1991. 'The Newsworthiness of International Terrorism.' *Communication Research.* 18(3): 333–354.

Weimann, Gabriel. 1987. 'Media Events: The Case of International Terrorism.' *Journal of Broadcasting and Electronic Media*. 31(1): 21–39.

Weissberg, Robert. 1976. 'Consensual Attitudes and Attitude Structure.' *Public Opinion Quarterly* 40(3): 349–359.

Weissberg, Robert. 1998. *Political Tolerance: Balancing Community and Diversity.* Thousand Oaks, CA: Sage Publications.

Whittaker, David. 2002. *Terrorism: Understanding the Global Threat.* New York: Longman.

Wolfsfeld, Gadi. 1997. 'Fair Weather Friends: The Varying Role of the News Media in the Arab-Israeli Peace Process.' *Political Communications.* 14(1): 29–48.

Wolfsfeld, Gadi. 1997. *Media and Political Conflict: News from the Middle East,* Cambridge, U.K: Cambridge University Press.

Wolfsfeld, Gadi. 2001. 'The News Media and the Second Intifada: Some Initial Lessons.' *The Harvard Journal of Press/Politics* 6: 113–118.

Wolfsfeld, Gadi. 2003. *Media and the Path to Peace.* Cambridge, U.K.: Cambridge University Press.

Wrightsman, Lawrence S. 1991. 'Interpersonal Trust and Attitudes Toward Human Nature.' In *Measures of Personality and Social Psychological Attitudes.* Eds. John P. Robinson, Phillip R. Shaver, and Lawrence S. Wrightsman.

Zaller, John R. 1992. *The Nature and Origins of Mass Opinion.* New York: Cambridge University Press.

Zelizer, Barbie and Allan Stuart. Eds. 2002. *Journalism After September 11.* London: Routledge.

List of Tables and Figures

List of Tables

List of Figures

List of Contributors

Sean Aday is Assistant Professor of Media and Public Affairs at the George Washington University. His research on media effects, political communication, and public opinion has appeared in *Journal of Communication, the Harvard International Journal of Press/Politics, The Annals of the American Political Science Association,* and *Presidential Studies Quarterly.*

Ted Brader is Assistant Professor in the Department of Political Science and Associate Research Scientist, Center for Political Studies, University of Michigan. Ph.D., Harvard. His research and teaching interests include public opinion, media effects, political psychology, campaigns and elections, and political parties. Although most of his work is in American politics, his general concern with questions of political behavior invites research in comparative politics as well. Professor Brader is currently writing a book on the impact of emotion in campaign advertising.

Paul Brewer is Assistant Professor of American Politics at George Washington University. His research on American public opinion, political communication, and political psychology has appeared in the *Journal of Politics, Political Communication, Political Psychology,* the *Harvard International Journal of Press/Politics,* and elsewhere.

Robin Brown is Senior Lecturer in International Communications at University of Leeds and Director of the Institute of Communication Studies. He is Chair of the International Communication section of the International Studies Association. His current research focuses on the impact of communication technology on international politics. His publications include *From Cold War to Collapse: Theory and World Politics in the 1980s* (Cambridge University Press, 1992) [co-editor] as well as articles in *Information, Communication and Society* and the *Journal of Information Warfare.*

Tim Cooke is Head of Broadcasting at BBC Northern Ireland, responsible for commissioning and scheduling all television, radio and online programming. Previously he ran the BBC's newsgathering operation in Northern Ireland. In spring 1998 he was a Goldsmith Fellow at the Joan Shorenstein Center, John F. Kennedy School, Harvard University.

Mansour O. El-Kikhia is Associate Professor of Political Science at the University of Texas, San Antonio. He received his Ph.D. from the University of California at Santa Barbara. Dr. El-Kikhia teaches courses in International Political and Economic Relations with special emphasis on the Middle East. His latest work is *Libya's Qaddafi: The Politics of Contradiction* (1997).

Anat First is Associate Professor of Mass Communications at Netanya Academic College and she also works as a lecturer in the School of Journalism and Mass Communications at Hebrew University of Jerusalem. Her main interests include the role of the media in constructing reality and the representation of the "other" in the media, especially women and Arabs.

Stanley Feldman is Professor of Political Science at Stony Brook University. He has published extensively in the fields of political psychology, public opinion, and political communications.

Doris A. Graber is Professor of Political Science at the University of Illinois at Chicago. Her Ph.D. is from Columbia University. Her fields of interest are political communication, information processing and management, and public opinion. A prolific author, selected publications include *The Politics of News, The News of Politics*, 1998. *Media Power in Politics* (March 2000, 4th ed), *Mass Media and American Politics*, (2001, 6th ed), and *Processing Politics: Learning From Television in the Internet Age* (2001). She is Editor Emeritus of *Political Communication*.

Kimberly Gross is Assistant Professor of Media and Public Affairs at the George Washington University. Her research on political communication and public opinion has appeared in the *British Journal of Political Science, Political Psychology* and *Journal of Communication*.

Leonie Huddy is Associate Professor of Political Science at Stony Brook University. Her fields of interest are political psychology, public opinion, and intergroup relations. She is co-editor of the *Handbook of Political Psychology* (2003), and *Research in Micropolitics: Political Decision-Making, Deliberation, and Participation* (2002). She has also published in many books and journals, including articles on public reactions to 9/11 in *Public Opinion Quarterly* and *Political Psychology*.

Ronald Inglehart is Senior Research Scientist, Center for Political Studies, Institute for Social Research, and Department of Political Science, University of Michigan. His Ph.D. is from the University of Chicago. Professor Inglehart's ongoing research focuses on cultural change and its consequences. He coordinates a worldwide survey of mass values and attitudes, the World Values survey. A prolific author, his most recent books include *Value Change on Six Continents* (Ann Arbor: University of Michigan Press, 1995); *Modernization and Postmodernization: Cultural, Economic and Political Change in 43 Societies* (Princeton: Princeton University Press, 1997); *Human Values and Beliefs: A Cross-Cultural Sourcebook* (Ann Arbor: University of Michigan Press, 1998); and *Rising Tide: Gender Equality and Cultural Change* (with Pippa Norris) (New York: Cambridge University Press, 2003).

Amy E. Jasperson is an Assistant Professor of Political Science at the University of Texas, San Antonio. Her research focuses on political communication, especially political advertising and political campaigns. She has published in journals such as the *Journal of Advertising, Political Communication,* and *Polity.*

Marion Just is a Professor of Political Science at Wellesley College and a Research Associate at the Joan Shorenstein Center on Press, Politics, and Public Policy at the Kennedy School of Government. Her research focuses on politics and media. She is a co-author of several books, including *Crosstalk: Citizens, Candidates and the Media in a Presidential Campaign, Common Knowledge: News and the Construction of Political Meaning,* and *The Election of 1996* as well as numerous journal articles and contributions to edited volumes.

Montague Kern is Associate Professor of Journalism and Media Studies at Rutgers University. She is the author *Thirty-Second Politics: Political Advertising in the '80's,* and is co-author of *Crosstalk: Citizens, Candidates and the Media in a Presidential Campaign* and *The Kennedy Crises: the Press, the Presidency and Foreign Policy* as well as numerous articles and books chapters. She is currently writing a book on the role of mass media in the construction of candidate images.

Gallya Lahav is Assistant Professor of Political Science at the State University of New York at Stony Brook. She works on international migration and European integration and her articles have appeared in several books and journals, including *Comparative Political Studies, the Journal of Common Market Studies, Journal of Ethnic and Migration Studies,* and *Global Governance.* Her book, *Reinventing Borders: Thinking about Immigration in the New Europe,* gauges 20 years of public opinion and elite attitudes toward immigration in a Europe of changing boundaries (Cambridge University Press, 2003).

Tamar Liebes is Professor and Head of the Department of Communication and Journalism, Hebrew University. She has written extensively on the viewing of popular culture and coverage of terrorism in the Middle East.

Brigitte L. Nacos, a long-time correspondent for newspapers in Germany, is adjunct professor of political science at Columbia University. She is the author of *Mass-Mediated Terrorism: The Centrality of the Media in Terrorism and Counterterrorism* (Rowman & Littlefield, 2002); *Terrorism and the Media: From the Iran Hostage Crisis to the Oklahoma City Bombing* (Columbia University Press, 1996); *The Press, Presidents, and Crises* (Columbia University Press, 1990).

Pippa Norris is the McGuire Lecturer in Comparative Politics at the John F. Kennedy School of Government, Harvard University. Her research compares elections and public opinion, political communications, and gender politics. She has published almost thirty books, including a series of related volumes for Cambridge University Press: *A Virtuous Circle: Political Communications in Postindustrial Societies (2000), Digital Divide: Civic Engagement, Information Poverty and the Internet Worldwide* (2001), *Democratic Phoenix: Political Activism Worldwide (2002), Rising Tide: Gender Equality and Cultural Change Around the Globe* (with Ronald Inglehart, 2003), and *Electoral Engineering: Voting Rules and Political Behavior* (2003).

Frank Louis Rusciano is Professor and Chair of Political Science at Rider University and a former visiting Professor at the University of Mainz. His books include *Isolation and Paradox: Defining "the Public" in Modern Political Analysis* (Greenwood, 1989), and *World Opinion and the Emerging International Order* (Praeger, 1998). His articles have appeared in journals such as the *International Journal of Public Opinion Research, Comparative Politics, Current World Leaders: International Issues, Western Political Quarterly,* and *The Harvard International Journal of Press/Politics.*

Todd M. Schaefer is Associate Professor of Political Science at Central Washington University. His research interests are in the areas of elite political rhetoric, mass media, political communication and public opinion, and his work has appeared in journals such as *Political Communication* and *Journalism and Mass Communication Quarterly.*

Oscar Torres-Reyna is Ph.D. candidate in the Department of Political Science at Columbia University.

Charles S. Taber is Associate Professor of Political Science at Stony Brook University. He is interested in cognition, affect, and political decision-making, and has published widely in the fields of foreign policy decision-making, public opinion, and political cognition, including in the *American Political Science Review, Political Psychology,* and *Political Analysis.*

Michael W. Traugott is Professor and Chair of the Department of Communication Studies, University of Michigan. His research interests include the mass media and their impact on American politics. He focuses on media coverage of political campaigns and its impact on voter behavior, use of the media by political candidates, and the use of political surveys and polls to cover campaigns and elections. Professor Traugott is a past president of the American Association for Public Opinion Research. In 2000, he published his ninth book, *The Press, The Polls and Democracy*.

Index